Money and the Corrosion of Power in Thucydides

The Joan Palevsky  Imprint in Classical Literature

In honor of beloved Virgil—
"O degli altri poeti onore e lume . . ."

—Dante, *Inferno*

Money and the Corrosion of Power in Thucydides

The Sicilian Expedition and Its Aftermath

Lisa Kallet

UNIVERSITY OF CALIFORNIA PRESS
Berkeley Los Angeles London

The publisher gratefully acknowledges the generous contribution to this book provided by Joan Palevsky.

University of California Press
Berkeley and Los Angeles, California

University of California Press, Ltd.
London, England

Library of Congress Cataloging-in-Publication Data

Kallet, Lisa, 1956–.
Money and the corrosion of power in Thucydides : the Sicilian expedition and its aftermath / Lisa Kallet.
p. cm.
Includes bibliographical references and index.
ISBN 0–520–22984–3 (cloth : alk. paper)
1. Thucydides. History of the Peloponnesian War. 2. Greece—History—Peloponnesian War, 431–404 B.C.—Historiography 3. Sicilian Expedition, Italy, 415–413 B.C.—Historiography. 4. Greece—History—Peloponnesian, 431–404 B.C.—Finance. 5. Sicilian Expedition, Italy, 415–413 B.C.—Finance. I. Title.

DF299.T6 K32 2001
938′.05—dc21 00–067237

Manufactured in the United States of America
10 09 08 07 06 05 04 03 02 01
10 9 8 7 6 5 4 3 2 1

The paper used in this publication meets the minimum requirements of ANSI/NISO Z39.48–1992 (R 1997) (*Permanence of Paper*). ♾

An earlier version of chapter 3 appeared in the *American Journal of Philology* 120 (1999) under the title "The Diseased Body Politic, Athenian Public Finance, and the Massacre at Mykalessos (Thucydides 7.27–29)." I thank the Johns Hopkins University Press for permission to reproduce it, with changes.

To K.

CONTENTS

ACKNOWLEDGMENTS

This book is the product of nearly a decade of thinking and continual rethinking about Thucydides that itself followed well over a decade of interest in this historian—not quite, then, but almost, the length of the Peloponnesian War. The project started out as a mere continuation of my first book on money and naval power in Thucydides and grew into something different and broader, as I shall explain in the introduction. The fertility of the subject led me down unexpected paths, and, consequently, to the hope and expectation that, in the best of worlds, I would be opening up a discussion; much more on this subject remains to be explored and said. Kenneth Dover has put it best: "It is the common experience of people who study Thucydides intensively over a long period that one goes on indefinitely noticing things in him which one has not noticed before . . . ; in the case of Thucydides there always seems to remain the possibility that something really important is still waiting to be noticed" (*Thucydides* [Oxford: Clarendon Press, 1973], 44).

It is a special pleasure to acknowledge the friends, colleagues, and students who have greatly benefited my thinking. Many provided equal doses of generosity with their time, encouragement, and stimulating criticism and suggestions; some were guides when the book led me in directions in which I lacked expertise. The book would not be what it is, for better, without them; for worse, I take full responsibility. For reading and commenting on earlier versions of individual chapters and/or for oral conversations and feedback, I thank Thomas Figueira, Christian Habicht, Stephanie Moorhead, Robert Morstein-Marx, Martin Ostwald, Philip Stadter, Ronald Stroud, Peter van Alfen, and the students in my Thucydides seminar of fall 1999 not already mentioned. I am particularly grateful to three friends who have helped me in multiple ways in the final stages of this book over the last few years:

Jack Kroll, for his editorial acumen and encouragement; Paula Perlman, for written comments, and for her unstinting willingness to be a sounding board; and Emmet Robbins, especially for helping me to see the humor in all this. Carolyn Dewald, Simon Hornblower, and Christopher Pelling read and commented on the entire manuscript; like the Athenians at the end of the Peloponnesian War, I shall be permanently in debt, though in my case gratefully, to them. Needless, though necessary, to say, none of the above should be presumed to endorse any of what follows. Finally, I thank Jessica Miner for her research assistance; Christopher Lovell for indexing help; and Kate Toll, classics editor suffecta, and Cindy Fulton, project editor, at UC Press.

I am very grateful to the following institutions for their financial support and to individuals associated with them: the Center for Hellenic Studies, where I began this project at the end of my stay in 1991–1992, and its director at the time, Zeph Stewart; the Institute for Advanced Study, where I completed a first draft in 1994–1995, and Christian Habicht, who provided a supportive climate there for my research; and the University of Texas for a Dean's Fellowship in fall 1997. Finally, a University Fellowship from the National Endowment for the Humanities in 1998–1999, supplemented by a grant from the University of Texas the same year, allowed me to complete the manuscript. Additional grants from the University of Texas in 1999–2000 and 2001 enabled me to obtain further support for final preparation for publication. I am also grateful to Dr. Charalambos Kritzas, Director of the Epigraphical Museum in Athens, for his kind assistance and permission to examine inscriptions on several occasions.

The bibliography on Thucydides is enormous and has grown rapidly over the past few years. I regret that I have not been able to take account of or incorporate fully all relevant discussions.

NOTE ON TRANSLATION AND TRANSLITERATION

In the text, I alternately transliterate, provide the original Greek, and translate, following these general principles. I transliterate Greek terms and phrases (e.g., *periousia chrematon, gnome, dunamis*) when they recur throughout the book, and adopt a mixed system for citing names (sometimes using Latinized names, other times not, depending on what is likely to be most familiar to the reader). I use the original Greek for terms that come up rarely (or might look odd when transliterated) and for terms that are essential to a philological argument. I translate any Greek I quote extensively and where the reader does not need the Greek to understand my argument. Inconsistency is inevitable at times.

All translations are my own, except where otherwise noted.

ABBREVIATIONS

Arnold	Thomas Arnold. ΘΟΥΚΥΔΙΔΗΣ. *The History of the Peloponnesian War.* Vol. 3. Oxford and London: Parker, 1882.
ATL	Benjamin Dean Meritt, H. T. Wade-Gery, and Malcolm McGregor, eds. *The Athenian Tribute Lists.* Vol. 3. Cambridge, Mass.: Harvard University Press for the American School of Classical Studies at Athens, 1950.
Classen-Steup	Johannes Classen and Julius Steup, eds. *Thukydides.* Vols. 6–8. Berlin: Weidmann, 1963.
HCT	A. W. Gomme, A. Andrewes, and K. J. Dover, eds. *A Historical Commentary on Thucydides.* Vols. 1–2, 4–5. Oxford: Clarendon Press, 1945–1981.
IG I^3	D. M. Lewis, ed. *Inscriptiones Graecae.* 3d ed. Vol. 1, Fascs. 1–2. Berlin: Walter de Gruyter, 1981–1993.
LSJ	H. G. Liddell, R. Scott, and H. S. Jones. 1968. *A Greek-English Lexicon.* 9th ed., with suppplement. Oxford: Oxford University Press.
Marchant	E. C. Marchant. *Thucydides: Book VI.* London: Macmillan, 1914.
ML	Russell Meiggs and David Lewis, eds. *A Selection of Greek Historical Inscriptions.* 2d ed. Oxford: Oxford University Press, 1988.
Money	Lisa Kallet-Marx. *Money, Expense and Naval Power in Thucydides'* History, *1.–5.24.* Berkeley and Los Angeles: University of California Press, 1993.
OCT	Oxford Classical Text.
Tod	Marcus N. Tod. *A Selection of Greek Historical Inscriptions.* 2d ed. Vols. 1–2. Oxford: Clarendon Press, 1946–1948.
Tucker	T. G. Tucker, ed. *The Eighth Book of Thucydides.* London and New York: Macmillan, 1892.

Introduction

This book continues the examination of Thucydides' treatment of the role of money in relation to naval power begun in my earlier study on the subject.[1] Its focus is on the later books in the *History,* and it is thus in part a sequel, although its concerns and character differ to a large extent.[2] This examination deals more broadly with power, and perceptions and the meaning of power, and also relates Thucydides' treatment of money to other prominent themes in the *History;* it is much more a study of Thucydides' thought as a whole and attempts to locate his thought about money and wealth in its broader intellectual context.[3]

The shape of the book has above all been guided by the different nature of Thucydides' own treatment of the subject in books 6 through 8 of the *History*. When I began this examination, I had every expectation that I would encounter an unchanged approach and treatment in this part of the work, and I thought that my own approach and presentation would mirror that of my earlier investigation. Accordingly, on this somewhat unhappy premise, I was motivated more by a sense of duty to complete the study

1. Lisa Kallet-Marx, *Money, Expense and Naval Power in Thucydides'* History, *1.–5.24* (Berkeley and Los Angeles: University of California Press, 1993), hereinafter referred to as *Money*.

2. In one respect, this is due to the hope that I have already demonstrated both the depth and nature of Thucydides' interest in the subject of money in the context of naval war and of *dunamis* (power) more broadly, as it informs the narrative, speeches, and his own analytical sections. Thus in the present study I have felt less compulsion than before to deal comprehensively with virtually every morsel of financial information in order to demonstrate its function in the work.

3. There is much more to be done in the latter area than could be accomplished in this book. Here I offer a beginning.

promised in the first book than by the expectation of new revelations or greater understanding of how Thucydides was thinking about money. Initially, I was not disappointed: my examination of the rest of book 5, from where I left off at 5.24 (the end of the Archidamian War and the beginning of the account of the Peace of Nikias), confirmed, in the dramatic drop-off of financial information, that Thucydides' interest in money was chiefly related to naval power and war, since book 5 contains no significant discussion of naval warfare and, with the exception of the land battle of Mantinea, is occupied instead with treaties and diplomacy.

Also unsurprising was that financial information picked up dramatically in book 6 with the Sicilian expedition. However, I immediately found that while the level of Thucydides' interest in the subject was as high as in the earlier half of the work, the character of his approach and presentation had a radically different feel. First, the historian employs a wide variety of narrative techniques and devices with great frequency and shows much more explicitly (though by using implicit methods) and vigorously the interrelation of other themes as they affect, and are affected by, the theme of money. Second, his presentation of financial material has a fundamentally negative flavor.

To expand briefly on these two observations, it is precisely the explicit manipulation of the narrative so evident in books 6 through 8 that reveals the intensity of Thucydides' interest in the financial theme. His use of, for example, narrative anticipation and delay to achieve emphasis, counterfactuals, vivid and highly visual scene painting, and impressionistic description encourages the reader to approach the text more visually, as a spectator judging an event; the effects of this technique are all ways of making the reader focus more sharply on the subject of money than might otherwise be the case. Items of financial information that at first might seem to be included simply for the sake of the objective historical record have a charged rhetorical nature and function, to be put to the service of a larger historiographical agenda. Moreover, passages in which financial information or scenes describing money occur are almost always laden with irony, intended to be read against earlier sections of the work, as well as to give enhanced understanding to the latter.[4] Thus this book deals frequently with earlier parts of the *History,* especially the first three books, to show their interrela-

4. See Mink 1987, 49–50, on the necessity of "grasping together" the whole of a historical work, an act that is required for full comprehension, that is, for historical understanding. At the same time, the *History* contains multiple levels or layers of comprehension, from which the reader benefits in different respects. The Archaeology, for example, is comprehensible without knowing what happens later on in the *History* (yet it has a certain predictive power). On the other hand, its full historical meaning is revealed only when the end is reached and the reader "grasps together" the whole and thinks about the Archaeology, "Ah, *that's* what that is all about."

tionship with the later books, and leads toward an assessment of how the theme of money works in Thucydides' *History* as a whole. Finally, intertextuality, especially with reference to Herodotos' *Histories* but also Homer, plays a major role in this examination, since it constitutes an especially prominent technique by which Thucydides further intensifies lessons about historical events that center around money; even more, intertextuality is fundamental to his view of the historical process.[5]

The contrast between Thucydides' aims in roughly the two halves of his work can be put succinctly. Earlier in the *History,* especially in books 1 and 2, the historian sets out to demonstrate the essential role of money in the creation and increase of naval *arche,* to foster a positive reading of the notion of expense (*dapane*), and to imply the unprecedented success under Perikles of combining *periousia chrematon,* "financial surplus," *gnome,* "acute judgment," and leadership; in the last three books he systematically shows the dismantling or unraveling of this process. Through an extended and highly complex argument in which the historian links the subject of money to other prominent themes in the narrative—the role of the passions, greed, morality, and the interpretation of vision—money becomes, paradoxically, the engine not of Athenian power, but of the corrosion of Athenian power, as the Athenians and their leaders fail to know how to use the ample resources they have, and fail to recognize that money, not wealth in precious objects, is the necessary prerequisite and indicator of military power. They become motivated by greed and profit. Thus the first part of the *History* functions as a foil for the narrative of the end of the work, and the larger issue is the capability of the democracy in running an *arche* and especially in fighting a naval war.

To summarize the general result of my earlier examination and to set the stage for the current study, it is clear from the treatment of public and war finance in the first half of the *History* that Thucydides is saying something new about wealth and power. His originality in treating a theme that con-

5. I should emphasize that this is not a narratological or intertextual study or a theoretical analysis of Thucydides' deployment of rhetorical and other techniques. As it concerns the theme of money, Thucydides' narrative contains multiple layers, and to unpack these layers I approach the *History* in as many ways as I can. My thinking has often been stimulated by scholarly studies in narratology, intertextuality, and rhetoric, as applied to both primarily nonclassical literary texts (narratology: e.g., Genette 1983, 1988, 1990; Bal 1981, 1990, 1997; Bronzwaer 1981; Banfield 1973, 1978; Chatman 1986; Nelles 1990; narrative in history: e.g., White 1981; rhetoric: e.g., Booth 1974; McGee 1980; Shapiro 1986; Parker 1990) and classical literature (intertextuality: e.g., Conte 1986; Thomas 1986; Lyne 1994; Pelling 1991, 1999; Hinds 1998; Rood 1999; narratology: e.g., de Jong 1989; Hornblower 1994a; Rood 1998). My examination contains little explicit theoretical apparatus that might create confusion for the contemporary reader (not to mention bafflement for readers in the future), given the continuing inconsistency in terminological usage and meaning.

sistently occupies much of Greek literature from Homer on lies in his argument that the expenditure of money specifically is the sine qua non of military strength when naval power is at issue. Thus he implicitly contests and redefines traditional notions about wealth and power, in which nonmonetary wealth and its display are essential to the expression of power, and about military power in general, which hitherto had not involved the large outlay of public wealth in any form. Moreover, and perhaps most conspicuously, whereas in earlier authors the subject more often than not evokes anxiety and moral unease for its potential and perceived dangers to society, Thucydides makes the case that money is a positive as well as a necessary instrument, lacking any intrinsic negative power that threatens traditional morality.

Thucydides' liberation of money from the moral sphere is on the face of it an astonishing construction, given that in Athens' case it is not just money that is at issue, but its vast accumulation, ripe material for moral unease in other authors. Thucydides, however, is not making a general case. Rather, he rigidly delimits the sphere and the terms in which this positive construction of money is located. The sphere is public and military, and the terms are its necessary, unprecedented accumulation expressly for the purpose of expenditure on naval power—with an extra ingredient added, namely, the expertise and knowledge on the part of the city's leaders of how best to obtain and then to deploy financial resources in this sphere.

Thucydides' account of the downfall of Athens in the great Sicilian expedition has received enormous attention. Yet just as scholarship has tended to undervalue the extent to which money and public finance form part of Thucydides' larger narrative concerned with the rise and exercise of Athens' power, and of power generally, it has not sufficiently appreciated to what extent the subject also informs Athens' fall. In the latter books, Thucydides' use of the theme or subject is cast more negatively, and it is also, for the first time, tinged with moral implications. Not coincidentally it is embedded in and informed by a narrative whose character has changed, one that focuses more on individuals, on the relationship between private and public spheres, and on the consequences of the presence of enormous monetary wealth, floating free from proper guidance and leadership. In Thucydides' construction, money is unproblematic if used for the city's power and in the right way; it becomes morally problematic in the military and public sphere when military ventures are undertaken for individual gain, or when individuals, not the state, profit as a result—in other words, when public and private become blurred.

Related to this negative, moral casting of the theme of money is another phenomenon, namely, the transformation of the nature of the *arche* brought about both by the acquisition of vast wealth and by the necessary function of money in the exercise of power. In the introduction to my first book I noted the importance of distinguishing between motives for the creation of *arche* and those for perpetuating it.[6] In the beginning of the *arche,* money was a means to an end. The Athenians created a power relationship for which, for the first time on any large and enduring scale in the Greek world, money was the essential ingredient for success, used in the service of an alliance in which the polis that possessed financial resources was able to exploit them to exert political control. In a gradual and doubtless complex process, the economic facet of the *arche,* always present in its revenue-generating structure, became more prominent as the Athenians appropriated the resources of the Aegean world in diverse ways and aimed at controlling the grain trade; by the Peloponnesian War it moves in effect into a primary position in which the *arche* is now regarded as a method of obtaining wealth more than power per se. This is a transformation that Thucydides implicitly abjured as a perversion of power.

Thucydides' approach makes clear that the theme of money and finance continues to have a fundamental place in his *History,* but it also seems to have increased in vigor, intensity, and complexity as the war continues. Thucydides' strategy in writing about the financial aspect of the war at this stage is intended, through largely implicit means, to guide the reader to draw inferences and conclusions. This is of course true generally; in the case of the theme of money, however, the interpretation he fosters is fundamentally critical of Athenian democracy and is achieved partly by locating the theme within contexts and linking it to other themes that are themselves presented negatively—for example, those of ostentatious display, the passions and irrational states generally, and finally ignorance and bad judgment.

In arguing that Thucydides quite consistently intends his readers to draw *a* certain conclusion, I need to clarify what I mean by using the words "complexity" and "ambiguity" in discussing his approach. As is clear throughout the speeches and narrative of the *History,* less so in his explicitly analytical sections (e.g., the Archaeology, 1.95–96, 1.99) or where, unusually, he invokes the first person (e.g., 8.87.4) or clearly endorses a statement (e.g., 8.98.2), Thucydides makes possible different readings and interpretations in order to expose dilemmas, to underscore the complexity or ambiguity inherent in historical situations, and to play with the relationship between perception and reality. This approach is particularly pronounced in the paired speeches and in the Melian Dialogue.

His approach operates, as in any text, within a series of embedded hierarchical levels that are important to distinguish. On the level of the historical addressees of speeches, for example, responses would have varied given the heterogeneity of the audiences' status, attitudes, and views. The Funeral

6. *Money,* esp. 7–8.

Oration, for one, is a masterpiece of the way in which a speaker—in this case, Perikles—pushes buttons to appeal, at one time to elites, at another to the poor, at others to the politically engaged or the politically aloof, each of whom would have responded differently to a given part of the oration. Responses of readers of the *History* would have been expected to differ as well, depending on the views and ideologies brought to the reading of the text. In one respect, these are beyond the control of the author; on the other hand, if we turn specifically to Thucydides' objectives as historian-narrator, he composes the narrative precisely to encourage different ways of looking at an issue, by showing that different interpretations are certainly sustainable.

It is also clear, however, from the way that he constructs the narrative that he endorses certain interpretations. Individual sections of the work in themselves prompt a given response or diverse responses, but through a cumulative approach in the larger narrative, Thucydides also sponsors and privileges one response over the other. This is of course what historians and analysts do, not necessarily always on the level of an individual event or issue, but through the ways these resonate with the larger picture. When it comes to the subject of money in the public, military sphere, Thucydides vigorously presses one interpretation that for him is devoid of ambiguity and toward which he intends to guide the reader; it concerns the proper uses of money and the hierarchy of status among different types of wealth. In the composition of the narrative he explicitly shows different ways of looking at this subject but then privileges, through his higher narrative authority and through the cumulative effect of his development of the theme, a further interpretation—his own.[7]

Given the emphasis in this study on the way that Thucydides was using the subject of money to criticize developments that he regarded as fundamentally at odds with the health and power of the polis, I concentrate on books 6 through 8 and omit discussion of the few scraps of financial details in book 5,[8] even though they are details that are indeed valuable for under-

7. See, for example, his treatment of Alkibiades at the beginning of book 6 (see chap. 1, pp. 35–42).

8. 5.31.2: One talent paid by the Lepreans to Olympian Zeus until the Peloponnesian War. This is part of a detailed explanation of a quarrel over money. The Lepreans had owed one talent annually to Olympian Zeus but used the war as a pretext, according to Thucydides, to stop paying; when the Lepreans appealed to the Spartans and the Eleians refused arbitration, the latter formed an alliance with Argos. 5.47.6: Three Aiginetan obols per hoplite, light-armed soldier, and archer and an Aiginetan drachma a day for cavalry, stipulated in the truce between the Athenians, Argives, Mantineians, and Eleians. 5.49–50.1: Another dispute involving money. The Eleians refused the Spartans access to the temple of Olympian Zeus on the grounds that they had failed to pay a fine imposed on them by the Eleians for attacking Eleian territory during a truce, in accordance with Olympian law. Thucydides specifies the amount of the fine:

standing the historian's keen interest in specific and precise financial information (significantly, because often they seem not, in the degree of their detail and specificity, to be essential to the understanding of the historical events).

Because of the nature of Thucydides' treatment of the financial aspect of war, my focus in this study is largely historiographical. His aims, and the often highly rhetorical ways in which he embeds the subject of money and financing in the narrative, necessitate an examination of passages concerned with financial information in their narrative context, instead of regarding them as factual nuggets that can be plucked out of context and used as if they came from a list or as if Thucydides were writing a history of Athenian war finance. In order to understand the nature and meaning of such items of information, we must begin by understanding his purpose in including them. This helps in understanding the reasons for the absence of information in the *History* that we would want to know, as part of the financial history of the *arche* and the Peloponnesian War.

It is also important to follow the text sequentially, since Thucydides' treatment of money in books 6 through 8 constitutes part of a developing argument that can be fully appreciated only by analyzing it as it proceeds. Thus, as in my earlier study, my approach is both reader- and author-based. At the same time, I have adopted a combined thematic and sequential approach for the account of the Sicilian expedition, for as I worked through the text the subject of money seemed to be linked with themes that became especially prominent in specific parts of the *History* and could be useful in those

---

"2,000 minas, 2 for each hoplite, according to Olympian law." The Spartans disputed that the truce was in effect, the Eleians insisting that it was. The Eleians made two proposals, both of which were refused: (1) if the Spartans gave them back Lepreon, they would themselves pay the money owed to the god; (2) if the Spartans swore at the altar of Zeus in front of the rest of the Greeks to pay the fine in future, they would grant them admittance. 5.63.2: Following the aborted battle at Nemea between the Spartans and the Argives. Thucydides tells us that the Spartans were infuriated and impassioned because of Agis' failure to conquer the Argives when he had amassed an army of such high caliber (endorsed by Thucydides in 5.60, where he refers to it as τὸ κάλλιστον); they wanted to demolish his house and fine him 10,000 drachmas, but on Agis' promise to distinguish himself on the next occasion, they let him off and instead created a law that he should be accompanied in future by ten advisors and be deprived of independent authority. 5.67.2: Explaining the high quality of troops from Argos; they had received extensive training at state expense (δημοσίᾳ). (The use of χρήματα in 60.6 seems to designate "property" more generally.) The inclusion of these passages is not gratuitous, but most of them, in their specificity, arguably also go beyond what might be required of the narrative, and thereby reveal the scope of Thucydides' interest in the role of money, extending to, in this case, inter- and infrastate relations. They are thus similar in nature to passages elsewhere in the *History* where Thucydides chooses to relate with specificity the role of money in, for example, ransoming between poleis or within a polis (e.g., 4.65) and payment of money by the Camarinians to Syracuse for Morgantina (3.70, the beginning of the Kerkyraian stasis).

contexts as an interpretative framework and organizing principle. Thus chapter 1 concentrates on 6.1–46; chapter 2, on the remainder of book 6 through the first part of book 7 (with some discussion of passages from the rest of book 7); chapter 3, on 7.27–29; and chapter 4, on the last half of book 7. Yet the themes do not limit themselves tidily to these demarcations, and so I examine their presence more broadly in the narrative where necessary. Some repetition inevitably results, but, given the multiplicity and complexity of the thematic layers and techniques that are embedded in the narrative that concern money, it seemed best and less confusing to begin by examining them separately, in order eventually to appreciate their full significance.

At the end of the Sicilian chapters I consider the relationship between Thucydides and some of the central epigraphic evidence from Athens that bears on his text and vice versa in order to explore the historical value and implications of his treatment (chapter 5). I decided to present this material as a unit, given the thematic and historiographical emphasis of the preceding chapters, which would have been disrupted unnecessarily by an extended epigraphical examination; moreover, the analysis of the epigraphical texts against Thucydides' narrative made most sense if it followed and assumed an initial examination of the entire account of the Sicilian expedition. Finally, I follow the narrative of book 8 in the last chapter (chapter 6) in a sequential format similar to that in my first book.

PRELUDE

The Demonstration of Power and the Ambiguity of Expense in the Melian Dialogue

In 416, an Athenian-led expedition sailed to the island of Melos in the Aegean. Its purpose was to force Melos, a neutral state, to submit to Athens. Thucydides presents a dialogue between Athenians and Melians in which he highlights the nature of power, and the place of arguments about morality, justice, and divine favor—to name just a few—in that context. From the thematic standpoint of money and power, the Melian Dialogue (5.85–111) looks both backward in the narrative, in its function as a showcase of Athenian power, and forward, foreshadowing with deep irony the Sicilian expedition and its aftermath. It is itself pivotal, establishing and marking a shift in the character of Thucydides' treatment of this theme in the second half of his *History* that is ambiguous and complex. In one respect, the Melian Dialogue parallels the Funeral Oration: in both, Athens' power is the subject on display; and underlying both *logoi* is the unspoken basis of that power —*periousia chrematon,* "financial surplus."[1]

Similarly, by the point when the Athenians assert in the Melian Dialogue that "the strong exert their power and the weak submit" (5.89) and "by a necessity of nature we know that humans rule wherever they have power" (5.105.2), the reader knows that Athens' extraordinary financial muscle underlies these major premises, and makes the appropriate inference: although Athens had lost its financial strength in the Archidamian War, if the polis is as powerful as it is presented as now being, then ipso facto it must

1. It was unnecessary for Thucydides to have Perikles in the Funeral Oration dwell specifically on the financial basis of Athens' power because he had made the point abundantly in the preceding narrative. We see in the Oration—and in Perikles' last speech—the result and the significance: unprecedented reserves of money lead to unsurpassed power (*Money,* 111–12).

have regained it.[2] Thus, while Thucydides has been quiet throughout book 5 on the issue of Athens' financial recovery from the Archidamian War during the Peace of Nikias, he elegantly and implicitly can establish the point, in a highly dramatic context: Athens' finances have been renewed at this second stage of the war, and its power is at a second "greatest" height.[3]

At the same time, however, the effect of the Dialogue is, paradoxically, to foreshadow weakness and to suggest that the power may be illusory. This negative aspect dominates Thucydides' presentation of Athens at this renewed stage of the war and ultimately concerns the relationship between expense and *gnome,* and, conversely, irrationality. The shifting significance of the notion of expense is critical. Whereas expense above all has occupied a positive position in Thucydides' analysis of power—expense is the key to *dunamis*[4]—the obvious corollary is that expense is a drain, especially if it is not backed up by additional resources and good judgment, and if the state does not take steps to replenish the loss. Hints of the ambiguous nature of expense emerge as early as book 3;[5] parallels between these earlier instances—in particular, the Mytilenaian Debate and the Melian Dialogue—illuminate the thematic links.

While the correspondence in historical circumstances is not exact—the Athenians are after all deciding Mytilene's fate after a revolt by an ally, whereas Melos is resisting being brought into the empire[6]—the two episodes, the Debate (especially Diodotos' speech) and the Dialogue, are closely linked thematically and enhance each other's meaning;[7] one common element is the economics of empire. Indeed, in an important respect the Dialogue follows logically from Diodotos' speech, in which the orator excluded the issue of justice—Kleon's preoccupation in his speech—and urged the Athenians to consider the fate of Mytilene from an argument of economic self-interest. So too in the Melian Dialogue, the Athenians exclude arguments from justice and demand that the Melians, like themselves, focus on self-interest (i.e., preservation).

2. Though the city, I have argued, was not bankrupt; see *Money,* 179–80, 203.

3. Cf. 1.1.1.

4. A passage like 1.99, Thucydides' analysis of how the Athenians grew so powerful, makes the point explicit; cf. 1.83.2.

5. They appear in an allusion to the enormous costs of great power (3.17), and in the Mytilenaian Debate (3.37–48); on 3.17, see *Money,* 133–34.

6. The argument of Treu 1954 (cf. also Raubitschek 1963) that Melos had been a tributary member of the empire since 425, based as it is on the association of an undated fragment of an inscription restored to make Melos tributary with the 425 reassessment decree, is unconvincing (see the objections of Eberhardt 1959; Kierdorf 1962).

7. So Stahl 1966, 166: "Durch die Bezugnahme auf die Diodotos-Rede gewinnt die Situation der Melier allgemeine Bedeutung, oder, so sagen wir besser (um nicht zu abstrahieren), Symbolkraft;" see also Macleod 1983, 55–56.

In both, lenience is presented as an economic argument. Diodotos emphasizes to the Athenians the need not to jeopardize the revenue from the allies, "on which their strength depends," by causing them in the future (if Athens is harsh in the case of Lesbos) to sustain a revolt to the bitter end at great cost to the Athenians. The ally would have nothing to lose, knowing that punishment would be equally brutal no matter when in the course of the revolt it surrendered (3.46.2). Similarly, the Athenians are willing to be "lenient" to the Melians in order to gain financially, offering them survival in return for voluntary submission to tributary status.[8] The Melians, who naturally do not see the offer in the same light, ask: "Where does the advantage lie for us in being enslaved, as it does for you to rule?" (5.92). The Athenians reply: "In this: you would live, as subjects, instead of suffering the most terrible consequence, while we would profit (κερδαίνομεν) by not destroying you" (5.93). It is highly significant for understanding Thucydides that this "political thesis"[9] is put in economic language and terms. Moreover, the material advantage to the Athenians is perhaps emphasized further by the almost gratuitous nature of the comment, for the Melians are not really questioning or unclear about what gain the Athenians derive from a new subject; rather, they wonder what could possibly be advantageous about such a status for the newly conquered.

Finally, passion and reason inform the Mytilenaian episode and are linked to the theme of money. The Athenians made an initial decision in a state of passion (*orge,* 3.36.2) to kill the Mytilenaian men and enslave the women and children. They changed their minds, in Thucydides' account, on the basis of rational calculation of the economic benefit of leniency: in order to decrease the chance of costly sieges in the future. In 416, the Athenians' starting point is the desire to avoid a costly siege. Upon the Melians' resistance, however, they engaged in a lengthy siege and then put the Melian men to death and enslaved the women and children. But Thucydides' account suggests that the act was motivated by cold logic, not passion,[10] and resulted

8. But cf. Macleod 1983, 62: "Indeed at Melos the Athenians, though they use Diodotus' method of argumentation, go clean against his policy of conciliation." See also, for example, Bartoletti 1939, 306; Schwartz 1919, 140; and most fully, Bosworth 1993, all of whom see the Athenians here and generally in the Dialogue as offering fair terms.

9. De Romilly 1963, 286.

10. The Athenians themselves enhance this impression by foreshadowing the consequence in 5.95, as Bosworth (1993, 36 n. 30) notes, against de Ste. Croix (1972, 21), who reads 5.93 differently: "In regard to Melos, in particular, it must be evident to anyone who reads Thucydides without preconceived ideas that there is no reference whatever *in the Dialogue,* direct or indirect, to the appalling sequel—even *ta deinotata pathein* in v 93 need imply no more than the horrors that would anyway be likely to attend a desperate but hopeless resistance." This ignores completely the δὲ clause, which is explicit about what *ta deinotata pathein* means: namely, that the Athenians "would destroy" the Melians (ἡμεῖς δὲ μὴ διαφθείραντες ὑμᾶς).

in matter-of-fact, brutal punishment.[11] Yet the Athenians then embark on the Sicilian expedition, guided by passion (e.g., *eros,* 6.24.3; *agan epithumia,* 24.4); this time they are not motivated by a passion for revenge but by a lust for conquest, money, and the exotic.

The reemergence of passion and emotion brings us back to Diodotos' speech. In a crucial passage he asserts: "Hope and desire (*eros*), being everywhere, the one leading, the other following, the one conceiving a plan, the other suggesting an easy success, do the greatest harm and, being invisible, are far stronger than the dangers that are seen" (3.45.5). This passage resonates so closely with both the Melian Dialogue and the account of the Sicilian expedition that the parallels cannot be accidental;[12] while it does not itself concern money directly, it provides a useful segue to a discussion of the relationship between the Dialogue and the account of the Sicilian expedition, where the subject of money is more closely linked to hope and the passions.

As Cornford first showed, the Dialogue and books 6 through 7 are closely linked thematically.[13] Chronology may have dictated that Thucydides place the description of the attack on Melos right before the account of the Sicilian expedition;[14] but, as K. J. Dover rightly reminds us, that Thucydides "treated the occasion as deserving of a six-page debate . . . reflects his choice."[15] Indeed, the Dialogue, as is now well appreciated, is essential to the understanding and interpretation of the account of the Sicilian expedition, and, as I shall argue in chapter 6, its aftermath as well. It can be no accident that Thucydides highlights themes in the Dialogue that will be prominent in the account of the Sicilian expedition; he emphasizes the theme of

11. Cogan (1981, 90), for example, thinks the harshness of the punishment was in fact motivated by a passion (anger), because of the length of the siege; but given Thucydides' emphasis on the anger motivating the original decision about the Mytilenaians (3.36.2), and his simple allusion to the punishment of the Melians, I would argue that Thucydides at least is presenting it as a calculated, not impassioned act.

12. For the parallels, especially between 3.45.5, 5.103, and 6.24.3, see Bender 1938, 40–41 n. 109; Hornblower 1991a, 436, citing Saar 1953, 81–83.

13. Cornford 1971 [1907]; the intentionality of their juxtaposition has long been noted: e.g., Jebb 1907, 436; Schwartz 1919, 138; de Sanctis 1930, 308; Méautis 1935; Bartoletti 1939, 315–16; Finley 1942, 323; Murray 1944, 1–2; Wassermann 1947, 30, 36; Liebeschuetz 1968a; Parry 1981, 198–200; Macleod 1983, 59–60, 67; Connor 1984, 158 (cautious); Orwin 1994, 97–141; but cf. Andrewes 1960, 10: the Dialogue as a whole is "very little concerned with Sicily."

14. I say "may have" because Thucydides can engage in temporal manipulation, delaying the narration of an event, when it suits his purpose: e.g., 6.46, on which see chap. 1, pp. 69–79, below; also cf. Rood 1998, 109–30.

15. Dover 1973, 41. Cf. the one sentence devoted to the similar attack on Skione and its fate, 5.32; see Connor 1984, 147 with n. 20 on fourth-century B.C. attitudes toward Skione; also Lateiner (1977, 43), who sees *pathos* in Thucydides' description of the attack.

financial resources, for instance, and interweaves it with such other themes as sight and seeing, present and future, and hope and fear.[16] The Melians have reached a desperate stage in the argument, grasping at fortune or luck (*tuche*) and hope for the future (5.102); it is the Athenians who control the present. The text at 5.103 is critical. The Athenians seize hold of the Melians' reliance on hope and turn it into an economic argument, part metaphorical, part real:

> Ἐλπὶς δὲ κινδύνῳ παραμύθιον οὖσα τοὺς μὲν ἀπὸ περιουσίας χρωμένους αὐτῇ, κἂν βλάψῃ, οὐ καθεῖλεν· τοῖς δ' ἐς ἅπαν τὸ ὑπάρχον ἀναρριπτοῦσι (δάπανος γὰρ φύσει) ἅμα τε γιγνώσκεται σφαλέντων καὶ ἐν ὅτῳ ἔτι φυλάξεταί τις αὐτὴν γνωρισθεῖσαν οὐκ ἐλλείπει. ὃ ὑμεῖς ἀσθενεῖς τε καὶ ἐπὶ ῥοπῆς μιᾶς ὄντες μὴ βούλεσθε παθεῖν μηδὲ ὁμοιωθῆναι τοῖς πολλοῖς, οἷς παρὸν ἀνθρωπείως ἔτι σῴζεσθαι, ἐπειδὰν πιεζομένους αὐτοὺς ἐπιλίπωσιν αἱ φανεραὶ ἐλπίδες, ἐπὶ τὰς ἀφανεῖς καθίστανται μαντικήν τε καὶ χρησμοὺς καὶ ὅσα τοιαῦτα μετ' ἐλπίδων λυμαίνεται.

> Hope, that inciter to danger, does not utterly ruin, even if it harms, those who use it from a position of abundance. But for those who gamble their existing resources entirely on it—for it is expensive in nature—they see it for what it is only when they are destroyed, and it does not fail as long as there is a chance that someone will guard against it after recognizing it for what it is. This is what you, being weak and at the mercy of a single balancing of the scale, do not want to suffer, nor want to become like the many, who, when it is in their human power still to be saved, whenever manifest hopes fail them when they are hard-pressed, fall for invisible ones—prophecy and oracles and all that nonsense that causes ruin when accompanying hopes.

The Athenians rephrase and reinforce chapter 103 at the end of the Dialogue, recalling it through similar language as they caution the Melians: "Your strongest arguments lie in the future and are based on hope, but your actual resources are too small to allow you to prevail over those who are arrayed against you (ὑμῶν τὰ μὲν ἰσχυρότατα ἐλπιζόμενα μέλλεται, τὰ δ' ὑπάρχοντα βραχέα πρὸς τὰ ἤδη ἀντιτεταγμένα περιγίγνεσθαι). You will therefore show great irrationality of judgment unless, after allowing us to withdraw, you decide on something more prudent than this" (111.2).

Scholars have noted echoes of this section of the Dialogue in the Sicilian expedition narrative.[17] A. W. Gomme and others saw a resonance with 5.103

16. As Parry (1981, 198) notes with respect to present and future, "the meaning of μέλλοντα and παρόντα in the Sicilian campaign can be understood only from the Melian conference."

17. E.g., Cornford 1971 [1907], 182–85; Andrewes 1960, 2–3. Gomme, in *HCT* 4, ad loc.; Kitto 1966, 335; Orwin 1994, 118 n. 2. Liebeschuetz (1968a, 75) regards the chapter as containing a "clear if unintended reference to the Athenians" in Sicily; on the contrary, surely it is entirely intentional.

in 6.9.3,[18] where Nikias notes that the Athenians will not be inclined to listen to his warning that they "not risk what they have on invisible and future [hopes]."[19] Similarly, Clifford Orwin cites the parallel with a later passage in Nikias' speech, in which the general attempts to enlist the support of older Athenians against the expedition: "Do not have desire for the far-off that the young suffer; recognize that success comes least by desire and most by foresight, and on behalf of the country, which is emphatically risking the greatest danger ever, vote against the expedition."[20]

One additional narrative pattern needs to be appreciated before examining the significance of the parallels. In 5.102, the Melians state that they will rely on hope, and the Athenians respond in 103. In chapter 104, the Melians respond to the Athenians' statements on the folly and dangers of hope by asserting that the gods will surely help them. In 7.77.1–4, his final speech to his men after their defeat in the Great Harbor of Syracuse and their retreat, Nikias asserts—astonishingly—that he still has hope: "Athenians and allies, even in our present circumstances we must have hope. . . . I am hanging on the same danger as the lowest among you; and yet I have lived my life with great devotion to the gods and with much justice and without reproach toward men. Therefore, despite all, I have hope that the gods will have kinder judgments now, for we are more worthy of their pity than of their envy."[21] Thus the progression of hope, a belief in the gods' help, and utter destruction operates in both passages.

Although the element of hope in 5.103 has received the most scholarly attention, we need to appreciate fully the economic argument and its implications. The Athenians locate hope in the context of economic and commercial activity as it applies to both strong and weak players. The *periousiai,* "abundances," which will allow those possessing them to survive, should they employ hope, have a strong financial component, given the theme and argument of the chapter. This element emerges more explicitly in the next clause: "But for those who gamble their existing resources (τὸ ὑπάρχον) entirely on it—for it is very expensive[22] in nature," etc. Finally, a weighing metaphor in the phrase ἐπὶ ῥοπῆς μιᾶς ὄντες, "hanging on one weighing

18. Gomme, in *HCT* 4, on 5.103; Kitto 1966, 335; Orwin 1994, 118 n. 2.

19. μὴ τοῖς ἑτοίμοις περὶ τῶν ἀφανῶν καὶ τῶν μελλόντων κινδυνεύειν.

20. 6.13.1: μηδ', ὅπερ ἂν αὐτοὶ πάθοιεν, δυσέρωτας εἶναι τῶν ἀπόντων, γνόντας ὅτι ἐπιθυμίᾳ μὲν ἐλάχιστα κατορθοῦνται, προνοίᾳ δὲ πλεῖστα, ἀλλ' ὑπὲρ τῆς πατρίδος ὡς μέγιστον δὴ τῶν πρὶν κίνδυνον ἀναρριπτούσης ἀντιχειροτονεῖν, καὶ ψηφίζεσθαι τοὺς μὲν Σικελιώτας οἷσπερ νῦν ὅροις χρωμένους πρὸς ἡμᾶς, οὐ μεμπτοῖς, τῷ τε Ἰονίῳ κόλπῳ παρὰ γῆν ἤν τις πλέῃ, καὶ τῷ Σικελικῷ διὰ πελάγους, τὰ αὑτῶν νεμομένους καθ' αὑτοὺς καὶ ξυμφέρεσθαι. See Orwin 1994, 118 n. 2.

21. See Stahl (1966, 168), who equates the nature of the Melians' and Nikias' hope.

22. δάπανος is unequivocally negative here, given the context.

of the scale," whether coin or commodity, includes the notion of financial risk through a transaction in which the value cannot be assured.[23]

What is straightforward in both cases described in 5.103 is that hope is expensive: thus when the reader discovers to what extent the Athenians relied on hope as they set out for Sicily (6.31.6), it is immediately clear that that expedition will be especially expensive. There is a striking ambiguity in this chapter, though, when considered from the perspective of the subsequent narrative. We are at first led to identify the Athenians with the category of those people who use hope but from a position of *periousiai*—clearly meaning financial strength, given the argument of the chapter—and the Melians as those who will be destroyed because of resources insufficient to engage in risky ventures. They will in effect be gambling with their money, and thus gambling away their lives; and the risk will be greater because they will have only one chance to "weigh" their decision. In the reversal of the Sicilian narrative, however, in which the Athenians meet with total disaster (πανωλεθρίᾳ, 7.87.6), they become like the Melians,[24] but not quite. As Peter Pouncey reminds us, unlike the Melians, the Athenians were not utterly wiped out.[25] Moreover, there are elements of the Athenians' statement about the weak that resonate as much with their own situation as with that of the Melians: "But for those who stake everything they have on [hope]—for it is expensive in nature—they see it for what it is only when they are destroyed, and it does not fail as long as one guards against it having been recognized for what it is." Antony Andrewes comments, "In particular, δάπανος γὰρ φύσει is much more appropriate to the Athenian than the Melian situation."[26] Adam Parry focuses on the clause preceding the Athenians' comment on the weak:

> The primary meaning of the passage is that the Melians have no margin of safety, and hence cannot take chances, as the Athenians can. But there is another less obvious and ironic sense of the words. The difficulty and unexampled construction of τοῖς δ' ἐς ἅπαν τὸ ὑπάρχον ἀναρριπτοῦσι may be due to Thucydides' desire to suggest this secondary sense. ὑπάρχον is the Athenians' word; it is an equivalent of παρόν, the thing they want to put all

23. There is an interesting paradox in the use of this metaphor, if the argument of Wallace 1989 is accepted, that in weighing (electrum) coins, the smallest, not the largest, denominations are weighed most carefully (i.e., repeatedly), since it is in the case of small weights that one would want to make sure, through repeated weighing, that a piece absolutely had as much metal as it was supposed to. Transposed to decision making, does this have the effect of suggesting that the Melians should not be forced to make a snap decision?

24. E.g., Cornford 1971 [1907], 184–85; see also Connor 1984, 154–55; Orwin 1994, 118–41.

25. Pouncey 1980, 91; also Liebeschuetz 1968a; and chap. 6, pp. 230–33, below.

26. *HCT* 4, ad loc.

> their trust in. And so the gambling metaphor of the second clause insensibly reverts to the Athenians themselves. It is they, to twist the uncommon Greek idiom slightly, who are staking their all on immediate reality, and staking it with a recklessness of danger which is far greater than that of the timid but stubborn Melians, greater because they have so much more at stake, and because they are doing it so deliberately.[27]

Thus by themselves (i.e., without the Sicilian narrative) the financial language used and its link to the element of the present place the Athenians in both categories. But the reader does not have to wait until the end of the Sicilian account for the irony planted in 5.103 to be more fully revealed. It is already blatant and powerful at the beginning of the account of the Sicilian expedition. In 6.31.6, concluding the vivid description of the appearance of the fleet about to depart for Sicily, Thucydides remarks: "The expedition was famed no less for the marvel of its daring and the brilliance of its appearance than for the magnitude of the force compared to that against which it was sent, and because it was the largest expedition attempted away from home and was sent out with the greatest hope in the future compared with their existing resources."[28] The echo is patent in the language Thucydides uses.[29]

Fundamental to the portrait of the interplay of money, hope, and risk, 5.103, then, foreshadows the Sicilian account. Thus it is no surprise that toward the end of the expedition there is both an emphasis in the narrative on danger, desperate hope (especially given to the figure of Nikias), and attention to money at dramatic moments.[30] Moreover, as we shall see in chapter 6, Thucydides begins his account of the aftermath of the disaster with language that evokes 5.103 yet again. 5.111 is also linked closely to the Sicilian account through the themes of hope and resources, but it adds the

27. Parry 1981, 197.

28. καὶ ὁ στόλος οὐχ ἧσσον τόλμης τε θάμβει καὶ ὄψεως λαμπρότητι περιβόητος ἐγένετο ἢ στρατιᾶς πρὸς οὓς ἐπῇσαν ὑπερβολῇ, καὶ ὅτι μέγιστος ἤδη διάπλους ἀπὸ τῆς οἰκείας καὶ ἐπὶ μεγίστῃ ἐλπίδι τῶν μελλόντων πρὸς τὰ ὑπάρχοντα ἐπεχειρήθη. Commentators translate πρὸς τὰ ὑπάρχοντα variously but usually understand it to mean "circumstances." But given Thucydides' interest in the issue of the resources with which the Athenians fought in Sicily, his interpretation, to be explored in chapter 2, that they did not use enough for their intended aims, the fact that τὰ ὑπάρχοντα often means "resources," and above all the similarity to 5.103, it seems likely that he is referring to resources here. Parry (1981, 74–75, 79) stresses the similarities between the ὑπάρχοντα/μελλόντα contrast in the Melian Dialogue and 6.31.6; see also chap. 1, pp. 63–65, below.

29. De Romilly 1963, 293 n. 2; Parry 1981, 77, and see chap. 1, pp. 63–65, below.

30. As, for example, Hunter (1973, 111) notes, the Athenians, through their reliance on hope and fortune in place of *pronoia* and *gnome* by the end of the expedition, are "all but reduced to those straits to which they once brought the Melians (cf. especially 5.102–104)." See chap. 4 below.

element of irrationality, itself a thematic thread woven throughout books 6 and 7.[31]

The Melian Dialogue sets the stage for the theme of money and power in the account of the Sicilian expedition in two additional and fundamental respects. The Dialogue is meant to be read on two levels, as portraying a great display of power, on the one hand, and, paradoxically, as an ironic recognition of the issues of cost and loss, on the other, on the part of the Athenians.

First, let's look at how the Dialogue portrays the display of power. The Athenians, as we saw, invoke an argument about money and power early on when they state that the Melians' peaceful submission would benefit both sides: the Melians would be saved, and the Athenians would profit by not undertaking a siege. Thus, as mentioned above, whereas earlier in the *History* the expenditure of money is linked to the (positive) increase of power (*auxesis*), in the Dialogue the only argument Thucydides permits explicitly concerns the elimination of expense for power (5.95). While Thucydides downplays the positive notion of spending to exercise and extend power, he builds the impression that the Athenians are interested above all in the demonstration or display of their power.

The differing presentation is important. In the Dialogue Thucydides obscures the not-insignificant power and relative prosperity of Melos—the Athenians assessed the Melians 15 talents in the 425 reassessment decree,[32] failed to conquer them in the Archidamian War, and did so in 416 only after a ten-month siege that required reinforcements from home—and instead presents Melos as poor and weak and Athens as rich—implicitly and through analogy (5.103.1)—and strong. Relatively speaking, this is accurate, but the downplaying of Melos' own resources must be deliberate. The image, upon the Melians' reduction, of an elephant stomping an ant suggests not so much an *increase* in the power of Athens as a *show* of power. This interpretation is explicitly advanced in the Dialogue itself, when the Athenians argue the necessity of conquering the Melians, and the reasons they furnish have primarily to do with how their power *looks* to other Greeks. In 5.95 they assert, in response to the Melians' desire to remain neutral: "Your enmity does not harm us as much as your friendship shows to our subjects an example of weakness, while your hatred shows an example of power" (οὐ γὰρ τοσοῦτον ἡμᾶς βλάπτει ἡ ἔχθρα ὑμῶν ὅσον ἡ φιλία μὲν ἀσθενείας,

31. This is presented most strikingly first in the assembly scene following Nikias' second speech before the expedition, in which the Athenians are collectively presented as being struck by *eros* and *epithumia* for the expedition, with the common people fixated on the financial rewards of the conquest of Sicily (6.24). See chap. 1, pp. 44–45, below.

32. Sanders (1984, 262) comments that "the fertility of the island may . . . explain why ancient Melos, before its fall to Athens in 416 B.C., was assessed at such high tribute in relation to its size."

τὸ δὲ μῖσος δυναμέως παράδειγμα τοῖς ἀρχομένοις δηλούμενον). The phrase "Your hatred shows a *paradeigma* of power" makes the emphasis on the display of power especially chilling, since the Melians are neutral and cannot be said to deserve the fate that the Athenians destine them for as an example to others.[33]

The Athenians continue in 5.97 by making the point that if they leave others independent, it is (in the allies' eyes) from fear. The statement that "so that, apart from extending our empire (ἔξω καὶ τοῦ πλεόνων ἄρξαι), we would gain security (τὸ ἀσφαλές) in your conquest" likewise reveals their concern with the appearance of their power to others, since fear and concern for security relate directly to others' perception of their power;[34] as de Romilly comments, "in order to keep [the allies] at bay she needs to *show her strength.*"[35] The Melians respond by saying, "How can you not make enemies of all who are currently unaligned, when they look (βλέψαντες) at our case and believe that you will at some point come against them?"

The appearance of Athens' power—the primary basis of its position, in which the actual extension of empire is secondary[36]—is crucial to the narrative of the Sicilian expedition. Thucydides develops the idea of the appearance of power primarily in the first half of book 6, as we shall see in the next chapter. In the Sicilian expedition narrative, the appearance of power leads to questions about the reality of the power itself: is the expedition an exercise and extension of power, or merely the demonstration, the look of power? Thucydides provides an answer in the case of the Athenians in 415, when he concludes his description of the launching of the expedition, which emphasizes the appearance of power, with the comment "To the rest of the Greeks it looked more like a display of power and resources than a military expedition" (ἐπίδειξιν μᾶλλον εἰκασθῆναι τῆς δυνάμεως καὶ ἐξουσίας ἢ ἐπὶ πολέμιους παρασκευήν, 6.31.4), noting in addition that the expedition was renowned for the "brilliance of its appearance" (ὄψεως λαμπροτάτη, 6.31.6).

Thucydides' presentation of the display of power at the beginning of the account of the Sicilian expedition is fundamentally ambiguous, as we shall see more fully in the next chapter. Its ambiguous presentation in the Melian Dialogue emerges as the Dialogue is read not only on the level of the appearance of power but also on the level of cost and loss. As mentioned above, the Dialogue and the narrative concerning the aftermath of the expedition

33. See de Romilly 1963, 288 with n. 1.

34. Macleod (1983, 58) views the Athenians' fear of their own empire as the primary motive for the conquest of Melos; cf. Cogan 1981, 92 with n. 10.

35. De Romilly 1963, 287 (my emphasis).

36. The Athenians say, "Apart from ruling more"; de Romilly 1963, 289; see also Seaman 1997, 390.

decidedly do not foster the positive interpretation supported in earlier sections of the *History*—namely, that spending brings power. Rather, one gains the impression that the conquest of Melos, motivated by the need to demonstrate power, will cost Athens dearly. At 5.95, the Athenians argue that they will profit (κερδαίνομεν) if Melos submits voluntarily. But the negative corollary lurks just below the surface: the military reduction of Melos will *not* profit the Athenians. A positive point makes a negative point at one and the same time; we recall Diodotos' emphasis on the tremendous cost and the drain on power of sieges (3.46.2–3).

To confirm the point implicitly, Thucydides tells what resulted from the failure of "negotiation." The Athenians did not easily bring down the Melians, as their envoys' arguments in the Dialogue encouraged us to think; on the contrary, they succeeded in reducing Melos only after a ten-month siege with reinforcements from home (5.116). Moreover, having been successful, they did not impose a result that brought them any long-term profit in the end. They neither demanded that the Melians pay an indemnity, nor made them tributary; they killed the men, sold the women and children—hardly significant compensation for the cost of the siege—and colonized the island. One recalls again the case of Lesbos. There, Thucydides explicitly noted that the Athenians, upon finally deciding what to do with the islanders, "did not impose tribute" but instead converted the island into an Athenian cleruchy (3.50.1), making the point through his negative presentation that the Athenian state did not benefit greatly from the siege. Thus while in one respect the Athenians won, in another important respect, from the standpoint of the rhetoric of the Dialogue, they lost; they did *not* get what they said they wanted most of all, what they described as being in their greatest self-interest—that is, profit through the Melians' voluntary submission to tributary status.

Finally, as scholars have long recognized, as a prelude to the account of the Sicilian expedition,[37] the Melian Dialogue is itself a beginning. In this light, there are both parallels and reversals when the beginning—the Melian episode—and its end—the aftermath of the defeat at Syracuse—are read against each other, and these may help explain the "historian's choice." The Athenians offer the Melians their lives in return for money (5.111), but to no avail. After Nikias is forced to surrender his men, he offers to repay the cost of the war to the Syracusans and casts the repayment in terms of men for money—one hostage per talent spent—also to no avail.[38] The Melians could have saved their lives in return for tributary status; Nikias tried and failed to save the lives of his men in return for money. Thucydides

37. E.g., Wassermann 1947, 34, 35.
38. 7.78.2; see chap. 4, pp. 176–81, below.

may have decided to include the description of Nikias' attempt to ransom his men, I suggest, partly to evoke and contrast the Athenians' attitude toward and treatment of the Melians with Nikias' solution to human loss and violence at the bitter end of the Sicilian expedition.

In conclusion, both the implicit emphasis on the cost and drain of the siege of Melos and the presentation of Athens as displaying its power to other Greeks, then, set up and foreshadow the Sicilian expedition with emerging irony, for Thucydides composes the narrative of the expedition by linking the two elements, first and most strikingly in 6.31, and then again as the expedition drags on. In both the Dialogue and the Sicilian account the presentation is fundamentally negative, read not as a use of money to extend power, which is the positive construction offered in the Periklean sections of the *History* and in the Pentekontaetia, but as a costly demonstration that will, in Sicily, have catastrophic consequences.[39]

39. This economic reading of the negative aspects of Athenian policy parallels and dovetails to some extent with de Romilly's political reading with its emphasis on the costs of Athens' strategy based on fear: "If the empire really obliges Athens to be constantly showing her strength in order to keep her subjects obedient, and if this continual show of strength perpetually increases the number of her enemies, then the remedy is simply making the situation worse; by giving rise to more numerous and sharper enmities, it is making the trial of strength at one and the same time more necessary and more dangerous" (1963, 295); see also Macleod 1983, 58–59; Hussey 1985, 127.

CHAPTER ONE

Optical Illusions

Wealth and the Display of Power in the Beginning of the Sicilian Narrative

The presentation of money and wealth in the opening stage of the Sicilian expedition (roughly the first half of book 6) constitutes an inversion of the same theme as treated in the earlier books of the *History*. The Sicilian narrative takes Perikles' comment in the Funeral Oration, "We use wealth more for action than for show" (2.40.1), which implies criticism of those who do the opposite, and turns it on its head. I shall argue in this chapter that a central theme of Thucydides' account of the Athenians as they prepare to go off to Sicily is the ostentatious display of their wealth and the implication that this display is a substitute for the exercise of real power—"action."[1]

Thucydides interweaves the subject of money with other thematic elements, some of which we have seen to be prominent in the Melian Dialogue: chiefly, the relationship between hope and resources, and sight and seeing, as well as Athenian ignorance and gullibility, the blurring of public and private, and the passions. The historian devotes considerable attention to the financing and expense of the expedition. He was not compelled to do so by some notion of generic necessity; rather, he embeds financial details in highly rhetorical contexts designed to evoke irony and to encourage the reader's criticism of the way the city's leaders and the Athenian collective are thinking about and using metallic wealth.

Sight (*opsis*) figures especially prominently in Thucydides' treatment. It has often been noted that the Greeks had a cultural preoccupation with sight and its relationship to knowledge—"to see" and "to know" are etymologically related—and, like other fifth-century writers, Thucydides displays

1. See also Jordan (2000), whose study in a number of places parallels my discussion but appeared too late to be incorporated.

an intense interest in the relationship between vision and knowledge (and vision compared with other sensory faculties, especially hearing).[2] *Opsis* in Thucydides can be an essential tool, or it can be useless,[3] and at worst, fundamentally and dangerously deceiving.[4] *Opsis* always involves interpretation; it is a participatory, reciprocal act in which the relationship between subject and object is fluid. *Opsis* is fundamentally ambiguous: it can be illusory or real, but even in the latter case, it must be interpreted correctly.[5] The interpretative difficulty inherent in *opsis* relates to Thucydides' didactic approach in treating the problem of *opsis:* his narrative is constructed in such a way as to provide lessons in how to read and interpret visual signs. These lessons consist in part of explicit instruction of his own, followed by glaring examples of misreading. Much like hope, explored in the prelude, *opsis* is often truly understood only at the moment of destruction.[6]

2. Debates about the value of optical perception (often in comparison with auditory perception) began with the pre-Socratics and continued through the classical period and beyond. The issue was of special interest to Plato and Aristotle, who had different theories about the optical process and came to little consensus except about the problematic nature of sight in relation to knowledge. For Greek theories of vision, and for general discussion, see, for example, Snell 1953; O'Brien 1970; Simon 1979; Jonas 1982; Meyering 1989, 21–36; Jay 1993, 21–33; Segal 1995; Goldhill 1996; for the relationship between sight and knowledge in the tragedians, see Goldhill 1986, 17–19 (Aeschylus), 199–221 (Sophokles); Zeitlin 1994 (Euripides); Gregory 1985 (Euripides). Visual evidence and the usefulness of seeing as a historiographical tool to draw in the external audience were preoccupations of Roman historiography as well as Greek; see Marincola 1997, 63–86, and e.g. for Livy, Feldherr 1998, 1–50. On the culture-specific nature of sight and theories of and attitudes toward vision in various historical periods, see esp. Wartofsky, e.g., 1979; 1981; also Jay 1993; Brennan 1996; de Bolla 1996. I have benefited from discussion with Stephanie Moorhead and from her master's thesis on vision in Herodotos and Thucydides (University of Texas, 2000).

3. E.g., 1.10, on which see below. On the rejection of visual observation of *phainomena* as useful evidence in Greek science, medicine, and philosophy, see Lloyd 1979, esp. 129–38 (but also passim).

4. As Marincola (1997, 68) notes, Thucydides recognizes the insufficiency of even his own autopsy (1.22.2); Hartog's claim (1988, 272) that "for Thucydides, historical knowledge is founded above all on *opsis*" misses the subtlety in Thucydides' attitude toward the value of *opsis* (Thucydides can also be more positive about *akoe,* "tradition," than Hartog credits him). Neither Marincola nor Hartog wrestles sufficiently with the issue of Herodotos' concern, and Thucydides', with the ways in which *opsis* is problematic as an interpretative tool in the case of actors in their respective histories. Cf. also Hedrick (1993, 1995), who also assumes a greater contrast between the two historians than may be accurate. The same struggle with the problem of vision and its relation to knowledge that is pervasive in Greek texts is evident in both historians' works. For a nuanced discussion of *opsis* in Herodotos, Dewald 1987.

5. See also Ober 1998, 114 n.114, on *opsis* in connection with the launching of the fleet (6.31.1, examined below): "The masses' false confidence from seeing demonstrates that . . . visual perception can be just as misleading as verbal persuasion."

6. See chap. 4, pp. 168–69, below.

Both Herodotos and Thucydides describe wealth in a way that focuses the reader's attention on its visual impact.[7] Both encourage interpretation on the part of both actors and readers, but Thucydides' originality lies in his particular attention to the problem of money versus other wealth in a military context. Thucydides presents scenes focusing visually on non-monetary wealth in which his actors consistently misinterpret its meaning and make ultimately catastrophic decisions. This is especially evident in his description of the fleet that sailed to Sicily in 415 (6.31) and in the story of the trap that the Egestans set for the Athenians (6.46). These passages highlight his attitude toward the relationship between sight and money and wealth.

The intricacy of Thucydides' narrative of the origins, launching, and early stage of the Sicilian expedition lies partly in the interrelationship of the historian's presentation, the audience/reader, and contemporary, competing interpretations. His narrative technique sets up an assumption and an awareness of Athenian *dunamis* on the part of actors, spectators, and readers, only to make it ambiguous. He constructs ambiguity partly through prominent use of the word *paraskeue,* "preparation," "preparedness,"[8] a crucial component of which is Athens' financial resources. Thus Thucydides highlights Athenian preparedness at this second beginning of the war, as at the beginning of the Archidamian War in 431 (1.1.1), to create the assumption that Athens once again had extraordinary financial resources to muster. But he simultaneously represents Athens' power as a kind of paradox. He manifestly shows it as great, to create the expectation of strength and success, and then, by emphasizing the display and suggesting that the appearance of power through a show of wealth can be deceptive, he raises the question of its reality, and, finally, with the help of irony achieved through implicit comparisons with earlier parts of the *History,* he rapidly unsettles the assumption of strength and instead presents Athenian *paraskeue* as fundamentally ambiguous.[9] Before examining these techniques fully, however, we need first to consider the opening of book 6, in which financial resources are conspicuously absent.

7. E.g., Hdt. 1.50–52 (Croesus' dedications at Delphi and the shrine of Amphiaraos), 7.83.2 (Persian equipment); Thuc.1.13.3–6 (Athens' wealth), 6.31 (description of the fleet), 6.46 (treasures and drinking vessels).

8. See Allison 1989, 66–120, on the prominence of *paraskeue* in books 6–7.

9. This is a technique Thucydides has employed elsewhere: e.g., 3.16–17, with *Money,* 129–34; and 6.63–93, as Dewald (1975, 195–97) has shown by looking at the way in which Thucydides constructs the account both to emphasize Athenian power and to control, and then undercut it: "Within this large-scale picture of Athenian optimism, Thucydides has placed a second, subtler development designed to cast doubt on all Athenian plans" (196), resulting in "subtle interpretive ambiguity" (197).

ARCHAEOLOGIES AND COLONIES

After concluding the Melian Dialogue and the account of the siege, Thucydides begins his Sicilian narrative abruptly,[10] referring to the Athenians' desire to conquer the island, despite their ignorance of its size and inhabitants (6.1.1).[11] While the Melian Dialogue is a prelude to the Sicilian expedition, Thucydides signals that the expedition is itself a new beginning, meant to be compared with the first beginning—that is to say, with book 1. Hunter Rawlings has demonstrated the close structural relationship between the openings of books 1 and 6: the similarities in the first four sentences of each; followed by an argument about the past, introduced by *gar,* to support a statement about the present (the Archaeology in book 1 [1–19] and the second "archaeology" in book 6 [1–5]); finally, the appearance of the unparalleled phrase *alethestate prophasis,* referring to the "truest explanation" for the Peloponnesian War and the Sicilian expedition, respectively (1.23.6, 6.6.1).[12] The correspondences can only mean that Thucydides intends the reader to draw comparisons and contrasts.

One conspicuous difference between the two archaeologies (the term is used as a convenience) is that while the argument in book 1 aims above all to demonstrate the relationship between money and power, the opening of book 6 sends no such clear message. As Rawlings observes, since Thucydides had fully laid out the general development of power in book 1, "in book VI there is no need for extended analysis of the benefits that money, walls, stability, and ships confer in creating *dynamis.* . . . Instead, the primary concern of the second archaeology is to familiarize Greeks with the size of Sicily and the number of its cities. . . . Both archaeologies are thus concerned, though in different ways, with a question of size and power."[13] Given Thucydides' interest in the role of money in acquiring power, his silence about the Sicilian cities', and in particular Syracuse's, command of financial resources is surprising, for he must have regarded such resources as crucial to their ability to become powerful.[14]

It is important to remember, however, that Thucydides in fact has already explicitly commented on power and wealth in Sicily: in a discussion about tyrannies in 1.17, he notes that in contrast to mainland tyrannies, those in Sicily "advanced to a great height of power," and he had previously made clear (1.13) that tyrannies emerged because of the presence of substantial

10. Connor 1984, 158: "Suddenly . . . the reader is plunged into a new undertaking of major proportions and awesome implications."

11. Some scholars dispute the accuracy of the charge of ignorance: e.g., Kagan 1981, 165; Buck 1988.

12. Rawlings 1981, 65–70.

13. Ibid., 66.

14. See Hornblower 1991b, 53.

material resources. It would be out of character for the historian to repeat this. Different aims explain the contrasting flavors of the two introductory arguments. The purpose of the first is to reveal the components of power, especially sea power, and then underrate all earlier attempts at amassing it. Since Thucydides' chief criterion for power was the accumulation of financial resources—the sine qua non of ships and unity—it was essential for him to dwell on this aspect of power, and to signal that this element would be central to his historical analyses and interpretations more generally. In the introduction to book 6, his aim is to highlight and prove the Athenians' ignorance of the magnitude of their plans for Sicily by showing its size and number of inhabitants.[15] Yet what is so striking about the introductory chapters of book 6 is that Thucydides deals with the size of the island in one sentence and then does not simply list the number of inhabitants; he makes colonization the central theme of the section.[16]

In my view, H. C. Avery has put his finger on the underlying function of the second "archaeology." By writing, in effect, a history of colonization in Sicily, immediately following book 5, the last sentence of which refers to the Athenians' colonization of Melos following its reduction, Thucydides implicitly presents the expedition to Sicily as a colonizing venture,[17] encouraging such an interpretation by referring to the Athenian presence on the island as another "city."[18] Yet the theme of colonization also supplies a link to the Archaeology in book 1 and both implicitly and indirectly to the theme of money through the figure of Minos: "Minos was the first, according to tradition, to have acquired a navy and conquered most of what is now called the Hellenic Sea. He ruled the Kyklades Islands and was the first to colonize most of them . . . ; and it is likely that he purified the sea of piracy to the extent possible, in order to increase his revenues" (1.4).

The analysis of Minos' power in book 1 is as striking and bold as that of the Trojan expedition, to be discussed below in chapter 2, and as odd. Like his discussion of why it took the Greeks so long to win the Trojan War, Thucydides' interpretation of Minos' activities and aims derives not from traditions about Minos but instead must have been influenced by Thucydides' own understanding of contemporary events and the motivations underlying

15. Thucydides "characteriz[es] ignorance by supplying the facts not known" (Stahl 1973, 70).

16. For discussion of Thucydides' treatment and accuracy, see Dover 1953; *HCT* 4: 198–210.

17. Avery 1973, 8–13; cf. also Green 1970, 131.

18. E.g., 6.37.2; 7.75.5; 7.77.4; cf. 77.7. So also, implicitly, Aristophanes' *Birds*. I agree wholeheartedly with Arrowsmith (1973, 143–144): "The equations [between the play and the Sicilian expedition] are relentless; whatever else Aristophanes' fantasy of Cloudcuckooland may be, it is not escapist, but a fantasy-mirror of Athen[s]."

them.[19] There are loose resonances with Minos in the opening of the Sicilian campaign, just as there clearly are in the Pentekontaetia, in which Thucydides charts the development of Athens' thalassocracy in the Aegean, paying close attention to conquest, money, and colonization.[20] Thucydides links Minos with conquest, colonization, and the desire for increased revenue. He applies this combination of themes to Athens in the Pentekontaetia and again in the Sicilian expedition. He does so there through the Sicilian "archaeology" (6.2–5), his flat statement about the Athenians' desire to conquer the island (6.6.1), and his claim that money was the motivating factor for most Athenians in the conquest of Sicily (6.24.3). Moreover, in his narrative of the final year of the expedition (413), in relating the Athenians' decision to abolish tribute and impose a maritime tax in order to increase revenues, his phraseology again recalls Minos' "likely" purification of piracy in order to increase revenues.[21] There is an additional, implicit resonance with Minos, I suggest, because, according to tradition, the mythical king of Crete went to Sicily, where he met his end.[22]

Thus the second "archaeology," in which explicit concern with money and power is absent, has a fundamentally different aim from the first. In its function of underscoring Thucydides' charge of ignorance on the part of the Athenians, it takes on a critical nuance. By placing Athens' venture in 415 in the context of successful attempts at colonization, Thucydides is arguably encouraging a positive interpretation of the Athenian decision; indeed, one suspects that such thinking may have been in the air at the time. Yet by embedding this section within a narrative implicitly critical of the Athenians, and planting in it the suggestion that the Athenians are after gain in their

19. As Hornblower (1991a, 21) comments: "When Th. speaks of Minos he is importing an idea from the world with which he was familiar;" cf. Branigan 1981, 33: "The case for Minoan colonialism, albeit of a modified and moderate kind, has still to be proved." Branigan suggests that Ayia Irini, Phylakopi, and Akrotiri, for instance, "if Minoan colonies," were motivated or enabled by economic rather than military factors (31–32). On 1.4, see *Money*, 24–27; see also Kleinlogel 1990, 195–96, on Minos and the way in which Thucydides both accepts myth and distances himself from the traditions.

20. See esp. 1.98–99.

21. 7.28.4. See chap. 5, pp. 198–201, below.

22. Hdt. 7.170; only a few fragments of Sophokles' play *Kamikioi* survive. In the story of Minos lie the origins of what Malkin (1998, 134–35) classifies as a "quasi-historical heroic myth of migration": after Minos was murdered, "his now leaderless Cretans escaped from Sicily and ended up as settlers in Iapygia, in southern Italy, and it was their descendants whom the Greek colonists of the eighth and seventh centuries met upon their arrival." Yet what Malkin means by "quasi-historical" is unclear and unsupported; excavations have revealed no trace of Minoan settlement in that period; on this, and for good discussion of the traditions and the archaeological evidence, see Sjöqvist 1973, 3–13. There seems also to be a conflation (or compression) of the traditions about the Cretans who eventually settled in Iapygia (Hdt. 7.170; Diod. 4.76–80). Cf. also Aristophanes' *Daidalos*, which Maxwell-Stuart (1973, 400–401) would place at the time of the Sicilian expedition.

desire for conquest—a suggestion that will become explicit as the narrative proceeds—Thucydides fosters a critical appraisal of the Athenians.

THE EGESTANS' OFFER

Following the account of Sicilian colonization, Thucydides reiterates the Athenians' desire to conquer Sicily by contrasting their real motive for intervention, to rule the island, with the pretext of assisting their allies, the Egestans, in their war with Selinous (6.6.2). But Thucydides writes the account to make it quickly clear that two can play the game of deception, and that money is the bait. Thucydides' narrative techniques are particularly conspicuous in his account of the Egestan trick.

As the episode opens, Egestan envoys are in Athens attempting to persuade the Athenians to come to their aid, indicating inter alia, Thucydides points out, that they have "sufficient money" (ἱκανὰ χρήματα) to pay for the expedition (6.6.2). In response, "envoys were sent out to investigate whether the money in the public treasury and in the temples existed" (εἰ ὑπάρχει). The form of the indirect question is striking: the Athenians were to investigate not the Egestans' claim of sufficient funds, but rather whether their public and sacred wealth existed *at all.* Thus Thucydides immediately encourages the reader to question the truth of the Egestans' claims and continues a theme introduced in the Melian Dialogue: the visible versus the invisible. The reader is left wondering whether the Egestans are representing something in their *logoi* that does not actually exist.

The Egestans later return to Athens with "60 talents of uncoined silver" (ἑξήκοντα τάλαντα ἀσήμου ἀργυρίου) as pay for sixty ships for one month (6.8.1). To the Athenians in the assembly who received the news, the Egestans had now confirmed the truth of their statement in 6.6.2—their *logoi* were genuine. Thucydides, however, wants the reader to know differently: the Egestans, having produced the money, said "many seductive and untrue things, especially about the money, that it was sufficient for the war" (6.8.2). What is significant about this comment is not only the unusual use of anticipation, but also that Thucydides signals his single-minded focus on the financial issue above all others: he lets the reader know that there were "many seductive and untrue" things said, but mentions only the money.[23]

23. Cf. also, similarly, 2.13.3–9: Thucydides presents Perikles' speech (in indirect discourse), focusing first, and most prominently, on Athens' finances, and making clear that Perikles made other arguments on that occasion (2.13.9) but choosing conspicuously to omit them. Note that his use of indirect speech in contrast to direct speech allows him to draw attention to his selectivity; in this case and others, he makes a historiographical decision to focus on money and finance. On 2.13, see *Money*, 96–107; Kallet-Marx 1994, 238–39 with n. 44. This is a technique Thucydides will also employ in book 8: e.g., 8.76, 82.1; cf. 8.45. See chap. 6 below.

While the Athenians now think that the Egestans' *ergon* matches their *logos,* the 60 talents, although real and visible, in fact represent something that does not exist; *logos* and *ergon* match each other as part of a grand deception.[24] Two questions immediately arise: first, is it significant that the Egestan envoys brought bullion rather than coined money? Second, why does Thucydides bother to include this detail? To answer these questions, perspective is important; in fact, the sentence is packed with ambiguity. On a practical level, bullion, rather than Egestan coinage,[25] might well have suggested good faith to the Athenians: the Egestans were supplying the most immediately usable form of metallic wealth, and Egestan coinage certainly lacked any international authority and would have had to have been reminted in Athens before being spent.[26] Yet why does Thucydides bother to specify that the talents were of uncoined money? Such a reference is unusual: normally he simply uses *chremata, argurion,* or the like.[27] In fact, only once elsewhere in the *History* has he distinguished between coined and uncoined money, in the indirect speech by Perikles listing Athens' financial resources on the eve of the Peloponnesian War (2.13.3–4).[28]

This may be no coincidence. In his speech, Perikles enumerates all the wealth available to the Athenians, in descending order of importance, in two categories, revenue and reserves. Under reserves, he lists first the coined money on the Akropolis (ἀργυρίου ἐπισήμου), then the uncoined gold and silver (χρυσίου ἀσήμου καὶ ἀργυρίου). His use of the phrase "apart from" (χωρίς) to refer to the gold and silver bullion confirms that it has a lower status than coined money and is less immediately usable. In the case of

24. I find intriguing Thucydides' remarkable attention to the Egestan "gift" and its deceptive nature and the fact that he accepts the Egestans' (half-) Trojan lineage (6.2.3)—thus Trojans, instead of Greeks, bearing gifts. An Anatolian origin has often been questioned: e.g., Leighton 1999, 217; Spatafora 1996. On the traditions, see van Compernolle 1950/1951; Nenci 1987; Mele 1993/1994; Malkin 1998, 172, 198, 199.

25. The Egestans had been minting silver didrachms since the second quarter of the fifth century; but they also produced a tetradrachm series as well as bronze coinage later in the century: Kraay 1976, 227, 231; also Lederer 1910. However, we have no way of knowing from the numismatic record whether any series was continuous or sporadic.

26. As Jack Kroll has commented to me, "Egestan coinage outside of Sicily must have been as enticing as boxes of Yugoslavian dinars would be to a Texas bank." Coin hoards outside of Sicily yielded an Egestan coin (Kraay and Mooney, 1981). Moreover, it was hardly a prestigious coinage within Sicily. This is not to say that local coinages did not regularly travel in the context of military expenditures (e.g., the Spartan war fund (*IG* V.1.1+) or, more frequently, trade.

27. Often he leaves it strictly open by referring simply to *argurion* (nineteen times: e.g., 1.27; 2.13.3; 8.76.2) or *chremata* (passim); but with the exception of the use of *chremata* in the Archaeology for periods before coinage, he is almost certainly regularly referring to coined money.

28. Howgego (1995, 89–90) suggests the unusual, because rare, nature of allusions to coined money in literary texts generally.

Athenian currency (or within any local context by this time), coined money signifies the highest financial power because of the immediacy of its use, and this explains why Thucydides/Perikles mentions it first. But this is not the case in an international context, as noted above, and thus more at issue here from a narrative standpoint is that Thucydides is specific when he wants to distinguish between coined and uncoined money. The distinction clearly has value for him.

In the passage in book 6, no explicit distinction is made between coined and uncoined money, but Thucydides' specific reference to "uncoined" money, in the place of a simple reference to "talents," "money," or "silver," implies a tacit distinction, not least because of the placement of this second occurrence of *asemon* in the text. The parallels in the narrative between the opening of the first stage of the Peloponnesian War and this second beginning, along with the unique dual instance of the word *asemon,* in 2.13.4 and 6.8.1, lead the reader to recall the resources on the eve of war and, most important, to remember how Thucydides chose to present them through Perikles.

The reference to *argurion asemon* in 6.8.1 constitutes a reversal from 2.13.3–4. In 2.13, an Athenian context, coined money is better than uncoined, whereas in the international context of 6.8, uncoined is preferable to coined. Perikles hides nothing in 2.13.3ff.; his list reflects the Athenians' actual resources—thus his *logoi* are matched by the *erga.*[29] The narrative of the Egestan offer, on the other hand, is inscribed with ambiguity and irony. The Egestans' gift of 60 talents of bullion is real money, but it also has been presented as *representing* the resources that are going to be available to the Athenians for the coming war in Sicily; and those, Thucydides allows the reader to know, do not exist.[30] Thus while the *logoi* and the *erga* mesh in one respect, in another, they clash strongly.

Another way of looking at Thucydides' treatment of the meaning of the Egestan silver is to consider it from the popular Greek antithesis of visible (φανερά) and invisible (ἀφανής). Louis Gernet, in commenting on the distinction as applied to property, notes the great variety of application and meaning of this antithesis.[31] The "invisible" can be what is concealed, or, in law, what is as yet imaginary, potential, as in the case of rights. In general,

29. On the other hand, there may be irony, as Perikles similarly alludes to expected annual revenue from the empire consisting chiefly of tribute, while in fact the Athenians proved incapable of sustaining the tribute levels necessary: in that sense, then, the expected financial resources in both 430 and 415 are similar in their illusory nature.

30. Beyond, that is, 30 talents, an inconsiderable sum in this military context (6.46.1; cf. 6.46.5, εἴη ἐν τῇ Ἐγέστῃ τὰ χρήματα).

31. Gernet 1981, 343–51; on property and wealth, see also Schuhl 1953; Fantasia 1973; Gabrielsen 1986; Kurke 1991, 225–39.

the "invisible" can be what does not exist, or, conversely, what, while hidden, is the real truth, apprehensible from visible signs if one knows how to read them.[32] The Egestan money, as we have seen, is itself real and visible yet it also represents what does not exist, that is, what is not real—the nonexistence of which the Egestans are concealing by the visible gift. In another sense, it is also a tacit pointer to the real: the reality is that Egestan money at home does not exist.[33] Thus when the Athenians go to Sicily and discover the deception, the unreality (the lack of money) becomes real (they discover the truth).

Indeed, it could be argued that the gift of bullion makes the Egestans' deception deeper rather than more transparent.[34] They are offering something that could be interpreted as good-faith and most practically useful. Yet the fact that the gift was bullion, not coinage, obscures ownership, for bullion lacked the backing of state authority;[35] who was to say that it was really Egestan money? Moreover, Thucydides' reference to the nature of the money, like Perikles' reference in 2.13, concentrates the reader's attention on the visual aspect to a far greater extent than simply saying "money" would have done. This correlates with his general focus on the visual display, the look, of money and wealth in his account of the expedition (see 6.31, 6.46, 7.82.3). Bullion makes a far more powerful presentation than coin: large chunks of silver ingots would have been much more impressive—and therefore more psychologically potent for the deceivers[36]—than tiny coins of unknown weight and quality.

Thus in the account of the Egestans' offer of money Thucydides clearly foreshadows the speciousness of the promise and reveals his deliberate choice to focus on the financial issue. He will continue to keep it in the reader's mind, in both of Nikias' speeches (6.12. 1, 22), and then, finally, in the description of the story of the deception, delayed in the narrative until

32. E.g., *Regimen* I 11, 12; Anaxag. frag. 21a (D-K); Jouanna 1999, 291–322.

33. See Stahl (1973, 72), who neatly brings out the interchangeable nature of real and unreal as Thucydides' narrative unfolds.

34. The logic connecting the untrue words (οὐκ ἀληθῆ) and the money that represents something that does not exist and is therefore invisible (ἀφανής) recalls 1.23.6: "the truest explanation but most hidden" (ἡ μὲν ἀληθεστάτη πρόφασις, ἀφανεστάτη λόγῳ). Here it is hidden and untrue.

35. Of course ingots may have been stamped, as are examples from the Selinous hoard, but this is still removed from the authority of coinage. For some examples of ingots, see, for example, Arnold-Biucchi, Beer-Tobey, and Waggoner 1988, pls. 13–15 (from Selinous); Howgego 1995, pl. 183 (= pl. 14D, in Arnold-Biucchi et al.; a cake ingot that weighs 597 gm).

36. Cf. 6.46: the Athenians visiting Egesta, Thucydides notes, had a profound emotional reaction to the sight, described as μεγάλη ἔκπληξις, a highly unusual use of ἔκπληξις in this context; see below, pp. 78–79.

the moment of discovery by the Athenians after they had arrived in Sicily, for reasons that I shall examine below.[37] Perhaps nowhere else in the *History* (with the exception of the episode at Pylos) is the "commentator Thucydides" so conspicuous as in the account of the Sicilian expedition, where his emphasis on public ignorance, misinformation, and deception pervades the narrative from the start. Scholars have noticed the emphasis on ignorance; what has not been appreciated is the extent to which what Thucydides chooses to illuminate is public ignorance about finance: the demos knows its importance to military success yet, as we shall see, lacks the guidance that had to be coupled with it to achieve military success. They are easily fooled by false indicators of power, like showy wealth—a criticism that will become acute in 6.31 and 6.46. In the intervening narrative, however, Thucydides develops the argument in other ways.

NIKIAS' SPEECH (6.9–14)

Following the return of the envoys, the Athenians voted to send an expedition to Sicily. The narrative continues with a presentation of an assembly meeting at which Nikias and Alkibiades, among others, spoke.[38] Nikias has often been seen as a wise advisor, or tragic warner, in Thucydides' characterization, because he seeks to dissuade the Athenians from embarking on the invasion of Sicily, yet the portrait of the general is considerably more complex.[39] As W. Robert Connor and others have noted, the arguments and proposals brought forth by him seem less than wise.[40] Nikias begins by cautioning against involvement in an enterprise urged by people of other races, with insufficient deliberation in proportion to its magnitude (9.1). Before he addresses those points more fully, however, he injects into his discussion arguments that speak to broader themes of the *History*, arguments that are illuminating in the interplay, and indeed blurring, of collective and individual values, and public and private wealth.[41] These reveal contrasts and inversions when read against earlier parts of the narrative.

37. I defer treatment of 6.46 until after I have examined the intervening narrative, since Thucydides intended it to be read in that sequence.

38. On the debate, see the analyses of, among others, Tompkins 1972; Stahl 1973, esp. 64–72; Yunis 1996, 103–9; Ober 1998, 104–18.

39. Von Fritz 1967, 728; Hunter 1973, 131, 179; Marinatos 1980. See Lattimore 1939, 35 n. 31: "If Nicias . . . may be taken as [an] example of the tragic warner, yet the contrast between good and bad advice is far less clearly marked."

40. "As Nicias' [first] speech continues . . . the policies he urges are inappropriate and implausible" (Connor 1984, 163). See chap. 4 below.

41. I am using the term "wealth" rather than "money" to allow for the inclusion of nonmonetary wealth; but an implicit emphasis on monetary wealth is, I would argue, predominant.

In order to remove the charge of self-interest, Nikias explicitly notes the honor that would accrue to him personally from the expedition: "In fact I myself am honored by such an enterprise, and I fear less than others for my person—although I believe that a good citizen can equally be one who takes forethought for his person and his property (τοῦ σώματός τι καὶ τῆς οὐσίας προνοῆται);[42] for such a man would wish for the city to prosper because of his own [property and person]" (6.9.2). Several features of this sentence stand out. First, Nikias introduces private considerations into a political context: he speaks of personal honor (a theme picked up again later on and intensified in 9.2, where he notes that "being honored above [others] has not in the past made him speak contrary to his judgment, nor will it now") and personal safety and property. But such considerations and values, earlier seen as belonging to the collective, have been transferred now to the individual. It is not that honor, the body, and property are exclusively collective—far from it—but rather that earlier in the *History* the polis was the privileged site of those values and concerns.[43] Now it is Nikias himself.

Moreover, Nikias inverts the "Periklean" definition of the good citizen, in which the polis will flourish only by being placed first, with individuals benefiting only by accepting its primacy.[44] In Nikias' variant, even if one puts a concern for one's own person and prosperity first, one can be a good citizen, for that individual will be more likely to act on behalf of his polis in order to protect his own prosperity. But even more interesting is that Nikias has inserted a reference to his lack of fear for his body, and he has put wealth in close juxtaposition to his fearlessness. Farther on, he reminds the Athenians of their still recent respite from the plague and from war "so that our money and bodies have been increased" (ὥστε καὶ χρήμασι καὶ τοῖς σώμασιν ηὐξῆσθαι, 12.1).[45] Here I would suggest that Nikias is referring to both public and private contexts of the body and wealth. His comment

42. Is there perhaps irony in the use of the verb προνοέω in view of Thucydides' association of πρόνοια with the statesman (e.g., 2.65.6; cf. 2.65.13)?

43. For example, the Athenians' reference to honor in their speech to the Peloponnesian assembly (1.75.3); and in the Funeral Oration, where the honor and admiration belong above all to the polis, and the body is the citizen's body (e.g., 2.39.4, 41.1, 4).

44. As in, for example, the Funeral Oration and his last speech (2.40.2, 42.3; 2.60.2). Bender (1938, 54) and Kohl (1977, 9–13) interpret Nikias' view negatively, comparing it to the Periklean version. Rood (1998, 186 n. 12), following Dover (*HCT* 4, ad loc.), stresses the concessive nature of the comment: "Although I think that a man who takes some thought," etc. This does not diminish the presence of the inversion. But cf. Musti 1985b for a critique of the argument that the Funeral Oration privileges the public sphere above all else and denigrates the private sphere.

45. Classen argued that of the pair χρήμασι καὶ τοῖς σώμασιν was more important because of the definite article; Steup raises doubts but cites 1.143.5 in support; Marchant cites Dem. 16.22; 22.55 as parallels.

seems clearly to relate to the city's collective and fiscal health,[46] but his previous attention to the private sphere and the ambiguity residing in "money" through the linkage with the body, as well as subsequent blurring of public and private motives in the decision to invade Sicily (6.24), suggests that both public and private contexts pertain.[47]

Nikias' attention to private wealth continues in chapter 12, where he charges the unnamed Alkibiades with a desire for personal profit from the expedition, in such a way that illuminates the kind of criticism Thucydides is making about the expedition as a whole.[48] Nikias links Alkibiades' private extravagance (πολυτελεία) and desire to gain brilliance (ἐλλαμπρύνεσθαι) with risk to the city.[49] Both Thucydides, in his introduction to Alkibiades' speech, and Alkibiades in his speech will pick up on, reinforce, and broaden the linkage to a comment about the Athenians, or, in the case of Alkibiades, contest it;[50] thus Nikias' comment has an important programmatic function for the subsequent narrative. In particular, the use of the word *poluteleia,* "extravagant cost," is significant, for not only is it rare in Thucydides, but almost every instance of its usage appears in rhetorically loaded contexts, sometimes tinged with sarcasm, in which the underlying judgment is critical.[51]

Thus concern for private wealth in a public context (being a good citizen, especially in connection with war), articulated through the voice of Nikias, has both acceptable and unacceptable facets. Nikias advocates a rec-

46. Cf. especially the verb ηὐξῆσθαι, which evokes the "increase" or growth in power used (negatively) in the Archaeology: e.g., 1.2.6 (which may or may not refer to Attica, on which, see *Money,* 24, with bibliography) and 1.99.3 (of the Athenians; he goes on to note the folly of using their "money and bodies" on behalf of the Leontinioi).

47. The linkage between money and the body will resurface in intriguing ways later on (7.28); see chap. 3 below, but also below, p. 80.

48. Gribble (1999, 61–62) brings out nicely the assumptions in Nikias' speech that the kind of private spending one engages in is an indicator of the kind of leader one will be. His discussion of the public aspects of private spending complements my arguments here. Yunis (1996, 104) sees Nikias' allusion to Alkibiades' horse raising in 6.12 as "not relevant." Yet it is not idle mud-slinging, or merely "useful invective," since this chapter of the speech raises critical issues aobut the relationship between public and private. Undeniably it also underscores, as Yunis emphasizes, the change in political debate since Perikles (101).

49. Διὰ δὲ πολυτέλειαν καὶ ὠφεληθῇ τι ἐκ τῆς ἀρχῆς (6.12.1); cf. Plut. *Nik.* 12.3. Dover (*HCT* 4, ad loc.) comments: "either (i) 'as his expenditure necessitates, gain (sc. in money)', or (ii) 'by means of his expenditure (sc. in command) gain (sc. in political prestige)'"; and rightly prefers the first alternative; clearly financial gain is at issue. So also Classen-Steup: "Weil das aber viel Geld kostet, (hofft er) von seinem Heerbefehl auch einigen Vorteil zu ziehen"; see. also Kohl 1977, 68–69 n. 3.

50. See. Kohl 1977, 68 on the verbal linkages between Nikias' and Alkibiades' speeches. On the linking of private and collective behavior as it relates to the implicit construction of the "democratic tyrant," see also below, pp. 79–82.

51. 1.10.2; 2.65.2; 6.12.2, 31.1, 3. The passages 7.27.2, 28.1 are more problematic cases. I shall return to discussion of this word below.

onciliation and wedding of public and private concerns, and he does so partly by using the same language in both the context of the collective polis and the private context. As we saw, the language of honor and the concern for private wealth and the safety of his body emerge, if defensively, as creditable in his case; using Alkibiades as a foil, however, he portrays his colleague as a negative counterexample of the confusion of public and private. Moreover, the polis can be justly admired for its show of power (θαυμαζόμενα, 11.4), but Alkibiades should not, he implies, be admired (θαυμάσθῃ) for his horse raising, a source of his personal power (12.1).

I suggest that the development of the narrative at this stage and its relationship to earlier parts of the *History* are intended to foster unease in the reader about the role of private wealth in public contexts. If so, this may help to explain a striking instance of "conspicuousness by absence" in the *History:* namely, the omission of reference to the trierarchy, a use of private wealth often seen as fundamental to the development of Athens' naval power.[52] Instead Thucydides stresses to its exclusion the role of public moneys, emphasizing imperial revenue. When considered against the historian's treatment of private wealth and private considerations in the origins of the Sicilian expedition, this omission may reflect a deliberate attempt to downplay the positive role that another writer might have ascribed to private wealth.

Nikias' speech has much to do with the preservation of resources, both human and financial. Resources ready at hand should be used to combat obvious and existing risks, not the obscure, or invisible (6.9.3; cf. 2.62.5). Clearly, what troubles the general is not whether the Athenians can afford to embark on the expedition, but whether they should spend their resources to do so. Nikias' secondary proposal to the Athenians, should they insist on sailing to Sicily, seems on the face of it to be commendable and compelling to his listeners. If they must go, they should then simply return home, "having made a display of their power" (δείξαντες τὴν δύναμιν); what is faroff and makes the "least test" of one's reputation is greatly admired (θαυμαζόμενα) by others. Indeed Nikias prefaces these points with the claim that most Greeks in Sicily would be "astonished" or "terrified" (ἐκπεπληγμένοι) by this show of force (11.4).[53]

This strategy might seem innocuous and safe, and even compelling to the internal audience of the *History,* Nikias' contemporaries; but, I suggest, from the perspective of the reader, the strategy is intended to be interpreted

52. See Gabrielsen 1994. Thucydides' implicit downplaying of the role of the institution of the trierarchy in enabling Athens' naval *dunamis* is countered by his explicit attention to the extravagant expenditures of individual trierarchs in 6.31. See below, pp. 53–54.

53. Cf. Kagan 1981, 178: "This argument, with its dubious psychological assumptions, ignores the possibility that the Athenians might win, thereby enhancing their reputation in a forceful way and acquiring a certain means of deterring an attack from Sicily."

in a more complex fashion. Not only has the Melian Dialogue introduced the ambiguity inherent in a "show of strength," but Thucydides will develop the argument, perhaps most conspicuously in 6.31, that the display of power is not the exercise of real power, but rather mere appearance and illusion. Thus when Nikias reiterates the desirability of this option when the fleet arrives in Sicily (6.47), it has a negative resonance and reminds the reader that the general has been advocating a strategy that puts resources, however less than they would be for the exercise of power, into mere show.[54]

It is thus noteworthy that Nikias, and by implication Thucydides as well, has made Athens' finances a feature of Nikias' speech, and a reason for changing his fellow citizens' minds about going to Sicily. This tells us that public finance was an important subject in the assembly, figuring not just in explicitly financial matters, but in political and military decisions. To judge from Thucydides' representation of the Mytilenaian Debate, this was true as well in the Athenians' deliberations after the suppression of the revolt of Lesbos, where the question of what to do about the island was connected closely with the financial benefits or detriments of the revolt and consequent treatment.[55]

THUCYDIDES' INTRODUCTION OF ALKIBIADES AND ALKIBIADES' SPEECH (6.15–18)

Others made speeches after Nikias. Thucydides chooses to include Alkibiades' speech and through it continues to exploit financial issues and to develop the themes of the relationship between display and power and the transferal of the language of the public sphere into a private context. But he introduces the speech with a preface unique in the *History* both for its length and for its nature: detailed biographical information about Alkibiades, with special attention to his spending habits and their public consequences. Thucydides introduces Alkibiades by connecting his extravagant lifestyle with Athens' downfall; both the introduction and the speech that follows again link private and public concerns and motivations,[56] as in the case of Nikias' speech, connecting them through money.

Nikias invoked his fellow citizens' concern for their private wealth as a

54. Thus I disagree sharply with Ellis (1979, 53), who observes regarding Nikias' reassertion of his proposal in 6.47 that "it seems safe to infer that Thucydides' own view was . . . that if [the Sicilian expedition were undertaken] it should have amounted to no more than an economical but impressive display of strength." Cf. Bender 1938, 39 on the proposal: "Das ist schon rein militärisch falsch, nicht nur politisch."

55. 3.37–50; see *Money*, 143–49.

56. As generally in his presentation of Alkibiades, as has often been noted; see, for example, Finley 1942, 218; Seager 1967, 8–9; Westlake 1968, 212; Forde 1989, 72; Bloedow 1990, 4. n.14; 1992.

reason to rescind the decision to invade Sicily (6.9.2–3, 12.1), yet at the same time he noted that it was precisely (the unnamed) Alkibiades who would attack Sicily *for* private enrichment (6.12.2). Thucydides endorses this accusation in his introduction and uses familiar, highly charged vocabulary in contexts and combinations that immediately produce unease about the man as a leader. Alkibiades, we are told, "especially desired and hoped (ἐπιθυμῶν καὶ ἐλπίζων) for the command" and from it "to benefit privately in money and reputation" (τὰ ἴδια ἅμα εὐτυχήσας χρήμασί τε καὶ δόξῃ ὠφελήσειν). Thucydides continues:

> ὢν γὰρ ἐν ἀξιώματι ὑπὸ τῶν ἀστῶν, ταῖς ἐπιθυμίαις μείζοσιν ἢ κατὰ τὴν ὑπάρχουσαν οὐσίαν ἐχρῆτο ἔς τε τὰς ἱπποτροφίας καὶ τὰς ἄλλας δαπάνας· ὅπερ καὶ καθεῖλεν ὕστερον τὴν τῶν Ἀθηναίων πόλιν οὐχ ἥκιστα. φοβηθέντες γὰρ αὐτοῦ οἱ πολλοὶ τὸ μέγεθος τῆς τε κατὰ τὸ ἑαυτοῦ σῶμα παρανομίας ἐς τὴν δίαιταν καὶ τῆς διανοίας ὧν καθ' ἓν ἕκαστον ἐν ὅτῳ γίγνοιτο ἔπρασσεν, ὡς τυραννίδος ἐπιθυμοῦντι πολέμιοι καθέστασαν . . . (6.15.3–4)
>
> For, being held in high esteem by the city men, he indulged his desires to a greater degree than his existing resources allowed with respect to horse raising and the rest of his expenditures; and this contributed in no small part to the downfall of the city later on. For the many, frightened by the extravagance of his transgressions with respect to his own body and his way of life and by the (suspect) intention that he exhibited in whatever he was engaged in, thinking that he was desiring tyranny, became his enemies.

The clustering of the language of desire, the body, private profit and expense, and the relationship between public and private contrast strikingly with earlier sections of the narrative. Thucydides preconditions a negative reading of Alkibiades' speech, at least as it pertains to his wealth and power, through both repetition (his endorsement of Nikias' charges) and the location of a higher narrative authority, his own, immediately preceding the speech.[57] His commentary is obviously not neutral, but is rather highly critical, emphasizing personal power, greed, and desire as motivating factors in Alkibiades' public life. Thus Thucydides implicitly endorses Perikles' dictum in 2.60 that citizens must look to the health of the polis first. This would seem correspondingly to undermine Nikias' reconfiguration of the "good citizen." Yet in another respect, Alkibiades is a foil for Nikias' formulation: Alkibiades illustrates the most extreme example of private over public interests; his behavior is cast in terms of moral transgression.

In Thucydides' portrait, Alkibiades' desires and ambitions were destructive of his body and his money; moreover, as has been noted, Thucydides makes a direct connection between Alkibiades' spending habits and the

57. On narrative hierarchy, see, for instance, Bal 1997, 52.

downfall of the city.[58] Yet there is even more to it, for Alkibiades and the collective Athenians ultimately mirror each other in their aims, desires, and expenditures. The Athenians will also have a passionate desire to invade Sicily; in the case of many, this desire will be connected with private enrichment. The Athenians collectively will actively waste away their money on displays of wealth that they think will bring them great power. Ultimately, bodies and money, replenished and increased during the Peace of Nikias (emphasized in the narrative through repetition and different voices [6.12.1, 26.2]), will be destroyed in the course of the campaign. Thus in his introduction Thucydides is interested not only in showing the grave public consequences of Alkibiades' private behavior, with an emphasis on his expenditures, but also in foreshadowing the continued transferal of desires and behavior from the individual to the collective.[59]

While Nikias and then Thucydides in his own voice suggest the inappropriateness of the public/private link, and the historian introduces Alkibiades by explicitly stating that his private expenditures caused great damage to the state, Alkibiades turns the tables. At the beginning of his speech, he asserts: "The Greeks have considered our polis to have much greater power than it actually has because of my magnificence at the Olympic festival, whereas before they expected that the city would have been completely ruined, because I entered seven chariots—a feat no private individual had ever accomplished before—and I won, as well as coming in second and fourth, and prepared everything (παρεσκευασάμην) else in a style worthy of victory.[60] For by custom such displays are regarded as sources of honor (τιμή), and from the action, at the same time power is also conjectured (δύναμις ἅμα ὑπονοεῖται, 6.16.2).

Alkibiades links his personal expenditure with not only his own but also his city's power, but in doing so, he blurs individual and polis power. The language with which he begins his speech—his worthiness to command (ἄρχειν . . . καὶ ἄξιος ἅμα νομίζω εἶναι, 6.16.1), and his references to honor and his private "preparations" (τιμή; παρεσκευασάμην, 16.2)—is the language of polis power.[61] He continues the link between his expenditure and the city's power in 16.3: "And as many times as I was *choregos* . . . I brilliantly distinguished myself (λαμπρύνομαι), which naturally brought envy to my fellow citizens, but to outsiders it appeared to be a sign of strength. So this madness of mine is not useless in the case of one who benefits not only himself by his private expenditures but the polis as well."

58. Gribble 1999, 70.

59. See also below, pp. 79–81.

60. Cf. also Plut. *Alk.* 11–12.

61. E.g., 1.75.1 (the Athenians at Sparta): Ἆρ' ἄξιοι . . . ἀρχῆς; παρασκευή in Thucydides is used above all in a public context, as the treatment of Allison 1989 makes clear. On honor see above, p. 32 with note 43.

Thus while Nikias urges caution and preservation of one's own wealth to maintain the strength of the polis, Alkibiades suggests that personal extravagance enhances the power of the polis.

These arguments are hardly outrageous. After all, it would not have been unusual for an elite speaker to expect to convert prestige-expenditure to leadership in the polis; indeed, Alkibiades' claims provide a brilliant illustration of the role of aristocratic display in a civic context.[62] Yet the effect is fundamentally unsettling, for the underlying ideology is precisely what Thucydides aims to contest. He does this in a number of ways. First, as we have seen, his preface to the speech conditions a negative reading. Second, he embeds a filter of unreality through which Alkibiades' remarks are to be interpreted, giving a decidedly illusory aspect to Alkibiades'—and by extension the polis'—power.[63] Alkibiades' own greatness, Thucydides points out, was built on credit, not on his own wealth (ταῖς ἐπιθυμίαις μείζοσιν ἢ κατὰ τὴν ὑπάρχουσαν οὐσίαν ἐχρῆτο, 15.3), so that in a sense Alkibiades' symbolic capital was not derived from his own real capital, and it was fueled by his desires. Moreover, the polis' power, as Alkibiades puts it, "was conjectured" (ὑπονοεῖται); it lies in the conceptual, not the tangible, realm and thus by extension it has an illusory quality about it as well.[64]

The negative emphasis on power as illusion or at least as ambiguous in Thucydides' rendering of Alkibiades' speech fits into broader themes and arguments of the *History*. The first has to do with the evidence by which one can distinguish real power from (mis)perceived signs of power. A passage from the Archaeology (1.10), crucial for understanding Thucydides' ideas about signs of power, helps elucidate the significance of Alkibiades' comments for the narrative. In the passage, which concerns the power of Mycenae, Thucydides contrasts real *dunamis* with appearances of power (ὄψεις), asserting that one must not judge the real power of a polis by visual display of, so he argues, false indicators of power. But this kind of comment can be read to imply an opposing, and likely more common, belief that such displays are real tokens of power;[65] Alkibiades illustrates the point. Given that

62. Kurke 1991, 172. But contrast the comment of Millett (1998, 244): Alkibiades' "calculated expenditure as a positive 'lever to office' is . . . problematical," with his discussion on the passage (244–45).

63. Forde (1989, 79) comments that Alkibiades' "personal profligacy creates an appearance of power in the city, which by itself increases the effective power of the city. *The appearance becomes the reality*" (my emphasis); this is exactly what Thucydides is rejecting.

64. Cf. also 6.31.4 and below, pp. 55–59.

65. In commenting on Thucydides' preference for the poetic tradition over monuments, and thus the ear over the eye, Hedrick (1993, 28) may overstate when he says that this "contradicts contemporary Greek thought." For one thing, Thucydides is focused, as mentioned, on a specific issue—power—and not making a generic statement about oral vs. autoptic evidence; second, while there was undeniably a pattern of preference of sight over sound, the

the passage in the Archaeology contains Thucydides' own views about real versus illusory power, we can see that he is weaving an implicit argument in this part of book 6, his point being that although people take Alkibiades' display-expenditure as evidence not only of *his* power, but also of the power of the city, this kind of thinking about power is false; moreover, by establishing the correct criterion of power in 1.10 and contrasting it with popular belief, Thucydides implies, as elsewhere,[66] that people generally should be able to make correct inferences and assessments. That he is rendering a critical judgment on them for failing to do so, I shall develop below, returning to a discussion of 1.10.

Second, Thucydides' remarkable attention to the relationship between private expenditure and polis power, and even more, the way in which he illustrates the relationship, brings out an essential—and highly polemical—argument of the work: namely, that private wealth does not equate to polis power. In the earlier books of the *History,* in his own voice, in the personae of speakers like Archidamos and Perikles, and in comparative analyses of other states or rulers, Thucydides makes clear that polis power is dependent on public not private wealth, to the extent that Perikles, in the last speech Thucydides gives him, virtually devalues private wealth.[67]

Finally, the relationship between private wealth and polis power relates to the more general argument that private considerations have no proper place in public decision-making; that this is Thucydides' position here is implicit from his discussion in 2.65. Both Nikias and Alkibiades consider the Sicilian expedition from the standpoint of private considerations. This rubs against not only Periklean ideals but also Thucydides' own views, to judge from the praise he gives to Perikles through criticism of his successors for the intrusion of private motives into a political context (2.65.7).[68] Accordingly, even Alkibiades' relatively innocuous claim to power because of private aggrandizement is tacitly suspect.[69]

---

richness of sources concerned with the problems of interpretation of vision suggests that Greek thought was not quite so monolithic.

66. Most notably, in 1.20 and in the Peisistratid digression (6.54–59).

67. 2.62.2–3; Archidamos' comment at 1.80.4 implies the same thing. Thucydides will implicitly make the same point again in 6.46, the description of the Egestan deception.

68. Cf. Bloedow (1992), who stresses the similarities between the positions of Perikles and Nikias.

69. The Athenian envoys, speaking before the Peloponnesian assembly at Olympia, base their claim of worthiness to rule (1.75) on military actions that demonstrated their power, specifically, their part in repelling the Persian invasion; they also note that they were asked to take over the hegemony from the Spartans. Thucydides implicitly denies Alkibiades' justification the same validity as that of the Athenian envoys; the reason is clearly that the former's was based on private, not public, considerations. This implication is not affected by the Spartans' de facto denial of validity to the envoys' claims.

Thucydides develops Alkibiades' arguments concerning the relationship between money and power toward the end of the speech, but focusing now on the broader public and imperial context. In 6.18 Alkibiades explains why the Athenians, responding to the appeals of allies and kinsmen, should invade Sicily, but he emphasizes the significance of such an action for the Athenians' possession of empire. He notes that empire is not won or maintained by holding back—thus appealing to the acquisitive nature (*tropos*) of the Athenians, so well constructed both by Perikles in the Funeral Oration and by the Corinthians at Sparta in book 1 (1.70). Empires are won by a readiness to come to the aid of all, Hellenic or barbarian, since if the Athenians were to keep quiet or make distinctions between those they should and should not help, they would hardly add possessions to their existing empire and would endanger what they have: "It is not possible to control the extent of the rule we desire, but there is necessity at work, given the fact that we have come this far, to plot against some and not to let others go, since there is a risk of being ruled by others, unless we rule others ourselves" (18.3).

In this remarkable passage, with its expansionist doctrine, the language of finance and public economy is employed to enhance the link between money, power, and empire. Alkibiades uses the verb *tamieuesthai*—literally, "to be treasurer of"—but rather than "supervising," "managing," or "controlling" the (extent of a) treasury, here it means "to control the extent of an empire," and when he insists that fixing limits is impossible, he invokes necessity, *ananke.*[70] It is reasonable to suggest that this financial metaphor carries an implicit idea of financial gain from the extension of empire, especially since this is a point made explicitly elsewhere (6.12.2, 15.2, 24.3). Then follows another metaphor, borrowed from accounting: "Therefore, calculating (λογίζομαι) that we shall increase (αὐξήσειν) further what we have here, should we sail against them, let us make this voyage, in order to level the pride of the Peloponnesians" (6.18.4). The link between "calculation" and "expansion" inherent in the vocabulary used, and the resonance of *arche* in the vocabulary of expansion, connect the idea of material, financial gain with (the extension of) empire.

Alkibiades' doctrine of unlimited expansion is not in itself a novel idea in the history of the *arche,* or, more to the point, in Thucydides; indeed, it bears striking similarities to an observation the historian attributes to Perikles in his final speech in the *History.* In 2.62.1–2, Perikles is attempting to cheer up the Athenians, who are suffering from the effects of the plague. He

70. See Ostwald (1988, 38–42) on what he calls "imperial *ananke.*" See also the apposite remarks of Connor (1984, 176 n.45), apropos Alkibiades' use of this metaphor: "This metaphor links the attack on Sicily to the 'expenditure' of lives in the war." See also chap. 4 below.

makes a remarkable observation about their power, commenting: "I shall explain something that you yourselves have apparently never realized, that concerns the magnitude of your *arche*. . . . You have absolute mastery over the sea, to such an extent that it is not only over your present holdings but also any extension for which you may wish."[71] There are clear parallels between Perikles' statement and that of Alkibiades. Both leaders assert the unlimited nature of Athens' *arche,* which presupposes the assumption that the Athenians manifestly have the power to extend it where they may.

There are, however, more points of contrast. First, whereas Perikles implies that the Athenians would be in control of any extension, Alkibiades denies the possibility: the Athenians have no control over the limits (οὐκ ἔστιν . . . ταμιεύεσθαι) because "necessity" governs or rules them. This reinforces on another level, and through another narrative voice, the theme of the Athenians' lack of self-control and loss of agency that will be developed later on. Second, whereas earlier in the *History,* wealth is to be used for power, in Alkibiades' formulation there is a sense in which the relationship has become inverted: driven by necessity, the Athenians will use their power to increase their wealth. Alkibiades' use of financial metaphors in connection with imperial *auxesis* creates the impression, as mentioned above, that the purpose of imperial expansion is the desire for, if not the necessity of, financial profit—*auxesis* is material, as well as political, increase. Thucydides endorses this as a motive in his own voice (6.15.2, 24.3). If this interpretation is valid, then Thucydides is mapping a pivotal, and destructive, shift from the beginning of the war, under Perikles' guidance, to the subsequent stages under his "successors": the possession of *arche* leads to a loss of control through the exercise of power for wealth.

Is Thucydides at the same time saying something about human nature? In the Melian Dialogue, certainly, the case for power and its extension is phrased deliberately and explicitly to suggest a "law of human nature";[72] thus the issue of responsibility in that rhetorical setting can be rendered moot. But I suggest that there is a subtle difference between these other expressions concerning the Athenians' actual or potential extension of power and the remarks attributed to Perikles and Alkibiades; in the latter cases, by making these two individual leaders express their views on the extension of *arche,* and by making their views particular to Athens' *arche,* rather than to *arche* generally, Thucydides inscribes these individuals with moral responsibility for Athenian political and military behavior. In the case of Alkibiades, Thucydides' treatment of his character, his motivations, and his playing upon the equally unlimited desire for wealth encourages the inference that

71. For a fuller discussion of this passage, see *Money,* 114–15.

72. E.g. 5.105; cf. the Athenians' comment to the Spartans at 1.76.2.

Alkibiades' pronouncements on the nature of the *arche,* unlike those of Perikles, are irresponsible and insidious. The speech by Nikias that follows does nothing to improve this impression.

NIKIAS' SECOND SPEECH AND ITS EFFECT (6.20–26)

Passion for the expedition was apparent to Nikias. Aware that the old arguments from prudence would fail, Nikias decided, Thucydides tells us, to exaggerate the extent of resources the Athenians would require in Sicily (παρασκευῆς πλήθει, 19.2), in the hope that he might prompt a change of heart. Thus the purpose of this second speech is specifically to present an argument based on Nikias' assessment of his audience's ability to be deceived, and deceived into making a decision at the core of which lie the city's resources, financial and other.[73] Scholars examining the speech have focused primarily on its cogency, or lack thereof.[74] Ultimately, of course, it was a rhetorical failure. Underappreciated, however, is the deliberate messiness of the presentation of information.

Nikias' main rhetorical strategy is, first, to emphasize the odds and, second, following from that, to stress the need for increased resources. But he does so not by presenting a clear, lucid accounting; rather, since his primary hope is to make the totality appear as cumbersome and complicated as possible as a deterrent, he instead presents a confusing jumble of information that is as conspicuous for its ultimate vagueness as for its detail.[75] As for the chief targets of the expedition, Selinous and Syracuse, he notes that in those places there are many hoplites, archers, and javelin throwers and many triremes and men to man them; in addition, "they have private wealth, and riches also in the temples at Selinous (χρήματά τ' ἔχουσι τὰ μὲν ἴδια, τὰ δὲ καὶ ἐν τοῖς ἱεροῖς ἐστι Σελινουντίοις), and the Syracusans receive first fruits from some of the barbarians" (20.4).[76] "But their special advantage over us," he points out, "is that they have plenty of cavalry, and grain, not having to import it."

Then comes a sentence whose beginning is remarkable, at least to an Athenian audience: "Against such a power as this the navy and paltry army[77]

73. I fail to see the force of Bloedow 1990, 15 n. 38, defending Nikias against Dover's critical assessment (HCT 4, *ad loc.*) of both Nikias' and Alkibiades' speeches and arguing that because Nikias' exaggerations were "deliberate," he is making correct arguments.

74. See, for example, Kagan 1981, 186–90 and von Fritz 1967, 728; see Bloedow 1990 for opposing assessments.

75. In these respects, the speech has much in common with 6.31, to be discussed below.

76. See Ampolo 1984 and Musti 1985a on the relationship between this passage and the inscription from Temple G at Selinous, which mentions 60 talents.

77. Crawley's translation wrongly takes φαῦλος with ναυτικόν.

are not enough (πρὸς οὖν τοιαύτην δύναμιν οὐ ναυτικῆς καὶ φαύλου στρατιᾶς μόνον δεῖ); we need also to sail with a sizable infantry" (6.21.1). The word order, juxtaposing *dunamin* and *ou nautikes* at the beginning of the sentence, would have been unexpected to Athenians accustomed to think of their navy as invincible; the negation—emphasizing that although they would be attacking an island, their navy would be useless—will have jarred.[78] Nikias continues to relate the extraordinary needs of the expeditionary force beyond the navy and army. Remarkably, he details the nature of the provisions and supply services required, noting the kinds of grain needed and the necessity of bakers from the mills who would have to be conscripted to work for a proportionate amount. As for the money they will need, he says simply: "We will especially have to bring as much money as possible (μάλιστα δὲ χρήματα αὐτόθεν ὡς πλεῖστα ἔχειν), since," he forewarns, "you should recognize that the alleged offer of ready cash from the Egestans is readier in word than in reality" (τὰ δὲ παρ' Ἐγεσταίων, ἃ λέγεται ἐκεῖ ἑτοῖμα, νομίσατε καὶ λόγῳ ἂν μάλιστα ἑτοῖμα εἶναι, 6.22). In this last clause Thucydides keeps the Egestan offer in the reader's mind.

The speech stands out because of the sheer jumble and quantity of items listed by Nikias, heaped on one after the other and including a number of words that are unusual in the elevated context of deliberative oratory in the *History* (e.g., κριθάς, "barley"; μυλώνων, "mills").[79] He concludes, thinking that he will either have dissuaded the Athenians from making the expedition because of the sheer extent of preparation (τῷ πλήθει τῶν πραγμάτων), or, if compelled to sail, that at least they will do so as safely as possible (6.24.1). But the Athenians, Thucydides continues, "were not shaken from their desire for the voyage by the troublesomeness of the preparations (ὑπὸ τοῦ ὀχλώδους τῆς παρασκευῆς). On the contrary they were even more eager, and the result was the opposite of what Nikias intended: they decided that he had given good advice and that accordingly they might now go forward in complete safety. Indeed, passionate desire for the expedition infected all, the older among them thinking that they would either conquer

78. I thank Simon Hornblower for alerting me to this nuance of the sentence. If Dover (*HCT* 4: 260; 1954/1955, 6–8) is correct in his interpretation and translation of this difficult sentence (i.e., we must be "a match for them—except, mind you, not for those forces which really do the *fighting,* their hoplites," 6.23.1), the statement further strengthens the paradox. Cf. also Archidamos' speech in 1.80–85, which makes an equally jarring, and equally unsuccessful, argument that Spartan hoplite strength will not win a war with Athens; see also Allison 1989, 83.

79. Possibly the internal audience (Nikias' contemporaries in the assembly) would also have found the words atypical. One can imagine discussion of army maintenance in wartime deliberations, but it would not have been the usual stuff of political decision making. See Tompkins 1972 on the general complexity of Nikias' speeches in contrast to Alkibiades' paratactic style; see also Kohl 1977, 68.

the enemy, or at least come to no harm given their great strength; while those younger had a craving for foreign sights and spectacles. And the majority of the common soldiery thought it would bring money (ἀργύριον) for the present and an acquisition of power whence they would have everlasting pay" (ἀίδιον μισθοφοράν, 24.3).[80]

Thus the points that Nikias made to engender anxiety and to prompt a change of heart had the opposite effect. Most paradoxical, the "crowdedness," or "troublesome extent" of the preparations—ἡ ὀχλώδης τῆς παρασκευῆς—only made the Athenians feel safer. Thucydides chooses the word ὀχλώδης, a *hapax* in the *History,* to bring out the tangled complexity of Nikias' speech. This is his assessment of the items he has Nikias mention in his speech, whereas the assembled citizens listened to the complex details and interpreted them as indicators of success. But the word also neatly plays on the demos' feeling of safety in numbers, as if mere quantity guaranteed success.[81] Moreover, perhaps most damning is that Nikias induces the Athenians to confuse the enhancement of resources with the display of resources, as we shall see below.

Just as Alkibiades claimed that "necessity" would impel the Athenians inexorably to limitless goals, implying in a sense that it was not in their power to resist, so Thucydides explains that "passionate desire" (ἔρως) for the expedition "attacked" (ἐνέπεσε) the Athenians,[82] thereby suggesting not only the involuntary nature of the condition, but also its definition as a sort of disease.[83] Through a cluster of words denoting powerful emotion (ὥρ-

80. On the profit motive of the Sicilian expedition, see Finley 1986, 77.

81. It seems reasonable, given the emphasis on the paradoxical nature of the assembly's positive reaction to Nikias' speech, to suggest that the amount of detail and kinds of things mentioned were unusual, not the sorts of things that a general might normally relate in a speech before the assembly. If so, then it follows that the assembly was not accustomed to hearing this degree of detail, nor to learning the extent of the preparations necessary. That Nikias expected his audience to be persuaded by exaggeration says much about their relative knowledge in these areas: they collectively knew enough to be expected to be impressed; that they were impressed to the extent that they reached a conclusion that was the opposite of what Nikias expected does not weaken the point.

82. 6.24.3; cf. 6.13.1 (from Nikias' speech): Nikias implores the Athenians not to be δυσέρωτας τῶν ἀπόντων, "in love with the far-off."

83. For *eros,* often personified, as a disease violently attacking its victims, cf., for example, Eur. *Hipp.* 38; Winkler 1990a, 82–93; Faraone 1999, 43–49. The theme of *eros* in the account of the Sicilian expedition (including the Peisistratid digression) has received a great deal of scholarly attention: e.g., Hunter 1973, 124; Connor 1984, 178; Loraux 1985, 15–21; Scanlon 1987; Forde 1989, 31–37, 39, 50, 66, 119; see also Arrowsmith 1973 for comparisons between the "erotic politics" of the Sicilian expedition and Aristophanes' *Birds.* See also de Romilly (1963, 326–27), who notes the contrast between reason and passion in this section of the work in her discussion of the pathology of empire.

μηντο, 24.2; ἔρως, πόθος, εὐέλπιδες, 24.3; ἄγαν ἐπιθυμία, 24.4), Thucydides drives home the extent to which the Athenians had submitted to passion as they made this momentous decision to invade Sicily. Moreover, he links passion explicitly with sight, though paradoxically, sight not yet seen.[84] The vocabulary of passion and the use of the verb "attacked," with both medical and military nuances, suggests that, like war itself, passion—that is, the irrational—can inflict violent harm on its victims.[85] It is important to note that in the following explanation of the specific objects of the Athenians' *eros,* Thucydides cites money as a chief factor for the common soldiery and throng (ὁ πολὺς ὅμιλος καὶ στρατιώτης, 6.24.3).[86] Love of money—greed, then—impelled the majority toward Sicily.[87] Far from having the quality of an "almost comically pedestrian" longing,[88] Thucydides' presentation of the motivation of the majority is deadly serious and central to his construction of the perniciousness of the relationship between money and emotion.

This is not the the first time that Thucydides has connected money and passion. Consider 2.13, Perikles' indirect speech, cited above. Perikles instructs his fellow Athenians to feel strong emotion—"He exhorted them to feel emboldened" (θαρσεῖν)—with a list of the city's financial resources; Thucydides closes this section of the speech with the comment "Thus he emboldened them with respect to their wealth" (13.6). The narrator Thucydides makes the link between passion and money by framing only this section of Perikles' indirect speech with the verb *tharsein* (θαρσεῖν τε ἐκέλευε, 2.13.3; χρήμασι μὲν οὖν οὕτως ἐθάρσυνεν αὐτούς, 2.13.6); in 2.13.6–8 he relates the other advantages in resources that the statesman mentioned the Athenians possessed, such as hoplites, light-armed troops, cavalry, and triremes, but they are outside of the frame. It is tempting to suggest that *oratio obliqua* is used for this particular speech so that Thucydides can step into the narrative to guide the reader's interpretation. At least it is significant that

84. The younger of the Athenians had a "desire for the faraway sight and beholding" (τοῖς δ' ἐν τῇ ἡλικίᾳ τῆς τε ἀπούσης πόθῳ ὄψεως καὶ θεωρίας, 6.24.3). Sight and emotion are linked again in 6.31, and ironically in 8.1, on which see chap. 6 below.

85. Hope can perform the same destructive function; cf. 5.103, and the prelude, pp. 13–16, above.

86. Gomme (1920) is right to take ὁ πολὺς ὅμιλος as a reference to "the common people" generally: i.e., those staying in Athens and not identical with the στρατιώτης.

87. It becomes clear why most Athenians saw Sicily as a huge treasure chest when Thucydides relates the Egestan deception in 6.46: the Athenian crew (the same social stratum as ὁ πολὺς ὅμιλος καὶ στρατιώτης) go "out of their minds" (μεγάλη ἔκπληξις) upon seeing the gold and silver with which they were entertained in Egesta. Cf. Ar. *Birds* 592: the Chorus-leader asks, "How will we give [humans] wealth? For that's what they love exceedingly" (σφόδρ' ἐρῶσιν).

88. Forde 1989, 49.

he does not simply report the speech in indirect discourse from beginning to end but rather editorializes and guides as Perikles goes along.[89]

The linking of money and emotion here, filtered through the Periklean lens, is positive; the Athenians were to be emboldened because they knew that their wealth would be put to use, expended on the exercise of naval strength in war—that was its sole purpose. Another passage, from Perikles' Funeral Oration, is even more striking, if indirect. While not making an explicit connection between money and passion, it nonetheless reveals the larger issue with which the historian is concerned in linking money and passion. In this speech Perikles reflects on Athens' *dunamis,* and, as in 2.13, the reader is presumed to come to this section of the work with the preceding narrative context in mind. Thus, as mentioned in the prelude, Perikles' emphasis on *dunamis* in the Funeral Oration presumes the reader's recognition of the underpinnings of that power, money and ships, which the historian has elucidated in his own analyses (especially in the Archaeology and Pentekontaetia) and in speeches like those of Archidamos and Perikles. Thus when the statesman instructs his fellow citizens in 2.43.1 to "gaze on the power of the city and become its lover" (τὴν τῆς πόλεως δύναμιν καθ' ἡμέραν ἔργῳ θεωμένους καὶ ἐραστὰς γιγνομένους αὐτῆς), there is, I suggest, another implicit link between money and passion, here a positive one.[90]

What stands out about these two passages is that Perikles is *instructing* the Athenians to experience an emotion. He instructs them to marshall passions and press them into the service of enhancing the feeling of power. He points out that power (*dunamis*) is gained, and is to be exercised, through decisions reached in a rational environment (e.g., through the exercise of *gnome* and the proper use of *periousia chrematon*). By contrast, in the post-Periklean period, when Thucydides in a variety of ways is writing a critique of Athenian leadership, the link between money and passion has changed: emotions attack the Athenians like disease, and they make decisions in an afflicted and irrational state, which appear ill fated to the reader precisely because they are made in an emotional climate.[91] Thus as he has done with the presentation of expenditure, Thucydides plays with inversions of the passions: whereas earlier in the work the Athenians are empowered by the passions, which are applied to constructive use, now love and lust for victory

89. As he does also in 2.13.3, when he steps in to gloss Perikles' comment about the total resources available in 431. See n. 23 above.

90. On the ἐραστής metaphor in this passage and the ambiguity of the antecedent of αὐτῆς, see Hornblower 1991a, ad loc.

91. Luginbill (1997, 129–30) rightly notes the contrast between Thucydides' emphasis on the passions in decision making and Perikles' style of "sober, well-informed deliberation." See also below, chap. 3.

attack them and ultimately place their very possession of money, and power, at risk.[92]

To return to the narrative, Thucydides continues his account of the climate in the assembly following Nikias' second speech by noting that finally one (unnamed) Athenian[93] came forward and asked Nikias to specify the preparations (*paraskeue*) on which the Athenians should vote. Nikias replied that he would have rather decided this together with the other generals[94] but would answer that they needed no fewer than one hundred triremes and not less than five thousand hoplites all told from themselves and the allies, and more if possible; and the rest of the force (*paraskeue*) should be levied in proportion, archers from home and from Crete and slingers and anything else that seemed fitting (25.2). So the Athenians voted to give the generals full powers, with reference both to the size of the army and to the whole fleet. After this the preparations (*paraskeue*) were undertaken, made easier by the recent recovery from the plague, but also by plentiful financial resources because of the truce. At this juncture Thucydides confirms through the narrator's voice what was hinted at before by Nikias (as well as in the Melian Dialogue): the Athenians had achieved an "accumulation of money" (ἄθροισις χρημάτων). Thus, he concludes, they were in a state of preparation (*paraskeue,* 26.2).

The frequency with which the word *paraskeue* appears in this section highlights an important fact about Athens' *dunamis.*[95] The Athenians have the ability to equip a huge fighting force swiftly: they do not have to scramble or delay to put together a sizable expedition, and the financial resources are there in a centralized place to be used immediately. As at the beginning of the war (2.13), one again gets the impression that the odds will be heavily stacked in the Athenians' favor; the image is of a powerful city at the ready. And yet there is something troubling about this *paraskeue,* for, in Thucydi-

92. Thucydides' presentation has much in common with Giambattista Vico's formulation (*New Science* 1725, pts. 132–33; cf. 130, 135) of passions that can lead men astray or be harnessed for the strength and prosperity of the state, as well as with seventeenth-century debates concerning the relationship between the passions and economic interest; see Hirschman 1977, 40ff.

93. Plut. *Nik.* 12.4 (cf. *Alk.* 18.2) names a certain Demostratos, who rose in the assembly and stated that he would "stop Nikias from making excuses," and who proposed the decree to give the generals full powers: see further below. Might the "unnaming" have a significance similar to that which Pelling, cited by Hornblower 1996, 137 n. 35, suggests for the Spartan judges at Plataia—i.e., to make them stand for Sparta as a whole? See also Pelling 2000, 255–56 n. 4.

94. Is the implication that decisions like this were usually not made in the assembly? Or presented to the assembly only after consultation?

95. As Allison (1989, 84) puts it (with reference to 6.19.2): "*Paraskeue* is to be identified with, and in fact subsumes, *dynamis.*"

des' account, the expedition was decided on hastily, both Nikias and Alkibiades were guilty of exaggeration and misrepresentation before the people, and Nikias quickly and without proper deliberation had to voice specific recommendations. Moreover, the expedition was decided on under the influence of passion.[96] The irrationality creates a sense of unease about the nature of the decision, as does Thucydides' inclusion of Nikias' first speech urging that a previous decision be rethought.[97] Athenian *paraskeue* may once again be at its height; yet Thucydides' narrative is layered with ambiguity and represents the Athenians as confusing the display of power with its augmentation. These features are no more clearly revealed than in one of the most fascinating chapters of the *History*—6.31.

6.31: THE EXODUS OF RESOURCES AND THE APPEARANCE OF POWER

> Thucydides did not much go in for descriptive writing, but he did write a brilliant description of the fleet that assembled in the Piraeus, so impressive, so costly: how the captains poured out from goblets of gold and silver libations.... He tells us that the rowers were paid a drachma a day by the state.... Yet with such incomplete figures we are unable to calculate how the expenditure on the fleet compared with the total revenues of the city: because Thucydides had no complete figures and would not guess? I doubt it. Surely he could have got reliable figures from somebody, had he wanted them. He was not thinking of finance, but like this: "It did not look so much like an expeditionary force as like a demonstration of the power and greatness of Athens, and an expression of the most far-reaching hopes." The fleet was carrying with it the pride, the power, and much of the wealth of Athens; that is what was filling the mind of Thucydides, not the precise cost of the expedition. It may be the wrong way in which to write history, but it is the way in which Thucydides thought and wrote it.[98]

This comment captures much of the essence of Thucydides' remarkable description, yet in one sense it misses a fundamental point. Thucydides *is* thinking about money and war finance, and that is why, as we shall see, he paradoxically devotes so much attention to constructing a portrait that emphasizes non-monetary wealth and the display of power and wealth. Thucydides' description is brilliantly vivid; the fact that the historian was not present to see it makes the emphasis on its visual impact especially ironic.[99]

96. See Allison 1989, 85.

97. Cf. also its similarity to Thucydides' presentation of the mood after the suppression of the Mytilenaian revolt, in which passion leads to haste and regret (3.36).

98. Kitto 1966, 335–36.

99. See Regenbogen 1968, 11–17 for a detailed stylistic analysis of the chapter, drawing attention to key expressions and phrases.

In this respect his narrative is similar to descriptions of the power of sight in Homer, Herodotos, and the tragedians, pertaining to which, Charles Segal suggests, "we the audience become, in effect, spectators of the power of vision itself."[100] And like the spectacle and sight highlighted in Herodotos and tragedy, in Thucydides the vision itself obscures the true meaning of the event witnessed.[101] But Thucydides' description of the launching of the fleet is not intended to evoke the expectation of divine envy, as does Herodotos' description of the appearance of Xerxes' army, following his presentation of the King's words and acts of hubris.[102] If "Greek thought tends to privilege vision as the primary area of knowledge and even of emotion,"[103] Thucydides constructs his narrative to contest the power of vision, or, to put it another way, to instruct his audience about how one reads and interprets what is seen; his example in this case is the interpretation of costliness (*poluteleia*).

Consider the beginning of the description, which relates the emotional state of the Athenians present, both those about to leave and those left behind. The armada is assembled at the Peiraieus, and flocks of spectators have come to see it off; Thucydides dissects the group into Athenians, allies, and foreigners. The inhabitants of Attica, he notes, came down feeling both "hope and grief" as they thought about those leaving (30.2–31.1):

> καὶ ἐν τῷ παρόντι καιρῷ, ὡς ἤδη ἔμελλον μετὰ κινδύνων ἀλλήλους ἀπολιπεῖν, μᾶλλον αὐτοὺς ἐσῄει τὰ δεινὰ ἢ ὅτε ἐψηφίζοντο πλεῖν· ὅμως δὲ τῃ παρούσῃ ῥώμῃ, διὰ τὸ πλῆθος ἑκάστων ὧν ἑώρων, τῇ ὄψει ἀνεθάρσουν. οἱ δὲ ξένοι καὶ ὁ ἄλλος ὄχλος κατὰ θέαν ἧκεν ὡς ἐπ' ἀξιόχρεων καὶ ἄπιστον διάνοιαν. παρασκευὴ γὰρ αὕτη πρώτη ἐκπλεύσασα μιᾶς πόλεως δυνάμει Ἑλληνικῇ πολυτελεστάτη δὴ καὶ εὐπρεπεστάτη τῶν ἐς ἐκεῖνον τὸν χρόνον ἐγένετο.

> Indeed, on the present occasion, as they were about to leave each other, the dangers became clearer to them than when they voted for the expedition. However, in their present strength, because of the huge size of all the individual things that they saw, they cheered up from the sight. The foreigners and the rest of the crowd came down for the spectacle thinking that it was worth seeing and an incredible intention. For this first expedition that was sent out was undeniably the most extravagant and beautiful Hellenic force to be sent out by one city up to that time.

This introduction is cumbersome in its syntax and redundant in its vocabulary; Thucydides is packing in lots of words of sight and seeing. Dover

100. Segal 1995, 185. On *opsis* in Greek thought, see also above, pp. 21–23.

101. On vision and the interpretation of objects in Herodotos, see Dewald 1993.

102. As Segal 1995, 189 implies; see also Forde 1989, 52.

103. Segal 1995, 191. See also Connor 1985, 10–11, on the importance of vision in Thucydides and its linkage with emotion. See also Walker 1993 on vividness in Greek historiography.

and others have been troubled by the repetition and awkwardness of the passage, especially its first part. Dover, for example, comments: "If ῥώμη means material strength, διὰ τὸ πλῆθος ἑκάστων is tautologous. Whatever ῥώμη means, the accumulation of two datives of different point with ἀνεθάρσουν is stylistically objectionable. This last objection is removed by punctuating not after ἑώρων but after ὄψει: 'which they saw with their own eyes', distinguishing between what they saw and what they felt"; but he also notes that "the tautology remains."[104] Yet I suggest that both the complexity of the syntax and the repetition are deliberate, or perhaps inevitable: Thucydides wants to make as emphatic as possible the relationship between sight, feeling, and power, and deliberately to correlate emotion and sight. Let us consider the passage more closely.

First, as it had shortly before, the narrative evokes 2.13, examined above. Emotion and wealth are closely linked in both, for Thucydides makes clear that the power of the vision resides in its costliness. The phrase "They cheered up because of the sight" (τῇ ὄψει ἀνεθάρσουν) resonates especially, since forms of the verb *tharsein* open both sections. However, whereas Perikles wanted to embolden his fellow Athenians positively through *hearing* about their financial resources, knowing they would be put to use in the exercise of power, here Thucydides stresses the sense of sight.[105] I think this is significant. The wealth to which Perikles refers existed, to be seen, but he intrudes in his role as filter, or interpreter. He instructs the Athenians on the proper interpretation of the wealth, including precious metal objects: it is there to be spent on the exercise of military power. In 6.31, because the Athenians are directly viewing the fleet, defined by Thucydides in terms of the wealth that went into its appearance, their interpretative faculty is unmediated: they must interpret what they see, unaided on the spot; but they had had instruction (in the time of Perikles). They chose to ignore it, and, as Thucydides will imply, their consequent interpretation is dubious.

Moreover, in 431, the Athenians were united, about to embark on a war with their resources concentrated. In 6.31, Thucydides draws attention to the moment of fracture: men and resources are about to separate (ἀπολιπεῖν ἀλλήλους), and about to create two cities.[106] He highlights the reci-

104. Dover notes that it cannot mean "confidence" or "energy," since Thucydides has "just described [the Athenians] as struck with apprehension" (*HCT* 4, ad loc.). Yet in fact this may be part of Thucydides' point: their apprehension was immediately overridden by a sense of confidence because of the size; on the use of ῥώμη see also chap. 4, p. 169, below.

105. Cf. Macleod 1983,144: "As often in his accounts of battles, Thucydides is sensitive to the effect of what men see on their morale, and so too on events themselves."

106. Avery 1973; and above, p. 25. Thucydides will emphasize the idea of separation with reference to the city's financial resources at the end of the chapter in 31.6, on which, see below.

procity of the gaze: the sight cheers up both spectators and participants; and later on in the passage, following a detailed description of the look of the fleet and reference to the army engaging in a kind of beauty contest, then a competition among the trierarchs on the ships to see who looked the best, comes the judgment of the observers (31.3–4), a passage to which I shall return below.

Dover's comment about the meaning of the word ῥώμη ("whatever it means") nicely makes the point that it does not entirely comfortably fit in its context. The noun is usually associated with bodily strength (as well as with morale); here it is used with reference to size and emotion. I suggest that its appearance is intended to draw attention to the emotional effect of sheer size on the spectators, but also to evoke ironically a previous passage as well as to foreshadow the subsequent narrative. Recall that Nikias' aim in his second speech was to try to deter the Athenians by emphasizing the size of the expedition (6.19.2); but his plan backfired, and the Athenians only grew more eager. As the narrative of the expedition unfolds, Thucydides will implicitly highlight the problem of size in relation to resources, in order to demonstrate the danger inherent in escalation unsupported by sufficient resources.[107] At the same time, the word occurs at the end of book 7, in a passage with close parallels to 6.31, which relates the scene after the final defeat, preceding evacuation, in which Thucydides focuses on the size of the camp and the failing bodily strength of the soldiers.[108] Accordingly, it is likely that Thucydides uses it in 6.31 to help the reader think about the relationship among size, resources, and strength.

The second part of this introductory passage is as revealing of Thucydides' historiographical agenda as the first. Here Thucydides contrasts the emotional state of the Athenians with the motivation leading the rest of the observers to watch: they came down to see the spectacle because it was a "sight worth seeing and an incredible intention" (οἱ δὲ ξένοι καὶ ὁ ἄλλος ὄχλος κατὰ θέαν ἧκεν ὡς επ' ἀξιόχρεων καὶ ἄπιστον διάνοιαν). Then he explains why it was worth seeing and incredible in its intention: "For this first *paraskeue* that was sent out was emphatically the costliest and most beautiful Hellenic force (*dunamis*) to be sent out by one city up to that time."

This section looks both backward and forward in the narrative. The vocabulary used to refer to the "crowd" and the "preparation" (ὄχλος . . . παρασκευή), especially in such close proximity, evokes the unusual expression "the crowdedness of the preparation" (τοῦ ὀχλώδους τῆς παρασκευῆς) in

107. This is a point that will emerge as well in book 8 with reference to the Spartans; see below, chap. 6, p. 271.

108. 7.75; see below, chap. 4, p. 169.

6.24.2. There, the Athenians' passion was increased by their audial perception, as they listened to a description of a preparation that seemed "crowd-like" in its unruliness. In a sense, then, the described preparation mirrored them: it did not make rational sense. In 6.31 the sense of the irrational continues as the crowd marvels at the sight of the now-realized preparation and finds it "an incredible intention."[109] Here vocabulary of the mind ("intention," διάνοια) is qualified by the irrational, the incredible (ἄπιστον). The "incredible" nature of the sight of Athenian *paraskeue,* and by extension, *dunamis,* also anticipates a later passage (7.28.3), in which Thucydides again refers to the "incredible" nature of Athenian power, which constituted a *paralogos* to other Greeks.[110] The impression created thereby is one of ambiguity: Athenian power defies conception; but perception seems to confirm its reality—or does it?

June W. Allison draws attention to the unusual combination of the noun *paraskeue* and the adjectives *polutelestate* and *euprepestate.*[111] She observes that Thucydides is emphasizing the extravagance of the *paraskeue,* but also points out that *euprepestate* can have the connotation "specious." Thucydides is, of course, also connecting *dunamis* with the adjectives;[112] thus he not only immediately highlights the extravagant look of the expedition but suggests a sense of unreality about both the *paraskeue* and the *dunamis.*[113] Indeed, it needs to be stressed that the adjectives *polutelestate* and *euprepestate* are a very odd, one might say inappropriate, way to talk about power and *paraskeue;* moreover, the historian will use these two adjectives again in 6.31 in close combination (31.3). Thus Thucydides is highlighting that what is so "worth seeing" and "incredible" is not the power itself, but its costly and beautiful/specious appearance; this is what is unreal. Why it is so will become clearer as the chapter progresses.

Thucydides develops and intensifies the ambiguity as the narrative proceeds. He continues by immediately qualifying what he means by saying that the expedition was the costliest and most beautiful. It is not as much the size (numbers of ships and hoplites) that justifies the superlatives,[114] as the fact that earlier expeditions had been sent on shorter campaigns and with unimpressive (φαύλη) *paraskeue:* "By contrast, this expedition was intended to

109. This resonance may also account partly for the repetition of the vocabulary of optical perception: Thucydides is reinforcing the contrast between two different kinds of sensory organs and interpretation based on them.

110. See below, chap. 3, pp. 128, 135, 136.

111. Allison 1989, 92.

112. See Thompson 1968, 121.

113. Allison 1989 well brings out both the ambiguity and the irony of Thucydides' use of *paraskeue* in book 6 generally. See also Stahl 1973, 72–74 on the aspect of unreality generally in this part of the account of the expedition.

114. See chap. 2, pp. 100–101, below for the significance of this remark in connection with Thucydides' analysis of the Trojan War.

be long-lasting and involving both sea and land operations" (31.3). Then follows a lengthy description of the fleet:

> The fleet had been elaborately equipped at enormous cost (μεγάλαις δαπάναις) to the trierarchs and the state; the treasury giving a drachma a day to each sailor and providing empty ships, sixty warships and forty transports, and the best crews, while the trierarchs gave pay in addition to the state wage to the *thranitai* and *hyperesiai*, and in other areas they spent lavishly on figureheads and costly equipment (κατασκευαῖς πολυτελέσι); each one undertook with the greatest zeal to make his ship the most beautiful (εὐπρεπείᾳ) and fast. Meanwhile the land forces had been picked from the best muster-rolls and vied with each other in paying great attention to their arms and personal accoutrements. From this not only did a rivalry among themselves in their different departments result, but also it was conjectured by the rest of the Greeks that it was more a display of power and resources than an armament against an enemy. (6.31.4)

This section of the chapter is remarkable for its degree of specificity and detail. It provides valuable details: for example, that the sailors (*nautai*) received a drachma a day from the state and additional pay from the trierarchs. But Thucydides does not relate any of this information for the sake of providing a matter-of-fact list of resources for the expedition. For one thing, he is clearly not concerned to be comprehensive—for instance, he specifies only the rate of state pay received by the sailors, not the total after the additional money from the trierarchs, and numbers of ships but not cavalry or troops—nor is the information he does provide presented in a neutral way.

Recall that the function of these pieces of information is to elaborate on his statement that this *paraskeue* was the costliest and most beautiful force that one city had ever sent out. But even the decision to single out certain costs while remaining silent on others seems deliberately designed to foster a negative impression. For example, Thucydides specifies only the pay for the common oarsmen, and not that of other members of the campaign. Why? Though daily rates of pay likely fluctuated in accordance with the situation and the rank of the crew,[115] a drachma for the ordinary sailors was high; that it was "topped off" by the trierarchs makes the sailors' wage even more extravagant. Moreover, consider the attention to costly aspects of the fleet's appearance that have nothing to do with its ability to fight:[116] the trier-

115. There has been a lively debate over standard rates of pay: Gabrielsen (1994, 110–18) believes that they fluctuated; Jordan (1975, 113–15) distinguishes between a normal rate of 1 dr. for *nautai* and 3 ob. for *hyperesiai;* the arguments of Pritchett 1971, 23–24 (3 ob. normal), Dover, *HCT* 4: 293 (1 dr. normal), Rhodes 1981, 306 (more than 3 ob. normal), and Loomis 1998, 55–56 (1 dr. normal) assume, to my mind wrongly, a standard wage independent of rank and status.

116. Forde 1989, 52: "The lavishness with which the fleet was outfitted in fact bore little relation to the purely military task at hand."

archs "spent lavishly on figureheads and other costly (πολυτελέσι) personal equipment" and vied to make each ship "beautiful" (εὐπρεπέια); we learn later (32.1) that officers and men poured libations from each ship from gold and silver vessels.[117] The second appearance of the adjectives *poluteles* and *euprepes* evokes the costly but wasteful nature of the display, as well as its misleading aspect, to which I shall return.

A conspicuous feature of this section is that Thucydides devotes far more attention to the fleet than to the land forces. The description is intended to support his statement that this expedition would be long-lasting and was prepared for both sea and land campaigns. Then comes the nine and a half-line *men* clause regarding the fleet, followed by the two-line *de* clause referring to the land forces, containing no specifics except to say: "Meanwhile the land forces had been picked from the best muster-rolls and vied with each other in paying great attention to their arms and personal accoutrements" (31.4). Thucydides' cursory treatment of the land forces, with concentration once again on the visual, and conspicuous silence regarding the specific costs of the army and cavalry demand explanation. If we recall Nikias' surprising comment in his second speech, that the war would be won "not by the fleet" (21.1), the criticism becomes pointed: the Athenians are not putting money where Nikias told them it mattered most.[118] Besides the implicit charge that the Athenians are wrongly spending on display, the additional sting is that the Athenians are making beautiful and extravagant what will not even be especially useful in the war. Nikias had argued that expenditure be put into the cavalry and land army. The conclusion is, therefore, that such extravagance was misplaced, unnecessary, and therefore utterly wasteful.

Thucydides' focus on the competitive nature of the launching of the expedition is especially noteworthy, and his choice of vocabulary provides a clue to its nuance. In referring to the soldiers' competition to see who looked the best (31.3) he uses the verb ἁμιλλάομαι; then in 6.32.2, in describing the departure of the fleet, he tells us that "after singing the paean and finishing the libations, they put out to sea, and sailing away at first in column formation, they held a race (ἅμιλλα) as far as Aigina."[119] The emphasis on costly show and competition leads the reader naturally to expect a reaction from the "judges"; Thucydides obliges. The "rest of the Greeks conjectured that it was more a display of power and resources than a mili-

117. Diod. 13.3.2 adds the detail that silver craters lined the entire circuit of the Peiraieus. See Vickers and Gill 1994, 39.

118. As Pelling points out (*per litteras*), Nikias mistrusts the fleet (which leads him to exploit it less vigorously), and thus his comment becomes in effect a self-fulfilling prophecy; but this did not necessarily have to be the case.

119. See chap. 2, p. 86, below for the Herodotean resonances in this section.

tary expedition" (ἐπίδειξιν μᾶλλον εἰκασθῆναι τῆς δυνάμεως καὶ ἐξουσίας ἢ ἐπὶ πολεμίους παρασκευήν, 6.31.4). This judgment captures and illuminates the essence of all that has preceded; or, to put it another way, in an important respect, 6.31.1–3 has been constructed implicitly to lead to this point. It reiterates, but now explicitly, the interpretation of display and power toward which Thucydides has been guiding the reader; but instead of presenting it as his own perspective he focalizes it through "the rest of the Greeks." Why do this, and to what effect?

The simple and obvious answer to the first question is that he was not himself present. The focalization, however, accomplishes an important function. Stepping back and letting other Greeks offer the perspective in a sense confirms and lends weight to Thucydides' own critical appraisal of the scene—namely, that the culmination of the Athenians' *paraskeue* looked most of all like a big show. By distancing himself from the narrative he in fact buttresses his own position, enhancing the credibility of his negative emphasis on appearance and *opsis* by asserting that others had a similar view. By this means, his implicit interpretation is thus given a sense of objectivity and thus authority over competing interpretations.

Indeed, while we know by now from the larger narrative context that Thucydides is prejudicing negatively the interpretation of the appearance of the expedition, it by no means follows that all spectators judged it equally negatively. The ambiguity is built into their perspective through the "more than" construction (μᾶλλον ἤ); it is not that it did not look like a military expedition, but that it looked more like a display of power and resources. In fact, this accords with Thucydides' own presentation, which interweaves *paraskeue* with the notion of display as unreal power.

The use of the verb εἰκασθῆναι is crucial for understanding Thucydides' purpose in including this comment. As Dover notes, citing 1.10, εἰκάζειν regularly means "infer" or "conjecture." "Yet no one is likely to have conjectured that the Athenians were not mounting a military expedition but merely making a display; the sense we need is 'it was *as if* they were making a display . . . ' and this requires εἰκάζειν = 'represent', 'portray'"; thus Dover rejects the parallel.[120] On the contrary, Thucydides not only uses the verb in its normal sense of "infer" or "conjecture" but he also does so, I suggest, intentionally to evoke 1.10. Indeed, I would go farther and suggest that the analysis of sight and power in 1.10, usually taken as a critique of Herodotos,[121]

120. *HCT* 4, ad loc.

121. E.g., Hornblower 1994b, 31–33 (though he says "perhaps" it was anti-Herodotean on p. 92). Commentators point to Hdt. 1.5.3, in which Herodotos introduces his history proper (the rise of the Mermnadai dynasty) by stating that he will deal with "the small and great cities of men equally, for those that long ago were great, the greater part of them have become small; while those that were great in my day were small in earlier times. Knowing that human happi-

may have been motivated in part by Thucydides' awareness of the false interpretations of power from *opseis* in the Sicilian expedition;[122] this makes 1.10 crucial for understanding Thucydides' comment in 6.31.4, and vice versa. I examined this chapter more briefly above, but now we need to explore it more fully to see how it illuminates 6.31.4 and 6.31 generally.

In 1.10 Thucydides contrasts the outward appearances of power in the physical makeup of a polis with the reality. His starting point is the small size of Mycenae:

> Καὶ ὅτι μὲν Μυκῆναι μικρὸν ἦν, ἢ εἴ τι τῶν τότε πόλισμα νῦν μὴ ἀξιόχρεων δοκεῖ εἶναι, οὐκ ἀκριβεῖ ἄν τις σημείῳ χρώμενος ἀπιστοίη μὴ γενέσθαι τὸν στόλον τοσοῦτον ὅσον οἵ τε ποιηταὶ εἰρήκασι καὶ ὁ λόγος κατέχει. Λακεδαιμονίων γὰρ εἰ ἡ πόλις ἐρημωθείη, λειφθείη δὲ τά τε ἱερὰ καὶ τῆς κατασκευῆς τὰ ἐδάφη, πολλὴν ἂν οἶμοι ἀπιστίαν τῆς δυνάμεως προελθόντος πολλοῦ χρόνου τοῖς ἔπειτα πρὸς τὸ κλέος αὐτῶν εἶναι (καίτοι Πελοποννήσου τῶν πέντε τὰς δύο μοίρας νέμονται, τῆς τε ξυμπάσης ἡγοῦνται καὶ τῶν ἔξω ξυμμάχων πολλῶν· ὅμως δὲ οὔτε ξυνοικισθείσης πόλεως οὔτε ἱεροῖς καὶ κατασκευαῖς πολυτελέσι χρησαμένης, κατὰ κώμας δὲ τῷ παλαιῷ τῆς Ἑλλάδος τρόπῳ οἰκισθείσης, φαίνοιτ' ἂν ὑποδεεστέρα), Ἀθηναίων δὲ τὸ αὐτὸ τοῦτο παθόντων διπλασίαν ἂν τὴν δύναμιν εἰκάζεσθαι ἀπὸ τῆς φανερᾶς ὄψεως τῆς πόλεως ἢ ἔστιν. οὔκουν ἀπιστεῖν εἰκός, οὐδὲ τὰς ὄψεις τῶν πόλεων μᾶλλον σκοπεῖν ἢ τὰς δυνάμεις . . . (1.10.1–3)
>
> And because Mycenae was small, or if some town of those at that time does not seem to be noteworthy, whoever would disbelieve that the expedition was as great as the poets say and tradition holds would not be using accurate indications. For if the polis of the Lakedaimonians were to become deserted except for temples and foundations of buildings, I think that people later on would have great disbelief in its former power compared with its fame (yet they occupy two-fifths of the Peloponnese and lead all of it and have many allies without; nevertheless, since there are neither temples nor costly buildings, but they live in villages in the old manner of Greece, they would appear to have been weaker than they are); whereas if the Athenians were to suffer the same thing, their power would be inferred to have been twice as great as it was from the manifest sight of the city. Therefore, it is not reasonable to be incredulous [sc. about Mycenae's power]; nor should one examine the appearances of cities more than their power.

Both the verbal parallels between 1.10.3 and 6.31.4, and the argument of 1.10 and 6.31 generally, are too close to be accidental: "conjecturing

---

ness nowhere stays in the same place, I shall make mention of both equally." The specific focus of Thucydides' comment on monuments and sight needs to be kept in mind: it is not a blanket statement about either monuments or sight; it is made, rather, in the specific context of power.

122. See chap. 2 below for an examination of 1.10.6–1.11 as motivated by his observations of the Sicilian expedition as well.

power" appears in both 10.3 and 31.4; the repetition of *opsis* in 1.10 mirrors the repetition in 31.1, and the following sections implicitly, with their emphasis on sight: the use of *axiochreon* appears in both 1.10.1 and 31.1, as does the reference to disbelief (1.10.1, 3; 31.1), and the use of *poluteles* (1.10.2; 6.31.1, 3). The similarity between inference, sight, and power in both 1.10 and 31.4 is precise. Moreover, the remark that "one should not look at the sight *of the cities* more than their power" has a special resonance with the expedition inasmuch as (following Avery), Thucydides (as noted above) presents the expedition as a new city moving off to Sicily. Thucydides' method in 6.31, as in 1.10, is to contest the method of inference commonly used to assess power. It is clear from both passages that in his view his contemporaries were inclined to mistake displays of wealth for accurate indicators of power. He points up the error in 1.10 with reference to physical monuments as indicators of power; in 6.31, he shows the error in action as he highlights the appearance of the fleet and the conclusions people drew from it.

The point in 31.4 is that Greeks are, *pace* Dover, making inferences from the look of the expedition, concluding that it looked more like a show of power and resources than a military expedition.[123] In both 1.10 and in 6.31, *opsis* is presented almost in opposition to power—"Do not look to the appearances of cities more than to their power" (οὐδὲ τὰς ὄψεις τῶν πόλεων μᾶλλον σκοπεῖν ἢ τὰς δυνάμεως)—but in a sense the central point is the irrelevance of *opsis* as a practical *criterion,* or as a sign. People who see Athens' power as twice as great as it really is and Sparta's as insufficiently great are misreading signs: they are looking at *phanerai opseis,* not *dunamis.* Likewise, the spectators (and the participants) are misreading the signs: they are looking at, and are impressed by, the *opseis* more than the *dunamis;* but this is because of the Athenians' own approach to their expedition. Thucydides' comment that the participants were "competing" with each other to look the best (ἁμμιληθέν; ἔριν, 6.31.3, 4) reveals that they themselves were consciously aiming at appearance; thus when the "rest of the Greeks" made the inference about display from what they saw, they were only deducing from the conclusion toward which the Athenians were leading them. Thucydides shows explicitly in 1.10 and by example in 6.31 that it is incorrect.[124]

Moreover, Thucydides' use of *poluteles* and its cognates clearly shows that the word has an elevated ideological status in conceptions of power that the historian seeks to undermine, and he accomplishes this by placing it in discussions of power only to contest its validity as a criterion. This sheds light on what has been seen as a glaring omission and an odd choice of vocabulary in one passage of the Funeral Oration. First, I suggest, Thucydides' im-

123. Dover misses the μᾶλλον ἤ construction.

124. They are doing what Dewald (1993) demonstrates Herodotos is doing with reference to Xerxes.

plication in 1.10 that costly buildings are not necessary indicators of power makes transparent why, in this speech on Athenian greatness and power, Perikles does not, to the surprise of most modern commentators, draw attention to the Parthenon and the rest of the magnificent buildings on the Akropolis. Such signs were clearly compelling and powerful to Thucydides' contemporaries—as 1.10 makes clear—and it may be that their absence from Perikles' speech may be a bit of silent polemic; certainly any mention of them by Perikles, whom Thucydides strongly appears to credit with the "right" way of thinking about power, would constitute a subversion of the historian's own program. Second, the famous phrase "We cultivate the beautiful with economy" (φιλοκαλοῦμεν μετ' εὐτελείας), followed by "We use wealth for action not for show" (πλούτῳ τε ἔργου μᾶλλον καιρῷ ἢ λόγου κόμπῳ χρώμεθα) at 2.40.1, has an especially pointed resonance—in particular, the word *euteleia*—when considered alongside both 1.10 and 6.31. The choice of the word has troubled many scholars, who have protested that the building program, for example, if an implied referent of Perikles' remarks, could hardly be considered "economical."[125] Yet the special usefulness of this particular word becomes clear when one considers it against 1.10 and 6.31. It is the antithesis of *poluteleia* and is another indication of the normally negative connotation of the latter word in Thucydides' framework. It is evident, then, that Thucydides is attempting to contest an entire ideology.

In this, however, he and Herodotos are not so far apart. I have noted above that scholars have usually seen 1.10 as a jab at Herodotos. Yet in its emphasis on drawing deductions from visible signs of wealth, from *poluteleia,* Thucydides' treatment is remarkably similar to Herodotos' account of Solon's visit to Croesus, and the latter's display of his treasury to the Athenian as a visible sign, in this case not of his power, but of his happiness. Herodotos tells us that after Solon's arrival, the Lydian king led him to his treasures. Solon gazed at and examined everything (θεησάμενον δὲ μιν τὰ πάντα καὶ σκεψάμενον, 1.30.2) but was not fooled into making the inference that Croesus desired. Thucydides picks up on this in 1.10: whereas Solon examined (σκεψάμενον) everything and was led to the correct inference (foiling Croesus' expectation), Thucydides writes that "one should not examine (σκοπεῖν) the appearances of cities more than their power." In both, examination should lead to deduction, not acceptance of common interpretations of the sight.[126]

Returning to 6.31.4, the verb "to conjecture" (εἰκασθῆναι) embodies the idea not of observation or representation but rather deduction from signs, in this case the *epideixis,* itself embodying both display and an indication. As

125. E.g., Gomme, *HCT* 2, ad loc.; Rusten 1989, 153; cf. Boedeker and Raaflaub 1998, 4 with n. 13; Kallet 2003.

126. See Konstan 1987 and Dewald 1993 on (mis)interpretations based on itemizing.

he did in his own voice in 1.10, Thucydides uses the perspective of the other Greeks to make a methodological point about how one draws deductions about power from appearances. This approach will become even more blatant in the manner in which he treats the story of the Egestan deception (6.46). But his own position also casts a critical light on Alkibiades' assertion that people "conjectured" Athens' power to be greater than it was through his displays (6.16.2); he does not deny that this is a common deduction; he suggests only that it is wrong.

One might think Thucydides has gone far enough to make patent his historiographical aim in writing up the scene of the fleet's departure patent. But he is not finished. He follows 31.4 with a lengthy comment, introduced by *gar,* in support of the inference of the other Greeks, thus implicitly endorsing the perspective. He does so, however, not by elaborating on the aspect of appearance, already treated amply, but by listing the *expenses* incurred:

> For if anyone had calculated the public expenditure of the city and the private costs to the soldiers, of the former [i.e., public outlay] as much as had already been spent as well as what the generals took with them, and of the latter [private expenses] as much as anyone needed for his personal outfitting and a trierarch, for his ship, and as much as he expected to spend in addition, apart from the travelling money which each likely provided for himself, not including his daily state pay, for such a long journey, and what the soldiers or traders brought with them for the purpose of exchange, a huge amount of money in all would have been discovered to have been taken out of the city (πολλὰ ἂν τάλαντα ηὑρέθη ἐκ τῆς πόλεως τὰ πάντα ἐξαγόμενα). (31.5)

Many scholars have been troubled by this passage, largely because of its unusual—for Thucydides—vagueness, coupled with the detail of categories of expenditure. And the final clause, "many talents would have been discovered to have been taken out of the city," might seem a bit of an anticlimax, as Dover comments on this passage.[127] But he adduces a parallel in Aristophanes' *Clouds* 1065, where the phrase πολλὰ τάλαντα also appears, meaning "a vast amount of money," and suggests that the phrase "can bear a lot of emphasis."[128] This seems to be the case in this passage, especially with the adverbial phrase τὰ πάντα, "in all." Even accepting the emphasis, however, one must still explain the vague nature of the passage as a whole, like the earlier part of 6.31, in which specific financial details are overshadowed by vague references to costs. This is especially true when it is contrasted, for example, with Perikles' list of financial resources on the eve of war, which overwhelms with specific figures and monetary totals. The latter shows that Thucydides was concerned and interested enough in financial

127. *HCT* 4, ad loc.

128. Ibid.

information to provide such details; thus his refusal to do the arithmetic here is conspicuous and deliberate.

A ready explanation is that the items included costs that might not have been available even to an industrious individual who did some research—namely, private costs to individuals. One could also argue that Thucydides did not have access to precise figures because of his exile, but could he not have located the information later? This is precisely the point, driven home by the contrary-to-fact condition: "if someone had calculated" implies that no one at the time did; the comment is, I suggest, loaded with sarcastic condemnation. The Athenians (publicly and privately) simply spent and spent on the expedition, without even accounting for it; and they spent not on real power, but on making the expedition look as good as possible, the result being the "costliest" expedition ever launched. No one researched the costs; when Thucydides ends the sentence with "it would have been *discovered* (ηὑρέθη)," there is an additional sting, for, as he will shortly make clear in the Peisistratid digression, the consequences of the failure to do research, to discover the truth, can be grave.[129]

The vagueness of the exposition, therefore, fits Thucydides' historiographical purpose. It is significant that the sole focus of this lengthy *gar* clause is the expenses incurred. Recall the purpose of this section, to explain and support how the expedition was inferred to be more an *epideixis* of power and *resources* than a military campaign. By writing only about the resources, Thucydides reveals his paramount interest in the financial aspect and consequences of the preparation of the fleet. As if the point needed making, he also makes clear that the purpose of relating the various ex-

129. Thucydides' emphasis on calculation and discovery in a passage concerned as well with sight and the interpretation of the visual, for which one requires *gnome,* bears an intriguing similarity to the Hippocratic treatise *Prognostic,* in which the author uses an accounting metaphor, λογίζεσθαι, to refer to the process of drawing judgments: e.g., "He who would make accurate forecasts as to those who will recover, and those who will die, and whether the disease will last a greater or less number of days, must understand all the symptoms thoroughly and be able to appreciate them, estimating (ἐκλογιζόμενον) their powers when they are compared with one another" (*Prog.* 25, Loeb trans.); cf. *Prog.* 15; *Ars* 7, 10. As Jouanna (1999, 302) observes, "In the pedagogical passages of the collection, where authors give advice about the way in which to conduct an examination of the patient, the list of senses is completed by mention of intelligence (*gnome*), or reason in the sense of faculty of calculation (*logismos*). Although in such passages the authors do not explicitly describe the role of this faculty, they regarded it as being on the same level with the other senses; it had to do—at least from the point of view of an author such as that of the *Prognostic,* who represents the most authentic version of Hippocratism—with reckoning (*logizesthai*) the relative value of the observed signs. This calculation consisted, first, of determining the value of each sign as a function of the various parameters that might have an influence upon its weight in comparison with that of the others." Thucydides has presented the signs to be judged—the appearance of the armada and examples of the costs incurred—and implies the inability to assess their relative value (i.e., not all are usable in the waging of war) and to calculate the total value.

penses is not to show how much was spent on real power, but on the display of power and resources; the ambiguity lies in the possibility that money has been spent on mere display. Contemporaries who likened the expedition to an *epideixis* may not have done so as a criticism; Thucydides' position is undeniably negative.[130]

There is an additional issue. The choice of verb at the end of the sentence is surely significant. Thucydides does not finish the list of categories of expenditure with the comment "If someone had calculated the public and private costs . . . he would have found that many talents had been spent"; rather he says: "He would have discovered that many talents had been taken out (ἐξαγόμενα) of the city." The vocabulary makes as vivid as possible the removal of vast wealth from the polis; the physical carrying away of the city's public and private financial resources serves as the negation, the undoing, of what they had just recently been able to accomplish—namely, the accumulation of money in a centralized place, made possible by the Peace of Nikias, which, as we have seen, Thucydides makes explicit in 6.26.2 (ἄθροισις χρημάτων).

I suggest that the purpose of 6.31, to highlight the element of wasteful display and the appearance or impression of power, accounts both for the absence of specific figures and amounts and for Thucydides' deliberate decision to use words that convey huge quantity, but in a vague way.[131] So, for example, if we want to evoke a sense of the opulence of something or someone's great wealth, we might say colloquially that the person has "loads of money." Or, to cite an ancient example, in Solon's visit to Croesus' treasury, Herodotos needs to convey the impressive extent of Croesus' wealth in order for the story to have its punch. He puts it this way: "Croesus' servants led Solon through his treasury and pointed out everything to him in its greatness and richness (πάντα ἐόντα μεγάλα τε καὶ ὄλβια, 1.30.1). "Solon gazed in wonder and examined everything" (τὰ πάντα, 1.30.2). To foster an impression, specific quantities are not necessary, though listing items is as rhetorically effective for making an impression as it is practically effective for providing precise amounts—thus the lists in 2.13 and 6.31. Thucydides' historiographical purpose in 6.31 may also explain why he chooses—I use the word *choose* deliberately—not to relate the exact amount of money taken on the expedition to be spent in the actual military campaigns; his focus is on the wealth that went into looking good, not on the money that would be used for fighting.

130. See Hedrick (1995, 86), who briefly discusses the use of ἐπίδειξις in this passage and in 3.16 and 6.46, as well as Thucydides and the interpretation of material culture. See also below.

131. It is important also to recognize the tragic techniques in this kind of vague approach; see Hornblower 1994b, 148; also Macleod 1983, 140–58.

Implicit in 6.31 may be a critique of the value of quantification and measuring. Thucydides counts those items that relate above all to *poluteleia* and then provides the implicit criticism at the end of the passage that no one precisely quantified the actual expenditures of the city. If we return to the story of Croesus and Solon, the latter can be said to draw an analogy to the implied quantifying of Croesus' treasure—the larger, the happier—and by his lengthy quantification of the days of a man's life (1.32), he underscores the uselessness of quantifying and measuring when it comes to the value of life.[132] Mere measurement does not reveal what is really at issue. Likewise, the quantifying, both precise and vague, in 6.31 does not add up to real power; Greeks wrongly infer from measuring and counting signs of power that the power really exists, or is even greater than it appears.[133] On the other hand, Thucydides implies that measuring and counting are valuable when the issue is *real* power (especially since in war it is necessary to maintain reserves and revenue to offset expenditure); that is why he allows Perikles to quantify, but leaves everything in 6.31 vague.

Moreover, an additional resonance helps to illuminate further the parallels scholars have drawn between the Sicilian expedition (and the Melian Dialogue preceding it) and the Persian Wars: specifically, the theme of excess greatness followed by downfall.[134] We have seen that the Athenians are presented as being at a renewed height of power. Donald Lateiner has examined a progression in Herodotos in which, in the instances in which he uses the verb *akmazein*, "to flourish" or "to be at a height," with reference to cities, he makes a point of alluding specifically to their great wealth, and then their downfall follows in the narrative[135]—a pattern that fits the causal nexus of hubris in the *Histories*. Thus, on the one hand, without the rest of the narrative, 6.31, in which Thucydides puts the Athenians' wealth—more than their power—on display, can be read by itself as a foreshadowing of the ultimate fall of the city.[136] On the other hand, by contrast with Herodotos, Thucydides' point is not to make a case about hubris but rather to show the Athenians' inability to understand the relationship between money and power, and to criticize those who mistakenly infer power from display.

Thucydides, then, fosters an essentially negative perception of the ex-

132. See Konstan 1987 on the significance of quantifying in Herodotos; also Hartog 1988, 232–35.

133. Cf. Alkibiades' speech, 16.1, examined above: he lists the number of his victories and ties them to perceptions of the city's power (as well as his right to be general).

134. E.g., Cornford 1971 [1907]; Marinatos Kopff and Rawlings 1978. See also below, chap. 2.

135. Lateiner 1982, 97–98. The instances are Sardis (Croesus), Siphnos, Miletos, and Sybaris.

136. In support is the ironic echoing of 6.31 in two passages at the end of the Sicilian narrative, 7.71 and 7.75, on which, see below, chap. 4, pp. 163–71.

penditure of wealth on display. But it needs to be emphasized that this is as much a construction, a contingent way of regarding display, as other ways of looking at wealth: another writer either might not have focused so intently on this aspect of the beginning of the expedition or might have cast it in positive terms, citing magnificence and display as measurements and evidence of power. For example, included in the list of costs in 6.31 are fully normal and justified expenses involved in preparing a military expedition. Thucydides prejudices the interpretation of those items, however, by putting them all into an explanation of why the expedition was inferred to be more an *epideixis* than an armament, and why it was so extravagant, thus making them appear wasteful and unnecessary.

In fact, Thucydides himself elsewhere speaks of the fine appearance of a military assemblage in positive terms. Consider how he refers to the army assembled at Nemea in 418: "This was the finest (κάλλιστον) Hellenic force that had been assembled up to this time, and it should have been seen (ὤφθη) especially when it was still gathered in Nemea, when there were . . . [a list of all the Peloponnesians represented follows]" (5.60.3).[137] Thucydides concentrates on the visual aspect, whose effect was lost because the army disbanded before there were any opponents to see it; they were all dressed up with nowhere to go, or rather, to fight. Why, then, is the appearance of the Peloponnesian army worth noting in positive terms, while such enormous attention is given to the appearance of the fleet in 415 in negatively prejudicial ways? There is no indication that the Peloponnesian fighting force was decked out in any extravagant or costly way; rather, the fact that they were all assembled and were picked men, all primed for battle, is what inspires Thucydides to use the term *kalliston;* the lost opportunity that brought such blame to Agis and others for not letting them fight resided in the fact that their enemies did not encounter their power (60.5–6), not the fact that nobody saw the display of it. By contrast, the fleet outfitted for Sicily was being equipped to look pretty, and the competition that ensued over who *looked* the best, as opposed to who fought the best, almost negates the military context of the occasion; indeed, the occasion seems more like a festival.[138]

To return to 6.31, the final sentence of the chapter considers the expedition from a distance:

> καὶ ὁ στόλος οὐχ ἧσσον τόλμης τε θάμβει καὶ ὄψεως λαμπρότητι περιβοήτος ἐγένετο ἢ στρατιᾶς πρὸς οὓς ἐπῇσαν[139] ὑπερβολῇ, καὶ ὅτι μέγι-

137. See the discussion of this passage in Stroud 1994, 289–92.

138. Cf. also Brasidas' speech, 4.126.4–5, on the appearance of an army—or in this case, specifically, barbarians—vs. the reality of its power; see Luschnat 1942, 57–63.

139. Rood (1998, 161 n. 7) notes that πρὸς οὓς ἐπῇσαν is a doublet of 2.65.11. Lugenbill's argument (1997, 130–31) that the grammatical construction in both cases is attraction of the relative is in my view implausible; moreover, his translation of 6.31.6 does injustice to

στος ἤδη διάπλους ἀπὸ τῆς οἰκείας καὶ ἐπὶ μεγίστῃ ἐλπίδι τῶν μελλόντων πρὸς τὰ ὑπάρχοντα ἐπεχειρήθη. (6.31.6)

Indeed, the expedition became renowned no less for the astonishment of its daring and brilliance of its appearance than for the superiority of its fighting force, compared with those against whom it was sent; and because this was the largest expedition away from home and attempted with the greatest hope in the future, compared with present resources.

Thucydides' language in this concluding sentence elegantly sums up 6.31 as a whole and encapsulates themes not only found in 6.31 but in the expedition more generally, as well as in the Melian Dialogue. Again, there is no blanket statement—"It was renowned for the astonishment of its daring and brilliance of its appearance, not for the strength of its armament." Rather, the ambiguous marker of power—appearance, show, which may or may not reflect reality—continues to be elevated to the same level or even a higher one than real power occupies. The comment—especially the phrase "brilliance of the appearance" (ὄψεως λαμπρότητι)—coming on the heels of the lengthily presented linkage between expense and display, focuses our attention above all on the aspect of sight; and λαμπρότητι recalls both Alkibiades' use of the verbal form (λαμπρύνομαι, 6.16.3) and Nikias', with reference to Alkibiades (ἐλλαμπρύνεσθαι, 6.12.2). Yet the brilliant—extravagant—appearance, present for all to see, is, as we have been guided to conclude, not entirely real, and not a true sign of power. And the extraordinary expenditure on display is further undercut by the following clause concerning hope and present and future.

Parry stresses the (modified) *logos/ergon* antithesis embodied in the μέλλοντα/ὑπαρχόντα contrast in this clause and links it to the Melian Dialogue. His remarks are worth quoting in full. "The opposition here is between μελλόντων and ὑπαρχόντα. μελλόντων, depending on ἐλπίδι, belongs in the realm of λόγος. ὑπαρχόντα are the real things that are, and are at hand, now; μέλλοντα are things one plans, hopes to get, things that exist only in conception. . . . This fits into a larger sub-pattern of Thucydides' work, one which begins with the Melian Dialogue." He cites 5.87, in which the Athenians reject the Melians' reliance on τὰ μέλλοντα and in-

the relationship Thucydides establishes between sight and extravagance. Rood translates the clause στρατιᾶς πρὸς οὓς ἐπῆσαν ὑπερβολῇ as "because of the extravagance lavished on the invasion force relative to the numbers who actually participated" (131). While this is attractive, given, as he notes, Thucydides' emphasis in 6.31 on extravagant display, it makes no sense when considered with the preceding clause, of which it is a part: "The expedition was no less renowned for its astonishing daring and brilliant appearance than for the extravagance lavished on the invasion force relative to the numbers who actually participated." Since the object of viewing in 6.31 is in fact the extravagant look, the notion of extravagance is already contained in the οὐχ ἧσσον clause.

sist that they look to τὰ παρόντα that they see before them. In 6.31.6, he notes, "the situation of the Melian Dialogue is being ironically inverted: now it is the Athenians who rely on ἐλπίς and τὰ μέλλοντα."[140] As Parry comments later on, "It is only because of what was said in the Melian Dialogue and by Nicias of μέλλοντα and ὑπάρχοντα, and because of what Diodotus says of ἐλπίς, that one recognizes the distinction as one of conception and actuality at all. But it is a statement of fundamental importance for the development of the latter portion of the *History*."[141] Finally, Parry remarks that "the phrase ἐπὶ μεγίστῃ ἐλπίδι τῶν μελλόντων πρὸς τὰ ὑπάρχοντα is designed to emphasize the divergence between conception and actuality which characterizes Athenian policy after Pericles' death and reaches a climax in the Sicilian campaign."[142]

It is important to appreciate the extent to which Thucydides, in writing about conception/perception and reality, has embedded Athens' financial resources in this antithesis and connected it in turn to the linkage among hope, present and future through 6.31 (and the Melian Dialogue). Ἔργον/ὑπάρχοντα concern power, made possible by resources; but Thucydides has undercut the perception even of the ὑπάρχοντα by emphasizing the expenditure on display and appearance, and by comparing the "greatest hope in the future" with present resources. This undermines to an even greater extent the reliance on the "greatest hope"; the very brilliance of the display, because of the waste it implies and its illusory nature as a true token of power, means that the Athenians, in relying on future hopes, are misleading themselves even more seriously than they are misleading the Melians (5.103). They have spent on present appearance; they should have saved for military expenditure for the future.

It will be useful to conclude and summarize this lengthy discussion of 6.31 by again considering the passage against 2.13, for the structural similarities between the two suggest that the reader is intended to connect the two. Both passages occur where the narrative focuses on the eve of a momentous event: the beginning of the Peloponnesian War in 2.13, and the departure of the Sicilian expedition in book 6. Both list resources on the eve of a major conflict, but in dramatically different ways and to different effect. Whereas the effect of Perikles' speech (in indirect discourse) is one of specificity and precision, Thucydides in 6.31 is detailed but vague overall. Although the emboldening and encouraging of the people through the sight of wealth are common to both passages, the differences between the two are profound. Perikles makes a deliberate attempt to encourage the Athenians with a list of financial (and other) resources; the statesman employed a skillful rhetori-

140. Parry 1981, 74–75.
141. Ibid., 77.
142. Ibid., 78.

cal strategy that would produce justified confidence in the impending conflict. By contrast, in 6.31, Thucydides comments that the Athenians were fearful of the coming enterprise but were encouraged by the sight and magnitude of the preparations. He writes the narrative in such a way, however, as to suggest that they are confident for the wrong reasons. Moreover, whereas Perikles relates not only the amount of the accumulated reserve, centralized on the Akropolis for military use, but also the quantity of money regularly coming in from the empire, in 6.31 Thucydides focuses on the enormous wealth that, having once again been accumulated, was now being taken out of the city, and implies that much of it was in the form of display, in order to make the fleet look good. And just as 2.13 may be read in an ironic sense—so much wealth was available, and still the Athenians failed to defeat the Spartans—in book 6, not even all the talents carted out of the city could overcome the Syracusans. The implication once again is that it is not simply abundant financial resources that win wars, but the ability to use them properly.[143] On the other hand, it is questionable that the "many talents" were in fact sufficient.[144]

THE SPEECHES AT SYRACUSE

Thucydides follows up his account of the exodus of Athenian resources with a debate at Syracuse, presenting speeches by Hermokrates and Athenagoras. These speeches constitute a valuable thematic link between the narrative of the departure and the Athenians' appearance in Sicily, and Thucydides makes the debate in Syracuse mirror that in Athens, as scholars have recognized.[145] Just as there was something ambiguous about the spectacle to those at the Peiraieus—was it really an armament, or just a glittering parade of floating resources?—so the speeches in Syracuse continue to focus attention on whether the Athenians are really coming, and, by extension, whether Athenian *dunamis* in Sicily will be real or illusory. Indeed, the speakers serve the crucial function of highlighting and even intensifying the ambiguity, as the certainty with which each speaks becomes clouded when read against the preceding narrative.

Thucydides introduces Hermokrates with the statement that the Syracusan came forward to speak "on the grounds that he thought that he knew the truth" (ὡς σαφῶς οἰόμενος εἰδέναι, 32.3). Hermokrates begins: "Perhaps I shall be disbelieved as much as others when I speak of the reality of

143. This issue is the subject of chap. 4 below.

144. See chap. 2, below.

145. E.g., Connor 1984, 168–76. Stahl (1973, 77) notes the similarities between Hermokrates' and Nikias' speeches; Allison (1989, 89–90) and Mader (1993b) see similarities in argument between the speeches of Nikias and Athenagoras.

the expedition" ("Ἄπιστα μὲν ἴσως, ὥσπερ καὶ ἄλλοι τινές, δόξω ὑμῖν περὶ τοῦ ἐπίπλου τῆς ἀληθείας λέγειν, 6.33.1), and he reinforces the notion that those who speak of a reality that seems incredible would be taken as irrational, indeed, out of their minds (ἄφρονες, 33.1). But he insists that the Athenians are on their way. There are clear echoes of 6.31 in his awareness that what he thinks is real may seem unbelievable to others;[146] one recalls the spectators' perspective that the expedition was an "incredible intention" (ἄπιστον διάνοιαν) at 6.31.1.

Hermokrates appears to know what he is talking about, an impression enhanced by subsequent vocabulary that echoes earlier parts of the narrative: for example, when he alludes to the Athenians' desire (ἐπιθυμία) to conquer Sicily and regards the aid to Egesta as a pretext (πρόφασις, 33.2).[147] Yet his very insistence and confidence, read against the earlier narrative, make the reader wonder whether Hermokrates' confidence is justified. He does not have the uncertainty or ambivalence about the nature of the expedition that the reader has; yet there is considerable uncertainty and irony built into the narrative. Thucydides introduces Hermokrates' speech with the conspicuous qualifier "thinking" he knew the truth, rather than with the unambiguous "knowing" the truth. Moreover, those who actually saw the expedition set out at the Peiraieus judged its nature and purpose as ambiguous; Hermokrates, for whom it was still invisible, possessed certainty. Thus the narrative casts doubt on the "truth" (ἀληθεία) of the power that he claims.[148]

In another set of verbal parallels, both Nikias and Hermokrates place the potential appearance of the Athenian fleet in the context of the terror it could inspire. But while Nikias, in his first speech, advised the Athenians either not to sail to Sicily, or if they did sail, to make a show of force and leave, as alternative strategies that he claimed would equally strike terror (ἐκπεπληγμένοι, 6.11.4) into the Sicilians, Hermokrates urges the Syracusans who believe him "not to be terrified" (μὴ ἐκπλαγῇ) by the Athenians' power and daring, and he insists that its magnitude will make the rest of the Sicilians, "through terror" (ἐκπλαγέντες), ally with them (33.4).

Uncertainty about Hermokrates' status as an accurate interpreter develops as he continues, again, paradoxically because of his certainty, and also because of parallels with a much earlier speech, that of the Spartan king Archidamos (1.80–85).[149] Just as Archidamos instructed the Spartans about

146. Disbelief and persuasion are repeatedly emphasized in 6.33: ἄπιστα, οὐ πείθουσιν, πείθων; cf. ἄφρονες, 33.1; ἀπιστήσαντες, 33.3; πιστά, 33.4.

147. Cf. 6.6.1; 24.4.

148. But cf. Bloedow (1996), who regards Hermokrates' speech as straightforwardly intelligent. This view denies any complexity to the preceding narrative.

149. Stahl 1973, 77; Frank 1984, 101–2; Rawlings (1981, 83–84) notes parallels between Athenagoras' and Archidamos' speeches.

the primary criterion of military success—"War is not so much a matter of men as of expense, through which men can succeed" (1.83.2)—so Hermokrates, in advising the Syracusans to seek help from the Carthaginians, notes that they possess the most gold and silver, "through which war, as everything else, flourishes" (6.34.2).[150]

On the other hand, while he refers to the Syracusans' slowness to act (similar in this respect to the reputation of the Spartans), Hermokrates urges immediate and swift action, by contrast to Archidamos, who recommended waiting before engaging the Athenians. The Athenians, Hermokrates notes, do not expect the Syracusans to resist them, since the Syracusans failed to help the Spartans at the beginning of the Peloponnesian War. If, accordingly, the Syracusans launch a fleet and set out to meet the Athenians at sea, the reaction will be great surprise: "If they should see the Syracusans daring beyond judgment, the Athenians will be more terrified by the surprise than by our actual power" (εἰ δ' ἴδοιεν παρὰ γνώμην τολμήσαντας, τῷ ἀδοκήτῳ μᾶλλον ἂν καταπλαγεῖεν ἢ τῇ ἀπὸ τοῦ ἀληθοῦς δυνάμει, 6.34.8). Yet, given the way in which Thucydides has crafted the narrative to stress the Athenians' passion and zeal in undertaking the expedition, their desire to conquer the island, their expectation that they were abundantly equipped for success, and their reliance on the "greatest hopes" (6.31.6), Hermokrates' expectation seems misplaced, but in a slightly different sense from that seen earlier. The effect is once again to reinforce the perception of ambiguity concerning Athens' actual power, for whereas in his preceding arguments he assumed the reality of Athenian power, here he seems to endorse its illusory aspect.

Hermokrates ends his speech by insisting that the Athenians are on their way. But Thucydides relates the contentiousness of the Syracusans, noting their differing and conflicting views about the Athenians, none of which supports Hermokrates' position. Athenagoras' speech follows. A man whom Thucydides describes as δήμου προστάτης, "leader of the demos," and at that time πιθανώτατος τοῖς πολλοῖς, "most persuasive among the many" (35.2), Athenagoras disputes Hermokrates' claim about the reality of the expedition, both by casting doubt on the veracity of reports (τῆς νῦν στρατιᾶς, ὡς φασιν, ἐπιούσης, 37.1) and by arguing on the basis of probability (εἰκός): with the Peloponnesians close by, the Athenians would hardly leave home to venture to Sicily (36.4). As Hans-Peter Stahl notes, Athenagoras' insistence on the Athenians' common sense "means, in Thucydides' eyes, a cynical judgment on their irrational vote for the expedition."[151] But, through

150. καὶ ἔστιν ὁ πόλεμος οὐχ ὅπλων τὸ πλέον ἀλλὰ δαπάνης, δι' ἣν τὰ ὅπλα ὠφελεῖ, 1.83.2; χρυσὸν γὰρ καὶ ἄργυρον πλεῖστον κέκτηνται, ὅθεν ὅ τε πόλεμος και τἆλλα εὐπορεῖ, 6.34.2.

151. Stahl 1973, 77.

Athenagoras' remarks, Thucydides also reinforces the "incredible" nature of the Athenians' intention (6.31.1), as well as foreshadowing the "incredible" nature of what they actually did (7.28.3), irrational though it was.[152] Moreover, Athenagoras' insistence and certainty, like Hermokrates', only lend support to the impression that he, apart from simply being wrong, has overstated the illusory nature of Athens' power. The two Syracusans reflect the two sides of the ambiguous judgment of the Athenian expedition offered by the Greeks in 6.31.4: that the expedition "was conjectured to be more like a display of power and resources than a *paraskeue* against enemies."

6.46: THE DISCOVERY OF THE DECEPTION AT EGESTA

We come now to the Egestan deception, which Thucydides has chosen to present not in its chronological place,[153] but instead at the moment of its discovery. As we have seen, in treating the Egestans' offer he has employed various techniques, both to challenge the offer's veracity and to keep the issue alive in the narrative. One of these techniques is repetitive anticipation, which is used in both narrative and speeches. As Stahl has pointed out, the issue of money is developed by Thucydides through a combination of speech and narrative, in which experience proves correct the statements made by Nikias.[154] The anticipation (6.6.3, 8.2, 22) is not the kind that "robs the narrative of suspense"; rather, it supplies a "tension which keeps the reader engaged."[155] Indeed, Thucydides employs it one final time (44.4), right before relating the story, now to prepare the reader for the climax. He notes that after, the Athenian fleet landed at Rhegion, the generals waited for the return of the ships that had been sent on ahead to Egesta to investigate whether the money promised by the messengers in Athens really existed (περὶ τῶν χρημάτων εἰ ἔστιν ἃ ἔλεγον ἐν ταῖς Ἀθήναις οἱ ἄγγελοι, 6.44.4).[156]

This statement comes as a surprise, since we were told at the beginning of book 6 that the Athenians had already been instructed to investigate the existence of the money before voting for the expedition, and the envoys who carried out the investigation had returned with the Egestans and their

152. He fuses irrationality with incredible feats also in the Pylos episode; some scholars see a link between his presentation of that event and that of the Sicilian expedition: e.g., Hunter 1973, 81; Wilson 1990; see also Mader 1993b for a careful discussion of the theme of rationality vs. insanity. On Athenagoras' speech, as intended to highlight the irrationality of the expedition, see also Bloedow 1996, 157.

153. As does Diodoros 12.84.4ff., which shows the different historiographical agendas.

154. Stahl 1973, 66–67.

155. Bal 1997, 95.

156. Note that he had not mentioned that this was a task of these ships; Dover, *HCT* 4, ad loc.

60 talents before the meeting recorded in 6.9–23. Thus a further allusion here—not a suggestion to go collect the money, which had already been ascertained (wrongly) to exist, but an open question regarding the money's existence—serves to remind the reader of the problem (almost in a resumptive, Herodotean way) and heightens the dramatic tension. Moreover, the tension underlying the repeated question ("Does the money exist?") to which the reader knows the answer is part of a criticism that will become more explicit in 6.46: namely, that the Athenians failed to do what was necessary to determine the answer.

The news that the Egestans had no funds to produce except for 30 talents was expected by Nikias, Thucydides tells us, but was "unaccountable" to Alkibiades and Lamachos.[157] Following the realization that no sizable funds existed, Thucydides turns to the deception itself. Scholars have wondered at the placement of the story,[158] and, indeed, it is important to ask: Why does it appear here?[159] Stahl attributes the story's placement to Thucydides' tendency "to characterize human moods and attitudes"; in this case he wants to explain the disappointment.[160] Hartmut Erbse emphasizes Thucydides' decision to keep the reader in the dark as long as the Athenians themselves are fooled by the deception and sees instructional value in the manner of relating the trick.[161] These points are indeed valid—although Erbse is wrong to claim that the reader is in the same position as the Athenians, for the reader, at least, knows that the Egestans had been lying (6.8.2) —but more needs to be said. First, it is far more effective from a dramatic standpoint to put the discovery of the deception at the point when the Athenians *realize* they have all been duped, rather than when the deception occurred; the narrative delay, prepared for by anticipatory comments, gives the story a much more powerful impact, placed in the narrative when the huge force, the "second city," is now far from Athens, on the spot, and now

157. ἀλογώτερα, 6.46.2. The choice of word is elegant in its economic nuance and ironic, since now there are no more words (*logoi*), only the fact itself.

158. E.g., Mader 1993a.

159. For a general comment on narrative delay, see Erbse 1989b, 43; Hornblower 1994, 139ff. (who calls it narrative displacement); Genette 1980, 40 ("analepsis"); Bal 1997 82 (more cumbersomely, "deviation in sequential ordering"). Cf. White 1981, 5, regarding "proper [narrative] history:" as "professional opinion has it, the account must . . . honor the chronological order of the original occurrence of the events of which it treats as a baseline." See Genette 1990, 757–60 on the problem of achrony from the standpoint of the relationship between fictional and historical narrative. Thucydides not uncommonly describes an event out of its chronological order, as Erbse (1989b, 43) notes, placing it "wo sie das Handeln der Beteiligten beeinflussen. Das besagt: Er ordnet solche Vorgänge einer Situation zu, die ihre historische Bedeutung am besten verdeutliche"; Erbse supplies some other examples (44). On temporal manipulation in Thucydides, see the sensitive discussion of Rood (1998, 130).

160. Stahl 1973, 74.

161. Erbse 1989b, 43–44.

finding themselves without visible means of expected support.[162] Related to this, the reader approaches the story far more intensely than if Thucydides had located it, as did Diodoros, in its correct chronological position. Finally, as we shall see, Thucydides clearly wants the reader to have encountered and thought about the questions raised in 6.31–32 about deductions from the sight (ὄψις) of costly display (πολυτελεία), and its parallels with the methodological lesson in 1.10 that is evoked in 6.31, so that the reader, too, can judge the story. Thus the story's placement has, as Erbse rightly notes, important instructional value. The decision to set up the story gradually and let it build to a climax, then, is made to achieve the greatest effect on the reader.[163]

Thucydides begins by relating that the ships sent to investigate the money returned and reported that only 30 talents could be produced. The generals were considerably disheartened; as noted above, Nikias was prepared for the bad news, but it took Alkibiades and Lamachos, his two colleagues, completely by surprise (46.1). Thucydides continues:

> οἱ δὲ Ἐγεσταῖοι τοιόνδε τι ἐξετεχνήσαντο τότε ὅτε οἱ πρῶτοι πρέσβεις τῶν Ἀθηναίων ἦλθον αὐτοῖς ἐς τὴν κατασκοπὴν τῶν χρημάτων. ἔς τε τὸ ἐν Ἔρυκι ἱερὸν τῆς Ἀφροδίτης ἀγαγόντες αὐτοὺς ἐπέδειξαν τὰ ἀναθήματα, φιάλας τε καὶ οἰνοχόας καὶ θυμιατήρια καὶ κατασκευὴν οὐκ ὀλίγην, ἃ ὄντα ἀργυρᾶ πολλῷ πλείω τὴν ὄψιν ἀπ' ὀλίγης δυνάμεως χρημάτων παρείχετο· καὶ ἰδίᾳ ξενίσεις ποιούμενοι τῶν τριηριτῶν τά τε ἐξ αὐτῆς Ἐγέστης ἐκπώματα καὶ χρυσᾶ καὶ ἀργυρᾶ ξυλλέξαντες καὶ τὰ ἐκ τῶν ἐγγὺς πόλεων καὶ Φοινικικῶν καὶ Ἑλληνίδων αἰτησάμενοι ἐσέφερον ἐς τὰς ἑστιάσεις ὡς οἰκεῖα ἕκαστοι. καὶ πάντων ὡς ἐπὶ τὸ πολὺ τοῖς αὐτοῖς χρωμένων καὶ πανταχοῦ πολλῶν φαινομένων μεγάλην τὴν ἔκπληξιν τοῖς ἐκ τῶν τριήρων Ἀθηναίοις παρεῖχε, καὶ ἀφικόμενοι ἐς τὰς Ἀθήνας διεθρόησαν ὡς χρήματα πολλὰ ἴδοιεν. καὶ οἱ μὲν αὐτοί τε ἀπατηθέντες καὶ τοὺς ἄλλους τότε πείσαντες, ἐπειδὴ διῆλθεν ὁ λόγος ὅτι οὐκ εἴη ἐν τῇ Ἐγέστῃ τὰ χρήματα, πολλὴν τὴν αἰτίαν εἶχον ὑπὸ τῶν στρατιωτῶν. (6.46.3–5)

> The Egestans had recourse to the following such stratagem at the time when the first Athenian envoys came to them to investigate the money. Bringing them to the temple of Aphrodite at Eryx, they displayed to them the dedications, plates, wine ladles, and censers and many other objects, which, being in

162. Delaying the presentation of information is a technique that Thucydides will continue to exploit in the narrative; see below, chap. 2, pp. 108–9.

163. The comment of the narrator in Laurence Sterne's *A Sentimental Journey through France and Italy* (1768) is apposite: "When I got to my hotel, La Fleur told me I had been enquired after by the Lieutenant de Police—The duce take it! said I—I know the reason. It is time the reader should know it, for in the order of things in which it happened, it was omitted; not that it was out of my head; but that had I told it then, it might have been forgot now—and now is the time I want it."

silver, provided an appearance greater by far than their actual minimal power in wealth. And they entertained the crews at private banquets, having collected all the gold and silver cups that they could find in Egesta itself and borrowed from the neighboring Phoenician and Hellenic towns, each bringing them to the banquets as if their own. Since for the most part they all used the same ones and everywhere they appeared to be so numerous, the Athenians from the triremes were completely stunned, and when they returned to Athens they spread it about that they had seen great quantities of riches. Those who had been deceived and had persuaded the others at the time, when the truth was revealed that there was no money in Egesta, were held in great blame by the army.

This story has a fundamentally Herodotean flavor to it; indeed, it bears a striking resemblance to Herodotos' account of the downfall of Polykrates, tyrant of Samos (3.123–4). Recall the earlier unfolding episodes of the Egestan story in Thucydides, in which the Athenians go to investigate about the money, the Egestans return with 60 talents of bullion, and Nikias (and Thucydides) warns the Athenians not to believe their offer. In Herodotos, Oroites, satrap of Sardis, who wanted to destroy Polykrates, learned that the Samian tyrant aimed to take control of Ionia and the islands. He sent a message to him, in which he offered to pay for the expedition, noting that even with just half of what he (Oroites) possessed, Polykrates would have riches enough to rule all Greece (εἵνεκέν τε χρημάτων ἄρξεις τῆς ἁπάσης Ἑλλάδος, 3.122.4). Then Herodotos has Oroites continue: "Polykrates, if you are in doubt about the money (ἀπιστέεις περὶ τῶν χρημάτων), you can send someone in whom you have the greatest trust, and I will produce it" (ἀποδέξω, or prove it). Polykrates was quite pleased with the plan, and since he greatly desired money (καί κως ἱμείρετο γὰρ χρημάτων μεγάλως, 3.123.1), he sent his scribe, Maiandrios, to investigate (κατοψόμενον). When Oroites heard that Maiandrios was coming to inspect, he filled eight chests with stones, leaving only enough room for a layer of gold on the surface (3.123.2). Maiandrios came and saw, and then reported back to Polykrates. Despite the warnings of his seers—and his daughter—Polykrates prepared to go to Oroites and was promptly killed in Magnesia at the satrap's instructions (3.125).

The deception itself looks like it could be a topos.[164] The structural simi-

164. Cf. Eur. *Hec.* 989–1172, a highly elaborate extended passage in which Hecuba lures Polymestor to a tent with the enticement of gold, to which he readily succumbs, and then kills his children, whom Hecuba instructed him to bring along, and stabs his eyes with brooches, blinding him. As Gregory (1999, 164) puts it, "In a sustained passage of stichomythia [989–1018] Hecuba accomplishes Polymestor's entrapment by playing on the greed that she correctly estimates to be his most vulnerable quality. The dialogue unfolds in three stages, corresponding to the three caches of gold described by Hecuba." Cf. also Nep. *Hannibal* 9, in which Hannibal deceives the Gortynians: *amphoras complures complet plumbo; summas operit auro et ar-*

larities to the Egestan deception suggest that this may have been the kind of "fooling people about the extent of your wealth" folktale that was plugged in where appropriate, to illustrate cunning.[165] But this need not mean that the story about the Egestans and Athenians is not true—although the absence of neighboring towns around Egesta[166] could seriously compromise that part of it. What matters for our purposes, however, is that Thucydides chose to include it and write it up the way he did. Let us first consider the similarities: (1) In both Herodotos and Thucydides, the ruse is concocted in order to give the appearance of greater wealth; (2) in both cases, the ruse follows an offer by the deceiver(s) to finance an expedition, and a test or investigation to see if the money existed; (3) there are verbal similarities, including κατασκοπή (Hdt. 3.123, Thuc. 6.46.3; cf. 6.6.3) and περὶ τῶν χρημάτων (cf. 6.6.3, 8.2); (4) the response to the deception is identical—Maiandrios and the Athenians at Eryx and Egesta are fooled, and Polykrates and the Athenians at home are fooled as well; (5) both Polykrates and the Athenians receive warnings, which they ignore; (6) both are concerned with how objects are read, though in different ways.[167] Indeed, if anything, Thucydides' account is *more* Herodotean in its comic aspect than 3.123–4.[168]

Next, let us consider the assumptions underlying the deceptions. Maiandrios is shown the chests and assumes that their contents will finance Polykrates' campaign. Recall that the ruse in Thucydides has two parts. In the first, the Egestans show the Athenian envoys the contents of the temple treasury at Eryx. But, just as the crews from the triremes were not thinking

---

gento. Especially intriguing and apposite for its resonances with Thucydides' account of the beginnings of the Sicilian expedition is the story in Tac. *Ann.* 16.1–3 about Nero's gullibility in the case of Dido's wealth. Duped by a Carthaginian, Caesillius Bassus, who alleged that Dido had hidden a treasure of gold, "not coin, but in ancient, unworked bullion," Nero, not bothering to investigate its truth, even exaggerated the claim (*auget ultro*) and dispatched warships to Carthage. The people (*populus*), Tacitus notes, bought the story; but those who were sensible (*prudentes*) disbelieved it. The enthusiasm of the people "increased Nero's extravagance": "Extravagance swelled by the vain hope, and existing resources were consumed as if those had been presented that could be squandered for many more years . . . ; and expectation of riches was among the causes of the national impoverishment." (Cf. Syme [1958, 1:310], who regards this "peculiar story" as designed as a "light interlude" between the Pisonian conspiracy and the next round of murders; cf. 2:473 n. 2). Aside from Nero's lack of investigation, this story fits the underlying interpretation of Thucydides to an astonishing degree, especially in the squandering of existing resources at home in the expectation of future riches.

165. Cf. also similar tales of cunning not having to do with currency, like Hdt. 1.22, which concerns Thrasyboulos of Miletos' ruse to fool Alyattes about the extent of food in Miletos; see Lateiner 1990, 230–46.

166. Dover, *HCT* 4, 6.46.3.

167. On this aspect of Herodotos, see Dewald 1993, 55–70.

168. One conjures up the vigorous back-door activity as the cups were conveyed from house to house. It seems to me that Thucydides took a little Herodotean-style delight in relating this story.

that they would use the gold and silver cups for military purposes, the envoys are not thinking that the Egestans will use the Eryx treasury for the expedition;[169] rather, the envoys are inferring—and the Egestans leave it to them and count on them to infer—that the display of silver dedications at Eryx *represents* greater wealth elsewhere. In the second part of the ruse, the Egestans brought 60 talents of bullion to fool the Athenians at home (6.8.1).

The purpose of the deception is similar in both cases: to dupe another or others into believing that the deceivers have more money than they really do. Both Polykrates and the Athenians want financial help, and their subsidizers set a trap, though Oroites' purpose is considerably more sinister, since its goal is Polykrates' death, while the Egestans merely want Athenian help. On the other hand, when read against Herodotos there is irony in the Thucydidean story as the Egestans are, indirectly, luring the Athenians to an equally fateful end. Greed is an element of both. Recall that Thucydides tells us that the common people and soldiery (ὁ ὄχλος) saw in the Sicilian expedition the prospect of eternal pay; and Alkibiades was hoping to replenish his private fortune as general in Sicily (6.15). In Herodotos, the Polykrates character is linked to the larger theme of hubris in the work, in which tyrants' love of money is a prominent feature.[170]

While both accounts share the notion of downfall through greed, there are illuminating contrasts. In the Sicilian narrative, it was perfectly reasonable for the Athenians to accept the offer of financial help from the Egestans. But whereas in Herodotos, Oroites pretends to offer his money believing that Polykrates has a cash flow problem, Thucydides has led us to believe that the Athenians have plenty of money at this point (cf. 6.12.1, 26.2); and, as it turns out, they do not absolutely need the Egestans' financial help.[171] Even after the deception is uncovered, Nikias suggests the existence of ample resources at home, although noting the undesirability of using them in Sicily (6.47).[172] Thucydides, then, does not employ the intertext to draw attention to financial need; his aim is different.

The Herodotean template allows Thucydides to underscore the role of ignorance, lies, and deception. He uses it to illuminate and develop an argument that shows the serious consequences of such circumstances, in ways

169. This is clear from the reaction of the generals at 6.46.1.

170. On the latter with reference to Persians, see Konstan 1987. Likewise, in his account of the Ionian revolt Herodotos does not imply that the Ionians, Naxian exiles, or Persians should have seen through Aristagoras' deception. For Thucydides' use of Herodotos' account, see below, chap. 2.

171. Oppermann 1985, 112; Mader 1993a, 184. But the issue of whether they needed the money, possessing sufficient resources at home, is different from that of whether they actually used what they could have in sufficient quantities; see chap. 2, pp. 101–18, below.

172. See chap. 2, pp. 102–3.

that depart from Herodotos. Indeed, Herodotos' and Thucydides' stories diverge considerably in their historiographical aims as regards accountability and responsibility. Within the larger theme of deception and ignorance, the emphasis shifts. Herodotos focuses on the act of trickery and the ulterior motives of the trickster,[173] as well as on individual behavior. He lays no overt blame on Maiandrios for failing to see through the deception: within the logic of the story he could not have been expected to know that he was being deceived; his role is therefore purely instrumental.[174]

By contrast, Thucydides concentrates attention to a much greater extent on those being fooled—the prominence accorded to the Athenian envoys and crew in 6.46 makes us focus more closely on them than we do on Herodotos' Maiandrios—and on the polis as a whole rather than on individuals, and the context is highly critical.[175] Thucydides implicates the Athenians: they should have known better than to be fooled by the Egestans, and to be fooled by their own false interpretation of what they saw. First, although it is not a criticism per se that the Athenian envoys were shown sacred wealth —for Greeks were used to thinking of such wealth as public wealth, temples as "reserve banks"[176]—the *presbeis* were shown only objects (*anathemata*), not money; Thucydides' choice of verb, "displayed" (ἐπέδειξαν), nods to the problem. They made two basic errors of judgment—thinking that the displayed wealth represented power, and that precious metal objects represented *dunamis chrematon*. Especially damning is that they were shown the treasures at Eryx, not Egesta. Dover comments that the envoys seem not to have recognized the international nature of the sanctuary.[177] This is too charitable. Even if, as Thucydides charges, the Athenians possessed insufficient knowledge about the peoples of Sicily, the envoys should still have been more than a little suspicious when they were shown treasures in a region different from Egesta. But there is also an implicit condemnation of the crews of the triremes for being so stunned by, and making the wrong inferences from, the private wealth they saw at the banquets.

Let us return to the scene at the temple of Aphrodite at Eryx. The meaning of the sentence "The dedications, being of silver, provided an appear-

173. On Herodotos' use of the trickster figure, see Immerwahr 1966; Lateiner 1990; Dewald 1993.

174. Elsewhere (3.148) Maiandrios himself plays the trickster, unsuccessfully.

175. This is a reversal of a related phenomenon, observed by Dewald (1985, 57), in which by contrast with Herodotos, "political actors" in Thucydides who "fail to see the extent to which their desires and fears have distorted their judgment" receive no censure from the historian "for *hubris,* or for assuming that their control over events is greater than it is."

176. As Bremmer (1994, 32) has noted in his valuable survey on Greek religion.

177. Dover, *HCT* 4, ad loc. It is even more absurd, therefore, than if someone supposed that the treasures at Delphi belonged to the Delphians; at least they lived by the sanctuary.

ance (τὴν ὄψιν) greater by far than their actual power in money" (δύναμις χρημάτων) has been regarded as problematic. There are two alternatives; the first, that the dedications are taken to represent, or correlate to, *dunamis chrematon*. Bétant, for example, translates the phrase as *pretium,* "value"; thus: "The dedications, being of silver, gave an impression that was much greater than their actual value, or worth." This latter translation causes difficulties, for it presumes that the Athenian visitors would not know the relative value of dedications used for exchange and converted into coin. Moreover, as Dover notes, in commenting on the emendation proposed by Meinike (τὸ ἐπάργυρα instead of ἀργυρά, "silver-plated"), it "entails the unlikely hypothesis that the majority of dedications in a famous sanctuary were of a peculiar kind."[178]

To be sure, silver- and gold-plated dedications do not constitute the majority in temple treasuries, though they are certainly not rare;[179] indeed, the emendation would make the correlation with Oroites' ploy tighter. But in general one should not emend the text where there is no textual justification for it, especially if it makes sense as it is. Elsewhere *dunamis chrematon* commonly means "power of wealth," or "power in money," and that is most likely its meaning here, especially given that the entire issue facing the Athenians is the absence of the great *financial* reserves they had been led to believe existed. Dover comments: "The point must be that the expensive dedications in the temple at Eryx did not reveal the comparative poverty of the state which controlled the sanctuary. Thucydides cannot mean that silver looks expensive but is not; the Athenian envoys, accustomed to live in a city which possessed both splendid dedications *and* a big financial reserve, wrongly assumed that one implied the other." This is correct, but incomplete. "Did not reveal" obscures a crucial point in the narrative: namely, that the envoys did not make the correct *deduction* from the sight of costly dedications; they looked at visible signs and made incorrect inferences about the reality behind them (the invisible).[180]

The phrasing of the sentence, and its point, closely recall the implicit argument in 6.31, as well as the explicit one in 1.10, concerning the relationship between appearance (ὄψις) and costly display (πολυτελεία). The buzzwords are there—*opsis, dunamis*—and the indicators (τὰ ἀναθήματα) from which the deduction (κατασκοπήν) is to be made. Here is a test of deduction from sight, one that the reader can pass more easily than the Athenian envoys, thanks to the instruction Thucydides has provided. Indeed, the description also tells us *how* the envoys were thinking: they were making a

178. *HCT* 4, ad loc., citing Meinike.

179. Cf., for example, *IG* I^3 343.11, 12, 16.

180. Cf. from the Hippocratic Corpus *De arte* 12; *Flat.* 3; see also Lloyd 1979, 134 with n. 47.

correlation between sacred wealth and the city's overall *dunamis chrematon,* "power in wealth"—a point as interesting as the fact that their thinking was false. But for the first time Thucydides is making a crucial theme of his *History* explicit: precious metal objects do not constitute *dunamis chrematon,* "power in money."[181]

Non-monetary wealth can of course be converted to military use—2.13 and other passages[182] show that. But as 2.13 and other passages make clear, "power in money," which underpins military power, means ready cash. Precious metal objects occupy a lower status in that context; when they are melted down and used for military power, in an Athenian contest, it is in the case of emergency. Most important, the very fact that the envoys are shown a kind of wealth that, for immediate expenditure in a military context, has an inferior status implies—and should have implied to the envoys—that coined money (or even bullion) did not exist. Thucydides has preconditioned the reader to recognize the necessity for money (and reserves of money, *periousia chrematon*), and has accordingly prepared us to make the important inference that on a point so crucial to success in war the Athenians sent to investigate should not have been duped. The same goes for other Athenians.

Thucydides also implicates the common soldiery for thinking that the gold and silver cups they saw at the banquets represented *dunamis chrematon,*[183] for an additional subtheme of Thucydides' treatment of money and power is that public, accumulated financial reserves, not private wealth, are essential for military success. This is implicit in the strong emphasis Thucydides places in the *History* on public money, in his near denigration of the public value of private wealth and its display—and possibly, as mentioned

181. I am not disputing the view that objects of precious metal—for example, silver phialai and other silver cups or plate—were movable wealth that could be considered a kind of currency (Amyx 1958, 208; Vickers and Gill 1994, 38–46). But for military purposes these are objects of last resort that would have to be melted down and minted, not ready cash. The view of precious metal objects as usable in a military context, but only as a last resort, is evident in Thuc. 2.13.3–5, where they appear last, as well as in temple inventories during the Peloponnesian War in which dedications of gold and silver were left untouched until the last years of crisis at the end of the war; cf. Harris 1991, 75–82. On the relationship between "old" wealth and "new" wealth, see von Reden 1995, esp. 171–84. See also the conclusion, below, pp. 291–93.

182. 1.121.3, 143.1; 6.70.4—though it is not explicit that these would consist only of objects; Thucydides simply says *chremata*.

183. Rood (1998, 168 n. 43) notes that the reference to the gold and silver cups recalls 6.32.1, the departure scene in which the trierarchs made libations from "gold and silver cups," the only other instance of the word ἔκπωμα in Thucydides; and he suggests the possibility that Thucydides intends an "ironic echo." Indeed this is surely the case and supports my argument that Thucydides wanted the reader to have read the departure scene before learning about the Egestan trick.

above, in the striking absence in his work of any reference to the importance of the trierarchy to Athens' naval strength, especially in conjunction with his implicit negative interpretation of the trierarchs' lavishness in 6.31. His comment about the soldiers at Egesta is most revealing: they were struck by great *ekplexis*. As noted earlier, *ekplexis* is an unusual word in this context. *Ekplexis* normally means "fear" or "terror" elsewhere in the *History*,[184] but here Thucydides manipulates its meaning. It has an ostensibly positive cast—the men are in a state of marveling astonishment[185]—but at the same time it embodies underlying criticism. Allison notes the unusual nature of *ekplexis* and *kataplexis* in the *History* generally, commenting that "[its] appearance [is] not casual. . . . Thucydides knew precisely in what contexts he had used them."[186]

We need to appreciate the force and the nuance of the word in its unusual context here. As Virginia Hunter has pointed out (though solely in connection with its application to the emotion of fear), *ekplexis* "implies a blow to the wits"; one comes "unhinged."[187] In this state, similar to that of an affliction by *eros*, the sailors were "paralyzed" by the *opsis* of the cups, and thereby rendered incapable of interpreting rationally the objects they gazed and marveled at. This clearly fits the relationship between emotion, sight, and power exploited by Thucydides in 6.31. But the use of the word is also heavily ironic and intended to be recalled at the end of the expedition, when it recurs twice to describe the Athenians' panic in the naval battle in the Great Harbor at Syracuse (7.70.6, 71.7). The *megale ekplexis* that the crew experienced from looking at beautiful objects that in part convinced their fellow Athenians to invade Sicily is transformed into terror at the end.[188]

Indeed, it is no accident that at precisely this point in the *History* we catch a rare glimpse of the thinking of diverse groups of Athenians.[189] Thucydides, unusually, tells us why different individuals and groups of Athenians de-

184. 2.94.1; 4.14.3, 34.2, 55.3, 112.1, 126.1; 6.36.2, 70.1, 98.2; 7.42.3, 69.2, 70.6, 71.7; 8.14.2, 15.1, 96.1.

185. Huart 1968, 77: here it has "la valeur d' *étonnement admiratif.*"

186. Allison 1997b, 63.

187. Hunter 1986, 418.

188. Its usage at the end of book 7 is also designed, as Thucydides makes explicit in 71.7, to evoke the Spartans' experience at Pylos.

189. This surely has to do with Thucydides' different focus in this part of the *History*, which was first noted by Westlake (1968, 308): "Thucydides devotes more attention in the second half to examining the personality of [leading] individuals and their relations with others, not because he has become more interested in biography, but because he is more convinced that their general qualities constitute a vital factor in determining the course of history." Likewise his breakdown of groups within the polis at crucial moments (6.24, 46) is a way of imputing responsibility for decisions and events with profoundly grave consequences; here, first, to the envoys and crew, who allowed themselves to be fooled by the sight of precious objects, which in turn helped persuade their fellow citizens at home to sail to Sicily, and, second, to the majority of Athenians at home, who were lusting for money.

sired the expedition, as well as their reactions upon learning of the deception. In fact, Athenians up and down the social spectrum were being fooled left and right: the envoys, ordinary soldiery, even some generals—both Alkibiades and Lamachos, recall, were surprised to find out that the money did not exist—and the majority back home.[190] No one escapes Thucydides' implicit censure—not even Nikias, though for other reasons.[191] All were unjustifiably fooled, not so much by the Egestans as by their own (false) interpretation of these precious objects, sacred and private. So we are back to those alluded to in 1.10, who would have inferred Athens' power to be twice as great as it was, back to Alkibiades' Greeks, who inferred greater polis power, back implicitly to the spectators at the Peiraieus and now to the Athenians in Egesta and at home. But by repetition, lessons, and examples, Thucydides has been developing an increasingly judgmental and particularized position: now it is the Athenians, not Greeks hypothetically or in the past, and it is their failure to read objects correctly that will have dire consequences, as they are stuck in Sicily, without local support.

DEMOS TYRANNOS

The various methods Thucydides employs to encourage particular interpretations of the Athenian collective and its wealth—notably, the transference of values and behavior from the individual to the collective that we saw operating in Nikias' first speech and in Thucydides' introduction to Alkibiades, and the Herodotean presence within the Egestan episode—comprise a means by which the historian can work another interpretative layer into the narrative, a layer that likens the collective demos to the figure of the tyrant.[192] In passages in which he explicitly mentions tyranny or tyrants in his own voice, Thucydides' position on tyranny appears almost neutral. The historian makes no equation between the collective Athenians and tyranny earlier in his *History;* indeed, he seems deliberately to resist setting up such an equation, as long as Perikles is still a presence in the *History.*[193] But all this

190. One intriguing—and maddening, given his interest in this story—omission from the account is an explanation of *how* the Athenians came to learn the details of the double deception.

191. There may be an additional layer of criticism in Thucydides' comment at the end of 6.46 about the reaction of the army in Sicily: they "greatly blamed" the envoys and the sailors who had been deceived; but his earlier comment about the lust of the Athenians for the expedition, specified as lust for money in the case of the soldiers (6.24.3), makes it easy to suspect that their anger was based on their greed; cf. also the explicit criticism in 8.1.1.

192. This implicit construction is different from the notion of the city or empire as a tyrant (2.63.2, 3.37.2; cf. 6.85.1).

193. See Kallet 2003.

changes. When the narrative reaches the Athenians' conquest of Sicily in 415, the characteristics of the stereotypical tyrant—a man of lustful, uncontrollable passions, who possessed enormous wealth, was in a state of perpetual greed in order to support his personal luxuries and excesses, and aimed at ever-greater conquests[194]—fit the Athenians remarkably closely. Thucydides uses a variety of techniques, in the service of a rhetorical strategy of identification, to set up an implicit equation or analogy between the collective demos and its wealth, on the one hand, and the characteristics of tyranny, on the other.

The first technique is a blurring of public and private as they relate to money and the body, which allows a reciprocal transferal of attributes and aims between the individual body and the collective body of individuals. Nikias' argument in his first speech before the assembly, examined above, that concern for one's individual body and wealth can justly take precedence over the collective health and wealth of the state (6.9.2), and his later proposal of an overabundance of expenditure and resources to insure the Athenians' own safety (6.19.2, 21–22), sound on the face of it innocuous and prudent, respectively; yet not only is the argument that looking out for one's own private prosperity and safety first arguably inappropriate for a city at war, it also ironically evokes a comment about tyrants that Thucydides makes in the Archaeology: "They looked out for their own interests both with respect to their body and the increase of their own household and made safety the primary concern of their administrations, and thus accomplished nothing worthy of record" (1.17). Nikias' primary concern for private wealth and the individual body (recall also his subsequent reference to the recent "increase in money and bodies," 6.12.1), the implication that expending resources should be partly for that end, and the desire for security echo the concerns of the Thucydidean tyrant and implicitly cast the Athenians in a tyrant-like role.

A second approach is more concrete. When Thucydides characterizes Alkibiades in 6.15, he essentially sums up the characteristics of a tyrant—sexual abnormality, excessive spending, and the desire for conquest as a way to increase his private riches in order to maintain his desired lifestyle.[195] Thucydides offers a paradigm of behavior that, while aiming to reveal the roots of the citizenry's fear of tyranny, at the same time, from the way that he constructs the surrounding narrative, paradoxically provides a framework within which to identify the Athenians as emulators of this tyrannical mode. Elements of tyrannical behavior punctuate the account: Alkibiades' role in the narrative reinforces our sense that the Athenians' striving for

194. See Davidson 1997, 278–308.

195. See Gribble 1999, 193.

power was uncontrollable and their imperial desires unlimited, a characterization too seductive for Nikias' earlier futile urging of "moderation" (*sophronoumen,* 6.11.7) to have any force. As the antithesis of the tyrannical mode, moderation itself sharpens the analogy between the Athenians and tyrants. Like Alkibiades and tyrants, the Athenians spend lavishly on display (6.31). They have *eros* for the expedition, with individual greed playing a prominent role (6.24).

Fundamental to this presentation are equations between actors in the Sicilian narrative at this stage—specifically Alkibiades and the *demos*—and those in the Peisistratid digression, in which Thucydides emphasizes the role of *eros* in the eventual undoing of the city's tyranny. Hipparchos' sexual excess, his murder by Harmodios and Aristogetion (which Thucydides labels an "erotic daring," 6.54.1), and the intrusion of private passions into the public sphere, all can be related to the Athenians in 415. In her discussion of the digression and the emphasis on sex, Victoria Wohl argues that the "sexuality of the tyrants was represented as antithetical to that of the democratic citizen."[196] I would contend that Thucydides constructs the *demos* in the Sicilian narrative context to reveal their synonymity. Hipparchos' sexual excess harms himself and the polis: the Peisistratids met their downfall as a result of *eros* and the erotic daring (*tolmema*) of Harmodios and Aristogeiton. The Athenians' individual (and collective) *eros* and *tolme*—words Thucydides explicitly uses in his account of the expedition (6.24.3; 6.31.6; 7.28.3) —likewise harmed themselves and the polis. The private *eros* of both Athenians—Alkibiades and, earlier, Hipparchos—have spectacularly destructive consequences for the state when played out on the public stage. The vocabulary and juxtaposition make the connection clear.

Finally, the implicit presence of Polykrates in the story of the Egestan deception (6.46), I have argued, associates the tyrant's greed with that of the Athenian collective. The similarity of the stories offers a means for Thucydides to implicate the Athenians, to liken them to a greedy tyrant. Farther on in the narrative of the expedition, Thucydides characterizes the Athenians again as impassioned (they are "in love with victory") and connects their passion with money and overextension. In their overextended state, the Athenians impose a tax measure on their allies typical of a tyrant—the *eikoste,* a five-percenter (7.28)—the exact term he uses in book six to refer to Peisistratid taxation (6.54.5). Finally, after the disaster in Sicily, Thucydides makes a point of using the verb *sophronein* (8.3) to refer to the ten advisors who are to impose self-restraint on the Athenians. The word underscores that the Athenians' behavior to that point has been unconstrained and impassioned, that is, tyrant-like.

196. Wohl, 1999, 361.

As should be clear, these rhetorical and narrative techniques are not mere stylistic devices: Thucydides employs them to get to the heart of the moral problem that he sees governing Athenian behavior and actions. Greed and passion, hallmarks of the tyrant, are literally a deadly combination. Because it comes at the cost of the real exercise of power, the Athenians' excessive desire to display, and thus waste, their wealth presents them in a tyrannical, and thus morally inappropriate, light.

CONCLUSION

Thucydides' treatment of the display of wealth and its relationship to power in the first half of book 6 reveals several interrelated themes, which are embodied in a programmatic vocabulary (*paraskeue, opseis, poluteleia, eros,* and *epithumia*) that produces a fundamental ambiguity in the narrative when combined. In a key respect Thucydides' concern with reading *opsis* as signs places him within an intellectual tradition shared by the pre-Socratics, Sophists, and medical writers, as well as Herodotos.[197] Moreover, his interest in the visual accords with a much broader fifth-century development evident in the theater and in the production of art.[198] Thucydides' approach is highly polemical, but also didactic: the purpose of his emphasis on *opsis* is to transport the external audience into a visual scene or episode that the internal audience is intepreting—in a sense, to say to the reader: Here is the visible; how are you going to interpret it? The case studies he cites (Mycenae, Sparta, and Athens, 1.10), the scenes he paints, and stories he tells (6.31, 6.46) are designed to drive home three important points.

First, Thucydides draws attention to the inappropriate role accorded to display, both public and private, in relation to polis power. The significance of this point cannot be overemphasized. Thucydides attempts to dismantle an entire ideology, manifest in both the aristocratic and civic spheres, as illustrated, for example, in Alkibiades' perceptions of his displays, in the reactions of Greeks to the display at the Peiraieus, and in the responses

197. In particular, 6.46 and its resonances with earlier passages like 6.24 and 6.31 bears striking similarities to Gorgias' *Helen,* in its concern with the interplay between sight and emotion (*ekplexis* and *eros*); see Hunter 1986; and, generally on Gorgias, Segal 1962, 106–9; see also Worman 1997 on the interplay of *eros* and *opsis* in relation to the figure of Helen in four literary texts, including Gorgias (171–80, esp. 179–80).

198. A comment of Zeitlin (1995, 175) on the growing interest in visuality in theatrical and artistic technique and modes of representation applies neatly to Thucydides: "Both ['art' and 'theater'] share the requirement of an attentive gaze as well as a[n] . . . informed mode of viewing, which, beyond its emotive qualities, engages the cognitive skills of spectators in learning how to recognize, evaluate, and interpret the visual codes of what they see." Thucydides' spectators, however, are primarily unable to prevent their emotive responses from impeding correct cognitive evaluation.

of both the envoys to the temple treasures and the common sailors to the gold and silver cups at the banquets.[199] Alkibiades does not deny but rather blithely embraces the notion that his displays create false perceptions about the city's power, but Thucydides constructs the narrative to contest and condemn this kind of thinking. Indeed, in a sense, he is trying to redefine markers of polis power; it is not some vague impression of power but the concrete exercise of military power that concerns him, and for that, only one kind of wealth is ultimately important: financial resources. Relapsing (as he sees it) into the creation and adulation of splendid appearance is not only wasteful but ruinous: Thucydides conveys this message explicitly in his introduction to Alkibiades' speech and implicitly, I suggest, in 6.31.[200]

A second point—the issue of real vs. illusory power (and real vs. illusory money)—relates to the first, for if the point is that display is a false indicator of power, and therefore illusory, it is therefore not clear whether real *dunamis* exists or not, since true signs (*semeia*) are lacking; moreover, if the money necessary for the exercise of power is illusory, as in the case of the Egestan offer, then the power is illusory as well. Diverse examples of these two elements include the Egestans' gift of 60 talents, Alkibiades' credit expenditures, Nikias' proposal to make a display of the fleet in Sicily and then return home (which in a sense suggests the appearance, not the reality, of power), the speeches of Hermokrates and Athenagoras, and the deception at Egesta.

Third, Thucydides' narrative in the first half of book 6, read against earlier books, is constructed in such a way as to impugn the Athenians as a collective, but also in their constituent groups, for incorrectly interpreting *opsis* in the context of power; that is, Thucydides implicitly shows that the Athenians had been capable of ordering forms of wealth into a hierarchy of value in a military context, only to reveal their reversion, in a sense, to a more traditional form of thinking about wealth and power; but they should have known better. Related to this, they fell victim to passion and greed, at which point, especially in the case of the former, they in one sense lost agency; again, the implicit argument is that they should have been able to resist.

At the same time, however, a central feature of the narrative we have ex-

199. In the last case, as mentioned above, they likely had in mind the riches they would themselves gain from the conquest of the island. It is significant that their response is emotional, not rational.

200. Cf. Arist. *Pol.* 1309a17 for a remarkably similar formulation (regarding liturgies) in the context of an argument that democracies—as opposed to oligarchies—ought to spare the rich from having to spend their money: βέλτιον δὲ καὶ βουλομένους κωλύειν λειτουργεῖν τὰς δαπανήρας μὲν μὴ χρησίμους δὲ λειτουργίας, οἷον χορηγίας καὶ λαμπαδαρχίας καὶ ὅσαι ἄλλαι τοιαῦται. See also Kurke 1991, 173 n. 24 for other references.

amined has been ambiguity. While I have argued that Thucydides has constructed his account to privilege the negative interpretation—that the signs by which people are judging power are misguided and that ostentatious display does not per se signify power—he weaves into it the possibility, accepted by his contemporaries certainly, that the Athenians were setting out on an expedition of manifestly great strength.[201]

Many of the themes introduced in the first stage of the Sicilian narrative will be developed as the account proceeds. As Thucydides begins to document the unravelling of Athens' power, we will have the opportunity in the following chapters to explore further the relationships between passion and wealth, and between *periousia chrematon* and *gnome,* as well as what happens when these relationships go awry.

201. Recall the reference to the "strength" and "size" of the expedition that cheered up the spectators in 6.31.1.

CHAPTER TWO

Intra- and Intertextual Patterns of Failure

Herodotos, Homer, and Thucydides

I shall be satisfied if those who wish to examine the clear truth of past events and of what will happen once again in such or similar ways in accordance with the human condition judge my work useful.

THUC. 1.22.4

We have examined the extent to which Thucydides in book 6 links money, deception, and misguided judgments and decisions; particularly useful are implicit back-references to earlier parts of his *History* and to Herodotos for understanding what Thucydides is saying about display and power. These intra- and intertextual relationships merit further investigation. Scholars have illuminated the parallels between books 6 and 7 and earlier parts of the *History* (in particular, book 1) and those between Thucydides and Herodotos; however, two subjects illuminate not only the theme of money but also the architecture of these books: Herodotos' account of the Ionian revolt (to my knowledge, still unmined in this respect), and Thucydides' analysis of the Trojan War (1.10–11).

HERODOTOS AND THUCYDIDES

Since Cornford, scholars have been struck by the intriguing parallels between Thucydides' Sicilian account and Herodotos' account of the Persian invasion of 480.[1] Certainly from the standpoint of the themes explored here in the narrative of the Sicilian expedition—money and the uses of wealth—Xerxes' invasion as handled by Herodotos offered a rich historical and historiographical exemplum for Thucydides; indeed, the parallels be-

1. E.g., Cornford 1971 [1907]; Marinatos Kopff and Rawlings 1978; Rood 1999. For a survey of scholarly attention to the correspondences between Herodotos and Thucydides and for general discussion, see Hornblower 1996, 19–38, 122–45.

tween Herodotos' Persian Wars and Thucydides' Sicilian expedition are too striking to be accidental.[2]

It will be useful to note three correspondences that are relevant to our purposes here. First, the rhetorical role of exaggerated, if not false, claims about the enemy (e.g., those found in the speeches of Mardonius and Alkibiades) is a key part of both accounts.[3] Second, the display of the forces at the Hellespont and that at the Peiraieus, in 480 and 415 respectively, with their emphasis on size and spectacle, are intriguingly similar. As noted in chapter 1, in 6.31.3, Thucydides refers to the competitive aspect of the launching of the expedition with the verb ἁμιλλάομαι, and then, in describing the departure of the fleet in 6.32.2, he tells us that "after singing the paean and finishing the libations, they put out to sea, and sailing away at first in column formation, they held a race as far as Aigina." Thucydides uses the word ἅμιλλα to refer to the race or competition held by the ships—the very word, Tim Rood notes,[4] used by Herodotos at the moment when the Persian fleet was assembled at Abydos: Xerxes sat on a promontory from which he could see both land and sea forces; "and he had a desire to see the ships hold a race (ἅμιλλα), which they did" (7.44). It is difficult to resist reading the Thucydidean passage within the Herodotean framework:[5] both concern the moment of setting out on a momentous expedition, both depict a celebratory or festal aspect of the event, and both focus on seeing and spectacle, a point to which I shall return as it concerns Thucydides.[6]

Finally, both historians stress the emotional element of the expeditions. With striking verbal echoes, Thucydides emphasizes the Athenians' desire for the Sicilian expedition, as does Herodotos in the case of Xerxes' desire to undertake the invasion of Greece. Rood notes that the urge for both expeditions increases in the narratives and "exploit[s] the gap between the expectations of participants and the reader's knowledge that the expedition will fail. This cognitive gap colors their descriptions of how the expedition's departures serve as vehicles for display."[7] But Thucydides will construct and exploit the correspondences in order to say something different

2. Rood (1999) argues the case most fully and compellingly.

3. Cf. also the similarities with the Persian council of war at 7.8–18, noted by von Fritz 1967, 727; Hunter 1973, 181 n. 7.

4. Rood 1999, 153.

5. Connor (1984, 175 n. 43) notes the parallel, but not the use of the word ἅμιλλα.

6. For this aspect of Herodotos, see Konstan 1987, 59–73. Cf. Flory (1978, 146) who considers the Xerxes anecdote in Herodotos and draws attention to Xerxes' almost childlike joy as he watches the spectacle, but his joy then turns to grief (i.e., wisdom). By contrast, the Athenians in Thucydides, when the moment of the launching of the expedition is upon them, feel fear and second thoughts, which are followed by confidence at the sight and reach a climax when the fleet sets sail and holds a contest.

7. Rood 1999, 153.

from, though by no means critical of, Herodotos. The similarities between the accounts help sharpen the contrasts, especially in connection with the absence of the gods, and the interplay of individual and collective responsibility, on the one hand, and irresistible human nature, on the other.

The Ionian Revolt and the Sicilian Expedition

Herodotos' account of the Ionian revolt exhibits equally fascinating similarities with Thucydides' narrative in the first part of book 6, and these parallels suggest an even deeper relationship between the two historians. The suggestion, however, immediately raises an important question: how certain can we be that Thucydides was familiar with Herodotos' description? One way to approach this question is to determine whether the Ionian revolt figures anywhere else in Thucydides in a way that specifically evokes Herodotos' account.[8]

In the course of describing the history of the fifth-century colonizing attempts at Amphipolis in Thrace (4.102.2), Thucydides relates the following details about Aristagoras: "Aristagoras the Milesian attempted an earlier settlement (when he fled from King Darius), but he was later driven back by Edonian Thracians . . . " He also dates the event to sixty years before the Athenians' successful settlement of the place called Ennea Hodoi in 437. This precise and specific information contrasts with Herodotos' rather vague and general mention of Aristagoras' demise in Thrace: "Aristagoras decided to go to Myrkinos [in Thrace] . . . ; there he gained control of the territory he was after, but on a subsequent venture, while besieging a neighboring town, he was killed by Thracians" (5.126.1–2). Herodotos neither names the city Aristagoras attacked nor specifies the Thracian tribe that killed him.[9] This has led commentators like Macan to suppose that Thucydides is correcting or amplifying Herodotos' account.[10] Indeed, the purpose of the Thucydidean passage supports this hypothesis: since Thucydides is above all concerned with relating the history of *Athenian* attempts on the site later called Amphipolis,[11] his digression on Aristagoras is essentially irelevant and difficult to explain except as a gloss on Herodotos.

Oddly at first sight, the Ionian revolt does not figure in the part of the *History* where one might most expect to find it, namely, in the Archaeology.

8. I am not convinced that the reference in 6.4.5–6 to "Samians and other Ionians . . . fleeing from the Persians" who expelled the original settlers of Zankle, necessarily evokes Herodotos specifically rather than a common tradition; but cf. Hornblower 1996, 144.

9. Note that Thucydides does not actually say that the Edonians killed Aristagoras.

10. Macan 1973, 268. See also Hornblower 1996, 34.

11. It is possible that Thucydides mentioned Aristagoras in 4.102 because his mind was on Herodotos in this section, specifically in 4.109, if Hornblower (1996 ad loc.) is right to see in that passage a correction of Herodotos.

Its absence there is especially noteworthy, since one conflict in the revolt, that off Lade (Hdt. 6.7ff.), was a significant naval battle, the very kind of event in which Thucydides is interested in that analysis of earlier demonstrations of power, especially sea power. The primary reason for the omission must lie in the purpose of the Archaeology, which is to relate and discount military engagements from the past regarded as the most significant by Greeks. Thus Thucydides brings up the Trojan War only to dismiss its greatness, and he does the same with the Persian Wars. The latter example is most telling for our purposes: for if Thucydides rather shockingly relegates to a sentence or two a conflict to which Herodotos devotes three books, we can hardly expect the Ionian revolt to warrant mention. On such a scale, it was a non-event;[12] most important, from the standpoint of the Archaeology, it was not considered a great military engagement of the past.

That Thucydides was aware of Herodotos' account of the Ionian revolt makes sense, given how manifestly familiar he was with the Persian War books. Additionally, the parallels that can be adduced between the two writers, which we shall now consider, make it highly likely that Thucydides was modelling his account, especially the portion of it concerning the origins of the Sicilian expedition, in part on Herodotos' story of the revolt.

Herodotos begins the story of the Ionian revolt by relating how some Naxian exiles, ἄνδρες τῶν παχέων—"men of the fat," that is, the wealthy—came to Miletos and approached Aristagoras, deputy ruler of the city, for help in restoring them to their island, citing their *xenia* with Histiaios, tyrant of Miletos and Aristagoras' cousin and father-in-law (5.30.1–2). Aristagoras accepted their plea, using their bond with Histiaios as an excuse; he really wanted to rule Naxos and thought he could accomplish that if he restored the exiles to power on the island (5.30.3). He told them he would ask for help from Artaphernes, Darius' brother, who controlled the coast. The Naxians told Aristagoras to promise Artaphernes that they would pay for the cost (δαπάνη) of the force he sent (5.30.5–6). So Aristagoras went to Artaphernes at Sardis and told him that Naxos was not a large island, but was full of wealth and slaves; it lay near Ionia, and if equipped with one hundred ships to restore the exiles, Artaphernes could win for the king not only Naxos but the Kyklades; and from there it would be very easy to attack and conquer Euboia, a "large and prosperous island"; finally, Aristagoras claimed to have "a great sum of ready cash to pay for it, over and above the actual costs (ἑτοῖμα...χρήματα μεγάλα, 31.2). Artaphernes, Herodotos tells us, liked the idea and even enlarged the size of the fleet to two hun-

12. It is not clear exactly when the Ionian revolt was considered an event in its own right, rather than a mere prelude to the Persian Wars; see Tozzi 1978, esp. 21–27, for a discussion of the terms used to define the Ionian revolt; Murray 1988, 461–66.

dred ships (31.4). And so, in the coming spring, as promised, the ships arrived at the coast under the command of Megabates; but the plan eventually failed after Aristagoras tangled with Megabates, who then sent word to the Naxians that they were about to be attacked.

The siege failed. Aristagoras was now in trouble: the money promised was not forthcoming and he had no way to pay the fleet (5.35). Thus began the Ionian revolt, notable both for its problems of organizing unity among its component parts and for the problems of financing it presented. Aristagoras went to mainland Greece for help, first to Sparta. He tells Kleomenes, the Spartan king, that the sons of the Ionians had become enslaved (5.49.2), and that he should save them, related by blood as they were (5.49.3). He asserts that Persian weaponry (and clothing!) was negligible against the might of the Spartans, and that therefore it would be easy to conquer all of Asia, and then elaborates in great detail on the unparalleled riches ("the good things," ἀγαθά, 5.49.4) that would be his for the taking, mentioning, among other items, gold, silver, bronze, and other wealth, the Lydians who are "richest in money" (πολυαργυρώτατοι, 5.49.5), and the treasury at Susa (χρημάτων οἱ θησαυροί, 49.7), gaining control of which would make Kleomenes rival Zeus in money.

Herodotos comments on Aristagoras' cleverness, implying that Kleomenes was persuaded by the Milesian's lies, since he agreed to lend help (5.50.2); but when the king learned that Susa was three months' journey from the sea, he instructed Aristagoras to get out of town by sunset (5.51). Aristagoras ultimately failed to get Spartan support, then, by telling the truth. He moved on to Athens, saying all the things he said in Sparta about the "good things" in Asia and the Persian style of fighting (5.97.1). This prompts Herodotos' famous comment: "It is easier to deceive many than one; for Aristagoras could not fool Kleomenes, but he did fool 30,000 Athenians" (5.97.2).[13] So the Athenians sent a fleet.

Now let us recall the relevant outlines of Thucydides' account. He notes the Athenians' intention to invade Sicily, despite their ignorance about its size (6.1.1). Envoys from Egesta come to Athens asking for help in their conflict with the people of Selinous, citing their alliance with the Athenians. The Athenians accept their appeal; but the real reason, according to Thucydides, was that they desired to rule the whole island themselves (ἐφιέμενοι μὲν τῇ ἀληθεστάτῃ προφάσει τῆς πάσης ἄρξαι, 6.6.1). The Egestans promised to provide χρήματα...ἱκανά (6.6.2). The Athenians vote to send envoys to Egesta first to investigate whether the money existed in the public treasury and the temples (6.6.3). The envoys return later with the Eges-

13. Herodotos is silent on whether Aristagoras told them the distance to Persia, as at Sparta.

tans bringing silver bullion but reporting falsely that there was χρήματα ἑτοῖμα in the treasuries and temples at home in Egesta (6.8.2). The Athenians' false knowledge about the promised money induced them to send an expedition. They appointed the generals Alkibiades, Nikias, and Lamachos and held an assembly to determine the necessary preparations (6.8).

Both Nikias and Alkibiades addressed the assembly. Significant for our purposes here is that both men either exaggerate or outright lie to the Athenians, chiefly about the enemy against whom and the place to which they would be setting out. Among other arguments, Alkibiades claims that the Sicilians have insufficient weaponry (6.17.3) and fewer infantry than the Greeks believe (6.17.5). Thucydides, in introducing Alkibiades, notes that he desired to conquer Carthage in addition to Sicily (6.15.2). We learn later, in a speech by Hermokrates, of Carthage's enormous wealth.[14] Recall that already in Nikias' first speech he had implored the Athenians not to be "hopelessly in love with the far-off."[15] In response to his second speech, in which he exaggerates the preparation needed, the Athenians vote for much larger resources than at first and are even more keen for the expedition (6.24); there is an implication that many thought their goal of conquest would be easily accomplished, since they were setting out with, they believed, a great margin of safety in their preparations (6.24.1). But when they get to Sicily, they find out that the Egestans' money is not there as promised (6.46).

The following list of the structural and substantive parallels is instructive.

HERODOTOS	THUCYDIDES
Naxian exiles come to Miletos and ask Aristagoras for help in restoring them, citing their *xenia* with Histiaios. (5.30.1–2)	The Egestans asked for help in their conflict with Selinous, citing their alliance. (6.6.2)
Aristagoras accepts their plea, using their bond with Histiaios as an excuse, because he wanted to rule Naxos (ἄρξει). (5.30.3)	The Athenians accept their appeal, but the real reason was a desire to rule the whole island (ἄρξαι). (6.6.1)
Aristagoras goes to Artaphernes to ask for a fleet and tells him that the island is not so big and that from there one can	The Athenians are ignorant about the size of Sicily (6.1.1); Nikias and Alkibiades both exaggerate about Sicily; Alki-

14. 6.34.2: χρυσὸν γὰρ καὶ ἄργυρον πλεῖστον κέκτηνται.
15. 6.13.1: δυσερῶτας τῶν ἀπόντων.

go on to conquer other places, among which was wealthy Euboia. (5.31.2)	biades wants the expedition partly to go on to conquer Carthage (6.15.2), which is wealthy. (6.34.2)
Aristagoras was ready to provide χρήματα ἑτοῖμα μεγάλα given by the Naxians. (5.30.5–5.31.2)	The Egestans promise to provide χρήματα ἱκανά (6.6.2), later referred to as χρήματα ἑτοῖμα πολλά. (6.8.2) They show up with 60 talents of uncoined silver. (6.8.1)
Artaphernes agrees to the expedition, but doubles the number of ships, to 200. (31.4)	The Athenians vote for much larger resources than at first. (6.24)
Aristagoras tells Artaphernes and Kleomenes that conquest (of Euboia and Persia respectively) would be easy. (5.31.2, 97.2)	Alkibiades implies that conquest of Sicily will be easy (6.17); the Athenians believe that they will have great safety. (6.24.2)
Aristagoras runs out of money to pay the fleet. (5.35)	The Egestans' money turns out not to exist. (6.46; cf. 6.8.2)
Aristagoras persuades the Athenians to sail over to Asia, having told them it would be easy to conquer but also that it was far away. (5.97)[16]	The Athenians, as Nikias puts it, should not be (but are) hopelessly in love with the far-off. (6.13.1)

Certainly a number of these elements and calculations on the part of one side or another are or could be commonplace, and the temptation then as now to supply the hidden but real motive for an action is almost impossible to resist. Nor do I want to fit Thucydides in some procrustean way into a Herodotean template. History may indeed repeat itself, but the historian or writer has a rich and varied palette at his disposal with which to reconstruct and structure his account, and to select particular items for emphasis. In Thucydides' case, I suggest, he chose to map his account onto another highly tendentious narrative[17] of the origins of a failed enterprise, in particular by drawing attention to the roles of deception and gullibility. Let us summarize the common themes: (1) ignorance of the respective islands on

16. I take this as implicit from the fact that Aristagoras mentioned the distance in Sparta, and Herodotos tells us that he repeated everything he said to Kleomenes to the Athenians.

17. But cf. Georges (2000), who argues for the essential accuracy of Herodotos' account.

the part of those authorizing the attack (Artaphernes, the Persian satrap, accepts that Naxos is small and close to the coast of Asia Minor, while in fact it is the largest island in the Kyklades and about one hundred miles from the coast of Asia Minor; the Athenian *polloi* do not know that Sicily is as large as it is); (2) deception and exaggeration by those seeking help (Aristagoras, the Egestans, Alkibiades, Nikias); (3) a request accepted for ulterior motives; (4) an offer to finance the expedition turns out to be specious or otherwise not forthcoming, although promised; (5) the magnified size of the expedition compared with what was envisioned or requested at the start; (6) personal motives (those of Aristagoras in the events culminating in the Ionian revolt and those of Alkibiades in the Sicilian expedition) (this point of similarity would not be worth noting were it not for the rarity of personal motives in Thucydides);[18] (7) some striking verbal similarities (e.g., χρήματα ἑτοῖμα in identical contexts; (8) the Athenians were easily fooled (by Aristagoras and by the Egestans); and finally, (9) the Athenians in both accounts are not deterred by the faraway.

The parallels are especially dense in the narrative dealing with the origins of the Sicilian expedition; but there are also sections later on, once the campaign is under way, that resonate with Herodotos' account and concern the financing of the expedition. In the narrative of the early winter of 415/14, the Athenians have finally engaged the Syracusans successfully (6.69–70); Thucydides stresses the generals' thinking that they were too short on money and cavalry to accomplish much,[19] and thus they remained inactive during the winter (6.71–72). In this context, he chooses to note the Syracusans' fear after their defeat that the Athenians might decide to raid the temple treasures at the Olympieion in Syracuse (6.70, 71). This comment is especially striking, since it reveals not an unfulfilled intention on the part of the Athenians, but rather an unfulfilled fear on the part of the Syracusans, for Thucydides then pointedly remarks: "But the Athenians did not go to the temple" (6.71.1). Similarly, in Herodotos (5.36), the Ionians at Miletos, in desperate need of money after the revolt has begun, fail to take the advice of Hekataios to raid the temple treasures at nearby Branchidai. Herodotos steps into the narrative to comment that the treasures, as he had previously noted, were considerable. It seems that he is implicitly endorsing Hekataios' proposal and implicating Aristagoras et al. for failing to recognize its merits. Likewise, Thucydides may be implicitly signaling criticism of the Athenians when he says: "The Athenians, however, did not go the temple."

18. In his account of the Sicilian expedition, Thucydides is elaborating on 2.65.7, in which he refers explicitly to the personal motives of ambition and gain of Perikles' successors.

19. Thucydides *may* be implying that although those in charge thought (ἐδόκει) they could not accomplish anything, they were wrong.

The presentation through negation suggests that the Athenians did not do what might have been expected or reasonable under the circumstances;[20] there is a lingering suspicion of a great opportunity mistakenly passed up, a suspicion that will increase as the narrative of the campaign proceeds and the Athenians, like the Ionians, continue to be in financial need (a point to which I shall return below).[21]

Another possible resonance is found in Nikias' letter to the Athenians, sent in the winter of 413. By now the Athenian situation is seriously compromised by the arrival of Gylippos and a Peloponnesian fleet, as well as by insufficient resources and the inability to use their whole force to meet the enemy, occupied as they were by the need to guard their fortifications. The letter emphasizes the insufficiency of the forces to face the reinforced enemy, and the Athenians' inability to procure needed supplies and money from Sicily. Nikias then abruptly comments: "But by far my greatest problem is that I, their general, am not able to prevent these problems—for your natures are hard to rule" (7.14.2).[22] This comes out of the blue; why bring up a subject that, as Dover observes, "appears to have no bearing on the difficulties of the situation as Nikias has described them"?[23] I would not press the point, but Nikias' remark is reminiscent of a section of Herodotos' account of the Ionian revolt that is as close to the revolt's end as Nikias' letter is to the end of the Sicilian expedition. With the looming threat of a naval battle against the Persians, the Ionian crews entrusted themselves to Dionysios, commander of the Phokaians, to train them for the imminent battle. As Herodotos recounts it, the Ionians toiled hard for seven days but balked at the rigorous training and henceforth refused to obey him (6.12). The result was that the Samians, seeing the lack of discipline among the Ionians, joined the Persian side. The similarity between Herodotos' portrayal of the Ionians' natural laziness and Nikias' almost gratuitous comment about the Athenians' "natural" indisposition (put in terms of their *tropos,* or character) is suggestive, as both precede a decisive naval defeat at the hands

20. Cf. 3.50.2: the Athenians "did not impose tribute" on the Mytilenaians after their revolt but rather converted Lesbos into a cleruchy. See *Money,* 144–49.

21. Of course, the temple treasures would have comprised the very kind of wealth—precious metal objects—Thucydides implicitly relegates to an inferior status (2.13, 6.31, 6.46), as discussed in the previous chapter; but context is critical to assessing how he is thinking about monetary vs. other wealth. Non-monetary wealth is not the wealth of first recourse in a military context, and it does not signify *dunamis chrematon;* but it can be melted down and used in emergencies, and in this case, the Athenians were experiencing financial hardship. See also below, conclusion, p. 292.

22. Cf. 6.9.3 for a similar comment by Nikias about the Athenians' nature; cf. also 7.48.4.

23. *HCT* 4, ad loc. Cf. Tompkins (1972, 196–97), who sees the function of the sentence as enhancing the stylistic complexity of Nikias' letter.

of their respective enemies, at Lade off Miletos in the Ionian revolt and at Syracuse in the Sicilian expedition.[24]

These parallels strongly suggest that Thucydides was making use of Herodotos' account of the Ionian revolt as well as his narrative of the beginnings of the Persian invasion of 480 in an architectural or structural as well as in a thematic way. By mapping the origins of the Sicilian expedition in particular onto Herodotos' account of the Ionian revolt, Thucydides could exploit the familiarity the audience would bring to the narrative through its resonances with Herodotos to drive home more effectively the specific points he wished to make about the Sicilian expedition. As C. B. R. Pelling notes, "previous narratives . . . prepare readers and condition their expectations . . . ; they provide the indispensable foothold to allow interpretation to begin."[25] How, then, was Herodotos' narrative useful for telling the story of the opening of the Sicilian expedition? Thucydides' predilection for thinking about his subject comparatively provides an answer. What better event than the Ionian revolt, at least as Herodotos relates it, to call to his audience's mind in an account of the origins of the Sicilian expedition?[26] Herodotos' narrative of that episode in Greek history served perfectly as an analogy. It was a blunder through and through from start to finish: ill conceived, ill executed, begun for personal reasons and ulterior motives, and involving a large armament that could not be paid for adequately or properly. It was a complete disaster—although the outcome of the naval battle off Lade was by no means predetermined. Similarly, the final battle at Syracuse could not have been predicted to be a defeat for the Athenians.[27]

Herodotos implicates Aristagoras for his personal motives in embarking on a major campaign that was based on the ulterior motive of conquest and involved subsequent escalation necessitating even greater financial resources, which were not forthcoming. Similarly, Thucydides' account stresses

24. There is some irony as well, since it was the Athenians' vigilance in the early days of the Delian League that led the Ionians to balk at their obligations of naval service, leading to the momentous change in the extent of Athenian power recorded by Thucydides (1.99).

25. Pelling 1999, 326; see also 344: audiences are "more inclined to find a story plausible when it maps on to a pattern which is already familiar." As Pelling notes, there is a larger issue here, for the purpose of such patterning is to relate a particular story to a recurrent pattern and enhance interpretation and meaning (344–48). I shall return to this below.

26. This point needs to be stressed, since Herodotos was not the only one to tell the story of the revolt; for Lysanias of Mallos and Phrynichos (at the very least) also treated it (Hdt. 6.21); see Hornblower 1994b, 22–23, 57; Murray 1988, 468–69. Cf. also 1.97.2, where Thucydides refers to τοῖς πρὸ ἐμοῦ ἅπασιν ἐκλιπὲς τοῦτο ἦν τὸ χωρίον καὶ ἢ τὰ πρὸ τῶν Μηδικῶν Ἑλληνικὰ ξυνετίθεσαν ἢ αὐτὰ τὰ Μηδικά.

27. Cf. 7.55.2: after their initial defeat by the Syracusans, the Athenians were despondent, for a defeat at sea "would never have been thought possible." Thucydides stresses other unforeseen factors leading up the naval battle (e.g., eclipses, taken as omens, 7.50.4).

the desire for conquest and a lust for riches, and, as I shall argue below, an insufficiently supported expeditionary force, which, like that of Aristagoras and his Ionians, once in the thick of military activities, either could not or would not pull back and avoid even more extensive losses until final disaster struck. Moreover, if we add the parallels between the Egestan deception and the story of Oroites, Maiandrios, and Polykrates, explored in the last chapter, it is clear that Thucydides is inserting criticism of the agents in his narrative, imputing responsibility to the Athenians for the deteriorating situation in which they found themselves.[28] Finally, both episodes were themselves beginnings: the Ionian revolt led to the Persian Wars, while the Sicilian expedition marked the beginning of the renewed and final stage of the Peloponnesian War, a stage in which the Persians would be prominent and their role decisive.

The Ionian Revolts in Book 8

Herodotos' Ionian revolt was useful to Thucydides not only in the composition of the Sicilian narrative, but also, I suggest, in the construction of his account of the aftermath, in book 8. I shall examine book 8 extensively below,[29] but it will be useful to bring out the Herodotean aspects of the narrative briefly here. They are embedded in the account in book 8 in the overall theme of the account, in the role and impact of key individuals, and in specific allusions designed to evoke Herodotos more directly. As is typical of the later historian, Thucydides uses Herodotos to underscore and suggest inversions, contrasts, and ironies, as well as to elicit comparisons.

Book 8 has strong thematic connections to Herodotos' account of the Ionian revolt. In fact, a major theme of book 8 is another Ionian revolt. Following the Sicilian expedition, the Peloponnesian War shifts largely to the eastern Aegean, and the players include not only Athens, Sparta, and Ionian cities but also, most aptly, the Persians. The Persians' role preceding the revolt in each work is similar: in Herodotos, Artaphernes, acting on behalf of the Persian King, lends military support in the form of ships to an effort (so he believes) to conquer Naxos and then Greece; in Thucydides, Tissaphernes, acting on behalf of the Persian King, promises military support in the form of money (and later ships) to the Spartans' war against Athens (8.5.5). The inversions are even more prominent. In 498, the Spartans refuse to help the revolt against Persia, and the Athenians agree; in 412, the Spartans, with Persian assistance, aid the Ionians in their revolts against Ath-

28. Thucydides, however, will complicate this conclusion by developing at the same time the idea of the Athenians as irrational and impassioned; I shall explore this more fully in chap. 3.

29. See chap. 6.

ens. It should be noted, however, as will emerge more fully below, that the efforts of the Spartans in 412–411 are ineffectual to a significant extent, and those of the Athenians in 498 are entirely so. What is more, in 412 and the years following, the revolts are sometimes initiated and carried out by the cities on their own with insufficient help from the Spartans.[30]

The similar role of individuals in Thucydides and Herodotos is also revealing. Both Aristagoras and Alkibiades—deputy tyrant and perhaps a wanna-be tyrant, respectively—act as middlemen between Greeks and Persian satraps. Both are completely unreliable, lie to their respective targets, and as the historians' attention to their ulterior motives makes clear, are out for themselves. Both Aristagoras and Alkibiades hold out the lure of wealth to both Spartans and Athenians, and in both cases, the Athenians, ultimately, are by far the more easily deceived, with grave consequences. Similarly, Aristagoras and Tissaphernes are unreliable paymasters, a detail that causes serious problems in both Herodotos and Thucydides.

In another area of similarity, Thucydides' treatment of a land battle in Miletos between the Athenians and Argives, on one side, and the Peloponnesians and Milesians, on the other, evokes Herodotos' account of the battle of Lade near the end of the Ionian revolt. In commenting on the mixed outcome of the battle in Miletos, Thucydides notes: "On both sides, it happened that Ionians won over Dorians; for the Athenians defeated the Peloponnesians arrayed against them, and the Milesians, the Argives" (8.25.5).[31] The Argives lost, he points out, because they were contemptuous of the Ionians and advanced in some disorder. In the Ionian revolt, of course, the battle off Miletos at Lade was a naval battle, which the Ionians lost; Herodotos stresses the stereotype the Argives had of the Ionians (6.12), which had led to defections to the Persians. The similarities here consist mostly of inversions and an emphasis on the Ionians and might be seen as coincidental or merely superficial. It is intriguing, however, that Herodotos ends his account of the fall of Miletos by recalling an oracle with two referents, one part pertaining to the Argives, one part to the Milesians (6.19). Thus it is tempting to conclude that when he composed his battle of Miletos, Thucydides was thinking of Miletos in the Ionian revolt (as Herodotos described it).

The suggestion of Herodotos' Ionian revolt in Thucydides' "Ionian revolt," like the parallels in the case of the Sicilian books, serves, through comparison, to underscore the interplay of financing, naval success, and the dangerous impact of individuals on events, especially where money—or its absence—is concerned. The similarities between Aristagoras and Alkibiades and their respective relationships to Athens allow Thucydides to cre-

30. See below, chap. 6.

31. On this passage see Alty 1982, 3.

ate a deeper layer of criticism about their gullibility and their ill thought-out desire for money in his narrative.

TROY AND THE SICILIAN EXPEDITION: THUCYDIDES AND HOMER AND HERODOTOS

Thucydides on the Trojan War and the Sicilian Expedition

Like the Ionian revolt, the Trojan War offered Thucydides a useful source for patterns and lessons for illuminating, among other things, the argument he makes in the narrative of books 6 and 7 about the financing of the Sicilian expedition. Indeed, Thucydides' interest in Troy in the Sicilian account is clear from the start. It is evident both in his catalogue of the earliest settlers, the Cyclopes, and the Laestrygonians in the Sicilian "archaeology" (6.2.1)[32] and in subsequent references to the migration of Trojans to Sicily following the fall of Troy, culminating in the founding of Eryx and Egesta (6.2.3). Drawing attention to the Homeric allusions in the account of the expedition, Allison observes that "when Thucydides turns to compose the events of the Sicilian Expedition, he allows the reader to dwell on parallels between it and its ancestral expedition to Troy. The parallels with the Homeric poems on a thematic level are large and obvious: the monumental Greek naval expeditionary force travels far in order to besiege a city."[33] Scholars have long noticed Homeric elements in Thucydides—or, better, ways in which Thucydides was patterning or modeling parts of his narrative on Homer and the Trojan War[34]—and have suggested that the Homeric and Herodotean intertexts help to bring out the tragic element of the expedition, or, alternatively, to reveal an almost Herodotean belief in the workings of a metaphysical force (*tuche*).[35]

32. See Frangoulidis (1993), who draws out parallels between the stories of the Cyclopes and Laestrygonians in the *Odyssey* and the Athenians in Sicily; he also sees a narrative frame in 6.2 and the end of book 7 in the use of ἀπενόστησαν (87.6).

33. Allison 1997a, 500; for the intent to invoke Homer directly, see also Mackie 1996.

34. E.g., Smith 1900; Strasburger 1968, 1972; Marinatos Kopff and Rawlings 1978; Hunter 1980; 1982, 40–41; Bowie 1993; Allison 1997a; Mackie 1996; Howie 1998; for resonances with the *Odyssey*, see Connor 1984, 162 n. 9; Frangoulidis (1993, 97–98), who sees the desire for material gain among the Athenians in Sicily (citing 6.90.3–4) paralleling *Od.* 9.548–57; Zadorojnyi 1998; but cf. Flory 1988 for the differences between Homer and Thucydides in the construction of counterfactual hypotheses. Homer, via Ais. *Ag.* 341–47, is likely embedded in 6.24, where Thucydides refers to the Athenians' passion for the expedition; for the passage and discussion, see Connor 1984, 167; Cornford 1971 [1907], 214. For another possible Aischylean level see below, note 79.

35. Allison 1997a; Marinatos Kopff and Rawlings 1978; Hornblower 1994b, 148; or to the *Odyssey* and the idea of the *nostos*, see Frangoulidis 1993, 102.

Whatever one's view of these interpretations, it is clear that Homer and Troy are present in the narrative on various levels. Thucydides' use of Homer, like his use of Herodotos, is highly complex: he will compare, contrast, show reversals, and, above all, stress ironies as he guides the reader toward the lessons he wants to be drawn. One such lesson intimately concerns the financing of an overseas expedition, and a clue that it is enormously important to Thucydides' historiographical agenda is that the historian's own radical reinterpretation of the Trojan War presented in the Archaeology emphasizes the link between Troy and Sicily as one of money and strategy.

When he uses the words ἀξιοχρέων, "noteworthy," and στόλος, "expedition," in conjunction in 6.31, the chapter describing the launching of the expedition, Thucydides may be evoking Mycenae and the expedition to Troy ironically; neither word is common in the *History* up to this point.[36] In 1.10.1 the historian comments that the power of Mycenae might not seem ἀξιοχρέων—a comment that then leads to his discussion of signs of power versus real power.[37] In 6.31.1 he notes that spectators came down to the Peiraieus to see the sight that was ἀξιοχρέων. He refers to the expedition as a στόλος twice, first in 31.3, and again, as he concludes his description of the fleet in 6.31.6; the same word was also used twice earlier in the *History* to refer to Agamemnon's fleet (1.9.2, 10.1).

In 1.9–11, Thucydides departs significantly from Homer to explain the motivation behind the united Greek expedition to Troy and the reasons for its protracted length.[38] His analysis of the war, like his allusions to other earlier Greek conflicts in the introductory section of the *History,* focuses on power and wealth, but his deductions about the length of the Trojan campaign are especially intriguing because of their unusual focus:[39]

> The number of those who sailed to Troy was not considerable, given that it represented all of Greece. The reason for this, however, was not so much a shortage of men (*oliganthropia*) as a shortage of money (*achrematia*). For due to insufficient sustenance (*trophe*), they brought a smaller army, thinking that they could acquire what they needed from the land while they were at war; but when, having arrived, they prevailed in battle (as they must have, for otherwise they would not have been able to construct fortifications around their camp), they appear not even from that point to have used all their strength; rather, they turned to farming the Chersonese and to plundering due to their insufficient supplies. . . . Whereas if they had come with a surplus of money (*trophe*) and, having drawn together their entire force, had waged war contin-

36. Ἀξιοχρέων: 1.10.1; 4.30.3, 85.6; 5.13.1; 6.10.2, 21.2, 31.1; στόλος: 1.9.2, 10.1, 18.2, 26.3, 31.1; 3.94.1; 4.60.2; 6.31.3, 6.

37. On this passage, see also chap. 1, pp. 38–39, 56–59.

38. See Erbse 1961, 22–23.

39. See also *Money,* 27–30.

uously, without resorting to pillaging and farming, they would easily have prevailed in battle and been victorious. (1.10.5–1.11)

What prompted this strange analysis? Hunter has argued that Thucydides' interpretation of why the Greeks at Troy took so long to gain victory was likely based on his own views about the problems faced by campaigns abroad, and that he was thinking of the Sicilian expedition in particular. She comments: "In spite of Nikias' warnings in the year 415 the Athenians departed for Sicily without a surplus of resources but confident that they would obtain supplies, food, money, and cavalry from their allies there. This miscalculation then produced grave difficulties, when they failed to achieve the prerequisite of all other success, the kind of victory at the outset that establishes a secure beachhead, and that in turn permits a united and unrelenting application of all one's forces to the siege and ultimately its speedy resolution in conquest."[40]

These brief observations deserve fuller consideration and elaboration, for if it is true that Thucydides' assessment of what went wrong in Sicily influenced his interpretation of what happened at Troy, then we should be able to use his interpretation of the Trojan War to understand better his account of the Athenians in Sicily.[41] The correspondences, which in fact go beyond those mentioned by Hunter, suggest the correctness of her observation: neither the Greeks at Troy nor the Athenians in Sicily brought enough money with them and thus were forced to rely on local provisioning; both groups were compelled to divide their forces because of the lack of supplies; both groups won a victory early on but failed to exploit it. Moreover, Thucydides' attention to the fortification he deduces the Greeks must have built in conjunction with their early, but unexploited victory compares with his emphasis on the Athenians' failure to construct a wall following theirs; correspondingly, the Greeks at Troy won, the Athenians lost. That Thucydides was likely motivated to write the Trojan analysis on the basis of his observations about the Sicilian expedition, and not the other way around, is suggested by the number of deductions he makes in 1.10–11; that is, he has not combed the extra-Homeric traditions and based his analysis on them but rather is making inferences about what must have happened, or, conversely,

40. Hunter 1982, 40–41. See also Hunter 1973, 165: "The *paradeigma* which throws most light on the probable experience of the Athenians is the Trojan expedition"; Hunter 1980, 203–4.

41. Thucydides would not have been the only one to draw such a connection between the Sicilian expedition and Troy, for even if Euripides' *Trojan Women* was only coincidentally produced in the same year as the launching of the expedition, it would certainly have fostered the connection as an effect of its production. For discussion and bibliography on the problem of the link between the play and historical context, see Croally 1994, 232–34.

what would have happened, and this kind of reasoning must derive from his own contemporary world.

There are two related points to be gleaned from the Trojan analysis that help us understand better the historian's focus in both 1.11 and the Sicilian narrative, accepting the hypothesis that the Sicilian expedition made him think about Troy in such an unusual way. The first has to do with the relationship between size and resources, and the second, with the level of initial resources and their consequences for the length of expeditions. Concerning the first point, reading the Trojan analysis and the Sicilian account together helps illuminate the motivation behind specific statements Thucydides makes that seem odd by themselves, as if the historian is making an unexpressed connection or thinking of something else. Two sentences in particular come to mind. Thucydides' deduction from Homer that the size of the Greek force at Troy was "not many" (1.10.5), considering that men came from all over Hellas, has long struck commentators as a decidedly peculiar claim, since the number the historian allows us to calculate—he does not do the arithmetic—is huge. Gomme thought that in this section Thucydides had not fully thought things out, and cites some troublesome sentence constructions as well.[42] Yet Thucydides' reconstruction becomes comprehensible and has all the appearances of being fully thought out when considered alongside an equally peculiar comment about the size and resources of the initial Sicilian expedition of 415.

In 6.31.1–2 the historian observes that the expedition of 415 was "emphatically the most extravagant and beautiful force ever to have been sent out." But then he adds: "In number of ships and hoplites it was no greater than that against Epidauros under Perikles or that against Poteidaia under Hagnon; but this one, however, was to last longer," and so on. Thucydides' elaborate description of the expenses involved in the expedition, examined in chapter 1, follows. Thus in both 1.10.5–1.11 and 6.31 Thucydides emphasizes the relationship between size and resources; but, more significantly, in both passages size is not really the point, or it is the lesser point. The chief point in both concerns resources. The historian forcefully makes the case that a larger force would not necessarily have helped at Troy: the crucial factor was the absence of resources from home to support the expedition, which made victory harder, because the men could not fight united but instead had to separate to forage and farm. It is quite clear, though more implicit, that a larger force by itself would not have helped the Athenians win

42. *HCT* 1, on 1.10.4–5. Howie (1998, 95–96) sees Thucydides' argument about the financial need of the Greek force and therefore its reduced size as an "elegant solution" to the implication of the epic: namely, vast depopulation.

in Sicily; it would have had to have been accompanied by a proportionately large *periousia chrematon.*[43]

If we turn to the second, related point, concerning the consequences of employing greater resources, Thucydides makes his position clear in 1.11 through a counterfactual hypothesis: "If [the Greeks] had come with plentiful *trophe* and, having drawn together their entire force, had waged war continuously, without resorting to pillaging and farming, they would easily have prevailed in battle and been victorious."[44] It is crucial to appreciate the extent to which Thucydides is going out on a limb by making a strong counterfactual statement concerning an "event" in the murky, distant past, something he does nowhere else in the Archaeology.[45] What gave him the confidence to make such a statement? Very likely, I suggest, his observations about the Athenians in Sicily.

This raises a critical question: did the Athenians have greater resources than they brought overseas on their expeditions? If so, the Sicilian narrative would contain another implicit argument and criticism: they had them to spend, and should have spent them; failure to do so significantly contributed to utter disaster. There are compelling reasons to answer in the affirmative. Recall that Thucydides draws attention to the (re)accumulation of money in Athens before the expedition set out, both in his own voice and in that of Nikias.[46] Recall also that Nikias advised the Athenians in his second speech in 415 to bring "as much money as possible from home."[47] So when Thucydides writes of the Greek force of 415 that it was not impressively large but rather impressively costly, and ends his description of the costs with the statement "Many talents were carted out of the city" (6.31.5), at first sight he would appear to be saying that the Athenians had overcome

43. Thucydides implicitly draws attention to the problem in connection with the Spartans at 8.80; see below, chap. 6, p. 271.

44. Flory (1988) has examined this technique in the *History,* concentrating on Thucydides' use of it in the narrative of the Peloponnesian War proper; but he is not concerned with deductions about the past, regarding them as those that tend to "reconstruct what happened rather than speculate on how the past might have been different" (45). Yet 1.11 does show Thucydides speculating on how the Trojan War might have gone differently; see also Dover 1988 [1981] on Thucydides' counterfactual judgments, with particular attention to 7.43.2; Hornblower 1994a, 158–59; Rood 1998, 278–80.

45. Flory (1988, 45) notes Thucydides' use of "must have been" deductions about the size of Agamemnon's navy (1.9.4); but his statement about how Troy might have gone differently is of a different order.

46. Preparations were easy, partly because the Athenians had an "accumulation of money" (χρημάτων ἄθροισιν, 6.26.2); Nikias comments that the respite from the plague and war "had increased their money and bodies" (χρήμασι καὶ τοῖς σώμασιν ηὐξῆσθαι, 6.12.1).

47. χρήματα αὐτόθεν ὡς πλεῖστα, 6.22.

the problem faced by the Greeks at Troy.[48] Yet the narrative, analyzed in chapter 1, also undercuts any expectation of success, because of the emphasis on expenditures that were either wasteful or nonusable in a military context; individuals were getting paid at an excessive rate,[49] and much wealth was used to make the force look good. They spent on the wrong categories; but that they also did not bring enough for expenditure on military power emerges from the subsequent narrative.[50] In the case of the Trojan War, Thucydides makes a deduction that Agamemnon had naval superiority because of inherited wealth from his father Pelops (1.9.2–3). Thus when the historian subsequently writes that the Greeks at Troy did not bring enough money, he seems to be implying, from the preceding attention to Agamemnon's financial resources, that they not only should have but could have brought more.

It needs to be stressed that Thucydides makes clear that the Athenians did not *intend* to bring a *periousia chrematon* from home for the campaign, but rather planned to acquire what they needed from Sicily and Italy—in fact, they expected the Egestans to fund the expedition. Gomme comments on the normalcy of this kind of strategy;[51] yet read against the Trojan analysis, Thucydides' narrative becomes negative and critical in tone. Let us follow the line of argument he develops, beginning with the Athenians' arrival in the vicinity of Sicily.

First, they divide up the force into three parts, not simply because that made sense given that there were three generals, but also because of anticipated supply problems (6.42.1;[52] after Alkibiades' recall, the force was redivided into two parts, 6.62.1). Next, upon discovering that the promised Egestan funds did not exist, save possibly for 30 talents, Alkibiades, Nikias, and Lamachos were in an agitated state[53] and debated what to do (6.47–9). The three generals offered different proposals, but a primary concern they

48. So Allison 1997a, 500.

49. On "standard" rates, see chap. 1, n. 115. In my view, the context of Thucydides' allusions to a *per diem* rate of one drachma implies strongly that he sees it as unusually high: as we saw in chap. 1 the argument of 6.31 is the costliness of the expedition, and accordingly the items the historian introduces in support should be regarded as unusually high; cf. also 7.27.2 in which the drachma rate for Thracian mercenaries is cited as *poluteles.*

50. However, in the narrative of the later stages of the expedition, Thucydides emphasizes the errors of judgment and absence of leadership that no amount of money would have rectified. See below, chap. 4.

51. Gomme, *HCT* 1: 114.

52. Rood (1998, 166) notes the emphasis in this part of the narrative on supply problems.

53. It is true that Nikias was not surprised to learn that the Egestan money did not exist, but Thucydides also explicitly comments that "*the generals* were immediately in a state of great distress (καὶ οἱ στρατηγοὶ εὐθὺς ἐν ἀθυμίᾳ ἦσαν)" upon hearing the report (6.46.2; my emphasis).

share in Thucydides' presentation is the need for funds to carry on the war. In other words, the huge force was now in Sicily, unsupported, having sailed manifestly without a sufficient *periousia chrematon* for the lengthy campaign anticipated.

Moreover, Thucydides makes clear that all proposals presumed the aim of obtaining money and grain from local sources: Nikias explicitly notes that they must not "endanger Athens by wasting its home resources," a fascinating because surprising comment coming from the man who had earlier advised the Athenians to bring "as much money as possible from home";[54] what is more, the comment will become ironic, given that the Athenians were endangered by not bringing greater resources from home. But Thucydides allows another interpretation of Nikias' insistence on obtaining resources locally in Sicily: he earlier had the general explicitly noting that sending for reinforcements would be "shameful" (αἴσχρον, 6.21.2)! In turn, Alkibiades spoke of making friends in the area in order to get "grain and troops," while Lamachos suggested that they might seize money from inhabitants of rural areas, whom they could surprise on the way as they removed their property into the cities, under fear of an Athenian attack.

The twofold concern with gaining allies and money suggests that the financing of the expedition was considered a significant problem and also that the Athenians had not intended to fund the expedition from their own sources; indeed, they do not request money from Athens until the winter of 415/14.[55] Instead they proposed strategies for ad hoc emergency financing, not for more secure and long-lasting *periousia chrematon,* which they possessed at home. Thucydides reinforces the point by having Alkibiades explicitly note in his speech at Sparta that the Athenians expected *not* to use home resources but to get what they needed in Sicily (6.90.4). A crucial turning point comes when in his letter to the Athenians (7.14) Nikias admits that the force in Sicily cannot rely on any local support and that they need plenty of money from home; yet this is in the winter of 413. Nikias' letter drives the point home that the Athenians had failed to sail to Sicily on this major campaign with *periousiai chrematon.* Thus Thucydides' narrative subverts completely the already ambiguous image constructed in 6.31 of a Greek force accompanied by a vast treasure.

Following Alkibiades' removal from the scene upon his recall to Athens

54. Ellis (1979, 49) sees Thucydides here as presenting Nikias with a case that is "developed logically from his earlier position"; while that applies to the example he gives (Nikias' advocating a show of force but not engagement), it does not apply to his position on the use of home resources.

55. For the implications of this point for assessing the epigraphic evidence associated with the Sicilian expedition, see below, chap. 5, pp. 189–91.

and subsequent escape,[56] Nikias and Lamachos were left as generals and, as mentioned, divided the army into two parts. Next they sailed to Selinous and Egesta, "wishing to know whether the Egestans would give them the money" (6.62).[57] The Egestans did hand over 30 talents, which the Athenians supplemented by selling the former inhabitants of Hykkara, newly conquered, for a total of 120 talents.[58] In its context, even the money raised by the sale of slaves is little more than a drop in the bucket; but attention to this act of cash raising, with specific figures supplied, is typical of Thucydides' larger concern with the financing of the expedition. It particularly reveals his negative treatment of war finance. The impressionistic vagueness of his description of the exodus of wealth in 6.31 contrasts with the supplying of specific pieces of information, as that in 6.62. This is money that will be immediately spent on military action, unlike the undefined amount in 6.31; Thucydides' description also underscores the fact that the Athenians are scrounging, as the subsequent narrative makes clear (6.70–74). Indeed, every piece of information that relates to the Athenians' financial problems in Sicily is laden with irony when the reader recalls Thucydides' comment at the end of 6.31, that "many talents were carted out of the city."

Thus, the Athenians, from the description of the thinking, decisions, and actions of Nikias and Lamachos, manifestly have arrived in Sicily without the surplus (*periousia*) necessary to carry on war effectively. They have divided their forces and have taken measures to attempt to provision themselves, as the Greeks did in Troy. Although they do not attack the Syracusans immediately, nevertheless in their first conflict with them in the winter of 414, they achieve victory (by a strategem, 6.64–70). The correspondences with the Trojan analysis are especially sharp here, for the introduction of the campaign proper, once the Athenians realized they were short of cash (6.62), is in effect a replay of the Greek experience at Troy as Thucydides describes it. The Athenians win an initial victory, but they do not make the most of it by following it up, instead wasting time procuring money and aid

56. One wonders whether there might be a Homeric resonance in the portrait of Alkibiades. Thucydides makes clear that Alkibiades' removal from command greatly damaged the Athenians (6.15.3–4; for the purposes here it does not matter significantly to what Thucydides is specifically alluding); likewise Achilles' withdrawal from the fighting damaged the Achaian side.

57. The tenor of this comment continues the sense of possible illusion—did the money exist?—as in 6.44.4; see chap. 1, pp. 69–70.

58. It may be significant that Thucydides now does not specify the form of the 30 talents—that is, whether coined or uncoined. Certainly in this case, there would be little rhetorical impact in the specificity, since he has already made the point more than sufficiently that the Athenians embarked on an enormous military enterprise, counting on a false promise of money.

and waiting for additional resources to come from Athens, which allows the Syracusans to gather strength.[59] There are ironies as well that look back also to Nikias' own statements before the expedition. In 6.23.2, Nikias counsels his fellow Athenians to be mindful of the fact that "he who undertakes such an expedition [amidst strangers and enemies] must be prepared to become master of the country the first day he lands, or failing in this, to know that they would find everything hostile to him." It is highly ironic, but also typical of Thucydides' portrait of Nikias, that the general has failed to follow his own advice. But the comment also contains resonances with the Trojan analysis.[60]

Thus it comes as little surprise that Thucydides' narrative of the early winter of 415/14 stresses the Athenians' inactivity and inability to accomplish much. His statement, analyzed above, that the Athenians failed to raid the temple treasures at the Olympieion in Syracuse, although this was the very thing that the Syracusans feared they would do (6.70, 71), reinforces the sense of immobility: they do not even become active to acquire resources that he implies they could have expropriated. Instead they remained idle in Catana and waited for horses and money to be sent from Athens and collected from the country (71).[61] Moreover, they needed to gather further supplies and win over more cities in preparation for a campaign in the spring; Thucydides' Greeks at Troy again are recalled. The Athenians then sailed to Naxos and Catana for the winter, failing to take Messina because Alkibiades had ruined their prospects by warning friends on the inside. They then sent a trireme to Athens to ask for money and horses, to join them in the spring. Thus the lack of resources has led to delays and a failure to achieve further military success.

An explicit condemnation of Nikias comes later in the narrative, in a controversial passage whose function may also be illuminated by reading it against the Trojan analysis. In 7.42.3, after Demosthenes has arrived with reinforcements from home in the summer of 413, Thucydides tells us of his intention to strike while the iron is hot, in order not to fare as Nikias had by delaying. He follows with a parenthetical comment containing his own

59. Allison (1989, 94) notes that Thucydides is presenting the deterioration of *paraskeue* in the second half of book 6 (6.45–105); but I disagree with her view (1997a, 500) that the Athenians in Thucydides do not face the problem of a protracted campaign. But cf. Avery (1973, 6–7), who argues that Thucydides is presenting the Athenians as acting with vigor when they do act.

60. As Gommel (1966, 39) notes, although he does not appear to regard the Trojan analysis itself as motivated by Thucydides' interpretation of the problems in Sicily.

61. It is possible that the ἐδόκει of 71.2 reflects Thucydides' belief that the generals could have done more than they did. See also above, p. 92 with n. 19.

opinion, but surely one that likely reflects Demosthenes' thinking as well.[62] He notes that Nikias' arrival had brought fear to the Syracusans, but his failure to attack immediately and instead to winter in Catana led the Syracusans to summon Gylippos and the Spartans. He presents a counterfactual hypothesis: "The Syracusans would not have summoned the Peloponnesians had Nikias attacked at once, for they thought they were sufficient to engage the Athenians and would have discovered their inferiority at the same time as they were walled off." The counterfactual hypothesis about an earlier victory and the specific mention of walls resonates intriguingly with the Trojan analysis, which contains a similar hypothesis. In 7.42.3 Thucydides assumes the construction of walls in conjunction with an initial victory, just as he does in the case of the Greeks at Troy. But the very fact that the Greeks at Troy were unable immediately to gain victory had to be explained; thus Thucydides invokes his financial argument. The Athenians in Sicily do not engage the Syracusans immediately and do not build a wall, but if they had, the help the Syracusans called in would have been less effective.

The parallels of course are not exact in every case, but they need not be in order for Thucydides to intend for the one to be read against the other. They help, I suggest, to explain the selective nature of the retrospection of 7.42.3. Important for our purposes is that the delay with which Nikias is charged in 7.42.3 is in other parts of the narrative directly connected to the problem of financial and other resources.[63] These parallels illuminate the

62. This passage has aroused great controversy over whether the opinion expressed is Thucydides' or Demosthenes'; see Dover, *HCT* 4, ad loc. for general discussion of the problems, which chiefly concern inconsistencies with the earlier narrative, since it omits any reference to Lamachos, to wintering at Naxos as well as at Catana, and to the initial victory. Most scholars seem to agree that the view expressed is Thucydides': e.g., Gomme, *HCT* 2: 196; Donini 1964; de Maele 1971, 25; Hunter 1973, 96; Hornblower 1994a, 134–35; Cawkwell 1997, 18, chiefly because of the use of the indicative in the parenthesis; moreover, as Dover notes, the inclusion of a *gar* clause in the midst of Demosthenes' reflections and in the course of Perikles' indirect speech in 2.13, in which Thucydides steps in to gloss a statement, leaves open the possibility that when he wants to provide elaboration or exegesis he will choose to present a speech in *oratio obliqua,* or, in this case, presenting Demosthenes' state of thinking rather than his spoken proposal. There is continuing disagreement over the extent to which Thucydides' and Demosthenes' views overlap, and the degree and significance of inconsistency between Thucydides' narrative of the winter of 415/14 and 2.65.11: e.g., Schneider 1974, 56; Dover 1988 [1981]; Connor 1984, 192 n. 19; Rood 1998, 67–68 n. 21; 159–73. Kopff's proposal (1976a, b) that the passage is an interpolation by Philistos has not won favor because of the weakness of its premise: i.e., internal inconsistency as justification to posit interpolation; cf. Dickie's rebuttal (1976); Andrewes, *HCT* 5: 425 n. 1; it is not even mentioned as a possibility by Maurer (1995). As Hornblower (1994a, 134–35) rightly notes, agreeing with Pelling, that the view is Thucydides' does not exclude it also being that of Demosthenes.

63. Relevant also is Thucydides' presentation of Nikias' thinking at the point in the narrative when Nikias decides to remain inactive: "it did not seem possible to carry on the war" un-

extent to which the historian is attuned in the Sicilian narrative to the relationship of the absence of adequate resources from home, delaying, and military success—the very issues and criteria he brings to bear in the analysis of the Greeks at Troy.

Meanwhile Hermokrates was now able to persuade his fellow Syracusans to prepare for war as he advised, and in accordance with his proposals, the Syracusans sent to Corinth and Sparta to ask for allies and to request that the Spartans engage in their war with the Athenians in earnest. That same winter, both Syracusans and Athenians went to Camarina, the Athenians hoping to get aid from them, and the Syracusans hoping to prejudice the Camarineans against the Athenians, and so the speeches of Hermokrates and Euphemos follow. The result was that the Camarineans decided not to support either side (6.88). The Athenians then proceeded to try to win over the Sicels, having more success with those in the interior, from whom they procured grain, and from some of them, Thucydides notes, "money, too" (καὶ εἰσὶν οἳ καὶ χρήματα, 88.4).[64] Meanwhile they also sent to Carthage, in the hope of help and friendship, and to the Egestans and the Sicels for horses; they planned the walling of Syracuse.

Thucydides continues to exploit the link with Troy as the narrative continues to explore the relationship between home resources and the expedition in Sicily. The historian notes the arrival of the Athenian trireme from Sicily to Athens requesting reinforcements: "And the trireme of the Athenians came from Sicily, which the generals had dispatched for the purpose of requesting money and cavalry. And the Athenians upon hearing the request voted to send the support for the army and cavalry" (6.93.4). Thucydides reiterates the specific request for "money and cavalry" (χρήματα καὶ ἱππέας) first noted in 6.71. The Athenian response that he records is striking: the generals in Sicily request *chremata;* but Thucydides tells us that the assembly voted to send *trophe.* The unusual nature of the word *trophe* here has not gone unnoticed;[65] Dover comments that *trophe* means "money for the purchase of food, as commonly."[66] W. K. Pritchett argues that Thucydides uses the terms *chremata, trophe,* and *misthos* indiscriminately as synonyms.[67] Yet, while the use of the definite article—"*the* support" (τὴν τροφήν)—shows that Thucydides intends us to understand that the Athenians were making a kind of equivalence, it does not follow that he regarded

til further reinforcements arrived (6.71.2); is this Thucydides' way of implying that it would have been possible?

64. I take that comment as a suggestion that the Athenians were not expecting financial support.

65. E.g., Figueira 1998, 262.

66. Dover 1965 ad loc.

67. Pritchett 1971, 3–6.

chremata and *trophe* as identical in composition and quantity. Thucydides uses the term *trophe* infrequently; indeed, up to this point in the work he has used it in the sense of "money for food" in five passages (a total of six times).[68]

I shall return to this issue below,[69] but for our purposes here, there is one crucial point to appreciate. The rarity of the word *trophe* hitherto in the *History* speaks to its deliberateness when it is used. I suggest that its occurrence here in 6.93, in conjunction with *chremata,* is intended to evoke Thucydides' analysis of the problems at Troy, in which he uses *trophe* twice in a passage whose concern is the *achrematia* of the Greeks.[70] In that passage, *achrematia* is the general condition of lacking money, which could be put to use for, among other purposes, *trophe,* the specific requirement of the men at Troy. Thus while *trophe* is *chrema, chrema* is not necessarily *trophe,* though it may include it.[71] In short, the words are not synonyms.

If the use of *trophe* is such a prompt, what is the point of the comparison here? The Athenians in Sicily have already had proved the difficulty of provisioning and of getting money from their allies in Sicily. It is therefore imperative that their fellow citizens at home support the force abroad fully. By explicitly noting that in response to a request for *chremata* the Athenians send *trophe,* Thucydides is, I propose, alerting the reader to the insufficiency of the home support: they send money only for food, not for the broader requirements of the navy, army, and cavalry abroad.

A conspicuous feature of the narrative of books 6 and 7 is the manner in which Thucydides lets the reader learn details about the financial and other support for the force and the extent to which he is forthcoming with specific details about the resources the Athenians are sending from home. An example examined in chapter 1 is the unfolding of the Egestan deception, in which Thucydides uses foreshadowing, narrative delay, and drops crumbs of details as the narrative proceeds to keep the reader focused on the question of whether the promised money exists, and then finally confirms that it does not. Similarly, the parceling out of details about the requests for, votes on, and dispatch and arrival of reinforcements from Athens here continues to heighten narrative tension over the central issue of the financing and provisioning of the expedition. Instead of conveying information in one place, he staggers the details so the reader is kept in sus-

68. 1.11.1 (twice), 2; 4.83.6; 6.34.4, 47.

69. See the appendix on the frequency of the term and its meaning in book 8.

70. On his usage of *trophe* and *misthos* in the Trojan War analysis, see also *Money,* 29–30.

71. See also 6.47.1 (contra Pritchett 1971, 4–5; Loomis 1998, 33), in which Nikias proposes that the Athenians request from the Egestans *chremata* for the whole army, but if not, at least *trophe* for the sixty ships. Here Thucydides is clearly contrasting *chremata* and *trophe,* but the passage also may be suggestive of Troy.

pense and keeps asking: What are the Athenians sending? Will it be enough? Accordingly, Thucydides first notes the relative incapacitation of the Athenians in Sicily, who needed to wait until money and cavalry could be sent from home; but he does not record the dispatch of the request. He next notes the arrival of the ship carrying the request for "money and cavalry" and the Athenians' vote of "*trophe* and cavalry" but does not specify the amount and numbers to be sent. Only when the ships arrive in Sicily does he give precise information: "250 horsemen with their equipment but without their horses, which were to be procured on the spot, 300 archers and 300 talents of silver" (6.94.4). Thucydides thus emphasizes the insufficiency of support by contrasting the request with the response, which was less than requested and would require the Athenians to use money for *trophe* on purchasing horses. In another piece of information provided in a staggered order in the narrative, Thucydides notes that the Athenians would have to procure mounts for the horsemen from the area, but waits to relate the result. As it turns out, the Egestans and Catanians supplied horses, and the Athenians purchased some as well (6.98); given the difficulties getting support from locals, evidenced most spectacularly by the Egestans, those at home could not have predicted any success.

The effect of Thucydides' decision to release these vital pieces of information piecemeal is threefold. First, it keeps readers focused on the financial aspect more than might otherwise have been the case; second, coming on the heels of the Egestan deception as presented by Thucydides, it raises questions about whether the money will be enough and whether correct decisions have been made; third, it puts the audience in the position of the force in Sicily anxiously awaiting the arrival of the ships then receiving only enough money for food and horsemen (with their equipment, he explicitly notes)—and a mere 250 of them at that—with no horses in sight. The implication is that the Athenians at home are inadequately supporting the expedition. Three hundred talents is not an inconsiderable amount per se; considering the number of men in the navy, land forces, and cavalry and the whole summer lying ahead, its impressiveness diminishes.

A rough estimate of the numbers in the field (including horses) and its relationship to the money the Athenians sent, 300 talents, supports the point. It suggests that, at the figure of one-half drachma per day (half of what the men were supposed to receive), the expedition could be fed for about four months.[72] While that might sound like an adequate amount, the

72. The initial force comprised 134 triremes (170 men), 2 pentekonters (100 men), 5,100 infantry, 480 archers, 700 slingers, and 30 horse (=60 mouths) (6.43); some unknown number died in the first battle (6.69–70); local aid was requested (6.88), but quantities are unknown; the reinforcements added 250 horsemen, who would have to obtain horses (=500 mouths), and 30 mounted archers (=60 mouths). This brings a total of 30,000 to feed; 1 talent would

men would be receiving only one-half of their expected pay (1 drachma a day), and the amount of money did not take into account anything unanticipated, such as additional mouths to feed or ships to repair, not to mention the purchase of horses, that would have to come out of this figure. And there are two other crucial points to appreciate. First, circumstances—the Egestans' failure to provide what they promised, the people of Rhegion's refusal to help—had already made abundantly clear that local financial support, provisions, and additional allies had to be considered unreliable. That local support was occasionally forthcoming or successfully coerced (cf. 6.88, 98) does not weaken the point. Second, it is important to remember the distance from home, and accordingly the length of time it would take for further reinforcements to be sent.

To continue with the narrative, the armament is newly strengthened, now with the reinforcements from Athens supplemented by three hundred additional cavalry from Egesta, and about one hundred from the Sicels, Naxians, and others (6.98.1).[73] Thucydides presents the Athenians as now working vigorously against the Syracusans. But at the same time we learn that Nikias was ill (102), and that Gylippos had finally reached Italy, after delaying because he thought that the Athenians had already completely invested Syracuse; meanwhile Nikias, who heard of his arrival, thought little of its threat and did nothing. Moreover, the inadequacy of money and other resources from Athens emerges in the narrative, as Thucydides notes the need for further provisions from allies in Sicily that summer in 414, and relates a letter written by Nikias at the end of the summer to the Athenians at home addressing precisely their deficiency.

The Athenians had had the advantage during the summer of 414. But with the arrival of the Spartans and Corinthians, they became increasingly hard pressed. As Thucydides tells it, Nikias had sent home frequent reports of the situation, but since by the end of the summer he thought that they were nearing a desperate state, he wrote a letter, instead of trusting his report to oral transmission (7.10). Thucydides produces the contents of the letter, in the characteristic way he has given out information elsewhere, not immediately, but, in this case, when it is heard.

Not surprisingly the focus of Nikias' concerns is resources (human and

---

support at this subsistence level 12,000 men a day, or 2.5 talents for the whole, and this number for four months. Obviously there are many unknowns (e.g., whether the cavalry helped to support themselves, cost of food, deaths, and additions, purchase price of horses in Sicily), but this estimate provides a ballpark figure.

73. Meanwhile in Greece, Thucydides notes (6.95.1), the Argives invaded the Thyreatid on the Argive/Lakedaimonian border and took booty that, Thucydides bothers to tell us, was sold for no less than 25 talents, a detail that, as elsewhere, reflects his interest in money, and another example of his concern to find out these kinds of details where possible.

material) and their present inadequacy. In sharp contrast to a year earlier when all three generals had discovered that their material supplies were insufficient, and advocated strategies of obtaining them from Sicily rather than from home, now Nikias makes clear the necessity—rather than simple desirability—of using resources from home, citing the present impossibility of acquiring men, goods, and money from Sicily. This again recalls Thucydides' counterfactual hypothesis in 1.11.2: "Had they brought sufficient *trophe* they would easily have conquered."

Nikias underscores the extent of the Athenians' distress by employing financial metaphors to talk about human resources: in 7.11.3, using the verb ἀπαναλίσκω, "to spend utterly," he notes that the Athenian force cannot even be deployed for offensive purposes, since a good part of it "was utterly spent" (or "completely consumed") in the defense of the walls. The metaphor emphasizes that even what the Athenians have to "spend" in Sicily—human "wealth"—is not useful for military success, since it must be spent in defense, not offense, but also that the lack of financial resources has a human cost.[74] In other words, the Athenians are unable to use their resources properly in the way in which they were intended, and are therefore wasteful of what they do have. In 14.2, Nikias again uses the same verb to refer to men, this time as he explains that the Athenians are forced to replenish the crews that have been "utterly spent" from what they brought with them from home, unable to recruit additional ones from outside their ranks. Indeed, Nikias' comments reflect the condition not of an invading force but of the invaded one. As he puts it, the besiegers—the Athenians—have become the besieged. He then notes that the Syracusans are aware that the ship hulls are rotting because they have been in the water for so long, and that the crew is wasting, thus compromising the superiority of the Athenian navy. He gives further details regarding the deterioration of the navy—their real strength[75]—countered not only by the Syracusans' strength in cavalry, but also by their growing efficiency at sea. He concludes by assuring them that against the original force, they were certainly not contemptible, but now that the enemy has been reinforced to a great extent, the Athenian side was in grave trouble. Nikias then asks to be relieved of his command, because of illness, or to have the whole force recalled or to have another fleet and army sent out as numerous as that sent out originally, along with "a great deal of money" (χρήματα μὴ ὀλίγα, 7.15.1).

After they heard the contents of the letter, the Athenians refused to accept Nikias' resignation and instead voted to send two generals, Menander

74. See 7.30.3, and chap. 3, p. 142 with n. 82, below.

75. Cf. his comment in 6.21.1, that the navy would not win the day, now a self-fulfilling prophecy, and ironic, because it is the Syracusans' navy that is now threatening the Athenian navy.

and Euthydemos, to Nikias immediately until the arrival of new colleagues, who were to be Demosthenes and Eurymedon. Eurymedon was sent off at once with ten ships and 120 talents of silver, and was to say that reinforcements were coming (7.16); Demosthenes stayed behind to make preparations, sending to the allies for troops and collecting money, ships, and hoplites at home; they would leave at the beginning of spring.[76] And so in early spring, right at the time the Spartans invaded Attica to fortify Dekeleia, Demosthenes left for Sicily with sixty ships, twelve hundred Athenian hoplites, and allied contingents.[77]

For our purposes, what is important about this part of the narrative is Nikias' insistence that even without the anticipated additions to the enemy side, the Athenians' resources were insufficient, despite what had been sent earlier and provided by allies (6.94.3, 98, 103.2). His comments also reveal that the Athenians' strategy abroad was still apparently based on local provisioning. It is also interesting that Thucydides fails to mention how much money the Athenians sent with Demosthenes, only noting the 120 talents accompanying the advance mission of Eurymedon. If there is any significance to be ascribed to this omission, it will be in connection with the information Thucydides provides about the Athenian financing of the expedition generally; he omits specific information to highlight insufficiency. Because their resources were inadequate, the Athenians were forced to delay and remain inactive, or attempt (unsuccessfully) to get money and provisions locally.[78]

Homer, Herodotos, and Thucydides

By following the narrative of the Sicilian expedition, I have noted the ways in which Thucydides' treatment of the financing of the expedition is closely linked to his larger interpretation of the inadequacy of funding from home, when the resources were there and could have been used, as an explanation for failure, and have suggested that his interpretation guided his analysis of the Greeks at Troy.[79] Thucydides forges two final links between Troy and

76. Ellis (1979, 54) misleadingly implies that the Athenians failed to respond efficiently to Nikias' request for reinforcements.

77. The effect of the juxtaposition of the "second war" being prepared for in Dekeleia, at the moment that the city sends away a large force to Sicily, is not lost on the reader.

78. This recalls not only the Greeks at Troy, but Perikles' comments at the beginning of the war about the Spartans' handicap in the war: their absence of money will result in delays (1.142.1). Now the Athenians are like the Spartans. On this reversal, see Rawlings 1981, 149–51, and on reversals more generally, see below, p. 114, and chap. 4, pp. 166–72.

79. I suggest the possibility that Thucydides thought the Greeks could have brought more *chremata* to Troy. Certainly Thucydides stresses Agamemnon's (inherited) wealth. Agamemnon led the expedition, in his view, "because he was preeminent in power and not because the suitors of Helen were bound by the oaths of Tyndareos. The most credible of Peloponnesian oral

Sicily at the climax of his narrative of the expedition; these also suggest that Thucydides was guided by the Sicilian expedition—though in this case not exclusively—to write the Trojan War analysis as he did. The most prominent part of the beginning of the description of the battle in the harbor at Syracuse is the catalogue of allies and enemies, whose purpose is to support Thucydides' statement that "this was the largest assemblage of peoples before a single city, if we except the total of combatants in the war" (7.56.4). He states that those participating on either side did so "not more out of any issue of right, nor because of kinship, but more so according to the circumstances relevant for each participant, either because of advantage or compulsion" (7.57.1). Later on, in relating the contingents who were not forced to participate, he makes a point of noting that hatred of Sparta more than alliance with Athens led the Argives to fight on the Athenian side.[80] As Connor observes, the unusual nature of this catalogue stems from the inclusion of the motives of the combatants. Thucydides uses the catalogue, a conventional and traditional form of narrative, to demonstrate "the dissolution of old relationships and the triumph of advantage and profit over traditional ties and loyalties."[81]

The catalogue reveals the size of the contingent on Athens' side (as well as Thucydides' wish to stress the size) and the motives of the Athenians' allies: they accompanied the Athenians on this great expedition not because of bonds of loyalty or kinship, but chiefly because of their power, or because of factors like fear. This detail is relevant to the historian's explanation of why the Greeks followed Agamemnon to Troy: it was not so much because they were bound by oath, and therefore loyalty, but because of Agamemnon's *dunamis* (1.9.1). Thucydides returns to this point, rephrasing and expanding on it in 1.9.3, significantly producing his own opinion: in his view (*moi dokei*), Agamemnon's (inherited) wealth, and a navy far stronger than those of his contemporaries, suggested that fear (*phobos*) was as compelling a factor as favor (*charis*) in explaining Agamemnon's command of the expedition. This conception fits into a broader pattern in the work in which Thucydides contests the strengths of traditional bonds elsewhere, most notably in his discussion of the development of the power of the Athenians in

---

tradition holds that Pelops first acquired power because of his great financial resources, which he brought with him from Asia to needy men" (1.9.2); "and Agamemnon inherited this wealth and had a more powerful navy than others" (1.9.3). For Agamemnon's wealth, cf. also Ais. *Ag.* 1638–639; cf. *Cho.* 135, 301; *Eum.* 757–58. Thucydides, I argue below, is also thinking about Agamemnon's wealth in *Iliad* 9 in relation to Nikias' at the end of book 7; see below, chap. 4, pp. 178–80.

80. Cf. Engeman (1974, 76–77), who argues for a close relationship between the motives attributed to the Arcadians and 1.10.3.

81. Connor 1984, 196; cf. Solmsen (1975, 217), who sees a tragic function of the catalogue at this point in the narrative and cites earlier discussions of the placement of the catalogue.

the Pentekontaetia, but its occurrence here in the description of the motivations of the participants before the great battle of Syracuse, and the manner of its presentation, strongly evoke the prior narrative about Troy, in a way that is related to Thucydides' interest in power.

As noted earlier, scholars have noticed the reversals that take place in the account of the Sicilian expedition. One such reversal may be connected to Thucydides' interest in keeping the Trojan War in the reader's mind at the end of book 7. When he relates the contingents on both sides before the final battle, he notes that the Syracusans provided the greatest number of ships on their side, "being the greatest and with the most to lose" (7.58.4); he is silent on the proportion of Athenian to allied ships, though it is clear that the Athenians too supplied the greatest number in their naval contingent. I suggest that he does this to shift the reader's focus, at this final stage, away from comparisons between the Athenians and the Greeks at Troy to comparisons between the Syracusans and Agamemnon, and, conversely, the Athenians and the Trojans. Indeed, as mentioned above, Thucydides explicitly makes the point in analyzing Agamemnon's power as leader of the Greek expedition that he had a greater number of ships than his contemporaries, and this point, like that concerning the relationship of size to resources examined above, suggests that another situation is prompting him to make such a deduction.

Thucydides' nod to Herodotos at the close of the narrative of the expedition may relate to this shift in focus as well. At the end of his moving description of the Athenians' fate, Thucydides famously writes: "[The Athenians] were beaten at all points and altogether; all that they suffered was great; they were destroyed, as the saying goes, with a total destruction, their fleet, their army—everything was destroyed, and few out of many returned home" (7.87.6, trans. Crawley). As N. Marinatos Kopff and Hunter Rawlings have shown, following a passing mention by Hermann Strasburger, Thucydides' term for "total destruction," πανωλεθρία, resonates with Herodotos, who uses the word to refer to the fall of Troy.[82]

Dover objected to the correspondence on the grounds of τὸ λεγόμενον, but his objection seems also to have been based on the belief that Thucyd-

82. Hdt. 2.120.5. Against Dover, *HCT* 4, ad loc.: Strasburger 1968, 529 n. 83; and Marinatos Kopff and Rawlings (1978, 332–33, n. 2), who argue that τὸ λεγόμενον is referring to a direct quotation, not to the alternative, a common saying. It seems to me likely that even if the context reflects a common expression, it is derived from the story of the Trojan War (though not from the *Iliad*) and celebrated in writing first by Herodotos. Marinatos Kopff and Rawlings also argue that Thucydides is importing the theological layer embedded in the term. See also Connor (1984, 208, n. 57), who follows Marinatos Kopff and Rawlings except to moderate their conclusions on the divine implications; Rood 1999, 163. See also Hornblower 1996, 145 with additional bibliography.

ides would surely have taken care to distance himself from Herodotean theology.[83] This view, however, forces the historian into an intertextual straitjacket. As we have seen here, Thucydides—like other authors making use of their predecessors—will use an allusion or an intertextual strategy for a variety of reasons, by no means necessarily intending simply to import wholesale the meaning and context of the original. Indeed, I would go farther and suggest that as we have seen Thucydides operating here, an aim of his intertextual and allusive strategies is precisely to highlight contrast, by "thinking with" another text. In this case, Thucydides can emphasize the utter destruction through the use of *panolethria,* and also once again evoke Troy, but differently. Specifically, the narrative moves the reader's attention from the previous analogies with Troy, which have paralleled the *Greek* side. Since the Greeks eventually won—and accordingly that focus of his attention is no longer viable—he exploits the fact that his readers will have been thinking of Troy to evoke now the Trojans, the losers who suffered *panolethria,*[84] accomplishing this also through the concentration of Homeric word usage at the end of book 7.[85] Certainly at this stage of the narrative Thucydides would not have feared that his readers would infer that he was now imputing divine causation to the Athenian disaster in Sicily, which would jar if not subvert not only the entire narrative of the expedition, but also the *History* as a whole.[86]

As we have seen, there is ample evidence to support Hunter's suggestion that Thucydides' analysis of the Trojan War was based on his view of the difficulties encountered by the Athenians in Sicily. In key respects the Sicilian narrative mirrors 1.11 but with ironic twists and inversions that allow Thucydides to criticize the Athenians. The unequivocal message Thucydides sends in 1.11 is that those who embark on major foreign expeditions need to bring the money they will need with them from home. His narrative utterly undermines the usefulness, and deepens the irony, of the *polla talanta* carried off to foreign shores.

2.65.11 AND THE NARRATIVE OF THE SICILIAN EXPEDITION

Reading the narrative of the Sicilian expedition against the analysis of the Trojan War may also afford insight into a highly controversial passage in the

83. *HCT* 4, ad loc.

84. So Mackie 1996, 113.

85. Allison 1997a.

86. At the same time, lurking in the background intriguingly may be Nikias' final speech to his men, in which he hopes for mercy from the gods (7.77). The use of the word *panolethria* would then have an even more richly nuanced flavor, by no means implying divine causation governing the expedition, but representing instead a rather sly intratextual answer to such fruitless thinking.

History: 2.65.11. Toward the end of his assessment of Perikles and his successors, Thucydides renders the following opinion about the mistakes the city made under the men who became leaders after Perikles' death: "There were many mistakes made, as happens in a great city that possesses an *arche,* and in particular, the Sicilian expedition, which was less an error in judgment concerning those whom they were attacking, than the fact that those at home did not make advantageous decisions for those on the expedition; instead, they made the waging of the campaign too blunt because of their private quarrels over the leadership of the *demos,* and threw the city into civil discord" (2.65.11). This sentence has elicited considerable controversy over two related issues, the translation and meaning of part of the sentence itself and its relationship to the actual narrative of the expedition, with scholarship divided over the question of whether the comment is in conflict or essential agreement with the narrative of books 6 and 7.[87]

The part of the sentence regarded as problematic describes the primary error in judgment: ὅσον οἱ ἐκπέμψαντες οὐ τὰ πρόσφορα τοῖς οἰχομένοις ἐπιγιγνώσκοντες. The difficulty lies in the translation and meaning of τὰ πρόσφορα. Literally "the suitable," or "fitting things" —that is, the appropriate, or "the advantageous things"—it has been taken by some scholars to mean, with the rest of the clause, that those at home failed to send the proper support to those in the field. Others have objected to this translation on the grounds of its inconsistency if not contradiction of the narrative of the expedition. So, for example, Gomme observes: "The reasons [Thucydides] gives in 2.65.11 . . . are not borne out by his narrative."[88] The Athenians, as H. D. Westlake and others point out, respond quickly with support.[89] The alternative has been to take *ta prosphora* almost as cognate with *epigignoskontes,* thus "make unadvantageous decisions"; and the primary, for many, sole decision to which Thucydides is alluding in this rendering is the recall of Alkibiades.[90]

Yet, if Thucydides had meant Alkibiades above all, why express this in

87. In conflict: e.g., Gomme 1951; 1956 ad loc.; Kagan 1981, 158; Buck 1988; Rhodes 1988, 245 ("the most serious inconsistency in Thucydides' *History*"); Bloedow 1992, 145. No contradiction: e.g., de Romilly 1963, 209 (correspondence but not "absolute coherence"); Westlake 1969, 161–73; Thompson 1971b; de Maele 1971; Rawlings 1981, 152 n. 40; Connor 1984, 158, n. 2; Erbse 1989b, 83–92; Luginbill 1997 (based on an unpersuasive grammatical reworking of πρὸς οὓς ἐπῆσαν in the first part of the clause); Rood 1998, 159–82; see also, for general discussion, Andrewes, *HCT* 5: 423–27.

88. Gomme 1951, 72.

89. Ibid.; Westlake 1969, 168; Hornblower 1991a, ad loc.; Gribble 1999, 178.

90. E.g., Hatzfeld 1940, 199–200; Brunt 1952, 60; Gomme 1951, 70–72; von Fritz 1967, 812; Liebeschuetz 1968b; Westlake 1969; de Maele 1971; Orwin 1994, 119; Cawkwell 1997, 76–77; Gribble 1999, 178.

such an opaque and coded way? Especially when he is completely explicit about the damage the recall of Alkibiades did to the city (6.15), there is no need to be vague or coy here. On the other hand, what about the first possibility, that he is referring to, or at least including, the support given those in the field by the Athenians at home subsequent to the departure of the fleet in 415? As noted, this possibility was discounted chiefly because of the view that the Athenians *did* support those in the field adequately, but if my arguments above are valid, Thucydides implies that they did not. Of the various ways in which he does so, recall Alkibiades' claim that the Athenians intended to obtain money and grain in Sicily (6.90.4). The full context of the comment in 2.65.11 is crucial. Thucydides elaborates on the consequence of *ou ta prosphora epigignoskontes:* they made the actual waging of war less effective, "blunter" (*amblutera*). This strongly suggests that Thucydides may well have been thinking primarily of the financial and military support given to the campaign. It is true that the Athenians do apparently respond expeditiously to the request for further resources (though it is certainly arguable whether Demosthenes sailed to Sicily as quickly as he could have in the summer of 413, months after Nikias had described the situation as desperate); but, as I argued above, his narrative strongly suggests that the Athenians did not adequately support the expedition with money (and provisioning generally).

It is important to keep in mind, as has been noted, that Thucydides is not denying in 2.65.11 that the expedition *was* a mistake in judgment about the enemy they were attacking.[91] Indeed, the formulation οὐ τοσοῦτον . . . ὅσον, because it is entirely relative, allows for the possibility that he saw the expedition as a huge mistake but was elevating to even greater prominence the explanation that the Athenians failed to support the force abroad adequately. On this understanding, then, it was bad enough that the Athenians embarked on such a misguided expedition; but it was even worse that, having done so, they failed to vote what was necessary to increase the chance of success, namely, *periousia chrematon.* There is, then, no inconsistency between the judgment in 2.65.11 and the narrative of books 6 and 7, and no reason to think that they were written at different times.[92]

It may also be implicit in 2.65, however, that some Athenians thought that they should have funneled more resources into the expedition, after it had been ascertained that local support would be unreliable. We may fill out Thucydides' comment about the internal dissension in Athens and speculate that though the fiscal conservatives won, others had argued that

91. Westlake 1969, 166; Hunter 1973, 139 with n. 20; Erbse 1989b, 83–84; Cawkwell 1997, 76; Rood 1998, 161 n. 8.

92. As Gomme (1951 and *HCT* 2, ad loc.) insisted.

the expedition should be supported more vigorously; Thucydides puts this in terms of rivalry over the leadership of the demos.

The end result was a failure, first, to make a strong and overwhelming first strike, and, second, once a substantial force was in the field, to make sure it was supported to the necessary extent. Contrast Thucydides' description of the Athenians' attack on Samos in 440. It is significant that this account is one of the few in which Perikles appears in the Pentekontaetia, and contains the most detail. The Athenians embarked on an overseas expedition, to the other side of the Aegean, with 60 ships; they were so successful in the initial siege, reinforced by 65 ships, that Perikles was able to divert 60 ships to Karia (to await a Phoenician fleet), which then returned, the fleet further reinforced by 90 ships (1.116–17); after a nine-month seige, Samos was reduced. In short, Perikles and his fellow generals did what was necessary to insure military success: they spent heavily and quickly.[93] The lesson is unmistakable: make an overwhelming and effective first strike, back it up as soon as necessary, not at the last moment, with amply supported reinforcements, and success will follow. It is a brief lesson, but one that makes the point elegantly, and simply.

CONCLUSION

An author enhances meaning by recalling and presupposing other texts. Thucydides' approach is consonant with his more general method in fostering historical interpretations and is fundamentally implicit in nature. He tends to make points, drive home lessons, and render and encourage judgments implicitly rather than explicitly, to let the inference or conclusion emerge from the narrative. Intertextual and intratextual strategies are valuable tools in this regard, allowing him to cast an interpretation more forcefully (as well as artfully) through more subtle patterning of his narrative on and against Herodotos, Homer, and his earlier analyses. From the reasons for becoming involved in Sicily to the eventual disaster, resonances with the Ionian revolt (not to mention the Persian Wars and references to the Trojan War in Herodotos) and the Trojan analysis encourage the conclusion that the Athenians are not only making a huge mistake but are also repeating mistakes from the past.

Pelling comments (on intertextuality in general): "Recurrence is crucial, and intertextuality is therefore crucial: in reading one historian we identify story-patterns which have occurred elsewhere."[94] Thucydides' use of He-

93. From *IG* I^3 363 we know that the Athenians spent some 1,400 talents in this brief period.

94. Pelling 1999, 347.

rodotos has a serious purpose that fits into his larger interpretation of the patterns of history. He need not, and does not want to, force events into a rigid, identical framework. Rather, it is his design to show similarities in order to reveal the truth of his famous statement in 1.22.4 that future events will bear similarities to past events, given human nature (for his statement, see the quotation at the beginning of this chapter). Indeed, I suggest that Thucydides' intertextual approach has a crucial methodological function and purpose: by mapping events of the past onto contemporary events he enables the reader to think about them together, in order to draw conclusions about history, and thereby the utility of Thucydides' *History;* in this way the reader gains the fullest knowledge and understands the truth (τὸ σαφές, 1.22.4).[95]

I have argued that the Ionian revolt provides a thematic structure in which to highlight ignorance, stupidity, deception, and the serious consequences of decisions based on ulterior, far-reaching motives; it was an apposite model for failure. In turn, the Trojan analysis illuminates Thucydides' historiographical agenda in writing about the financial underpinnings of the Sicilian expedition and the problems caused by the Athenians' decisions at home about financing the campaign; conversely, we can more easily understand why the historian focused on the financing of the Trojan War to the exclusion of all other details about it. Moreover, the results of our examination cast light on 2.65.11 and have allowed a reading of the latter which both does justice to the Greek and demonstrates its consistency with the Sicilian narrative.

The discussion in these first two chapters should already have made clear Thucydides' acute interest in the financing of the expedition; thus when the historian fails to mention specific details about the financing of the expedition we can be confident that the omission is intentional, not a reflection of lack of interest. But the nature of Thucydides' interest is what is most intriguing. His presentation of financial details, whether specific or vague, is deliberate and serves a historiographical purpose. When we come to categorize the appearances of financial details (and the provisioning of the armada in general), it is significant that Thucydides gives more attention to the attempts to finance and provision the force locally than to financing coming from Athens once the expedition is under way. In fact, Thucydides records money sent out from Athens twice in the entire account from the time that the Athenians arrive in Sicily, to a total of 420 talents; yet the Athenians undeniably received more. Again, Thucydides is parsimonious with details not because of lack of knowledge or interest; quite the contrary, the

95. Cf. *Anc. Med.* 2: "Full discovery will be made if someone is competent and conducts his research knowing the discoveries already made."

narrative is deliberately constructed to present the Athenians as inadequately reinforcing the land and naval force in Sicily. As we shall see in the next chapter, as the narrative proceeds, Thucydides both continues to develop some of the themes explored thus far and employs additional narrative techniques to expose the danger in the Athenians' financial decisions and handling of their resources.

CHAPTER THREE

Money, Disease, and Moral Responsibility

The Economic Digression and the Massacre at Mykalessos, 7.27–30

The section of the *History* that follows Nikias' letter and the Athenians' decision to send reinforcements to Sicily under Demosthenes and Eurymedon (7.12–16) builds on a theme addressed in chapter 1—namely, the relationship between money and the passions. I shall argue in this chapter that Thucydides continues to develop a critique of the Athenians' decisions about their monetary wealth, using the metaphor of disease in order to highlight, first, the emotional and psychological context in which the Athenians made decisions of a financial and economic nature and, second, the moral responsibility they held for the consequences of those decisions; his narrative strategies are put to a serious purpose, to link money/finance and human life.[1]

To pick up the narrative: at the beginning of the spring of 413, the Spartans invaded Attica and built a fort at Dekeleia (7.19); at that very time Demosthenes left for Sicily (7.20), but without his full complement of reinforcements, as we learn in 7.29, for only in the summer did thirteen hundred Thracian mercenaries, who had been intended for the Sicilian expedition, arrive in Athens. Rather than use them in Attica, the Athenians decided to send them home, "since," as Thucydides puts it, "to keep them for the Dekeleian war appeared extravagant; for each received a drachma a day" (7.27.2). There follows a lengthy excursus on the combined economic effects of Dekeleia and the Sicilian expedition (7.27–28), followed by the singular account of the Thracian rampage in Mykalessos (7.29).

Each part of this section of the narrative raises questions about the rea-

1. Much of this chapter appears in Kallet 1999 (specific acknowledgements to individuals from whose comments I benefited in writing the article may be found there), but the treatment here differs in the order of presentation and contains fuller discussion and bibliography.

son for its inclusion: the late arrival of the Thracians and the subsequent massacre at Mykalessos were events unarguably trivial to the course and outcome of the Sicilian expedition and the war; the economic digression concerns a historical process that could have been related at various points in the narrative. Why, then, does Thucydides pause in the midst of what is arguably the most unified, self-contained narrative of the whole work, the Sicilian expedition,[2] to dwell at such length and in such detail on the Thracians and on Athens' fiscal and economic condition? It is immediately clear that we are at a historiographically significant point in the narrative, and that Athens' financial and economic resources form a central part of what Thucydides wants to say about the Athenians.

First, let us consider the placement of the two-part digression. Much of the substance of 7.27–28 concerns, as mentioned, a gradual process of fiscal and economic deterioration that Thucydides could have placed anywhere in the narrative following the Spartans' arrival in Dekeleia (7.19). But it is in fact particularly necessary here, in order to explain his comment that "it appeared extravagant to keep the Thracians in Attica for the Dekeleian war."[3] The digression, however, goes beyond a narrow aim of providing supporting information to explain why the Athenians judged the Thracian mercenaries too costly to use; its purpose is also to paint a psychological portrait of the Athenians in order both to impugn critical financial decisions they made at the time and to underscore the grave human consequences that attended upon them.

Thucydides spells out the consequences dramatically and vividly in what follows, the massacre at Mykalessos. Most scholars would not adhere to Eduard Schwartz's view that the financial digression is irrelevant to the representation of the Thracians' savagery;[4] as Donald Kagan has noted, Athens' financial distress indirectly led to this enormity.[5] Nevertheless, the two sections have usually been examined separately, the financial digression by historians of the Athenian empire and finance[6] or by Thucydidean scholars

2. Finley 1967, 126.

3. Schadewaldt 1929, 79. The Athenians must have summoned the Thracians before the Spartans fortified Dekeleia, for Thucydides notes the simultaneity of Demosthenes' departure for Sicily and the Spartan invasion of Attica and fortification (7.19). It is clear, then, that the issue was not the acceptability of using the Thracians in Sicily and not at home per se, but rather that when the decision had been made to use the mercenaries, the Athenians had no idea that they would be facing the fortification of Dekeleia. On the other hand, there is a sense that the Athenians are privileging the expedition in Sicily over the need to defend themselves against the Spartans at home.

4. Schwartz 1919, 202. See Dover's comment in *HCT* 4: 404.

5. Kagan 1981, 293.

6. E.g., Böckh 1842, 325, 401–2; Cavaignac 1908, 147–48; Meiggs 1972, 369; Finley 1982, 55.

looking at the passage historiographically as one distinct from 7.29,[7] and the dramatic and shocking narrative of the massacre by Thucydidean scholars exploring its emotional resonances in the *History*.[8] There are, however, strong grounds for reading the sections together. Connor has laid out elegantly the ring composition linking the two sections,[9] but we can go even farther: in particular, a degree of detail in each not otherwise warranted by the narrative, a framing device, and the shared use of a vocabulary common in the description of disease all make clear that Thucydides was intentionally linking the two sections. By this linkage Thucydides not only creates a connection between Athenian public finance and human suffering but also develops themes central to the work as a whole: namely, those of moral responsibility, human nature, the conflict between reason and passion, and the nexus of finances, leadership, and military power. I want first to examine chapters 27–28 in detail in order to establish what Thucydides is saying about the connection between Athens' economic and psychological condition; then I shall show how this section links up with the description of the massacre at Mykalessos.

THE EFFECTS OF DEKELEIA AND THE SICILIAN EXPEDITION, 7.27–28

The economic digression (7.27–28) consists chiefly of an account of the debilitating effects of the fortification of Dekeleia on Athenian private and public wealth and on human lives. Thucydides notes, among other things, the desertion of slaves, the loss of animals, the expense of transporting cargo from Euboia by sea compared with overland as before, and the constant guarding of the countryside. He concludes the digression by noting the Athenians' remarkable decision to abolish tribute and instead to impose a 5 percent harbor tax, the *eikoste* (28.4).

Dover comments that the "sequence of thought in these chapters is notoriously obscure,"[10] because of vague or differing chronological pegs; at one point Thucydides seems to be thinking of 413, at another 415, at another still, looking ahead to some point in the future. The obscurity, however, may be overestimated. Thucydides has been describing a fixed point,

7. E.g., Bartoletti 1937; Erbse 1953, 38–46.

8. E.g., Grene 1950, 70–79; de Romilly 1963, 308; Stahl 1966, 137–39; Lateiner 1977; Pouncey 1980, 7, 94, 149; Quinn 1995; Crane 1996, 88, 90, 147. Those who have seen a connection but have not explored it in depth and tend to concentrate on either 7.27–28 or 7.29 include Schadewaldt (1929, 78–81), Reinhardt (1966, 184–218), and Orwin (1994, 133–36). Connor (1984, 158) does the most justice to the connection, but only briefly and schematically in an appendix.

9. Connor 1984, 158.

10. *HCT* 4: 400.

when the Thracians arrived in Athens. He then pauses to consider the grave effects of Dekeleia in general, in a passage that looks forward as well as referring to the present.[11] Then in 7.28.3, he remarks: "But what especially afflicted them was that they were fighting two wars simultaneously, and they came into a state of lusting after victory such that no one hearing about it would have believed, before it happened." What two wars? According to Dover, "as our attention has been diverted, in the course of reading 27.3–28.2, to 413/12–411, it is natural that we should interpret 'two wars' as referring to (i) the unbroken hostilities in Attica itself, τὸν ἐκ τῆς Δεκελείας πόλεμον, and (ii) naval operations in Asia Minor."[12] But Dover notes that the phrase "two wars" ill fits the context and points to Sicily as the other war besides that fought in Attica, and this is surely right. In fact, the natural way to read the passage is immediately to think of Attica and Sicily: Thucydides mentions one war, "the war operating from Dekeleia"; next, he describes its effects at greater length; then he mentions the "two wars at once," following up with a discussion of the war in Sicily (28.3) and the Athenians' decision not to withdraw when the Spartans occupied Dekeleia—these are clearly the two simultaneous wars. Likewise in 7.18.2, he mentions a "twofold war," explicitly referring to Attica and Sicily.[13] The sequence of thought is not obscure at all and should not be regarded as problematic. In the chronology the only uncertainty (and it is an important one) concerns the precise timing of the Athenians' decision to abolish tribute and impose the *eikoste.*[14]

As noted, however, the digression is also concerned with the extraordinary nature of the Athenians' behavior, as perceived by other Greeks; that is, Thucydides is deliberately constructing a link between the economic and psychological state of the Athenians,[15] in ways that tie in with his treatment of the exodus of wealth to Sicily in 6.31, analyzed in chapter 1. The information he relates, therefore, cannot be judged as if it is being presented neutrally or strictly objectively, but rather must be understood within the larger narrative context. For example, even the phrase "It appeared extravagant" (πολυτελὲς ἐφαίνετο, to retain the Thracian mercenaries in Attica)

11. How far forward is unclear; in particular, Thucydides' reference to "more than 20,000 slaves" has prompted much discussion, both over the figure and the temporal limit. See *HCT* 4, ad loc.

12. *HCT* 4: 401.

13. As Classen-Steup point out in their comment on 7.28.3.

14. But on the temporal manipulation in the chapter, see Rood 1998, 126. On the date of the *eikoste,* see below, chap. 5, pp. 218–22.

15. I see no good grounds for accepting Bartoletti's proposal (1937, 233 with n. 1) that the description of the Athenians' psychological state be separated from that of their economic distress by punctuating after εἶχον; thus: μάλιστα δ' αὐτοὺς ἐπίεζεν ὅτι δύο πολέμους. ἅμα εἶχον· καὶ ἐς φιλονικίαν καθέστησαν τοιαύτην; cf. Schadewaldt (1929, 81), who brings out the connection well.

is charged, narratively speaking. As we saw above, Thucydides rarely uses the word *poluteles,* and when he does, as, for example, in 6.31, it has a negative tinge, intended to suggest waste.[16] Moreover, the use of "appeared" rather than "was" casts some doubt on whether in fact it was extravagant,[17] but the choice of verb also underscores that this was the Athenians' thinking, not (necessarily) Thucydides' judgment. Indeed, there is considerable irony in the comment in its resonance with 6.31, with its strong implication of wasteful ostentation; for here, if the Athenians had decided to use the Thracians in Attica, the cost incurred would have been justifiable, given the seriousness of the Spartan presence in Dekeleia. To continue to fight the war in Sicily was extravagant; to deal with the Spartans at home was essential. And the decision both to remain in Sicily and to send the Thracians home proved wasteful and costly.

Thucydides describes the Athenians' behavior as follows in 7.28.3:

> What especially afflicted the Athenians was that they were carrying on two wars simultaneously and they lusted after victory to such an extent that no one hearing about it would have believed, before it happened. For could anyone have imagined that even when besieged by the Peloponnesians entrenched in Attica, they would still, instead of withdrawing from Sicily, stay on there besieging in like manner Syracuse, a town in no way inferior to Athens, and make the Greeks so greatly miscalculate their power and daring as to give the spectacle of a people who, at the beginning of the war, some thought might hold out one year, some two, none more than three, if the Peloponnesians invaded their country, now seventeen years after the first invasion, after having already suffered from all the evils of war, going to Sicily and undertaking a new war in no way inferior to that which they had already had with the Peloponnesians?

In this extraordinary piece of syntax, in which clause after clause tumbles forth as he describes the Athenians taking on more and more Thucydides draws attention to the breathtaking audacity of the Athenians.[18] The passage underscores not only their daring, but also their power, for that they were able to do what they did at all is testimony to an extraordinary and unprecedented *dunamis.* Thucydides illuminates its implications and consequences —specifically, how people who have it are impelled to use it[19]—and, related to this, describes the Athenian character (*tropos*) as it was continually constructed and reinforced by orators like Perikles, Nikias, and Alkibiades.[20] It is significant that only now in the Sicilian narrative are we given a clear state-

16. Chap. 1, pp. 52–58.

17. See, for example, Schadewaldt (1929, 78), who implies its factual nature.

18. Dover (*HCT* 4: 404) refers to the "syntactical audacity" of 7.28.3; see also Arnold on 6.31 and 7.28: both lack a main verb; cf. also Bartoletti 1939.

19. Cf. Alkibiades' comment in 6.18.3; also above, chap. 1, pp. 40–41.

20. 2.36–46; 2.62.2; 6.9.3; 6.18; cf. the Corinthians' comments in 1.70.

ment of Athens' real power, by contrast to the suggestions of its illusory nature earlier. But as we shall see, it is couched in a form and embedded in a context that raise questions not so much about its reality as about its morality and financial and human consequences.

This passage about the Athenian collective psychology has a two-part focus that relates to broader thematic interests in the *History*. The first point of focus is the perception of Athenian power by others, and the second is the Athenians' own behavior, motivated by their national character and its effects, especially as concerns the relationship between money and power.

PERCEPTIONS AND MISCALCULATIONS

In an important respect, Thucydides' remarks in 7.28 about the Greeks' expectations link up with and substantiate much earlier parts of the narrative, especially in books 1 and 2. More is at issue here than simply the Greeks' false expectations of Athens' prospects in a war with Sparta—that is, that the Athenians would not last more than a few years at the outside.[21] The reasons behind their false thinking and its implications are integral to Thucydides' presentation of the theme of the nature of Athenian *dunamis* and perceptions of it by others. What, in his view, caused the Greeks' miscalculation? As he sees it, it was their ignorance about the nature, reality, and potential of sea power. This judgment underlies the kind and amount of attention Thucydides gives to the theme of public finance in his work: in his own narrative voice (notably in the Archaeology; also 1.95–96 and 1.99) and through speakers like Archidamos, Perikles, and Hermokrates (e.g., 1.81.4, 83.2; 2.13.2–5; 6.34.2), Thucydides presents strikingly elementary and at times meticulously detailed "lessons" about the relationship of money and naval *arche*.[22] He also illustrates the Spartans' failure to appreciate the role of money in this war—one not played in previous wars—or, to put it another way, their failure to understand the nature of Athenian sea power and what they must do to stop it. The Spartans think in terms of traditional military power: that is, they are stuck in a way of thinking that equates power with hoplite and land strength, and do not see, or fully appreciate, the new, intimate, and inextricable connection between money and power.[23]

21. This view is attributed specifically to the Spartans at the end of the Archidamian War (5.14.3). On the significance of *paralogos* as a word denoting perceptions of others, see Finley 1967, 140–49; see also Rood 1998, 126 n. 64.

22. E.g., *Money,* 84–86.

23. For example, they took only a year to prepare for war against a sea power (1.125.2); Sthenelaidas, the Spartan ephor, was better able than Archidamos to persuade the Spartans by predicting that this war would be like any other (1.86); the Spartan general Alkidas is presented as a fool who could not even make use of opportunities laid in his lap to gain money and naval

This analysis is linked with Thucydides' famous comment on "the truest explanation" of the Peloponnesian War (1.23.6): "I believe that the truest explanation (*he alethestate prophasis*), though the one most obscured, was that the Athenians, increasing in power and engendering fear in the Spartans, compelled them to go to war" (τὴν μὲν γὰρ ἀληθεστάτην πρόφασιν, ἀφανεστάτην δὲ λόγῳ, τοὺς Ἀθηναίους ἡγοῦμαι μεγάλους γιγνομένους καὶ φόβον παρέχοντας τοῖς Λακεδαιμονίοις ἀναγκάσαι ἐς τὸ πολεμεῖν). In my earlier examination of the *History* through the end of the Archidamian War I argued that Thucydides was gradually unfolding and developing what is meant by the phrase ἡ μὲν ἀληθεστάτη πρόφασις, ἀφανεστάτη δὲ λόγῳ. The "truest explanation," which was "most obscure" or "least able to be articulated" (*aphanestate logo*), concerns, I suggested, the very nature of sea power, not its superficial fact. The subject of Athens' empire and power certainly did come up in speeches and was a topic of explicit and vocal concern. In itself, this was not obscured. Thucydides rather argues that Athens' power was something so unprecedented that although it could be seen, it could not immediately be seen for what it really was, and for its potential.[24] Thus, underlying the obscurity in articulation is a lack of understanding; arguably, the fear of not knowing was what drove the Spartans to declare war. The historian gradually reveals the nature of Athenian power throughout the work, especially in key places like the Pentekontaetia, 1.118.2, and 2.62,[25] so that it becomes less obscure and more intelligible to the mind.

Thucydides' comments at 7.28 fit into this developed argument and theme concerning the *alethestate prophasis* in two ways. First, by drawing attention to other Greeks' miscalculation (παράλογον) of the Athenians' activities in the war, Thucydides illustrates his point that the true nature of Athenian power had not been fully understood. It is clear that here he is describing a long-term perception: Greeks mistakenly thought that the Spartans would win in a few years (7.28.3), but their miscalculations continued even after the Archidamian War. The *paralogos* of 7.28.4 and the substance of the *alethestate prophasis* of 1.23.6 mesh neatly. The present participle in the phrase "the Athenians *growing* great" underlines an important aspect—the expansive nature of sea power[26]— through the command and expenditure of money. The use of the term *paralogos,* with its accounting nuance, nicely brings out not only the monetary underpinnings of Athenian power, but also

allies against Athens (3.30); see *Money,* 86–87, 91–93, 139–40, 204–5; see also Kallet-Marx 1994, 240–46.

24. Thus, in an important respect, it relates to Thucydides' arguments about the interpretation of *opsis* discussed above in chap. 1.

25. *Money,* 88–89, 114–16.

26. Note how Thucydides has Perikles exploit this by impressive rhetorical exaggeration in 2.62.2.

a sense that the enemy underestimated the extent and power of Athens' money. When Thucydides goes on to put the result of the Athenians' excessive behavior in terms of their incapacity in money (*adunatoi chremasin*), he underscores in a strikingly blunt way—here through inversion—the foundation of Athenian power.

THE ATHENIANS' COLLECTIVE BEHAVIOR: PASSIONS AND THE DISEASED BODY POLITIC

The second focus of 7.28 noted above is the Athenians' collective behavior; it serves to substantiate the perceptions of others. Indeed, the passage recalls and illustrates the Corinthians' appraisal of the Athenians in book 1 of the *History:* "The Athenians are darers beyond their power and risk takers beyond their judgment."[27] This is precisely the picture carefully constructed by Thucydides in his account of the Sicilian expedition in general. Whereas Alkibiades asserts that necessity impels the Athenians to expand their empire (6.18.3), Thucydides alternatively, or perhaps in a complementary way, throws the passions into the mix. One has only to recall the emphasis on the Athenians' lust and desire for the expedition in 415 (6.24); in 7.28 they are affected by *philonikia* so great that it seems "incredible" to observers. It is often assumed that Thucydides is admiring of the Athenians here;[28] I would argue that his presentation is considerably more ambiguous,[29] for he continues to highlight the Athenians' collective psychology in an extraordinary representation of the Athenians as diseased, through the use of a language that is medical in its overtones.

There has been a resurgence of interest in Thucydides' use of medical language in recent years, as scholars have argued, for example, for a more structural and pervasive debt to the medical writers than has been recognized, or have explored the way in which the historian's use of medical metaphors illuminates his interest in human psychology.[30] But while some scholars have noted individual instances of medical vocabulary in 7.27–28,[31] its

27. 1.70.3: οἱ μὲν ['Αθηναῖοι] καὶ παρὰ δύναμιν τολμηταὶ καὶ παρὰ γνώμην κινδυνευταὶ καὶ ἐν τοῖς δεινοῖς εὐέλπιδες.

28. E.g., Schadewaldt 1929, 79, 81. But cf. Orwin 1994, 134: "The implication is not of free and noble dedication but of all-consuming frenzy"; Orwin notes rightly that the context of Mykalessos "colors our reading of it."

29. When φιλονικία is used in later authors, the force of the related -νεικ derivation of the word (φιλονεικία, "contentiousness") is often felt, rendering it considerably more ambiguous; see Pelling 1997, 130–31; that there is a similar coloring here is not clear, though the usage in 3.82.6, in the context of the analysis of civil war, seems to lend some support to it.

30. E.g., Jouanna 1980; Hornblower 1994b, 131–35; Rechenauer 1991; Swain 1994. Interest in Thucydides' description of the plague has remained fairly steady since Page 1953 and Parry 1969.

31. Hornblower 1991a, 494; Swain 1994, 306.

frequency and concentration have not been equally appreciated, nor have the implications of its usage been carefully examined.

It must be acknowledged at the outset that much vocabulary found in the medical corpora is of course also used by other writers in nonmedical contexts, where it does not necessarily have an exclusively medical connotation. Thucydides, like his intellectual and artistic contemporaries in the fifth century, freely shared and exploited language common to other genres and modes of inquiry, whether medical, sophistic, or philosophical.[32] This was language in circulation, "in the air," not necessarily tied to any particular origin, as writers engaged in a "shared response" to the problems of the community and man's relation to it.[33] However, as I shall demonstrate, such a striking quantity of language in the chapters of the *History* at issue here is found not only in medical treatises but also in Thucydides' description of the plague that we must be open to the possibility that the historian intended a specifically medical resonance; if so, we need to explain its purpose.

In 7.27 Thucydides begins to describe the effects of Dekeleia on the Athenians. The fort enabled a permanent invasion of the geographical body, a sense conveyed by Thucydides' use of the common medical verb "injure" or "disable" (βλάπτω)[34] both at the beginning of his introductory section on the effects of the permanent fort in 7.27.3—"The garrison disabled them greatly"—and in his conclusion in 27.4—"The Athenians were greatly disabled." In between, he comments that "the destruction of wealth and loss of men particularly damaged their state" (καὶ ἐν τοῖς πρῶτον χρημάτων τ' ὀλέθρῳ καὶ ἀνθρώπων φθορᾷ ἐκάκωσε τὰ πράγματα, 7.27.3). Simon Hornblower notes that in this section Thucydides uses language "curiously appropriate to the effects of plague," and cites the intriguing similarity to 3.87.2 (especially in the use of ἐκάκωσε), which relates the recurrence of the disease in 428: "The second occurrence lasted no less than a year. . . . and nothing afflicted the Athenians and harmed their power more" (παρέμεινε δὲ τὸ μὲν ὕστερον οὐκ ἔλασσον ἐνιαυτοῦ, τὸ δὲ πρότερον καὶ δύο ἔτη, ὥστε Ἀθηναίους γε μὴ εἶναι ὅ τι μᾶλλον τούτου ἐπίεσε καὶ ἐκάκωσε τὴν δύναμιν).[35] Both animals and people physically suffered (horses: ταλαιπωροῦντες, ἐτιτρώσοντο, 27.5; people: ἐταλαιπωροῦντο, 28.2).

Mention of the physical suffering caused by Dekeleia leads Thucydides to shift to a discussion that ends in financial analysis: "But what was especially afflicting them (ἐπίεζεν) was that they were fighting two wars simultaneously, and they came into (καθέστασαν) such a state of lusting after victory (φιλονικία) that no one hearing about it would have believed, before it ac-

32. An excellent discussion of this phenomenon is Lloyd 1979, passim.

33. Goldhill's phrase (1986, 229), with reference specifically to tragedy and the sophists.

34. It occurs 103 times in the corpora; forms of the noun or adjective are used 49 times.

35. Hornblower 1991a, 494. He cites the use of ὄλεθρος and φθορά as well.

tually happened" (28.3). The verb "afflict" (πιέζω), used abundantly by the medical writers,[36] and by Thucydides four times in his description of the plague (2.52, 54, 58.2; 3.87.2),[37] again recalls 3.87.2: "Nothing afflicted (ἐπίεσε) the Athenians more than having the second occurrence of the plague on top of the first"; the allusions to two events causing special damage make the parallel exceptionally close.[38] Moreover, καθέστασαν, "they became" or "came into," may also have a medical resonance, especially in connection with the word *philonikia*, to which I shall return.

Clusters of vocabulary characteristic of descriptions of disease, used here metaphorically, as we shall see, in a highly original context, are also found in the final sections of 7.28. Thucydides uses the participle *tetruchomenoi* to describe the Athenians' condition after sixteen years of war: they were "worn down," "emaciated," yet they still undertook the invasion of Sicily. He continues: "Because of these things, since great harm was resulting from Dekeleia and the rest of the expenses befalling them were great (τῶν ἄλλων ἀναλωμάτων μεγάλων προσπιπτόντων), they became weakened in money." Liddell, Scott, and Jones (s.v., II.2), citing this passage, translate *prospiptonta* as expenses "to be incurred." But in view of its appearance in an extended passage (7.27–28) describing a kind of pathological condition affecting the Athenians, I suggest we should take *prospiptonta* not as a neutral metaphor, as "incurring" expenses connotes, but rather as one linked closely with illness: that is, the expenses are "attacking" or "striking" the Athenians. It is important to recognize that Thucydides' use of this verb in a financial context is unusual; it begins to appear regularly in such a way only in the third century B.C.

The "attacking expenses" render the Athenians *adunatoi tois chremasin*. Earlier in the *History* Thucydides sets up an argument that naval power (*dunamis*) depends on wealth—more specifically, on the expenditure of reserves of money (*periousia chrematon,*)—and therefore in one sense, in 7.28.4 the historian is referring to the Athenians' becoming "unpowerful." But this is not a factual statement that can be plucked out of the text to demonstrate that the Athenians were bankrupt.[39] Focusing on the narrative context and

36. Maloney and Frohn (1984, s.v. πιέζω) list 144 instances; a *TLG* search pulls up 161 uses (including compounds).

37. Thucydides uses πιέζω only 15 other times in a nonmedical context: i.e., it is not that common a verb for him.

38. There are a number of examples in the medical texts in which the presence of a second disease on top of a first makes the condition incurable (e.g., *Aphorisms* 4.46, 5.14, 6.35, 6.43), though there are also plenty of examples in which the second disease cures the first. The view expressed in *Places of Man* 38, that old diseases are harder to cure than new ones, is particularly interesting in the Thucydidean context being discussed.

39. As Dover (*HCT* 4: 400, 402) argues. It is true that the allusion to the Athenians' condition in 29.1 (παροῦσα ἀπορία χρημάτων) would seem to support this interpretation. How-

Thucydides' historiographical purpose, we need to appreciate how the historian may be, through another unusual expression, continuing the description of a pathological condition by using *adunatos* in a medical sense: expenses attack the Athenians like disease, with the result that they become *adunatoi*—"incapacitated" or "disabled" (as in, for example, *Regimen in Acute Diseases* 2.482.1 or Lysias 24, Περὶ τοῦ ἀδυνάτου, "On the Invalid").[40]

Thucydides then recounts the Athenians' decision to abolish tribute and impose a harbor tax, "thinking that they would increase their revenue by that means." He continues: "For their expenses were much greater than before, since the war had also grown; whereas their revenues were perishing" (αἱ δὲ πρόσοδοι ἀπώλλυντο, 7.28.4). Thucydides' choice of the verb *apollumi,* a favorite of the medical writers to describe the progress of disease,[41] is, especially given its proximity to the other words in 28.4 just examined, highly suggestive of the wasting away of a body from disease; here Thucydides is applying it to money in a way similar to the expression *adunatoi tois chremasin.*[42]

To return to the caveat I issued at the outset, while none of the vocabulary examined here is by any means exclusively medical in connotation, its frequency and especially its clustering strongly imply that Thucydides is aiming at a specifically medical resonance; if so, then to what end? It is significant that the context of such language is fiscal and economic, and this marks Thucydides' originality: he is the first to apply this kind of language to the realm of money and finances. The remarkable and unprecedented phrase *chrematon olethro* is especially notable. The word *olethros,* with its epic and tragic as well as medical resonances,[43] is normally applied to human, not inanimate, destruction;[44] likewise the equally remarkable *adunatoi tois chremasi*

---

ever, against these descriptions and allusions, which are, I am arguing, highly colored in their nuance, is the important fact that the Athenians have not yet touched the "Iron Reserve" of 1,000 talents established at the beginning of the war (2.24.1) and will not use it until the revolt of Chios in 412 (8.15.1), nor have they melted down dedications. So it is not that they lack wealth; rather, the phrase confirms that in Thucydides' view being powerful in wealth means having immediately usable cash, or money. See also below, chap. 4, p. 150 and chap. 5, p. 197. Cf. 3.19.1, referring to 428, a good example of a perceived need for cash at a time when the treasuries were far from empty; *Money,* 134–37.

40. Rechenauer (1991, 207 n. 19) would include a further resonance, the (false) prognosis about the expected length of the Peloponnesian War in 7.28.3. On *dunamis* in the medical corpus, see Plamböck 1964.

41. Maloney and Frohn (1984) cite 160 uses in the corpora.

42. Cf. Antiphon Soph. 54: ἀπολόμενον τὸ ἀργύριον; there, the meaning is "lost" in a literal sense.

43. There are 161 occurrences in the medical corpora (84 in Homer).

44. Only Aischylos uses it in connection with a thing (οἴκων ὄλεθρον, *Ch.* 862), and there it is clearly metonymic; however, as I argue below, in one sense Thucydides is constructing χρήματα as organic, not inanimate. But contrast a reference in a papyrus, probably from the

links money and the body in a way that is both metaphorical and nonmetaphorical, for lack of money acts as a kind of disease weakening the Athenians and causes actual human destruction.[45] Indeed, the concentration of this language associated with disease creates a kind of "medical field" within which Thucydides can represent the polis as a body—in this case, the body politic[46]—whose strength was nourished and measured by *chremata.* Thus the wealth itself becomes something organic.[47]

MONEY AND THE BODY

This kind of construction shares much with a larger Greek pattern of thinking that conceptualizes *chremata* as something in close connection with, at times as a kind of extension of, the body. This relationship is illustrated, for example, in the popular linkage *chremata kai soma* and in the trichotomy *chremata kai soma kai psuche.* A multitude of formulations, beginning with Hesiod and continuing throughout the classical period, place wealth and the body in close association. Consider, for instance, *Works and Days* 686: χρήματα γὰρ ψυχὴ πέλεται δειλοῖσι βροτοῖσι, "Wealth means life to wretched mortals"; or the proverbial χρήματ' ἀνήρ, found in Alkaios (frag. 360) and

---

early second century B.C., to a cloak that is being "destroyed" (γαυνάκης φθείρεται); see Sosin and Oates 1997, with their comment on the meaning of φθείρεται (258 n. 32). I thank Josh Sosin for the reference.

45. Cf. 1.25.4, where a similar phrase is applied to the Corcyreans: δυνάμει χρημάτων but with the abstract noun δύναμις in the dative dependent on the participle ὄντες rather than a personal adjective as in 7.28.

46. Of course Greeks equated the polis with its citizens, but the explicit expression σῶμα πολιτείας does not come into use until the fourth century (Din. 1.110, on which see Renehan 1982, s.v. σῶμα; Arist. *Pol.* 1302b34ff.). But there are a number of intriguing formulations in the fifth century that suggest the notion of the body politic; in Thucydides, Nikias calls on the *prytanis* to be a physician healing the state (τῆς δὲ πόλεως ‹ κακῶς › βουλευσαμένης ἰατρὸς ἂν γενέσθαι, 6.14, where the verb βλάπτω is also used); see Rutherford 1994, 62 with n. 39. It is also tempting to see in the use of the *erastes* metaphor applied to the city (e.g., Thuc. 2.43.1)—if it does indeed apply to the city rather than to the city's *dunamis* (cf. Ar. *Ach.* 143, *Eq.* 732, 1340–44)—as well as in the use of the word *philopolis,* "lover of one's city" (e.g., Ar. *Lys.* 546), a connection to the idea of the city as a body, as is implicit in 7.28 through the link with disease; cf. also the personification Demos in Aristophanes' *Knights* and the cult of personified Demokratia, though it is uncertain precisely when it was founded; see also Rutherford 1994, 62 with n. 38; for the citizen body represented artistically in this period, see most recently Stewart 1997, 133–51; for constructions of the citizen "democratic body," also Halperin 1990b; Winkler 1990b.

47. The conceptualization can go the other way; cf. the exploitation of political imagery by the medical writers: e.g., Alkmaion (frag. B4 D–K) speaks of health resulting from the ἰσονομία τῶν δυνάμεων, while μοναρχία is the νόσου ποιητική, whose prevalence is destructive (φθοροποιόν); cf. also the governing metaphors (δυναστεύειν, etc.) in *Anc. Med.* 16, 20; *Airs, Waters, Places* 12.10; cf. also *On Fleshes* 4: the brain as the μητρόπολις.

Pindar (*Isthm.* 2.11–12).[48] In a powerful chorus from Aischylos' *Agamemnon,* Ares exchanges ashes likened to gold dust for men: ὁ χρυσαμοιβὸς δ' Ἄρης σωμάτων | καὶ ταλαντοῦχος ἐν μάχῃ δορὸς | πυρωθὲν ἐξ Ἰλίου | φίλοισι πέμπει βαρὺ ψῆγμα, κτλ. (437ff.). The idea that money or wealth generally makes one *eugenes* (so, for example, Eur., *El.* 37–38) is of course often ironic and contested; but it too represents money in intimate connection with the body. Likewise Herodotos' Croesus comes close to regarding his wealth as an extension of himself, or as part of his self-definition, and clings to this notion despite Solon's arguments, which are designed in a sense to detach wealth from the body.[49]

Particularly suggestive is a passage in the anonymous writer quoted by Iamblichos in the *Protreptikos,* thought to date to the Peloponnesian War years, in which *chremata kai somata kai psuchai* experience misfortunes, *sumphorai.*[50] Here we are very close to the notion that *chremata* is in a sense an extension of the body and soul, a part of one's being. One would not be tempted to call this writer a major mind, nor is he, as Kathleen Freeman observes,[51] an original thinker, but that very fact makes it likely that his ideas, including the expression quoted, are derivative, and "in the air." Finally, in the fourth century, Plato, among others, is particularly fond of the collocation *chremata kai somata kai psuche* (e.g., *Republic* 366c2; cf. 442a6–8), while the Middle Comedy poet Timokles presents the especially apt formulation "Money is blood and life to mortals" (τ' ἀργύριον ἐστι αἷμα καὶ ψυχὴ βροτοῖς, frag. 35.1).

These passages obviously have different contexts and aims—some are contesting a claim, for example, that *chremata* is the man, or blood, some are concerned with moral implications, while others have more to do with economic ones; some are gnomic, others more delimited—but for my purposes the linkage itself is what is important. It makes clear that the representation of money as organic, and thus part of a person's "biological" makeup or an essential quality of a person, like beauty or wisdom, would not have been jarring to Thucydides' contemporaries, as it seems to us—after all, one's estate was represented as one's "being" (οὐσία) and one's interest as "offspring" (τόκος). Thucydides reconfigures such constructions, however, to place

48. See McLennan 1977, 133–34. See also Kurke's (1991, 240–56) analysis of Pind. *Isthm.* 2.11–12, in which she draws attention to the importance of the use to which money is put, and its positive or negative value.

49. Hdt. 1.29–32.

50. Τί δ' ἐστὶ ταῦτα αἱ νόσοι, τὸ γῆρας, αἱ ἐξαπιναῖοι ζημίαι, οὐ τὰς ἐκ τῶν νόμων λέγω ζημίας (ταύτας μὲν γὰρ καὶ εὐλαβηθῆναι ἔστι καὶ φυλάξασθαι), ἀλλὰ τὰς τοιαύτας, πυρκαιάς, θανάτους οἰκετῶν, τετραπόδων, ἄλλας αὖ συμφοράς, αἱ περίκεινται αἱ μὲν τοῖς σώμασιν, αἱ δὲ ταῖς ψυχαῖς, αἱ δὲ τοῖς χρήμασι, 99.5.

51. Freeman 1959, 414.

them on the level not of the individual, or even of the family, but of the collective (as he does more generally in his *History*):[52] *chremata*—which for Thucydides in the contexts at issue here (concerning expenditure on power) is always money[53]—is part of who the Athenians collectively are.[54]

MORAL RESPONSIBILITY AND THE DISEASED BODY POLITIC

The portrayal of *chremata* and the Athenians examined above has some intriguing implications. Above all, the medical template offers a useful means of highlighting the complexity of human agency and moral accountability. Simon Swain has argued that Thucydides departs from the medical writers in his focus on the psychological effects of disease;[55] 7.28 (and 7.29, on which see below) provides an excellent illustration of this concern. While in the earlier parts of his *History* Thucydides remarkably detaches wealth from morality,[56] in the framework of the Sicilian narrative we seem to be back in familiar territory, in that Thucydides reverts to more traditional representations by casting the launching of the Sicilian expedition in Solonian or Theognidean terms: as in the case of Solon's Athenians, the Athenians in 415, encouraged by Alkibiades and with him swayed by the lure of money, wish to ruin the city.[57] Looked at in these simple terms, the Athenians are morally responsible for what happens; they are the agents of their own destruction.

Yet at the same time Thucydides adds a twist to this time-honored and thus somewhat hackneyed construction by the way that he deploys the metaphor of disease. The medical field embedded in 7.27–28 fosters the conclusion that what the Athenians were doing, or what was happening to them, was in some sense beyond or out of their entire control, that they were objects being affected, not the collective agent. If we return to the passage in

52. On this, see most recently Crane 1996, esp. chaps. 3–5.

53. *Money,* passim. This is not to say that Thucydides cannot use the word in a nonmonetary sense, as von Reden (1995, 174) notes; only that in the realm of expenditure for power it is used with reference to money.

54. We have already encountered above passages in book 6 closely connecting money and bodies: e.g., 6.12.1; cf. 6.9.2, also 8.65.3.

55. Swain 1994. He examines this specifically with reference to Thucydides' emphasis on human nature. I shall return to this issue below.

56. *Money,* 16, where, however, I erroneously imply that morality and wealth are divorced throughout the work.

57. Thuc. 6.19 with 6.24; Solon frag. 4.5–6 West: αὐτοὶ δὲ φθείρειν μεγάλην πόλιν ἀφραδίῃσιν ἀστοὶ βούλονται χρήμασι πειθόμενοι. Thucydides' treatment, however, is in fact appreciably more complex, involving an intricate web of cause and effect. First, fear of Alkibiades' excesses turns *hoi polloi* against him; yet his excesses as they are linked to the expedition also arouse their greed and make them eager for the expedition; his speech in 6.16ff. plays upon this greed (as does Nikias', unintentionally).

which Thucydides describes the expenses "attacking" the Athenians (28.4), we see that representing money as disease is useful rhetorically, for it allows Thucydides to set up an interesting inversion in order to chart a shift (as he sees it) in Athenian power. Earlier in the *History* he makes explicit that power depends on the expenditure of money. As he states in 1.99, the Athenian navy grew strong at the expense of the allies. The Spartan king Archidamos puts it most succinctly: success in war is chiefly a matter of expense (*dapane,* 1.83.2). Earlier in the *History* the Athenians are the actors: they spend, and power results. Now they are objects or victims: it is the expenses that attack them, and as a result they become weakened—ill—in money. Thus, whereas expense had been an index of vital strength, and, in a sense, money as the food that nourished the body politic, it is now a disease draining that strength.

In support of this interpretation is the reference at the beginning of 28.3 to the Athenians' *philonikia.* As Dover explains, *philonikia* "is not something which one chooses, but something of which one becomes a victim, like love, fear, and grief."[58] This relates most obviously to Thucydides' account of the decision to go to Sicily in 6.24.3, examined in chapter 1, in which *eros* attacks or infects the Athenians—recall that the verb used is *empipto* (καὶ ἔρως ἐνέπεσε τοῖς πᾶσιν ὁμοίως ἐκπλεῦσαι)—so that the expedition itself becomes something out of their full control.[59] The Athenians become not agents but, in a sense, victims as they plan to invade Sicily. Similarly language of the passions is applied in 7.28 to the Athenian "body politic:"[60] *Philonikia* strikes the Athenians, making them behave as they do, with horrendous, violent consequences.[61]

In this state of affliction the Athenians inevitably act excessively, and Thucydides' syntax mimics this state in 28.4 (quoted above) as he describes the two wars. This excessiveness was "incredible" (ἠπίστησεν, 28.3) to other Greeks, and here too lies another possible link with the plague. Recall the well-known passage from 1.23. Thucydides is winding up an extended argument that nothing on the scale of the Peloponnesian War had ever previously occurred in Greek history, measured not only in terms of power but also in length and extent of suffering and catastrophe. He remarks: "Stories of things that had happened, handed down by tradition, that had not been directly experienced by those listening to them, suddenly ceased to be in-

58. *HCT* 4, ad loc.

59. This is not to deny rational considerations, but rather Thucydides' simultaneous stress on irrationality; see below.

60. Thus Thucydides continues the inversion of the treatment of money/power and the passions from its positive role under Perikles to a negative one (6.24, 31); see above, chap. 1.

61. Schadewaldt 1929, 81.

credible" (τά τε πρότερον ἀκοῇ μὲν λεγόμενα, ἔργῳ δὲ σπανιώτερον βεβαιούμενα οὐκ ἄπιστα κατέστη); he then mentions earthquakes, eclipses, drought, famine, and lastly and famously the plague (23.3).[62] If we compare this passage to 7.28.3 ("They lusted after victory to such an extent," καὶ ἐς φιλονικίαν καθέστασαν τοιαύτην ἣν πρὶν γενέσθαι ἠπίστησεν ἄν τις ἀκούσας), the similarity in thought and expression has some fascinating implications: it places the Athenians' behavior in 415–413 in the category of the incredible and may also suggest that, as in the case of the phenomena and calamities of 1.23.3, in some sense it transcends factors over which humans have control.

I have suggested thus far that by linking money and disease Thucydides is able to present the Athenians' behavior as complex: they are responsible for their actions in one respect, yet not in another. Moreover, as we have seen already, Thucydides is interested in not only Athenian collective psychology, but also its effect—fighting the two wars. I would like now to explore further the effects of the Athenians' psychological and diseased condition.

THE FINANCIAL AND ECONOMIC EFFECTS OF THE DISEASED BODY POLITIC AND THE *EIKOSTE*

In his lengthy discourse on the plague that struck Athens at the beginning of the war, Thucydides shows a demonstrable interest in the psychological and moral effects of real disease on people, including its effect on attitudes toward money and spending:

> Everyone dared with less restraint to do what he had previously hid his fondness for doing, seeing the abrupt change both among the wealthy who suddenly died and among those who previously possessed nothing, who immediately took the wealth of those who had died. The result was that they resolved to seek profits that were swift and gave them pleasure, regarding their bodies and their money (*tois somasin kai chremasin*) alike as ephemeral. (2.53.2)[63]

Thucydides then relates the plague's other effects on traditional morality: hedonism, lawless and irreligious behavior (2.53.3–4). What is interesting

62. On this and other reports of disbelief in Thucydides, comparing them to Herodotos and Xenophon, see Packman 1991.

63. It is difficult to know precisely what Thucydides means when he refers to those who previously had nothing and now "took the wealth of those who had died" (τῶν οὐδὲν πρότερον κεκτημένων, εὐθὺς δὲ τἀκείνων ἐχόντων). Certainly he is implying a "new rich" (Hornblower 1996, ad loc.), but how widespread this was and what it implies about the alienation of property more generally is difficult to say; the manner of expression and the context in which it appears, however, make it incautious to stake too much on it, as Fine (1951, 200) does, seeing it as a reflection of a systematic change in land tenure (for this criticism of Fine, see Hornblower, with whom I agree).

is that the historian charts similar effects in his treatment of the Athenians in a metaphorically diseased state. Indeed, much of the passage quoted above resonates in 7.28: the Athenians' pursuit of pleasure is implicit in the term *philonikia,* examined above, and they make a financial decision that will give them the means, they hope, to profit.[64]

Thucydides recounts that, around the time when the Athenians were suffering from the economic effects of the two wars, they decided to impose an empire-wide maritime tax, the *eikoste* (7.28.4). Thucydides' discussion of the *eikoste* is of obvious importance in the history of Athenian war finance in particular and that of the empire in general. Considering the significance of the tax—in one stroke it eliminated tribute, the innovation that made possible the first experiment in empire in the Greek world—it is frustrating that scholars have ultimately been able to do very little with it, for the simple reason that its success cannot be judged, and Thucydides is our sole source for its imposition. I shall deal more fully with the details of the tax itself in chapter 5; here I would like to focus on the historiographical significance of Thucydides' reference to it. I have argued above that Thucydides presents the Athenians as behaving excessively and irrationally. Yet one might object that although we have no information concerning the success of the new revenue system and cannot therefore properly assess the wisdom of dispensing with the old one, the decision to institute the *eikoste* was rational and based on extensive investigation into and discussion of calculations and estimates of maritime taxation. Taking an optimistic view of Athenian democracy, one might also argue that the very fact that the tax was instituted demonstrates that most Athenians judged it an effective and justifiable means of generating necessary increased revenue for the war.

However, did Thucydides (now in exile) share the majority view? First, central to understanding both Thucydides' view of the *eikoste* and the reason for its appearance in the *History* is the question, why are we learning about this piece of information here? The function of the digression as a whole, as I hope to have made clear, is not primarily to supply needed financial information with which to understand the financing of the war, nor is the specific reference to the *eikoste* included to fill out a description of the administrative mechanisms for generating imperial revenue. Thucydides mentions the fiscal decision at the close of a description of the Athenians' impassioned, "diseased" condition. Their decision to remain in Sicily after the Spartans had fortified Dekeleia was arguably mad, and certainly excessive—that is the whole point of Thucydides' emphasis on the "incredible" nature of the Athenians' "lusting after victory." Putting it in these terms (not,

64. Moreover, the ephemeral nature of bodies and money, when considered within the context of 7.28–29, as well as within that of the expedition as a whole, has an ominous, ironic effect.

as he could have done, regarding the two wars as necessary for the preservation of power or safety) helps us understand the inclusion of the *eikoste:* he casts it as a measure intended to enable the Athenians to continue to overextend. The discussion that leads up to and surrounds the decision to impose the *eikoste* does not encourage the view that the Athenians had pulled themselves out of their irrationality; rather, it shows them still deep in its throes.

Thus the narrative context is important. The way in which Thucydides describes the decision offers insight into his perspective. He uses a strong negation: "They created the *eikoste* instead of tribute (*anti phorou*) on their subjects."[65] It differs from a simple positive, or more neutral, statement, like this: "At this time the Athenians decided to institute a 5 percent tax, and they also stopped collecting tribute." Such a formulation would not adequately convey the relationship Thucydides wants to establish between the two measures. He does something similar in his account of the action the Athenians took following the revolt of Lesbos. He states that "they did not impose tribute but divided the land into 3,000 lots" (3.50.2); The statement implies the abandonment of a usual procedure in favor of a different one. As I argued earlier, the statement has a slightly critical tone: the Athenians did not do something that they should have done, and lost much revenue as a consequence.[66] In the case of the *eikoste,* Thucydides is explicit that the Athenians thought they would gain more money. While he does not make a negative judgment per se, when the general presentation in this chapter of the *History,* his distancing of himself from the Athenians' motives, and the parallel of his statement about the settlement of Lesbos are taken into consideration, censure is implicit.

Embedding the decision to abolish tribute and to impose the *eikoste* within a framework of (negatively) impassioned, diseased behavior, then, encourages the reader to see it *not* as the result of sound and sober fiscal planning —and extensive investigation into maritime commerce[67]—which another author might have presented as prudent and rational—but rather as the upshot of an emergency decision by the Athenians in a climate of irrationality in which they were beset by the uncontrollable consequences of their own human nature and passions; they were no longer true agents, or, to put it another way, they acted without an expert advisor at the helm.[68] Indeed,

65. See Hornblower 1996, ad loc.: this "instead" construction "is, we may say, the rhetorically strongest form of 'presentation by negation' in that it conjures up the diametrical opposite of what is being said not to exist or happen"; Hornblower 1994a, 157–58. See also above, chap. 2, pp. 92–93, and below, chap. 4, p. 168.

66. *Money,* 149.

67. See below, chap. 5, pp. 220–21.

68. Cf. also the decision to rescind the decree about the 1,000 talents set aside at the beginning of the war (8.15.1), presented as made in an irrational climate; see chap. 6, pp. 246–50.

Thucydides seems to be strongly implying that the decision was *not* working in the Athenians' economic or political/military self-interest because overextension and excessive behavior could lead only to downfall, not to increased power.[69] Thucydides, then, is encouraging his readers to assess the decision simultaneously, to abolish tribute and impose the *eikoste,* as misguided at least partly because of the use to which the increased revenue was to be used.

Whether this analysis provides a key to assessing the fiscal impact of the *eikoste* is, unfortunately, less clear, though Thucydides implies that the Athenians' belief that the tax would be profitable was misguided. However, the medical field, or template, may be usefully invoked again to clarify the qualities of the decision somewhat further. In one respect, as we have seen, in his unique variant of the money/body connection, Thucydides represents money as natural, inasmuch as it is part of the body politic. Likened metaphorically to disease, however, which attacks and disables the Athenians, it is both natural and unnatural: disease has its own nature, as is expressed, for example, in *On the Sacred Disease* and *Airs, Waters, Places,* but it is also, as G. E. R. Lloyd points out, "contrary or hostile to the nature of the organism."[70] The Athenians' financial sickness is fundamentally contrary to the healthy nature of the body politic.

This ambiguity has an intriguing relation to Aristotle's discussions about the nature of money in book 1 of the *Politics* and book 5 of the *Nichomachean Ethics.*[71] For Aristotle, money is both natural and unnatural; it is notoriously hard to pin him down to consistency,[72] but a crucial factor for him is the *use* to which money is put as a medium of exchange: if it is used to facilitate procuring necessary goods, it is natural and acceptable, but profit-oriented exchange, in which money is an end in itself and is unlimited, is unnatural (παρὰ φύσιν). It may be no accident that Thucydides presents Athens' fiscal planning in the part of the narrative in which money occupies an ambiguous position through its link with disease. In Thucydidean terms there is a moral problem in the Athenians' quest for more money in 413, not only because the majority, he tells us, have in mind the goal of obtaining greater wealth still, which suggests the idea of the limitless (ἀίδιον, "eternal," μισθοφοράν, 6.24.3), but also because their quest for more money will exact an enormous human toll, among Athenians and innocent Greeks alike.[73]

69. As Rood (1998, 126) comments regarding the financial burden of fighting two wars, "The daring that bred greatness is destructive of greatness." See also Schadewaldt 1929, 81.

70. Lloyd 1987, 13.

71. E.g., *Pol.* 1257 b10–17; *NE* 1133a30–b15.

72. Meikle 1995, 87–104.

73. Concern about the unlimited appetite for money and its moral implications goes back to Solon and Theognis; see Figueira 1995, 50, for passages and discussion.

It is no accident that Thucydides decides to follow the discussion of the Athenians' psychological state with a graphic example of some of those human consequences.

THE MASSACRE AT MYKALESSOS

Following the financial and economic digression, the narrative continues in 7.29.2 as the Athenian general Dieitrephes and the Thracians set out from Athens. They first attack Tanagra and later arrived at Mykalessos, a small town in Boiotia hardly fortified and with its walls in disrepair, since the Mykalessians did not expect an attack. Thucydides describes the scene:

> The Thracians fell on Mykalessos and pillaged the houses and temples and slaughtered the inhabitants, sparing neither old nor young, but killing everyone they saw, children and women and in addition cattle and everything else they could spot with breath in it; for the Thracian race, when it is filled with overbold confidence (θαρσήσῃ), is among the most murderous of the barbarian peoples. And then there was in general great confusion and every form of destruction occurred (ἰδέα πᾶσα ὀλέθρου): falling on a children's school, the largest in the area and into which the children had just gone, they butchered them all. Indeed, the misfortune that befell the entire polis was the greatest of any, and no other surpassed it in unexpectedness and horror. (29.4–5)

As in the financial and economic digression, the detail in this episode immediately stands out and gives the account of events at Mykalessos a prominence in the midst of the Sicilian narrative. This is noteworthy, since as shocking as the massacre at Mykalessos was, it was peripheral to the war, a minor event that could easily have been omitted or relegated to a sentence or two. It is relevant to note again in this connection Thucydides' very different treatment of Skione and Melos.[74] Though the causes differed, the Athenian response in those places, in 422 and 416 respectively, was identical—a siege and subsequent massacre of the males and enslavement of the women and children. Thucydides, however, relates the information about Skione in one sentence (5.32.1)—a mere passing mention—while he devotes many pages to Melos (5.84–116). He had obvious reasons for his handling of the event that have to do with his desire to elucidate the dynamics, the internal processes of the war. This applies as well to Mykalessos.

The prominence given to both the economic digression and what happened at Mykalessos through their similarly detailed narrative and especially their juxtaposition is by itself a sign that Thucydides intended that greater significance to be accorded to them, through their interrelation. The comparative example of Melos is again relevant; for one reason for its signifi-

74. See the prelude, p. 12 with n. 15.

cance lies in its juxtaposition to the Sicilian books (which explains why Thucydides would choose to highlight it, rather than the identical case of Skione). This is also the case in the juxtaposition of the Funeral Oration and the plague (and Perikles' last speech).

Thucydides constructs a link between the two sections by using the subject of the Thracian mercenaries as a framing device for his digression on the economic effects of Dekeleia: recall that in 7.27.1–2, the Thracians arrived in Athens too late for the purpose for which they had been intended, reinforcing the army in Sicily. The Athenians, Thucydides then explains, decided to send them home, because "to keep them for the Dekeleian War seemed very costly, for each received a drachma a day." Following the fiscal digression Thucydides emphasizes the connection with a resumptive sentence in 29.1 completing the frame that also recalls the fact that financial distress prompted their dismissal: "They sent home the Thracians . . . not wanting to run up expense because of their present lack of money." Thucydides thus immediately forges a clear and intentional link between the two sections at the narrative level; he then builds on this with an elaborate ring composition, as Connor has shown, clearly signaling further that these episodes are meant to be read and interpreted together.[75] Indeed, Thucydides' concern in mentioning the mercenaries at all is, significantly, not tied to the war in Sicily, except insofar as the mercenaries were intended for that arena; his attention is focused not at all on Demosthenes' need to make up for the lack of a considerable contingent of soldiers, which had been expected. Rather, the account of the Thracians is closely linked with a discussion about finances and the destructive effects of the war, financial issues intertwined with human ones.

The most illuminating link between these sections is the continued presence of vocabulary associated with disease, connecting money and financial decisions with the destruction of life. Dieitrephes is ordered to "disable" (βλάψαι) the enemy (29.1). The passage concerning the massacre is framed by the verb *empipto* (ἐπιπεσών, 29.3; ἐπέπεσεν, 29.5). Indeed *pipto*-compounds appear four times in 29.3–5,[76] which, in its close proximity to similar language in 27–28, deliberately echoes that passage; other verbs of attacking could have been more frequently used.[77] The phrase *idea pasa . . . olethrou* (29.5), with its distinctly (though not exclusively) medical resonance

75. Connor 1984, 258.

76. The other two instances are ἐσπεσόντες, 29.4, and ἐπιπεσόντες, 29.5.

77. In noting the use of this verb in 7.29, Swain (1994, 306–7) suggests that Thucydides uses *pipto*-compounds to bring out the uncontrollable nature of the phenomenon: "The point to grasp is that they are words used by Thucydides for a wholly unexpected visitation, one outside human control, which affects not only men's bodies but crucially their minds too." See also Edmunds 1975, 192.

in the use of *idea,* especially with a genitive,[78] directly recalls and expands *chrematon olethro* (27.3), linking financial disaster and human suffering. Finally, the Thracians are dominated by a passion, *tharsos*—the Thracian race is bloodiest when θαρσήσῃ—that makes them act out of control. These links, in addition to the fact that the Athenians' concern about their money led to the senseless slaughter, reveal that, far from treating public finance in a disinterested or arcane way, Thucydides is continuing not only to humanize the subject but also to connect it directly with human destruction.

As the narrative context revealed in the case of the *eikoste,* here Thucydides presents what could have been related as a sensible move—namely, sending the Thracians home as a cost-cutting measure—instead as something intimately bound up with excessive behavior and human destruction, both within the microcosmic framework of the economic digression and the report of the massacre at Mykalessos and within the larger account of the Sicilian expedition, which the historian sees as excessive from the start and closely linked with the passions. By means of all the links discussed, the historian closely connects (even if indirectly) decisions about finance and the decline of the city's financial resources with the horror at Mykalessos—his explicit reminder in 29.1 about the Athenians' shortage of money (διὰ τὴν παροῦσαν ἀπορίαν τῶν χρημάτων) shows that he wants to emphasize this point.[79]

The narrative of 7.28–30 contains enormous irony. First, as we saw in chapter 1, Thucydides' narrative in 6.31 focuses on the extravagantly wasteful (*polutelestate*) use of money on the appearance of an expedition, one goal of which was the acquisition of money (6.24). Now the Athenians' spending frenzy in order to obtain greater wealth in Sicily leads them to stint on a relatively minor scale, judging it "too extravagant" (*poluteles*) to retain the Thracians for use in Attica; yet this money-saving measure cost a whole town's lives.[80] Significantly Thucydides uses financial imagery to describe what happened in Mykalessos. He exploits a financial metaphor, *pheidomai,* ironically, in describing the Thracians' method of madness: "The Thracians burst into Mykalessos . . . and massacred the inhabitants, sparing neither young or old" (29.4).[81] He ends the account of the massacre with this comment: "A great number of the Mykalessians were utterly expended" (ἀπανηλώθη, 30.3).[82]

78. See Taylor 1911; Gillespie 1912.

79. A similar case is 1.95.1, in which Thucydides wants to emphasize that hatred of Pausanias was what led the Greeks to ask the Athenians to assume the command of the Hellenic League. The implication there is that it might not have happened otherwise. See *Money,* 40–41.

80. Reinhardt (1966, 207–8) comments on the disproportion of the contrast. See also Orwin 1994, 135.

81. Connor 1984, 258.

82. As Connor (1984, 258) notes, the application of language for human death to financial destruction and of financial metaphors to human death "suggests the incommensurabil-

It is relevant that this episode ends in death and suffering for the Thracians as well as in total disaster for the Mykalessians: when the Thebans learn of the slaughter they rush to the scene to engage the mercenaries, who lose 250 men and all of the plunder they had captured in the town (7.30).

ACCOUNTABILITY

We need now to return to the larger issue of political and moral accountability. Where, in Thucydides' presentation, does responsibility lie, both for Athenian behavior in fighting two wars and for the massacre at Mykalessos? Is the historian, by using the metaphor of disease and by his emphasis on the passions, letting everyone off the moral hook? The answer is in a limited way yes but, as we shall see, in the long term more emphatically no. If they are afflicted by something outside of their control, then, in their role as victims, one effect is to *remove* moral responsibility or blame from them. As in the case of many diseases, however, one can try to prevent the onset or at least, through knowledge and understanding of the illness, exert control initially and take steps to prevent a deterioration. Interestingly, Thucydides, both in the account of the plague and that of Athens' fiscal "illness," is concerned explicitly with effects, not causes, but there are elements of his presentation that encourage the reader to draw conclusions about responsibility for actions in the first place.[83] To determine the extent to which Thucydides' presentation suggests that the Athenians should have been able to prevent what happened to their fiscal condition and to the Mykalessians, we need to look at the larger narrative framework of the Sicilian account as well as at the specific sections concerned with Athens' fiscal deterioration and the massacre at Mykalessos.

Thucydides makes much of Athenian ignorance about Sicily; but an undercurrent of his narrative, especially pronounced in the first half of book 6, as we saw in chapter 1, is that they should have known better, specifically, that they should have investigated, and, where they did investigate, they should have done a better job. This suggestion pertains not only to his charges concerning the Athenians' lack of knowledge about Sicily and its inhabitants (6.1.1), but also to the specious offer by the Egestans to finance the expedition (6.6.3, 46), and then in their slackness in investigating the truth behind the accusations against Alkibiades for his role in impious events that preceded the Sicilian expedition. Thucydides argues not only that the masses readily accepted accusations by Alkibiades' enemies without investi-

ity of two thematic systems within the work—financial resources/expenditures and human resources/expenditures."

83. Thucydides, however, does not present the plague as something the Athenians could have prevented.

gating the truth, through fear that the flamboyant leader might aim at tyranny, but also that their ignorance in this matter was what destroyed the state (6.15.4). Not content to leave it at that, the historian then launches into the digression on the Peisistratids and the tyrannicides (6.54–59), one major purpose of which is to highlight Athenian ignorance and its consequences and at the same time, by means of a methodological tour de force, to show explicitly how one goes about investigating the truth, which he shows can be successfully undertaken even in the case of events that occurred a century before.[84]

Thus Athenians made decisions that caused enormous damage that Thucydides at least implies were mistakes that could have and should have been avoided with proper judgment, knowledge, and guidance. Likewise, as we have seen, Thucydides presents a critical portrait of the Athenians in 7.28 that presents their extension of power and financial decisions in a negative light.

There is more than a hint that he implicates the Athenians, and Dieitrephes as their agent in the massacre at Mykalessos as well for not exercising sounder judgment. First, the Athenians did not simply tell the Thracians to go home; their direction and their end goal were home, but Thucydides makes clear that the Thracians were being used in—and presumably paid for—a military campaign against Peloponnesian allies on the central Greek coast: "The Athenians ordered Dieitrephes to disable the enemy to the extent that he was able [literally, "where he had the power"] on their coastal voyage" (29.1). They attack Tanagra and then move on deliberately to Mykalessos (not on the coast, but inland). Second, a critical point left out of discussions of this passage is that Dieitrephes is the subject of every verb leading up to the massacre, verbs that appear in quick succession (over eight lines in the Oxford text) and that strengthen in their action as he approaches the town. He was to "disable" the enemy "to the extent that he was able." "He disembarked" them at Tanagra, "he effected some quick plundering," "he sailed" along the Euripus . . . , and, "landing them" in Boiotia, "he led them" to Mykalessos (29.2). "He spent the night . . . escaping detection," and at daybreak "he attacked" the city, and "he took" it, unwalled and the inhabitants not expecting an attack (29.3). Then, and only then, did the Thracians take over.

84. So Stahl 1973, 70, as cited above (chap. 1, n. 15) but useful to reiterate in this connection: "Characterizing ignorance by supplying the facts not known seems to be [Thucydides'] method." It is highly significant that in describing what really happened in the events surrounding the assassination of Hipparchos, Thucydides also shows—unusually—*how* he figured out the truth, quoting inscriptions, his primary sources for investigation and deduction (6.54.7 and 6.59.3).

So many action verbs in close succession, all with Dieitrephes as their subject, not only make his active role as a commander, and therefore his responsibility, clear; it also makes the Thracians, when they finally come into the story, appear merely as Dieitrephes' agents. There is more. In the midst of the graphic account of the slaughter, following his statement that they massacred the schoolboys, children, women, and even animals, and "anything with breath in it," Thucydides conspicuously intrudes in the narrative with a gnomic gloss about the Thracians: "For the Thracians are the most murderous of barbarians when they are filled with *tharsos*." And, one might add, having just been dismissed from what was to have been an extremely lucrative venture,[85] they certainly would have been ready to do damage. Thucydides' intrusion into the narrative to underline a widespread contemporary stereotype of Thracians as bloodthirsty savages implies strongly that Dieitrephes should have known what would happen: namely, a frenzied rampage culminating in total destruction.[86] Moreover, Dieitrephes was probably chosen as their commander because of his familiarity with Thrace and the Thracians: he next appears as a general in command of the Thrace-ward region and as one of the revolutionary conspirators in 411 (8.64.2).[87] Finally, the general was supposed to use the Thracians against coastal towns, while Thucydides points out that Mykalessos was inland. Thucydides does not explicitly condemn him, but the implicit condemnation—his favorite modus operandi— is unmistakable.[88] Dieitrephes sends the Thracians into

85. Not only would the Thracians have expected their share of plunder from the campaign in Sicily, but they were to have been paid 1 drachma a day, not an insignificant amount for a light-armed soldier. Cf. also above, chap. 1, p. 53 with n. 115.

86. Cf. Ar. *Ach.* 153ff. (a passage with extraordinary irony, given what happened in 413) and the presentation of Polymestor in Eur. *Hec.* (with Gregory 1999, 172). See also Archibald 1998, 100. There is surely an added layer of confidence in this comment, given Thucydides' personal knowledge of the Thracians, which he is fond of exhibiting (e.g., 2.95–101); he confirms his familiarity with and thus his authority to speak on the Thracians indirectly in 4.105.1. Thus I would agree with Badian (1993, 244) that this is Thucydides' own opinion, though he does not take into account the gnomic nature of the comment. Contrast the analysis of Grene (1950, 70–79), which focuses on the moral component of the narrative of Mykalessos and, like the present analysis, supposes that it could have been avoided, but stresses the chance nature of the catastrophe.

87. His role in the revolution was to put down the democracy at Thasos, which he did, although it was restored two months later. Thucydides goes into this episode in detail (8.64.3–5), completing it with the criticism that events at Thasos turned out contrary to expectation, and noting that this was the case in most of the allied cities where conspirators changed the government. It may be significant, then, that the two appearances of Dieitrephes in the *History* —very likely someone Thucydides knew, given his Thracian connection—are placed in a context of censure, one direct (Mykalessos), the other indirect (role in the coup).

88. Contra Quinn 1995; Archibald (1998, 100) recognizes the weight of the Athenians' instructions to Dieitrephes but also concludes that the historian "did not apportion blame."

Mykalessos, knowing their bloodthirstiness. Once they get started, he, their commander, disappears conspicuously from the narrative.

CONCLUSION

Another writer with a different viewpoint might have presented the decisions examined above—to continue two wars simultaneously, to impose the *eikoste,* and to return the Thracians—as necessary, as a neutral revenue-generating measure and as a prudent act of retrenchment, respectively. Thucydides does not. The decision to remain in Sicily is presented as an act of passion. The decision to abolish tribute and impose the *eikoste* is presented indirectly as a means to facilitate the Athenians' overextension and, ultimately, their destruction through overextension. Mykalessos is not thrown in simply to illustrate the tragedy of war but rather to show the ironies in and horrible consequences of decisions of a fiscal nature. The narrative context embeds them all in the realms of irrationality, disease, passion, and mistaken judgment.

The passages explored here are in many ways a microcosm of the narrative and interpretation of the Sicilian expedition as a whole,[89] and Thucydides constructs the link with the beginning and end of the account through vocabulary and thematically. We saw above that Thucydides connects 7.27–30 with the beginning of the expedition through the theme of the passions and money, and the decisions that resulted from the linkage. The relationship between this section of the narrative and the end is just as important; indeed, this section foreshadows the final disaster in ominous and ironic ways. Thucydides links *chremata* and *olethros* strikingly in 7.27, as we saw, and then recalls *olethros* in the Mykalessos narrative. The Thracians engage in "every kind of destruction" (ἰδέα πᾶσα ὀλέθρου); the Athenians, Thucydides writes in the famous final sentence of book 7, suffered *panolethria* (7.87.6)—a word that embraces the very kinds of *olethros* described in 27–29. Thus for Thucydides the linkage of money, fiscal distress, and human destruction is part of a larger argument about the costs of war. In the next chapter I shall continue to explore the relationship between individual responsibility, leadership, and money.

89. Stahl (1966, 137–38) makes the point with reference to Mykalessos.

CHAPTER FOUR

Periousia Chrematon, Gnome, and Leadership

Arguably the most important and certainly the most consistent theme overlaying Thucydides' presentation of the uses of money in all its varied forms is the relationship between *periousia chrematon* and *gnome,* "financial surplus" and "intelligent judgment," and their implementation under the guidance of a great leader. This combination appears explicitly first in book 2 and, significantly, is put in the mouth of Perikles, in his speech, reported indirectly, to the Athenians on the eve of war: "He said that their strength came from the revenue of the allies, and that war is chiefly won by a combination of intelligent judgment (*gnome*) and financial surplus (*periousia chrematon*)" (2.13.2). The statesman then enumerates the revenues and reserves available to the Athenians for the war (2.13.3–6). The implication is not subtle: for Thucydides it is the combination of *Perikles'* judgment and financial surplus that would enable the Athenians, under his leadership, to prevail over the Peloponnesians,[1] even in a protracted struggle.[2]

1. For the special association of *gnome* with Perikles, see Edmunds 1975; also Allison 1997b, 79. For the usage of this word in Thucydides, see Huart 1973; Allison 1997b. The word is ambiguous and admits of a range of meaning, from "judgment" to "resolve." I disagree with Rawlings (1981, 150 n. 37), who argues that the word means "resolve" in 2.13 (against Edmunds' [1975, 37] "intelligence"), chiefly because of the way that Thucydides implicitly develops the *periousia chrematon/gnome* theme. At the same time, in this military context, resolve is clearly part of "intelligent judgment," and thus, for example, Nikias' hesitation becomes a target of Thucydides' criticism. For these reasons and others presented in this chapter, the thesis of Luginbill (1999, 57) that "to the extent that *gnome* represents anything rational to Thucydides, it is a highly subjective and emotional sort of reason, fickle in the extreme" is simply untenable. That Thucydides *can* use the term in contexts where *gnome* goes awry or is not followed or is juxtaposed to *xunesis,* "intelligence," by no means justifies Lugenbill's categorical formulation. Cf. also Andrews (1994, 28–29), who sees *gnome* in opposition to emotions, and Perikles its champion, but also argues that Perikles can be closely associated with *orge.*

2. See also 2.65.12.

In my earlier study on the role of financial resources in the first half of the *History,* I argued that Thucydides uses the subject of Athens' financial resources to show the cogency of Perikles' gnomic statement, specifically by demonstrating what happens when one element of the pair is absent, and to prove Perikles' *pronoia* correct.[3] Power depends on money—the historian makes clear already in the Archaeology—but success in a major military conflict depends on having advisors who have the expertise and judgment to know how best to deploy the city's resources for power and to maintain the influx of revenue and who have the leadership ability to make judgments and resources effective. *Periousiai chrematon* alone, in short, will not ensure military success and power. This is a critical refinement of Thucydides' argument about power, for in book 1, in his own analytical sections (the Archaeology, the Pentekontaetia and elsewhere) and in the speeches, he focuses repeatedly simply on the equation, money equals power, in order to drive home the first important "lesson" of his *History,* that naval *arche,* and war with a naval power, must depend on the accumulation and expenditure of money. He allows a Spartan, King Archidamos, to express the best and most succinct statement of this fact: "War is not as much a matter of men as of expense, which makes men useful" (1.83.2), as if to say it is only the Spartans who need to learn this lesson.[4] But it is only in book 2, in Perikles' speech to the Athenians before the war, that Thucydides explicitly reveals a second, critical part of the formula for military success and power: namely, acumen, intelligent judgment (*gnome*).[5]

This interpretative agenda requires that he elucidate throughout the subsequent narrative, following the death of Perikles, the symbiotic relationship essential for victory. To achieve this he needs to give prominence to Athens' healthy financial condition to show the consequences of poor judgment—namely, the waste of resources and defeat[6]—so that readers come away thinking not "If only the Athenians had had more money," but instead, "If only they had exercised better *gnome* at home and in the field." This implicit argument reaches its climax in the narrative of the Sicilian expedi-

3. *Money,* 118–20, 150, 203–4.

4. By the end of book 7, however, it emerges, in one of the several reversals that occur in the course of the narrative of the Sicilian expedition, that the Athenians need the lesson (see below).

5. I stress the explicit aspect; as Parry (1989, 293) points out in reference to the development of dynamic power in the Archaeology, "each of these civilizations, these complexes of power, is seen as an order imposed by human intelligence"; yet I would downplay that it is actually "seen." Certainly also Thucydides believed that Themistokles possessed *gnome* as well, but only with Perikles does the combination *periousia chrematon* and *gnome* become explicit, because the historian is using the combination to draw a contrast between Perikles and his "successors."

6. This is not to deny the presence of other factors and causes in his narrative, but rather to show the significance of the money/judgment link operating in the *History.*

tion and is perhaps most important because the historian uses it to make the most fundamental criticism about Athenian leadership and ultimately democracy.[7] Implicitly Thucydides implicates the collective citizenry[8]—his narrative concerned with the Egestan deception, his description of the launching of the fleet, and, perhaps most of all, his construction of the narrative of 7.27–30 provide excellent illustrations—but he also lays blame squarely on the city's leaders, and his increased attention to individuals in this latter half of the *History* allows him to drive home criticism that was merely suggested earlier in the work.

To understand the significance of Thucydides' larger argument the reader must rely on implicit lessons, learned in the earlier books of the *History,* about the proper uses of wealth in the attainment and maintenance of *dunamis* and the role of financial expertise. To that end Thucydides provides us with opposing exempla through which he crystallizes for the reader the issue and the problem. One is positive, in the representation of Perikles as a leader who understood the necessity of combining financial power with sound judgment about how to use it, and who made clear that the key to success lay in insuring the flow of revenue into the city from the *arche,* and in not overextending the Athenians' power. Thucydides' discussion of Perikles in 2.65 confirms his approval of Perikles' understanding of Athenian power, in which the use of money occupies a central place. Both Nikias and Alkibiades in the Sicilian narrative provide negative exempla, as do the Athenians collectively.

Let us begin by considering the narrative concerned with the beginning of the expedition. Thucydides establishes for the reader in several ways that the Athenians have recovered their financial strength. Nikias notes in his first speech that the Athenians have recently been able to increase in "money and bodies" (χρήμασι καὶ τοῖς σώμασιν ηὐξῆσθαι, 6.12.1)[9] and makes that an argument for keeping the money at home. Thucydides next comments in his own person, in the context of the ease with which the Athenians were able to prepare for the expedition, that peace had allowed the Athenians again to accumulate money (καὶ ἐς χρημάτων ἄθροισιν διὰ τὴν ἐκεχειρίαν, 6.26.2). Then he explicitly stresses and makes vivid for the reader the costliness of the expedition in 6.31, with these framing sentences: "It was the most expensive and most beautiful of any that came before" and "If one had added up all the expenditures [public and private], . . . one would find that

7. As Macleod (1983, 141) notes, in writing about the tragic elements of Thucydides' *History,* "Thucydides' account of the character and motives of the Athenian attack on Sicily cannot be reduced to a trite moral or literary effect: it is essential to his analysis of the Athenian democracy and empire."

8. For example, by emphasizing their passions and their ignorance (e.g., 6.1.1; 8.2).

9. On the phrase, see also above, chap. 1, pp. 32–33.

many talents were carried out of the city." The implication of Alkibiades' comment that the Athenians intended to finance the expedition from Sicilian sources and not from revenues at home (6.90.4) is that they had money at home but preferred not to use it. This is confirmed when, after receipt of Nikias' letter, the Athenians (in the winter of 413) sent to their allies for an army, but they produced the money from *home* (αὐτόθεν, 7.17.1). Then we learn that in 413 the Athenians were able to send a force almost as impressive as the first (7.42.1); and in his arguments to Demosthenes against evacuating, Nikias implies the Athenians' financial strength (7.48.6).[10] To judge from Thucydides' account even the Sicilian expedition by no means obliterated the reserve; he notes that in the aftermath the Athenians decided, with the help of the newly formed *probouloi,* to economize, but he also presents them as being easily able to rebuild their fleet. Moreover, it is significant that they do not end up using the "Iron Reserve" of 1,000 talents until 412, and then only out of fear in response to the revolt of Chios—that is, their use of the reserve is presented as more of an emotional (and rash) response than a rational one.[11] This is noteworthy because while the Athenians were bound not to touch the reserve except in a situation in which they were being invaded by sea, that their eventual decision to release the money, and abrogate the penalty for doing so, did not fall under the terms of permissible use suggests that they could have used it the year before, even if with great difficulty.[12]

The allusions to Athens' *periousia chrematon* in 415, together with the frequency of the use of *paraskeue* in the first part of book 6, give the reader an unqualified expectation that the Athenians' starting resources are ample for such a venture as the expedition to Sicily, just as they were at the beginning of the Peloponnesian War. The *periousia chrematon* is there. But, as we have already seen, alongside this expectation Thucydides engenders a nagging sense that *gnome* is nowhere in sight by charging the Athenians with ignorance (6.1.1), by emphasizing their gullibility with unusual foreshadowing (6.8.2, 22), and by stressing the passion (the antithesis of *gnome*) with which the Athenians make their decision and prepare for the expedition (6.13.1; 24.3, 4). Moreover, although the *periousia chrematon* is available, and should be spent for power, the Athenians, as Thucydides represents them, make two

10. This impression needs to be considered alongside 7.28.4, where Thucydides explicitly notes that the Athenians' "revenues were perishing"; he refers to their *aporia ton chrematon* in 7.29.1. But the emphasis there is on revenue and on the implied fear of eating into the reserve; see also below, chap. 5.

11. 8.15.1. See chap. 6, pp. 246–50, below.

12. Thucydides stresses the effort it took the Athenians to prevent themselves from using it precipitously with the verb ἐγλίχοντο; see below, chap. 6, p. 248.

errors. First, they spend on wasteful or extravagant things—recall the trierarchs with their fancy plate and the desire to look as good as possible (6.31). They, like Alkibiades, covet greatness through display, but it is ephemeral and not real power. Second, as argued in chapter 2, they do not spend enough, even though they have it to spend and even after it is clear that the Egestans will not live up to their promise. The result is an enforced inactivity; and they squandered the chance to strike hard and fast.

The Athenians as a whole are implicated, but Thucydides also focuses on the roles of Alkibiades and, especially, Nikias. The historian marks Alkibiades' judgment as suspect from the moment he introduces his first speech, when he notes his personal motives for desiring the expedition, as well as his general profligacy. He is a man out for personal profit and glory; his extravagance has made the expedition necessary. His excessive personal spending (by borrowing, 6.15.3) unambiguously sets up the expectation that he will not be the kind of leader in whom the historian wants to build up confidence in the eyes of the reader. On the other hand, Thucydides complicates the picture by also remarking on the damage to the state caused by the removal of Alkibiades (15.3). The implication is that Alkibiades might be seen as a dynamic and effective leader, but he is irresponsible about how best to use money and operates on the basis of suspect motives.

THE CRITIQUE OF NIKIAS

The presentation of Nikias is different and more complex, and more central to Thucydides' argument—if only because Alkibiades was only fleetingly in Sicily. On the one hand, Thucydides initially presents the elder general as someone who appears to have both good judgment and financial acumen: he cautions against the expedition on the grounds that the war with Sparta is not truly over and that the city's resources are better spent at home (6.10, 12.1). He is attuned to the relationship between financial resources and power. He somehow knows that the Egestan offer of money is disingenuous, and in the speeches (direct and indirect), letter, and thoughts attributed to him, the issue of money is consistently present. On the other hand, Nikias' *gnome* proves in fact to be sorely lacking.[13] In connection with Nikias' arguments against evacuating at the final stage of the expedition, in which the general dwells on the insufficiency of Syracusan money, Dover comments: "Nikias betrays a certain obsession with the financial aspect of war, and this may explain some of the weaknesses of his strategy; he underrated the other

13. See Rutherford 1994, 62: "Nikias is a failure as a general and leader." His behavior in Sicily is in fact augured by his behavior in the Pylos campaign.

half of the Periclean dictum" (τὰ δὲ πολλὰ τοῦ πολέμου γνώμῃ καὶ χρημάτων περιουσίᾳ κρατεῖσθαι, ii.13.2)[14]

Dover's linkage of Perikles' comment to the narrative about Nikias is right on the mark, but it needs to be stressed that Thucydides is constructing the narrative in this way to keep the reader focused on the pairing of *chremata* and *gnome,* especially in the figure of Nikias, and increasingly so toward the climax of the expedition, in order to crystallize an issue that he judges essential to explain the Athenians' failure in Sicily despite their abundant starting resources. He can accomplish this aim so well in the person of Nikias precisely because of the impression he has built up about Nikias' knowledge of finances. This allows him to develop the theme of the importance of the combined use of monetary surplus, good judgment, and leadership. We see how Nikias cannot combine these elements, and this parallels Thucydides' construction of the broader narrative: as we saw in chapter 1, he also builds up a picture of Athenian *dunamis* only to erode it through an emphasis on display and appearance.

As the narrative proceeds, Thucydides brings out Nikias' inability to apply *gnome* and *periousia chrematon* to the expedition. Doubts surface immediately in connection with Nikias' second attempt to dissuade the assembly from sailing to Sicily. Thucydides tells us (6.19.2) that Nikias exaggerated the strength of the enemy so that the Athenians would be deterred by the size of the expedition—that is, when they considered the quantity of resources they would need. In other words, Nikias escalates the requirements of the expedition in the service of a rhetorical argument of deterrence.[15] In concluding the speech Thucydides adds Nikias' hope that if the assembly was still determined to proceed with the campaign, at least they would go more safely (6.24.1); but placed where it is in the narrative this comes as something of an afterthought,[16] and the overwhelming impression is of someone who not only was willing to put the city's resources on the line, irresponsibly, almost as a bluff, but also badly misjudged his audience and saw his plan backfire as a result.[17] As Parry observes, "Nicias in Thucydides' account is a prime ex-

14. *HCT* 4: 427. See also Bender 1938, 40 n. 108, on seventeenth-century Raimondo Montecuccoli's aphorism "danaro, danaro, danaro," "wobei er zu vergessen scheint, daß dazu noch ein anderer Faktor treten muß. Perikles sagt II 13, 2: 'Die Siege werden im Kriege durch Einsicht (γνώμη) und Überfluß an Geld gewonnen'. Aber was nützt das Geld, wenn wie bei Nikias die Einsicht fehlt!"

15. Ellis (1979, 57) disputes this.

16. See also Ellis 1979, 57: Thucydides "concedes [it as a] *lesser* aim."

17. There are clear similarities with the account of Sphakteria in book 4, although in that case Thucydides does not let the reader in on Nikias' expectations when the general told Kleon to take over his command (4.28).

ample of a leader as incapable of good planning himself as he is inducing it in others."[18]

In his speech Nikias also warned the Athenians that they must bring as much money as possible on the grounds that the Egestans' offer was in name only (6.22). Yet after the discovery of the deception Nikias, who after all is given prescience regarding the genuineness of the Egestan offer, is presented as being as much at a loss as the other generals regarding their current financial crisis; manifestly the Athenians came without "as much money as possible" (6.22). Either the Athenians did not listen to Nikias (as is likely since they expected Egestans to finance the expedition) or Nikias failed to stress this aspect adequately. Either way, it calls into question his competence as a leader, and his judgment. As we saw, he spoke of the importance of not committing resources from Athens to the expedition (6.47). I argued in chapter 2 that Thucydides advanced this policy as a primary cause of the Athenians' failure in Sicily, because it meant inactivity and delays as the force scrambled for resources locally and/or waited for help from home; and in the context of the portrayal of Nikias, it outright contradicts his statement that the Athenians must bring as much money as possible. Finally, Nikias' letter to the Athenians in the winter of 414 (7.11–15)—in which he finally emphasized the total inadequacy of local support—resulted in the further escalation of the force, which ultimately resulted in even greater losses and greater waste after his refusal to evacuate after the failed attempt on Epipolai. Thus Nikias is consistently presented as someone who is focused on financial considerations and yet lacks intelligent judgment. This amounts to a damning criticism, especially in light of Thucydides' representation of him as highly aware of the uncertainty of getting local financial support.

Just as Thucydides plays Alkibiades off Nikias in his implicit treatment of the relationship between *periousia chrematon* and *gnome,* so he continues to explore the relationship by contrasting Nikias and Demosthenes, after the latter's arrival in Sicily with reinforcements in the summer of 413. The historian notes the Syracusans' dismay[19] at seeing a second wave of combatants almost equal to the first expeditionary force, despite the fact that Dekeleia was being held by the Spartans (7.42), and following the Syracusans' victory at sea over the Athenians and given their hope of gaining superiority on land as well (7.36–41).[20] As Thucydides puts it, the Syracusans saw the "power of the Athenians appearing great in every direction" (ὁρῶντες . . . τήν τε τῶν Ἀθηναίων δύναμιν πανταχόσε πολλὴν φαινομένην, 42.2); the comment

18. Parry 1969, 109 [= 1989, 162]; also Connor 1984, 200 with n. 42.

19. The Greek is strong: κατάπληξις; see also below.

20. This recalls 7.28, which describes other Greeks' perception of the "incredible" nature of Athenian behavior under the circumstances of fighting the "two wars;" see above, chap. 3, p. 128.

recalls the link between sight and power brought out in book 6, and the ambiguity of the image: the *dunamis* of the Athenians looks and appears great, but is it really? Or, to put it slightly differently, Thucydides may be stressing the appearance of Athens' *dunamis* in order to demonstrate its inefficacy when it is not backed by sound judgment: here is impressive-looking power, but it is at present "static," and the central question is whether the generals have the *gnome* and leadership to exert it successfully.

In any case, in the course of the campaign in the narrative, Demosthenes' arrival with a new force marks a kind of second beginning. He determines that he has a chance to correct Nikias' blunder in 415 by making a swift attack. Thucydides, in a comment embedded in Demosthenes' thinking, offers an exegesis of Nikias' error at the outset of the campaign, his failure to make an immediate strike against Syracuse, as both a reminder and a more explicit analytical summary of the narrative of that time (7.42.3). I examined this passage earlier for the light that it shed on the Trojan war analysis;[21] for our purposes here, it is important because it gives prominence at this stage in the narrative to Nikias' earlier hesitancy and its consequences and shows it in a more explicitly critical light. Thucydides' attribution of responsibility to Nikias alone, excluding mention of Lamachos' role, is to be explained by his concern to highlight the issue of Nikias' inability to combine intelligent judgment and leadership in general in the Sicilian narrative. It also sets in relief Demosthenes' decision, upon his arrival with a force as impressive as the first, to make an immediate attack on Epipolai, and thus end the war in the shortest time possible, either in victory over the Syracusans or in being able, at the least, to lead his men out of Sicily, no longer squandering—here he uses a financial metaphor—the lives of Athenians and the whole city (καὶ οὐ τρίψεσθαι ἄλλως Ἀθηναίους τε τοὺς ξυστρατευομένους καὶ τὴν ξύμπασαν πόλιν, 42.5).

That Demosthenes' attack on Epipolai failed does not vindicate Nikias' earlier delaying. The reminder and the implicit condemnation remain in the reader's mind, and Thucydides' earlier comment (6.71.2), now recalled for the reader, that Nikias' inactivity was motivated by his assumption that he would be ineffective without additional resources, acquires an ironic tone when Demosthenes calls the strategy adopted by his predecessor "wasteful" (τρίψεσθαι) of the resources of the city. Thucydides initially presented Nikias as concerned about not consuming the city's resources (6.12, 47); yet his management of the expedition thus far only resulted in waste, waste that was only to increase.

Demosthenes' thinking about the most effective way to make use of the resources now at their disposal by an immediate strike was in principle fault-

21. See above, chap. 2, pp. 105–6.

less; but as it is presented as a reaction to Nikias' mistake, there may be a suggestion that Demosthenes was not giving equal consideration to the best timing for an immediate strike. Thucydides emphasizes the risky nature of the attack by including the reaction of Gylippos and the Syracusans: they experienced consternation because the attack was an "unexpected act of daring" (7.43.6). He then reinforces this with his own explicit comment that it was the only night attack during the war (7.44.1). It could have been a brilliant masterstroke, but, being untried, Demosthenes could not have been able to count on his men's ability to follow through, and this proved to be the problem: buoyed by their initial success in taking the Syracusans off guard, they fell out of order, and the night became their enemy (7.43.7). Thucydides writes similarly about the Syracusans' experience in a naval battle with the Athenians earlier in the summer. At first successful in their strategy of attacking at the mouth of the harbor when breaking through the Athenians' formation, they fell into disorder, became confused, and were defeated (7.23.3).

It is surely relevant that Thucydides took such care to present Demosthenes' equally novel strategy at Pylos in 425 as relying more on luck and hope than on sound judgment.[22] Moreover, the episode recalls the Corinthians' description of the Athenians as "daring beyond their power and risk takers beyond their good judgment" (παρὰ δύναμιν τολμηταὶ καὶ παρὰ γνώμην κινδυνευταί, 1.70.3), as well as Perikles' assertion in the Funeral Oration, after directing the Athenians to look upon the power of the city and become its lover, that "by daring and knowing what is necessary (τολμῶντες καὶ γιγνώσκοντες τὰ δέοντα) . . . they accomplished these things" (2.43.1). Thus there may be implied criticism, not in the idea of moving quickly against Gylippos now that the Athenians were reinforced, but in the execution and the motivation—presented as an almost-competitive reaction to Nikias—and, paradoxically, the concern above all not to squander more resources.[23] If so, the criticism is heightened by Thucydides' portrayal of the Syracusans upon the arrival of Demosthenes and reinforcements (7.42.2). Thucydides' choice of words is significant, conveying the impression that they were in an irrational state, ripe for easy defeat: "The Syracusans and their allies were immediately plunged into enormous terror" (καὶ τοῖς μὲν Συρακοσίοις καὶ ξυμμάχοις κατάπληξις ἐν τῷ αὐτίκα οὐκ ὀλίγη ἐγένετο). Thucydides comments further that in that state the Syracusans worried that "they would never see the end of freeing themselves from danger (εἰ πέρας μηδὲν ἔσται σφίσι τοῦ ἀπαλλαγῆναι τοῦ κινδύνου), seeing

22. On the parallels between the two episodes, see Hunter 1973, 103–5; Connor 1984, 197.

23. But the same criticism—not "knowing what is necessary"—applies to Nikias; see Bender 1938, 43: "Der militärischen Seite des γνῶναι τὰ δέοντα erscheint Nikias nicht gewachsen."

that, despite the fortification of Dekeleia, a new army had arrived in no way inferior to the first, and the power of Athens appeared great in every direction" (42.2). That is, at that point they think it even more remote that they will conquer the Athenians decisively. Here again the Athenians lose a chance through some less risky operation to take full advantage of the combination of their increased size and the Syracusans' emotional reaction, and thus vulnerability, to it.

The attack ended in disaster (7.43–45); not surprisingly, however, given his previous assessment of the Syracusans' state of mind, Thucydides relates that the Syracusans ascribed their victory to "an unexpected piece of success" (ὡς ἐπὶ ἀπροσδοκήτῳ εὐπραγίᾳ, 46). Afterward the generals consulted with each other about the next course of action. Demosthenes urged an immediate retreat of the Athenians. He returns to the theme of waste, this time explicitly the expenditure of money: "It would be much more useful to carry on the war against those who have built a fort on our own land than against the Syracusans, whom it is no longer going to be easy to overcome; in turn it especially makes no sense to waste a lot of money by besieging Syracuse (οὐδ' αὖ ἄλλως χρήματα πολλὰ δαπανῶντας εἰκὸς εἶναι προσκαθῆσθαι, 7.47.4). The *eikos* argument made by Demosthenes reflects and recalls the kind of argument that Perikles made about money and war, when he cautioned the Athenians against involvement in additional military activities when they were fighting the Spartans (1.144.1); they were emphatically not carrying on the war with the combination of *periousia chrematon* and *gnome* that Perikles said was necessary for victory (2.13.2). It also ironically recalls Nikias' own remark in his first speech that the Athenians should spend their "money and bodies" at home, not abroad (6.12.1).[24]

Just as Demosthenes has employed financial arguments—and even here

24. Demosthenes' comment is also of special interest not only because it sounds like something Nikias would have said in his earlier incarnation as someone concerned with the waste of financial resources, but also because it resembles closely a remark intended to be stinging, attributed to Eurymedon and Sophokles, and addressed to Demosthenes when the latter wanted to fortify Pylos, when he was accompanying the expedition to Corcyra and Sicily in 425. When Demosthenes' intentions became clear, Eurymedon and Sophokles objected, sniping that there were many deserted headlands in the Peloponnese if he wished to squander the city's resources (4.3.3: οἱ δὲ πολλὰς ἔφασαν εἶναι ἄκρας ἐρήμους τῆς Πελοποννήσου, ἣν βούληται καταλαμβάνων τὴν πόλιν δαπανᾶν). On this sentence, see Maurer 1995, 55–56. In both cases, financial considerations play a direct role, although in the case of Pylos, Demosthenes' comment is different in purpose and nature from the jibe leveled at him in 425, for it is part of a pattern of anxiety about spending home resources that Thucydides makes an important part of his Sicilian account by including comments such as Demosthenes' or Nikias' earlier in book 6 and by playing up the falsehood of the Egestan offer to fund the expedition. It is also highly significant that it is Demosthenes who is advising his fellow generals to direct their attention and resources to the war operating from Dekeleia, since he was the mastermind behind the fort at Pylos; see also Hunter 1973; Rood 1998, 188 n. 24 on the parallels.

it is not that they lack the resources but that they should not be wasted—as support for an evacuation, Nikias responds to Demosthenes with financial considerations as well (namely, that the Syracusans would be worn out by a lack of money should the Athenians persevere in the siege), which he brings up toward the beginning of his speech given in *oratio obliqua* (48.2). He returns to the same topic at much greater length at its end (48.5): "The Syracusans are much worse off than us because of paying for mercenaries, spending on guardhouses, and maintaining a large navy already for a full year; they were at a loss already and would be in further need. They had already spent 2,000 talents and incurred heavy debts besides, and they could not stand to lose any part of their present fleet by an inability to sustain it without destroying their strength, since they depended more on mercenaries than upon soldiers obliged to serve, like their own. So he urged that they should stay and continue the siege, and not depart defeated by money (μὴ χρήμασιν ...νικηθέντας), in which they were much superior" (7.48.6).[25] Thucydides continues by noting that Nikias was firm in his remarks partly because he had accurate information about Syracusan affairs, in particular their lack of money (*aporia chrematon*).[26]

We return to Dover's comment on this passage that Nikias underrated the importance of *gnome,* for as I hope to have demonstrated thus far, it applies to Thucydides' portrayal of Nikias throughout books 6 and 7. Nikias is presented as highly knowledgeable about war financing; he has troubled to find out detailed information about Syracusan finances and is portrayed as something of a financial authority. Yet Thucydides has also presented him as someone who wavers, hedges, and ponders decisions and strategy, as if in a hypothetical situation, not the center of a war, where the ability to come to a decision quickly is the requisite of a good commander. Moreover, Thucydides makes a point, both in introducing Nikias' first speech to the Athenians and here, before the indirect speech, of presenting Nikias as having an ulterior motive for making proposals and offering judgments. In this case, Thucydides tells us, he was concerned that if the Athenians evacuated, word might leak to the enemy and work to their own detriment (7.48.1); second, he also had grounds for thinking that Syracuse might be betrayed to the Athenians. But he gave none of these reasons publicly (τῷ ἐμφανεῖ τότε

25. Unfortunately it is impossible to assess the accuracy of the figure quoted by Nikias; Simon Hornblower has suggested to me that it has a "conventional" feel to it (cf. 2.70.2).

26. For the phrase, see also 7.29.1; as there, it does not mean literally that the Syracusans had no money. Diod. 13.27.3 refers to Nikias as *proxenos* of Syracuse, something mentioned by neither Thucydides nor Perikles. There is no need to accept it to account for Nikias' inside knowledge, and the attempts by those who do accept it (e.g., Ellis 1979; Trevett 1995) to explain Thucydides' omission of the detail must impute motives to the historian that in my view are highly unlikely; cf. also Green 1970, 4–5.

λόγῳ), saying instead that the Athenians at home would never approve the evacuation if it did not come before them for a vote. That is, once again he was misleading his audience. Thucydides explicitly comments that Nikias was at the very point of weighing options, that is, not yet firm, and yet he presented himself to his men as extremely confident (ἰσχυρίζηται, 7.49.4). But it is perhaps even more damning that he evidently kept his true thoughts to himself and did not share his intelligence with his co-generals.[27]

It is important to appreciate the implications of the fact that both Demosthenes and Nikias use the city's financial resources as the main argument for and against evacuation: Demosthenes thinks it is wrong to waste the city's resources in Sicily; Nikias insists that the Athenians should not be "defeated by money, in which they are far superior." Both are making money —not men, not power—the chief concern. Their elevation of financial considerations to a position of primacy perverts the Periklean dictum that *gnome* and *periousia chrematon* are to be used in combination for military success. At this final stage, they do not lack the resources on the spot; yet Demosthenes does not want to employ them, while Nikias insists that to give into a financial consideration is to be "defeated by money," not by the Syracusans. There is something misguided, not to mention ironic, about the thinking of both men. In fact, Thucydides makes clear that money is not at all the problem; rather it is disagreement among the generals, the privileging of money above other considerations, and the consequent lack of decisiveness. As he puts it, the disagreements between the generals resulted only in "diffidence and hesitation" among the men generally (7.49.4). The delaying and hesitation —over the issue of money—were what gravely harmed the Athenian force. And the phrase "defeated by money" has an ironic tone at the horrendous end of the expedition.

Only now, as the narrative is poised at the moment of the final disaster, does Thucydides imply the sufficiency of the resources on the Athenian side.[28] He does this not explicitly, in his own voice, but particularly in the speech of Nikias recommending that the Athenians stay and fight, in which the general alludes to the Athenians' financial superiority over the Syracusans. The point needs to be stressed: the clear implication is that only now, finally, after two years in Sicily, might the Athenians have sufficient resources, resources that had they been employed two years earlier might have brought victory; for then they would have had the advantage of a vigorous first strike against the Syracusans, who were not as experienced as the Athenians at naval war and who had not received reinforcements from the Spartans.

27. This is implied by 7.49.4: his fellow generals think that Nikias may know more than he is revealing.

28. The reality behind his remarks cannot be tested either by the information Thucydides provides or by epigraphic evidence; see below, chap. 5, pp. 193–95.

The Athenians may now have had greater financial and other resources than before, but there are several reasons why Thucydides chooses to draw attention to this fact at this climactic moment of the expedition narrative and at this point in the *History* as a whole. First, by implying the abundance of the Athenians' financial resources in Sicily and the sufficiency of their fighting force, Thucydides only heightens the sense of wastefulness: at the last minute, the Athenians escalate the campaign, and thus both the disaster and the waste will be twice as great. Second, he intensifies the irony: the Athenians now have an impressive force, backed, it is implied, by abundant financial resources, and yet the generals either want to evacuate and not use them (Demosthenes) or are hesitating and wavering (Nikias). This brings us to the third point, namely, Thucydides' interest in showing the interplay between financial resources and (the lack of) intelligent judgment.

Thucydides once again, at this final stage, brings money onto center stage as a foil of *gnome.* He shows that the problem is, now, not money or power ready to be exerted. Indeed, among the narrative functions of the striking catalogue of ships is the emphatic underscoring of the extent of the city's *dunamis* still remaining,[29] and thus the extent of resources the polis is still capable of mustering. The catalogue of ships also provides the motivation of the Syracusans in conceiving such a grand plan as closing the harbor entrance and preventing the escape of the Athenian armada: the presence of such a huge contingent, coupled with their confidence, explains their decision. "It was entirely reasonable," observes Thucydides after relating the entire list of combatants, "for the Syracusans and their allies to think they would gain great glory . . . if they could capture the Athenian side and prevent their escape either by land or by sea; . . . they conceived nothing small in any respect" (ὀλίγον οὐδὲν ἐς οὐδὲν ἐπενόουν, 59.3). Thus the size of Athens' ready power paradoxically worked *for* the Syracusans and *against* the Athenians: the latter's greatness became their undoing. As Connor notes, "throughout the account of the Sicilian expedition the greatness theme continues its transformation until it is fully disassociated from the measurement of Athens' power and fully applied to the totality of its defeat."[30] But for Thucydides this is not above all an abstract process from greatness to disaster; his emphasis on Athens' *dunamis* at this crucial juncture makes more glaring the failure of *gnome* on the part of the generals, and especially the failure of Nikias, whose characterization in the narrative contributes to the sense of what Connor has called the "grander reversal" of the Sicilian narrative.[31]

29. 7.57. See Connor's excellent discussion (1984, 161, 195–96).

30. Connor 1984, 161.

31. Ibid.

REVERSALS AND TRANSFORMATIONS

To set the context: while Nikias and Demosthenes were hesitating about the proper course of action, the Spartan general Gylippos arrived with a Peloponnesian force. The new arrivals made the Athenian generals decide to evacuate, but a lunar eclipse was taken as an ill omen by the majority of the men; they remained. Thucydides comments that Nikias, being overaddicted to divination, refused to consider a departure until twenty-nine days had passed, as the soothsayers had recommended (7.50.4). The Syracusans subsequently gained a naval victory (7.52–53). The Athenians, already despondent, became even more so upon this reversal: the acknowledged master of the sea had been defeated. The Syracusans then closed off the mouth of the harbor; the Athenians decided to try to fight it out once more. The final great battle in the harbor at Syracuse takes place (7.51–54). Thucydides' account of the devastating defeat and withdrawal of the Athenians justly stands as one of the most powerful and moving pieces of ancient Greek prose.[32] The narrative stresses the confusion and terror on the Athenian side and the difficulty of fighting in a confined space as factors in the defeat (7.70–71).[33] The Athenian survivors fled to shore, joined the rest of their force who had been watching, and prepared to try to escape by land.

In considering the parallels between books 2 and 7 that Rawlings notes, Nikias and the Athenians seem like the Peloponnesians at the beginning of the war. Just as Perikles predicted that the Spartans would have difficulties and face delays because of their lack of money, so money (and allies) was a serious problem for Nikias:[34] "In short, Nicias finds himself facing the same problems that Pericles had predicted the Peloponnesians would confront against Athens."[35] Like Nikias, so also the Athenians, collectively, are transformed, in a sense, into Spartans. It is they (and their leaders) who need Archidamos' lesson to his fellow Spartans in 432, when he asserted that war was primarily a matter of money (expense), not men (1.83.2). The Spartans failed to grasp this lesson at the time; they were far more responsive, because of its familiarity, to the equally pithy comment of the ephor Sthenelaidas: "The Athenians may have a lot of money and ships and horses, but we have brave men" (1.86.3). Now, however, the Spartans have, it seems, gotten the point, and, along with the Syracusans, have become more like Athenians while the Athenians are floundering as if in an unfamiliar world.[36]

32. Ibid., 198 and n. 36.

33. The historian explicitly marks the defeat as a reversal by drawing an analogy between the situation and what the Spartans had suffered at the hands of the Athenians at Pylos in 425 (7.71.7).

34. Rawlings 1981, 149.

35. Ibid., 151.

36. Connor (1984, 159 n. 5) makes a similar point.

Consider in this context Nikias' speech to the Athenians after their defeat in the harbor of Syracuse and before the withdrawal and final disaster. Scholars have often commented on the unlikelihood that Thucydides was able to obtain accurate reports especially regarding the late stages of the Sicilian campaign. Certainly in the case of Nikias, to whom Thucydides attributes thoughts and motivations not publicly expressed or acted upon,[37] we must suppose substantial inferences on the part of the historian.[38] Yet he could well have found out about the contents of this final speech from one of the survivors who returned to Athens, for it was given, he tells us, as Nikias walked along the ranks of soldiers, speaking as loudly as he could in a final attempt to encourage and console at the moment of greatest despondency. Although up to now Thucydides' portrait of Nikias has featured the general's inadequacies as an orator, leader, and military strategist, and has made it easy for the reader to hold him personally responsible for the disastrous consequences of his command in Sicily,[39] Nikias becomes in a sense, as has been noticed, a more sympathetic figure, as he poignantly comforts his men.

It is, I suggest, an image soon to be compromised in what follows. The substance of his remarks near the end of his speech is of most interest for our purposes. Addressing his men, Nikias asserts: "You yourselves are immediately a polis wherever you sit down (αὐτοί τε πόλις εὐθὺς ἐστε ὅποι ἂν καθέζησθε), and there is no one in Sicily who could easily resist your attack or expel you when once established" (7.77.4). He returns to the sentiment at the end of the speech: "In short, men, be convinced that it is necessary for you to become brave men (ἀναγκαῖόν τε ὂν ὑμῖν ἀνδράσιν ἀγαθοῖς γίγνεσθαι) . . . [and if successful in escaping] the Athenians among you will raise up again the great power of the city, although it is fallen. For men are the polis, not walls or ships empty of men (οἱ Ἀθηναῖοι τὴν μεγάλην δύναμιν τῆς πόλεως καίπερ πεπτωκυῖαν ἐπανορθώσοντες· ἄνδρες γὰρ πόλις, καὶ οὐ τείχη οὐδὲ νῆες ἀνδρῶν κεναί)" (77.7).[40]

37. Solmsen's view (1975, 223) is typical: "How could Thucydides know either the intimate thoughts or the openly stated reasons of Nicias when he opposed Demosthenes and after the attack on Epipolae had ended in failure?" See also Lang (1995), who notes that Thucydides gives Nikias the second greatest number of participially motivated actions, all but one (5.16.1) in books 6 and 7, and suggests that Thucydides was writing under Herodotean influence, employing the narrative technique of attributing motivations of a stock nature.

38. This is emphatically not to say that he is "freely inventing" Nikias; on the contrary, one could argue that Thucydides felt able to attribute so much motivation to Nikias precisely because he had known him well and felt that he knew what Nikias would say or think in a particular situation.

39. See Connor 1984, 200. It is, however, important to remember that he did ask to be relieved of his command.

40. Leimbach (1985, 127) notes the effectiveness of the ending. See also Luschnat 1942, 101–6. Expressions similar to Nikias' formulation can be found in Alk. frag. 112.10 (ἄνδρες

What immediately stands out is the contrast between Nikias' definition of the polis and the Periklean version presented in the Funeral Oration, in which the polis is an abstraction, an entity that makes men worthy as citizens, not the reverse.[41] That Nikias' formulation is the only one likely to have any force in this context does not obviate the need to appreciate that Thucydides has chosen to present and highlight this argument and to set it in the larger context of definitions of the polis. In fact, not only does Nikias here once again invert the Periklean vision,[42] but his words also help to perpetuate the sense of reversal at this final stage, in which the Athenians actually become more like Spartans. In a sense Nikias is trying to make his men more like Spartans: now off the sea they are forced to be soldiers on the land; now it comes down to men.[43] This hoped-for Spartanlike transformation may be implied in the phrase "You must become brave men,"[44] echoing as it does earlier comments made by and directed toward Spartans.[45]

γὰρ πόλι̣ο̣ς πύργος ἀρεύι̣οι), Ais. *Pers.* 349 (ἀνδρῶν γὰρ ὄντων ἕρκος ἐστὶν ἀσφαλές), and Soph. *OT* 56–57 (ὡς οὐδέν ἐστιν οὔτε πύργος οὔτε ναῦς | ἐρῆμος ἀνδρῶν μὴ ξυνοικούντων ἔσω); cf. Meister 1955, 33. These polemical assertions need to be read against the more prevalent notion that the city was defined by these things; see Croally (1994, 167–68), who sets these and the Thucydidean passage against the pervasive emphasis on walls as the defining characteristic of a city, citing most intriguingly, from the standpoint of Thucydides' interest in linking Sicily and Troy, references in the Homeric poems. The representation of the polis as ships, which Nikias' view strongly contests (in the form of "empty ships," which reinforces the point that men make the polis), goes back to Homer. But Thucydides' Athenian audience may have immediately thought of their own past and Herodotos' presentation of it at the beginning of the century. The oracle's advice "Flee to the wooden walls," interpreted as the wooden hulls of ships and famously supported by Themistokles, will have evoked the idea that the polis lies within ships, as before within city walls (Hdt. 7.143–44); cf. Hdt. 8.61.2: after the evacuation of Athens, in response to the Corinthian Adeimantos' jibe that Themistokles lacked a country (here *patris*), Themistokles retorted that he had a polis and a land as long as Athens had two hundred manned ships.

41. E.g., 2.40.2, 42.3, 60.2; cf. also 6.9.2 and above, chap. 1; for Perikles' views about citizenship and how they contrast with Nikias', see Edmunds 1975, 82–88. Cf. Rawlings (1981, 160), who sees parallels between this section of Nikias' speech and 2.64.3 (from Perikles' last speech) and notes, about the portrayal of Nikias generally in book 7, that "Pericles stands for the city, Nicias for the individual" (159).

42. As in 6.9.2; see above, chap. 1.

43. Recall also Nikias' second speech in the deliberations before going off to Sicily, where he says: πρὸς οὖν τοιαύτην δύναμιν οὐ ναυτικῆς καὶ φαύλου στρατιᾶς μόνον δεῖ (6.21.1); the emphasis is negative and unexpected; see above, chap. 1, pp. 42–43.

44. Athenians, of course, share hoplite values; the point here is that Nikias' *sailors* must adopt them.

45. Sthenelaidas contrasting the Spartans with the Athenians (1.86.3) and Brasidas at Amphipolis (5.9.9); see Luschnat 1942, 106. Nikias' comment is to be understood also within the more immediate context of the preceding narrative; in the description of the Athenians' despondent state, Thucydides likens the men about to evacuate—40,000 in all—to a "besieged city, and a large one at that" (7.75.5); see below.

Thucydides' description of the final battle scene and its aftermath, revealing the condition and perceptions of the Athenians in their desperate state, marks the culmination of the theme of reversal and transformation. It also contains an extraordinary concentration of highly charged vocabulary that he has used in developing the key themes that have layered the account of the expedition from its beginnings: vision (*opsis*), emotion, hope and fear, judgment (*gnome*) and preparation/preparedness (*paraskeue*). Thus, these chapters, especially 7.71, which concerns the perceptions and emotions of the spectators of the battle in the harbor, and 7.75, the dramatic description of the perceptions of the Athenians about to leave camp, stand out as especially significant in both a historiographical and a narrative sense,[46] as well as containing striking linguistic echoes of earlier sections that reinforce the sense of reversal and transformation.

7.71: Vision, Emotion, and Judgment

Thucydides has been relating the course of the naval battle, stressing the difficulties encountered by both sides and noting that this was the largest number of ships ever to have fought in such a small space (70.4).[47] He moves his reader's eye to land, to the army watching the naval battle from shore. His focus is on the connection among vision, emotion, and perception; through strong linguistic parallels that evoke the launching of the expedition, he engages the reader to interpret the perceptions of the crowd of spectators on shore.[48] When he comments that "since everything now rested on the Athenians in their ships, there was unprecedented fear about the outcome" (πάντων γὰρ δὴ ἀνακειμένων τοῖς Ἀθηναίοις ἐς τὰς ναῦς ὅ τε φόβος ἦν ὑπὲρ τοῦ μέλλοντος οὐδένι ἐοικώς, 71.2), the reader is led, by the juxtaposition of "ships" and "fear," to recall the emotional mood at the sight of the fleet at the outset of the expedition (6.31.1). Arising from the awareness that everything depended on the ships, that fear evokes Nikias' implied prophecy in his second speech before the expedition that it would not be the fleet that would win against such a power.[49] Thucydides' earlier reference to the unsurpassed size of the combined fleet intensifies the irony and

46. The number of *hapax legomena* (ἀθλιώτεροι, ἀντιβολίαν, ἐπιθειασμῶν, κατήφεια, αἰκία, κούφισιν, ταπεινότητα, παιάνων) or rare words, some of which appear here for the first time (e.g., τραυματίαι, οἰμωγῆς, δάκρυσι/δάκρυα, εὐχῆς) alone is an indication of its signal importance to Thucydides.

47. It is tempting to see a nod to the battle of Salamis in this passage.

48. See Walker's (1993) discussion of this passage, and of the recognition and imitation of Thucydides' vividness *(enargeia)* in antiquity. See also Connor (1985, 10) on the linkage between vision and emotion. See also 6.31.1, analyzed in chap. 1, pp. 50–51.

49. 6.21.1. The added irony is that Nikias at the time was implying the war would be won on land.

the tragedy: the Athenians, in the passage following Nikias' comments in the same speech, believed that the larger the fleet was, the better and safer.[50]

In his description of the crowd's reaction as they look upon the battle (ἔποψις, 71.2), Thucydides stresses both visuality and emotion: since the "seeing" (θεά) was close by, the men did not get a view of the whole; so that when some "saw" (ἴδοιεν) any of their side anywhere prevailing, "they cheered up" (ἀνεθάρσησαν); conversely, those looking at (βλέψαντες) others being defeated shouted and lamented (ὀλοφυρμῷ τε ἅμα μετὰ βοῆς),[51] and they "were enslaved in their minds by the sight" (ἀπὸ...τῆς ὄψεως καὶ τὴν γνώμην...ἐδουλοῦντο) of those fighting more than were those actually in the battle (71.3).[52] Both the link between vision and emotion and the language here hearken back to 6.31, although in reverse order: there the crowd of spectators first felt a mixture of lamentation and hope (καὶ μετ' ἐλπίδος τε ἅμα ἰόντες καὶ ὀλοφυρμῶν, 6.30.6), which changed to positive emotion as a result of the power of the visuality of size (ὅμως δὲ τῇ παρούσῃ ῥώμῃ, διὰ τὸ πλῆθος ἑκάστων ὧν ἑώρων, τῇ ὄψει ἀνεθάρσουν, 6.31.1). Now size indirectly brings fear, and the identical emotions occur alternately, depending on where the spectators are looking.

The focus on sight and seeing and its connection to emotion also ironically recalls 6.24.3: *eros* struck all the Athenians alike, and the younger among them wanted to go on the expedition out of a "longing for the far-off sight and seeing" (τοῖς δ' ἐν ἡλικίᾳ τῆς τε ἀπούσης πόθῳ ὄψεως καὶ θεωρίας). Moreover, the last part of that sentence, "and having great hopes of safety" (καὶ εὐέλπιδες ὄντες σωθήσησθαι, i.e., returning home alive) is contrasted with their hope of merely surviving. But it also resonates with the end of 7.71, when Thucydides notes their hopelessness at the prospect of surviving (ἀνέλπιστον . . . σωθήσεσθαι, 71.1).[53]

Worst off, Thucydides comments, were those who were looking at the part of the battle in which the outcome appeared in the balance. The language and combinations here again strongly evoke 6.31: "Others looking at any part of the naval battle that was equally balanced, because of the continuing indecision of the contest (τῆς ἁμίλλης), their bodies swaying in great fear equally with their assessment (τοῖς σώμασιν αὐτοῖς ἴσα τῇ δόξῃ περιδεῶς

50. 6.24.2: the "crowdlike" preparation (ὀχλώδης παρασκευή) gave them a sense of great safety (ἀσφάλεια νῦν δὴ καί πολλή). See chap. 1, pp. 43–44.

51. See also 71.4: ὀλοφυρμὸς βοή; also below on chapter 75.

52. See Gorgias' comments on the distinction between *opsis* and *logos* (*gnome* belongs in the realm of the latter term) in *On Not Being* (frag. 82 B3 D-K): *logos* embraces objects apprehended by nonoptical senses.

53. In 7.71 the hopelessness comes from seeing; cf. 8.1.2: when the Athenians *did not see* ships or men or money after the disaster, they felt "hopelessness at the prospect of survival" (ἀνέλπιστοι...σωθήθεσθαι). See below, chap. 6, pp. 233–34.

ξυναπονεύοντες), they were in the worst possible condition, for everything was just at the point of survival or destruction" (71.3). This remarkable sentence evokes 6.31 and 32 through a repetition of the rare word ἅμιλλα, "contest" or "race," which Thucydides used in the earlier passages. He used the verbal form to describe the competition (ἁμιλληθέν, 6.31.3) among the land forces to look the best, both in their armor and personal equipment (τῶν περὶ τὸ σῶμα σκευῶν), a competition conducted "with great enthusiasm" (μεγάλῃ σπουδῇ), and then, when the fleet departed, it held a "race" (ἅμιλλαν, 32.2) to Aigina. Especially striking is the connection between the body and emotion, and the competition in 6.31.3 and 7.71.3, since both passages concern the behavior of the land army, though in 7.71 the ἅμιλλα, naval battle, is the object of their observation. In 6.31 the men threw themselves wholeheartedly (μεγάλῃ σπουδῇ) into the contest to look the best, including with respect to their bodily equipment; now the same group throws themselves wholeheartedly into an experience terrifying both intellectually and physically.

In both 6.31 and 7.71 words of emotion are prominent, and while the latter passage emphasizes the differing emotional responses based on varying observations, the ultimate emotion for all becomes terror and hopelessness (ἔκπληξις, ἀνέλπιστον, 7.71.7).[54] Words of judgment in 6.31 are conspicuously absent: the Athenians as well as their observers are affected more by emotion—a continuation of the impassioned condition in which they entered the expedition. Now, at the end, when the results of their lack of judgment become overwhelmingly clear to the eye, Thucydides inserts words of judgment into the narrative, linking them alternately to vision and the body. The effect is to intensify the sense of reality, not illusion, as in 6.31. The Athenians are now able to observe and to comprehend: size now instills fear, not courage; the navy is not a beautiful object of wonder but an object that causes the response of hope or hopelessness, depending on one's vantage point. The emphasis on the body reminds us of the human consequences of this wasteful war.[55]

The battle ends in disaster for the Athenians, who soon come to a full understanding of the catastrophe based on their own observation and correct interpretation of the event. Thucydides' choice of language, which recalls the glitter and splendor of the expedition's beginning and the hopes with which they set out, results in the readers' powerful engagement in the

54. The ἔκπληξις, stressed also in chapter 75, examined below, recalls the reaction of the sailors in Egesta upon seeing glittering gold and silver cups (6.46); its connection with sight and emotion also recalls Gorgias' *Helen;* see above, chap. 1, pp. 78 and 82, n. 198. Conversely, the adverb λαμπρῶς is used to refer to the Syracusan side (7.71.5), evoking the ὄψεως λαμπρότητι of 6.31.6. which refers to the Athenian expedition.

55. See the "bodily" resonance in ῥώμη in 6.31.1. I shall return to this below.

text.[56] Chapter 75, employing much of the same vocabulary, continues to stimulate the reader's, along with the participants', recollection of the beginning.

7.75: The Greatest Reversal

In this extraordinarily moving passage, which is as vivid as any in the *History*, Thucydides describes the moment when the men break camp and begin their escape, ironically recreating the hopes, fears, perceptions, and expectations, and their relationship to judgment, that led the Athenians to embark on the conquest of Sicily. As the passage contains many thematically significant words, which are closely intertwined, it will be useful to quote it here in full.

"Thinking that they had prepared sufficiently" (ἱκανῶς παρασκευάσθαι), Thucydides notes, "[Nikias and Demosthenes] began the retreat on the second day after the naval battle." He continues:

> δεινὸν οὖν ἦν οὐ καθ' ἓν μόνον τῶν πραγμάτων, ὅτι τάς τε ναῦς ἀπολωλεκότες πάσας ἀπεχώρουν καὶ ἀντὶ μεγάλης ἐλπίδος καὶ αὐτοὶ καὶ ἡ πόλις κινδυνεύοντες, ἀλλὰ καὶ ἐν τῇ ἀπολείψει τοῦ στρατοπέδου ξυνέβαινε τῇ τε ὄψει ἑκάστῳ ἀλγεινὰ καὶ τῇ γνώμῃ αἰσθέσθαι. τῶν τε γὰρ νεκρῶν ἀτάφων ὄντων, ὁπότε τις ἴδοι τινὰ τῶν ἐπιτηδείων κείμενον, ἐς λύπην μετὰ φόβου καθίσταντο, καὶ οἱ ζῶντες καταλειπόμενοι τραυματίαι τε καὶ ἀσθενεῖς πολὺ τῶν τεθνεώτων τοῖς ζῶσι λυπηρότεροι ἦσαν καὶ τῶν ἀπολωλότων ἀλθιώτεροι. πρὸς γὰρ ἀντιβολίαν καὶ ὀλοφυρμὸν τραπόμενοι ἐς ἀπορίαν καθίστασαν, ἄγειν τε σφᾶς ἀξιοῦντες καὶ ἕνα ἕκαστον ἐπιβοώμενοι, εἴ τινά πού τις ἴδοι ἢ ἑταίρων ἢ οἰκείων, τῶν τε ξυσκήνων ἤδη ἀπιόντων ἐκκρεμαννύμενοι καὶ ἐπακολουθοῦντες ἐς ὅσον δύναιντο, εἴ τῳ δὲ προλίποι ἡ ῥώμη καὶ τὸ σῶμα, οὐκ ἄνευ ὀλίγων ἐπιθειασμῶν καὶ οἰμωγῆς ὑπολειπόμενοι, ὥστε δάκρυσι πᾶν τὸ στράτευμα πλησθὲν καὶ ἀπορίᾳ τοιαύτῃ μὴ ῥᾳδίως ἀφορμᾶσθαι, καίπερ ἐκ πολεμίας τε καὶ μείζω ἢ κατὰ δάκρυα τὰ μὲν πεπονθότας ἤδη, τὰ δὲ περὶ τῶν ἐν ἀφανεῖ δεδιότας μὴ πάθωσιν. κατήφειά τέ τις ἅμα καὶ κατάμεμψις σφῶν αὐτῶν πολλὴ ἦν. οὐδὲν γὰρ ἄλλο ἢ πόλει ἐκπεπολιορκημένῃ ἐῴκεσαν ὑποφευγούσῃ, καὶ ταύτῃ οὐ σμικρᾷ· μυριάδες γὰρ τοῦ ξύμπαντος ὄχλου οὐκ ἐλάσσους τεσσάρων ἅμα ἐπορεύοντο. καὶ τούτων οἵ τε ἄλλοι πάντες ἔφερον ὅτι τις ἐδύνατο ἕκαστος χρήσιμον, καὶ οἱ ὁπλῖται καὶ οἱ ἱππῆς παρὰ τὸ εἰωθὸς αὐτοὶ τὰ σφέτερα αὐτῶν σιτία ὑπὸ τοῖς ὅπλοις, οἱ μὲν ἀπορίᾳ ἀκολούθων, οἱ δὲ ἀπιστίᾳ· ἀπηυτομολήκεσαν γὰρ πάλαι τε καὶ οἱ πλεῖστοι παραχρῆμα. ἔφερον δὲ οὐδὲ ταῦτα ἱκανά· σῖτος γὰρ οὐκέτι ἦν ἐν τῷ στρατοπέδῳ. καὶ μὴν ἡ ἄλλη αἰκία καὶ ἡ ἰσομοιρία τῶν κακῶν, ἔχουσά τινα ὅμως

56. Plutarch comments on the battle description that Thucydides attempts to make spectators out of his audience (*Mor.* 347A, quoted by Connor 1984, 197). Cf. also Lucian *How to Write History* 50–51 on the goal of vividness in historiography generally; see also Walker 1993.

τὸ μετὰ πολλῶν κούφισιν, οὐδ' ὣς ῥᾳδία ἐν τῷ παρόντι ἐδοξάζετο, ἄλλως τε καὶ ἀπὸ οἵας λαμπρότητος καὶ αὐχήματος τοῦ πρώτου ἐς οἵαν τελευτὴν καὶ ταπεινότητα ἀφῖκτο. μέγιστον γὰρ δὴ τὸ διάφορον τοῦτο [τῷ] Ἑλληνικῷ στρατεύματι ἐγένετο, οἷς ἀντὶ μὲν τοῦ ἄλλους δουλωσομένους ἥκειν αὐτοὺς τοῦτο μᾶλλον δεδιότας μὴ πάθωσι ξυνέβη ἀπιέναι, ἀντὶ δ' εὐχῆς τε καὶ παιάνων, μεθ' ὧν ἐξέπλεον, πάλιν τούτων τοῖς ἐναντίοις ἐπιφημίσμασιν ἀφορμᾶσθαι, πεζούς τε ἀντὶ ναυβατῶν πορευομένους καὶ ὁπλιτικῷ προσέχοντας μᾶλλον ἢ ναυτικῷ. ὅμως δὲ ὑπὸ μεγέθους τοῦ ἐπικρεμαμένου ἔτι κινδύνου πάντα ταῦτα αὐτοῖς οἰστὰ ἐφαίνετο.

It was dreadful, not for the reason alone that they were retreating, having lost all their ships, and instead of holding out great hope, both they and their city were endangered, but also because the abandonment of the camp caused pain to the eyes and mind of each. For since the dead lay unburied, whenever anyone saw one of his friends lying there, he felt pain and fear, while the living, left behind wounded and sick, caused even more distress to those alive than the dead, and were more pitiable than those who had perished. For those left alive, turning to entreaties and wailing, were brought to a state of helplessness, wanting passers-by to take them along, and shouting out to each one of them, if they should anywhere see one of their friends or relatives, hanging on the necks of their tent-fellows who were about to depart, and following as far as they could, and whenever their bodily strength gave up, they kept appealing to the gods and shrieking aloud as they were left behind, so that the whole army was filled with weeping, and because of their inability to do anything, they found it difficult to set out, although they were in an enemy land, where they had already suffered far beyond tears and feared to suffer more in the invisible future. At the same time there was much despondency and blame among themselves. For they seemed like nothing less than a besieged town in escape, and no small one at that, the whole throng numbering no less than 40,000. . . . Nor had they brought sufficient supplies, for there was not enough grain in the camp. Moreover, their disgrace and the equal share of sufferings, even if lightened by being shared, still were not consequently regarded as easily borne at the present, especially since they had arrived at such a humiliating end after such a brilliant and vaunted beginning. Indeed, this was undeniably the greatest reversal for a Hellenic expedition. They had come to enslave others and were now going away in fear of suffering enslavement themselves; they had left with prayers and paians and now began their return under adverse omens; and they were traveling by land instead of by sea, and relying not on their navy but on their infantry. Nevertheless, the magnitude of the danger still in front of them made all this seem bearable.

As already mentioned, this passage brings together many of the key themes of the narrative of the expedition that I have been examining in conjunction with that of money. Yet money is conspicuously absent. Here, it appears, Thucydides wants to concentrate attention on the *consequences* of the misuse and insufficient use of financial resources (for discussion of the latter, see chapter 2). Thucydides' treatment of the massacre of Mykalessos, examined in chapter 3, is relevant here. It showed that the historian's interest in money is not abstract, nor is it focused on the dry, detached subject of military financing; rather, Thucydides is intimately concerned with the relationship of money to emotion and greed, and with the consequences of the misuse or insufficient use of money—that is, the waste of human life. In 7.75, money itself recedes, for the historian has already made his point. In fact, Thucydides concentrates on the human element—the soldiers and sailors—and at this crucial juncture detaches money from the issue of human lives even more explicitly in the preceding chapter: as he describes the preparation for evacuation, he notes that the men prepared to bring only what was "most useful" to them, defined in the next clause as "as much as was necessary for their bodily subsistence."[57]

The linkages with 6.31, the description of the launching of the expedition, are especially obvious. The most explicit echoes, although in the form of reversals, come near the end of 7.75 (see below), but they are suggested right at the beginning. In contrast to the *paraskeue* of 415 that was *polutelestate* and *euprepestate* (6.31.1), superior (ὑπερβολή, 6.31.6) compared with those against whom they were sent out, Nikias and Demosthenes broke camp "when they thought that they had prepared sufficiently" (ἱκανῶς παρασκευάσθαι); yet we learn a little later that in fact their preparation was not sufficient: "And they had not even brought sufficient supplies, for there was no longer grain in the camp" (ἔφερον δὲ οὐδὲ ταῦτα ἱκανά· σῖτος γὰρ οὐκέτι ἦν ἐν τῷ στρατοπέδῳ, 75.5). There is an additional layer of irony here: despite their extravagant preparations for the expedition in 415, the Athenians ultimately lack basic resources.[58] Moreover, now, by contrast with 415, when the expedition sailed "with the greatest hopes for the future" (ἐπὶ τῇ μεγίστῃ ἐλπίδι τῶν μελλόντων, 6.31.6), the remnants of the army are in the opposite state: "instead of holding out great hope they were endangering themselves and the city" (ἀντὶ μεγάλης ἐλπίδος καὶ αὐτοὶ καὶ ἡ πόλις κινδυνεύοντες, 7.75.2). The presentation through negation both evokes and emphasizes the reversal of the earlier passage.[59]

Yet what was terrible (δεινόν) was also the sight of those left behind, which caused "pain in the eyes and mind of each person leaving" (ἀλλὰ καὶ ἐν τῇ ἀπολείψει τοῦ στρατοπέδου ξυνέβαινε τῇ τε ὄψει ἑκάστῳ ἀλγεινὰ καὶ τῇ γνώμῃ αἰσθέσθαι, 7.75.2). The pointed use of *opsis* in this passage, as well as its juxtaposition to *gnome,*[60] has the effect of again evoking the be-

57. ὅπως ξυσκευάσαιντο ὡς ἐκ τῶν δυνατῶν οἱ στρατιῶται ὅτι χρησιμώτατα, καὶ τὰ μὲν ἄλλα πάντα καταλιπεῖν, ἀναλαβόντες δὲ αὐτὰ ὅσα περὶ τὸ σῶμα ἐς δίαιταν ὑπῆρχεν ἐπιτήδεια ἀφορμᾶσθαι, 74.1.

58. See chap. 2, pp. 100–102 on the insufficiency of support generally.

59. On this strongest form of negation, see chap. 3, p. 138 with n. 65.

60. See also 7.71.3, quoted above.

ginning of 6.31, in which, as noted in chapter 1, Thucydides clusters vocabulary of vision and links it to emotion. The sight of the fleet drove home the dangers (τὰ δεινά) to observers; nevertheless, "because of the present strength (ῥωμή), because of the size of what they saw, they were cheered up by the sight (6.31.1).

In 7.75, those whose bodily strength has failed produce in the spectators on shore extraordinary grief. But the juxtaposition of *opsis* to *gnome* at a point of great suffering and understanding—like that in 7.71.3 (though the effect differs there)—shows ironically that now *opsis* and *gnome* are, finally, in conjunction. The Athenians now, unlike in 415, correctly interpret *opsis.* Now, in disaster, seeing produces knowledge, not misinterpretation.[61] The use of *opsis* makes clear the participatory or reciprocal nature of vision in this passage. There is a curious reversal of the ordinary relations of the viewer and the object of vision (the men aboard ship). The latter are the passionately engaged agents, not just in the battle itself, but also in the engaged and agonized consciousness of those viewing the events from the shore (the superficial subjects of the narrative).

The resonances between this passage and 6.31 are intensified by further instances of identical vocabulary. First, the use of the word ῥωμή a little farther on in 7.75, applied to those being left behind, who tried to follow until their bodily strength gave out, recalls the use of ῥωμή in 6.31.1. While it is an obvious word to use in the context of 7.75, it is less natural in 6.31. Its use in 7.75 may be intended partly to enhance the nuance of the word in 6.31, to keep before the reader the connection between bodies/lives and money. But whereas the sight of the "bodily strength" of the fleet once cheered spectators, now the vision produces pain. Second, Thucydides remarks in 6.30.2 that relatives and friends who saw off the fleet went down with a mixture of hope and lamentation (καὶ μετ' ἐλπίδος τε ἅμα ἰόντες ὀλοφυρμῶν), the hope being that they would conquer Sicily, and the lamentation arising from wondering "if they would ever see" (ὄψοιντο) their dear ones again. Correspondingly, the men who were to be left behind when the camp made their escape turned to lamentation (ὀλοφυρμόν, 75.4). The added irony is that those lamenting in both cases are specifically those left behind. Finally, the use of *deinon/deina* in 6.31.1 ("the dangers" came home to them for the first time) is evoked in 7.75.2 ("it was terrible not only because of the absence of hope and presence of danger but also because of seeing those who were to be left behind").

61. This kind of "recognition scene," in which someone reaches understanding out of obstinate misunderstanding at the moment of catastrophe or destruction is a common motif—think of Oedipus—but even so, Thucydides' account is intriguingly similar to Herodotos' account of the fall of Croesus, who, finally and only at the point of his destruction, understands the emptiness of his wealth and the meaning of his conversation with Solon (1.86).

Resonances with 6.31 become more explicit toward the end of 7.75. The misfortunes of the army were hardly made easier by the fact that they were shared, "especially since they had arrived at such a humiliating end after such a brilliant and vaunted beginning. Indeed," as Thucydides sums it up, "this was undeniably the greatest reversal ever experienced by a Hellenic expedition. They had come to enslave others and were now going away in fear of suffering enslavement themselves; they had left with prayers and paians and now began their return under adverse omens" (75.6–7). The "brilliant and vaunted beginning" (ἀπὸ οἵας λαμπρότητος καὶ αὐχήματος τοῦ πρώτου) directly recalls 6.31.6 ("The expedition was marveled at . . . for the daring, and famed for the brilliance of the sight," καὶ ὁ στόλος... τόλμης τε θάμβει καὶ ὄψεως λαμπρότητι περιβόητος ἐγένετο), as does the reference to prayers.[62]

There are further parallels between 7.75 and 6.31; these also have links to statements made by Nikias in his speeches to the Athenian assembly before the expedition set out. In 7.75.5, Thucydides strikingly describes the camp as a "starved-out city," and "not a small one" at that, comprising no less than 40,000 men.[63] The soldiers each "carried as much as they could of what was useful" (χρήσιμον, 75.5).[64] In 6.31 Thucydides stresses the extravagant, costly appearance of the expedition; while making clear its size, he implicitly emphasizes the uselessness of the expenditures, as noted in chapter 1. Here Thucydides mentions only grain (σιτία, σῖτος). The implication is that whatever money the Athenians still had was itself useless; only sustenance mattered. For one thing, their naval power, for which money was necessary, was gone. As Thucydides concludes the description of the army departing he chooses to underscore the paradox: "They were traveling by land instead of by sea, and relying not on their navy but on their infantry" (πεζούς τε ἀντὶ ναυβατῶν πορευομένους καὶ ὁπλιτικῷ προσέχοντας μᾶλλον ἢ ναυτικῷ, 75.7).

The paradox expressed by ἀντὶ and μᾶλλον ἤ, evokes another earlier passage, again ironically, from Nikias' second speech (examined in chapter 1). As we saw there, Nikias pointedly told the Athenians that they would win not "by the fleet," but would need a large infantry force.[65] The Athe-

62. Put, as in the case of the reversal of the Athenians' state of hopefulness, as an "anti-state": ἀντὶ δ' εὐχῆς; the word εὐχή is used only here and in 6.32.1.

63. See Dover, *HCT* 4, ad loc. for discussion of the problem with this figure. It certainly is hard to reconcile with the fact that only 6,000 men were under Demosthenes' command. Dover suggests that Thucydides was including slaves in the figure; I'm not sure whether the fact that Thucydides explicitly draws attention to the number of slaves who had deserted compromises that.

64. See 74.1, cited above.

65. Πρὸς οὖν δύναμιν οὐ ναυτικῆς καὶ φαύλου στρατιᾶς μόνον δεῖ, ἀλλὰ πεζὸν πολὺν ξυμπλεῖν, 6.21.1.

nians now have a large land force—40,000 men—but one that is now a liability, unable to be supported sufficiently, and needing to be employed for the purpose of escape. Other ironic echoes of comments made by Nikias emerge in 7.75. In his first speech Nikias remarks that "his words would be weak (ἀσθενεῖς, 6.9.2), when set up against the Athenians' character, should he urge them not to endanger what is real and present for the invisible." Now it is men, not words, that are wounded and weak—that is, sick (τραυματίαι τε καὶ ἀσθενεῖς, 75.3). But the emphasis on illness also recalls the description of the Athenians in their "diseased" state in 7.28, examined in chapter 3. The ultimate result of their impassioned condition, becoming "diseased in money," is precisely and movingly laid out in 7.75. Metaphor has become reality.[66]

Nikias' worries have come true. Before the expedition sailed, he urged: "It is important to remember that we have only recently had a break from a great plague and from war, so that we have been strengthened in money and bodies"; then he asserted that it was wrong to expend money and lives on behalf of foreigners who, "if they fail, will drag their friends down with them" (6.12.1). The Athenians' character (τρόπος) has driven them into new dangers and destruction; under Nikias' leadership, though not solely his, they have expended money and lives, which had been replenished and strengthened after disease and war, on behalf of foreigners and have lost what they risked; once again they are victims of disease and war.

The resonances with Nikias' earlier speech have the effect of bringing Nikias to mind, and the recollection of his prophetic words make the general a more sympathetic figure when he addresses his men in a speech following 7.75. Both Nikias and Demosthenes spoke on this occasion, but Thucydides presents only Nikias' speech, relegating Demosthenes' to a mere allusion—"Demosthenes also spoke and said such and similar things" (7.78.1). That Thucydides explicitly alludes to his choice makes clear that he had special historiographical reasons for highlighting Nikias at this moment; one effect is to temper any positive expectations the reader may have of the historian's presentation of the general.

I have already examined parts of this speech above. Here I want to focus on its introduction and beginning. In the introduction to the speech, Thucydides describes the scene: "Nikias, seeing the army disheartened and in such a reversal, coming up to the front, cheered them up and offered consolation to the extent that it was possible under their present circumstances, raising his voice as he went along the ranks out of concern and wishing that his words might provide as much benefit as possible" (7.76). Here, as be-

66. See also Thucydides' attention to the destructive effect of disease in the camp, 7.47.1–2, 50.3.

fore, Thucydides links vision and emotion, introducing the theme of hope as Nikias begins.

Nikias insists that the Athenians must have hope, explaining: "Some have been saved from even worse dangers (δεινοτέρων) than these . . . and I am worse off in bodily strength (ῥώμῃ) than any of you—for you see how I am affected by the disease (τῆς νόσου)." He then gives further grounds for hope, namely, his devotion to the gods and just behavior toward men, which lead him to have "bold hope for the future" (ἡ μὲν ἐλπὶς...θρασεῖα τοῦ μέλλοντος, 7.77.1–3). With its references to vision and emotion, Thucydides' introduction is suggestive of 6.31, as is also his reference to the Athenians' "present circumstances," for Thucydides ends 6.31 with the comment that the expedition was the "largest sent away from home and was attempted with the greatest hopes for the future compared with their present circumstances" (6.31.6). Morever, the theme of illness—again real, not metaphorical—continues with Nikias' allusion to his own sickness.

The theme of hope and its link with Nikias' expectation of divine favor also strongly evoke the Melian Dialogue. There the Athenians scorned the Melians' reliance on hope; now Nikias has not only hope, but "bold hope." There the Melians hoped for favor from the gods because they were just men fighting unjust men; now Nikias thinks his proper behavior will merit divine assistance. Hope is now all the Athenians in their other "city" have; as Thucydides has emphasized, they have insufficient supplies. And, as the narrative continues, they will meet with the utter destruction they insisted would befall those who relied on hope without a surplus of resources.

THE FINAL DISASTER

We come now to the culmination of the narrative of the expedition, and of the theme of *periousia chrematon, gnome,* and leadership in it. After the Syracusan victory, Nikias and Demosthenes began marching their men in retreat while the Syracusans and their allies kept harassing them with missiles, assaulting them on all sides (7.78–79). Finally, in the night, Nikias and Demosthenes decided to change their plan and head for the sea, in the opposite direction from that guarded by the Spartans, hoping to meet up with the Sicels, who were to aid them. But in the panic that a night march through unfamiliar territory can engender, the two parts of the army became separated by several miles, and Demosthenes' army, in the rear, was pursued by the Syracusans until it was surrounded, and, pelted by missiles, was unable to defend itself (7.80–81).

After attacking the men under Demosthenes with missiles all day and finally seeing them wounded and weakened, the Syracusans and Gylippos made a proclamation, offering liberty to any of the islanders who chose to come over; and some did, though Thucydides makes a point of adding that they were "not many."[67] Under the terms of capitulation, Demosthenes' men were to lay down their arms on the condition that no one was to be put to death either by violence, imprisonment, or starvation. Thus they surrendered, Thucydides writes, "six thousand in all, laying down all the money in their possession; and they filled up the hollows of four shields and were brought to town" (7.82.3).

The next day, the Syracusans caught up with Nikias' force, told him that Demosthenes and his men had surrendered, and offered Nikias' army the same terms as they had offered to Demosthenes and his troops. Nikias disbelieved their report of Demosthenes' surrender, but after a herald confirmed the news, he sent a message to the Syracusans and Gylippos with an offer to repay the cost of the war, giving hostages as security. The result was, as Thucydides relates it, that "the Syracusans and Gylippos refused the offer and attacked Nikias and his army as they had Demosthenes and his men, encircling and assaulting them with missiles until evening" (7.83.2). Although he had been offered the same terms as Demosthenes and his men and was offered such terms *before* he and his men had suffered what the others had, Nikias rejected the tender and did not even surrender after being attacked as the others had been. Indeed, he surrendered only after additional harm had been inflicted on his men. Thucydides is especially graphic about his troops' fate as Nikias pressed them on: the men, pelted on all sides by the Syracusans, exhausted and thirsty, made for the river Assinaros, where great disorder resulted. The Syracusans and Peloponnesians, on the other bank, threw javelins at them; the water became bloodied, but the men kept on drinking, "most even fighting over it." By the end, many dead lay heaped in the river, others at its edge. Finally, Nikias surrendered; those of his men taken alive were made public property, but many were slaughtered (7.84–85).

The surviving prisoners who had not run away or been butchered or sold were thrown in the quarries, and Nikias and Demosthenes were put to death. The total number of prisoners Thucydides estimates at not less than seven thousand. He ends his account of the disaster with the following comment: "This event turned out to be the greatest of any in this war, certainly to my mind the greatest Hellenic event even known by tradition, both the most brilliant for the victors and the most catastrophic for the losers: for beaten everywhere in every way, they suffered nothing small in any aspect; indeed, as has been said, they experienced utter destruction (πανωλεθρίᾳ); their men, their ships, there was nothing that was not destroyed, and few out of many returned home. This is what happened in Sicily" (7.87.5–6).

67. 7.82.1.

The Four Shields

In the midst of the horror and the pathos of these final chapters of book 7 Thucydides brings money into the narrative of destruction and disaster in a remarkable way at two significant moments in the captures of Demosthenes and Nikias and their men. Let us consider Demosthenes' surrender first. The agreement stated that Demosthenes' men, six thousand in all, would hand over their weapons on the condition that they not be killed. But Thucydides makes a point of noting that after they laid down their weapons, "they laid down all the money in their possession, putting it into the hollows of shields, and they filled up four shields" (καὶ τὸ ἀργύριον ὃ εἶχον ἅπαν κατέθεσαν ἐσβαλόντες ἐς ἀσπίδας ὑπτίας, καὶ ἐνέπλησαν ἀσπίδας τέσσαρας). "Then," he says, "they were immediately conveyed to the city" (7.82.3). Thucydides mentions nothing in the agreement about handing over money; of course, a defeated city or individuals were always at the complete mercy of the victors, though in this case Demosthenes had negotiated an agreement that guaranteed his men's lives.[68] But given that Thucydides does not list the surrender of money as one of the explicit terms of surrender, the inclusion of this detail is noteworthy. It suggests that the historian had a special interest in including it, especially given the manner in which he describes the scene. What, then, is its function in the narrative?

First, note the slow pace of the sentence: instead of simply stating that they laid down their weapons, handed over their money, and were immediately conveyed to town, Thucydides details the steps. There are three stages and three verbs:[69] they laid down (κατέθεσαν) their money, putting it into (ἐσβαλόντες) the hollows of shields, and they filled up (ἐνέπλησαν) four shields. After the frantic scene of the retreat of Demosthenes' army, there is a certain calm in this scene. It provides a pause in the description of the horror; but it also contributes to the overall pathos of the terrible end of the Athenians' endeavor.[70] Moreover, this passage begins the end of the account of the Sicilian expedition. It needs to be read against the beginning, for its function is perhaps ironic above all: the glittering display of wealth and power constructed so brilliantly by Thucydides in 6.31, the "many talents"

68. Pritchett (1991, 203–4) notes the lack of any fixed or standard treatment and the spottiness of the evidence concerning the fate of captives. Cf. Xen. *Cyr.* 7.5.73.

69. More precisely one might speak of two stages, with the first in two parts, "1b" indicated by the participle.

70. The nature of the description in the narrative pause allows the reader to become a spectator; as Hornblower (1994b, 34) notes, " the precision [i.e., mention of the number 4] here makes it easier to visualise, and the enumeration adds pathos." The pause is part of the larger narrative description; time does not stop, but it slows down at this moment. Thucydides thus conjoins elements of what Bal (1997, 106–11) regards as separate techniques.

carried out from Athens to Sicily, now have come down to this: four shields' worth of silver coins, taken from six thousand men. As conspicuously here as in 6.31 Thucydides does not estimate totals, preferring to construct an impressionistic scene.

Yet the question immediately arises, how much money would four shields hold? Is this visually evocative scene intended to suggest a lot of money, to encourage the reader to think about how the opportunity to put that money to use had been wasted; or is it, alternatively, supposed to indicate a paltry amount, adding to the irony of the scene, when the extravagance and expectations at the beginning of the expedition are recalled? By my estimates, the latter seems more likely: each shield would probably have held only about 2.5 to 3 talents, making the total amount laid down 10 to 12 talents.[71] Thus by choosing to plant a visual image of money before the reader at the devastating end of the expedition, Thucydides reminds us of the destruction of the city's financial resources. It is no coincidence that both beginning and closing scenes of the expedition are highly visual; they make the reader focus on them. Significantly, Thucydides makes money part of the

71. This is of course a very rough estimate. There are many unknowns, such as denominations, whether the coins in the shields were heaped or level, and the exact diameter and depth of the shield. But the estimate can tell us at least whether we should be concluding "large" or "small." To arrive at an estimate, I used a shield radius of 40 cm. and 10 cm. deep on the basis of one of the few shields preserved (Blyth 1982). I arbitrarily chose a combination of tetradrachms and drachms and determined that 30 tetradrachms and 16 drachms had a volume of 100 ml. Using the following semiellipsoidal formula

$$\begin{aligned} \text{volume} &= \frac{1}{2}\int_{-40}^{40} 10\sqrt{1-\frac{x^2}{1600}}\,\sqrt{1600 - x^2 dx} \\ &= \frac{10}{40}\int_{0}^{40} (x^2 - 1600)\,dx \\ &= \frac{1}{4}\left(\frac{x^3}{3} - 1600x\right)\Big|_{0}^{40} \\ &= \frac{1}{4}\left(64{,}000 - \frac{64{,}000}{3}\right) \\ &= \frac{64{,}000}{6} \\ &= 10{,}667\ \text{m}L \end{aligned}$$

I established that the shield (leveled) would have held 10,667 ml. (= 14,507.12 dr. or 2.4 talents per shield). Since the coins may have been heaped, we can round up to 3 talents for a total of 12. I thank M. Shane Garonzik and Peter van Alfen for the semiellipsoidal formula and for the shield volume calculation, and Nina Amenta for formatting the formula. I also thank Jack Kroll and the Agora excavations for access to the coin collection and Malcolm Wallace for references and help in the earliest stage of these calculations.

destruction, the *olethros,* that the men felt was impending shortly before, when they witnessed thunder and rain (7.79.3)—a phenomenon that was, Thucydides caustically notes, common in autumn.[72] Thucydides wants to bring the loss of money, and lives, directly to the attention of his audience at this moment. The inclusion of money is intentional, not incidental. The loss of money will be part of the *panolethria* referred to at the end of the expedition, and the implicit link between *chremata* and *olethros* recalls the explicit pairing in 7.27, discussed above.[73] Thucydides thus reminds his audience of the destruction of both wealth and lives in this war. Money and lives frame the whole account of the Sicilian expedition.

Money and Human Life: Nikias' Offer

Thucydides chooses to focus attention on the financial resources of the army only in connection with the surrender of Demosthenes and his men. After the mass destruction of much of Nikias' force and their final surrender, the Syracusans presumably removed what money they could find; Thucydides refers only to the surviving men as being public property (*es ton koinon,* 85.3) and to the collection of spoils (*skula,* 86.1).[74]

However, as noted above, Thucydides does include a scene featuring money of a very different sort:

> The Syracusans overtook Nikias [at the river Erineos] and told him that the troops under Demosthenes had surrendered, and invited him to follow their example. Incredulous, Nikias asked for a truce to send a horseman to see and, upon the return of the messenger with the tidings that they had surrendered, sent a herald to Gylippos and the Syracusans, saying he was ready to agree with them on behalf of the Athenians to repay whatever money the Syracusans had spent upon the war if they would let his army go, and offered until the money was paid to give Athenians as hostages, one for every talent. The Syracusans and Gylippos rejected this proposition and attacked them, standing around and hurling missiles at them from every side until evening. (7.83.1–3)

Like the brief but powerfully ironic vignette of the four shields of silver, the inclusion of this episode demands explanation, for Thucydides could have reported simply that Nikias' offer of an indemnity was made and turned

72. The men felt the storm was "for the purpose of their destruction" (ἐπί τῷ σφετέρῳ ὀλέθρῳ); the phrase, as Simon Hornblower points out to me, has distinct implications of divine anger; it is also thus a beautifully economical and elegant response to Nikias' remarks in his speech immediately preceding that the Athenians had suffered more than enough and could hope for favor from the gods (77.3): the men did not buy it. Cf. also Parker 1997, 155–56.

73. Chap. 3. The linkage between money and lives in both cases is similar as well.

74. The *skula* would likely be chiefly armor; on the usages of the word, see Pritchett 1991, 132–47.

down, or he could have simply omitted both episodes, as did Diodoros (13.19).[75] On the face of it, Nikias' proposal seems quite reasonable; certainly Plutarch (*Nik.* 27.2–3) implies that he took it as such, to illustrate his general characterization of Nikias. In relating the response of Gylippos and the Syracusans, the biographer uses harsh language that reflects ill on them: "With hubris and anger they reviled and insulted him" (27.3). Plutarch's point in including this episode is clearly to contrast Nikias' humanity and concern for his men with the barbaric response of the victors.[76]

But did Thucydides include this episode to bring out Nikias' humanity and cleverness? The answer, I would argue, is clearly no. For one thing, he notes simply that Gylippos and the Syracusans rejected Nikias' proposal, and Nikias decided to press on, and thus to continue not to surrender. His proposal and refusal to surrender only resulted in greater carnage or in enslavement for his men. Indeed, such a proposal would have been highly unusual. Although it was common for the victor to demand indemnities or hostages, an offer on the part of those defeated to pay an indemnity and provide hostages as a security was not at all common. Moreover, Nikias doubtless had in mind leaving some of the men already there as hostages—that seems the reasonable assumption from the context—in spite of the fact that they were already de facto captives of the Syracusans; thus he wants to convert their status from captive to hostage.

In fact, the entire procedure he suggests has a strange cast to it; indeed it constitutes a kind of reverse ransoming. Instead of offering to ransom the men—using money as stand-ins for them—Nikias presents a variant: he wants to use the men as stand-ins—they are hostages—for money. His knowledge of the financial straits the Syracusans were in as a result of the war likely led him to propose an indemnity using men as hostages until the money could be raised;[77] but once again he miscalculated. Nikias continues to be, in Dover's words, obsessed with, fixated on, the financial element, and this is a fundamental part of Thucydides' criticism of the general. Nikias' refusal to surrender was implicitly motivated by his thinking that the Syracu-

75. Westlake (1968, 205) laments the brevity of the report, commenting that Thucydides "seems to have felt unable, or unwilling, to explain the reasons why Nicias took this action or to suggest to his readers, directly or indirectly, what conclusions they should draw from the incident." In my view, it is more useful to ask why he included what he did, for it may provide insight into the reasons for inclusion.

76. But note the critical comment about Nikias' behavior in the comparison of Nikias and Crassus at 5.4; Panagopoulos 1989, 133, with n. 3.

77. Thucydides notes later (7.86.4) that when Nikias eventually surrendered to Gylippos he counted on the Spartans to have goodwill toward him, because of his role in arranging peace with Sparta in 421. It is not made clear whether this would have entered into his thinking when he made the offer of the indemnity as well.

sans would be persuaded by money, because *his* mind was so focused on the financial element[78]—that is, his proposal is significant because it shows *how* he is thinking, namely, first and foremost about a financial strategy.

Moreover, Nikias' proposal of the equivalence of one talent per man is also striking, not because the men are valued at one talent, but rather the reverse: one talent is worth one man. Thus in Thucydides' presentation Nikias is revealing that money is worth more than men; paradoxically, then, he is devaluing the men, because he would be committing substantially fewer men to the precarious position of hostages than is customary in the case of ransom prices set for an individual.[79] Arguably, in a better-faith proposal Nikias would have offered more men, since such an offer would have underscored his awareness of the paramount importance of human life; it would have strengthened the sincerity of the promise. This does not mean, of course, that such an offer would have been accepted. As Dover comments: "The Syracusans, like Nikias, knew that Athens could raise money, and would raise as much of it as possible from subjects, but soldiers and sailors were not so easily replaceable."[80] In this case the Syracusans understand the value of human life; Nikias privileges, but miscalculates, the value of money in relation to men.[81]

The value of human life over material wealth is expressed more poetically by Adrastos in Euripides' *Suppliant Women:* "If you lose money, you can get it back, but no one recovers this expense: a human life" (*Supp.* 775–77, trans. Lattimore). The sentiment is expressed most famously by Achilles to the embassy presenting Agamemnon's offer of a "boundless ransom" (*Il.* 9.120): "[No wealth] is worth as much as my life, not even as much as they say is stored up in Ilion, . . . for cattle and fat sheep are there for the plundering, and tripods may be acquired, and tawny horses; but the life of a man, plundered or taken, cannot be brought back, once it passes the fence of the teeth" (*Il.* 9.406–9).[82]

This section of book 7 contains provocative resonances with *Iliad* 9 generally. Indeed, the backdrop of the *Iliad* may help partly to explain Thucydides' inclusion of the episode concerning Nikias' offer. There are significant parallels between Agamemnon's offer in the *Iliad* and that of Nikias.[83]

78. In like vein, Ducrey 1968, 76; in discussing the enslavement of the Athenians by the Syracusans, Ducrey sees the latter's motives as chiefly political and military, and only secondarily economic.

79. One to three mnai appear commonly in our evidence for the classical period; see Pritchett 1991, 245–61.

80. *HCT* 4, ad. loc.

81. See also Panagopoulos 1989, 142–44.

82. On the phrase, see Hainsworth 1985 ad loc.; Griffin 1995 ad. loc.

83. It has recently been argued by Zadorojnyi (1998), although without reference to this particular passage, that Thucydides' Nikias corresponds in a number of ways to Agamemnon;

In *Iliad* 9, Nestor appeals to Agamemnon to offer Achilles gifts (δώροισιν, 113); Agamemnon agrees but then refers to what he will offer as a "boundless ransom" (ἀπερείσι' ἄποινα, 120). He continues with a staggering list of gifts.[84] Agamemnon's reference to a ransom is especially noteworthy, since, as Emmet Robbins has observed, it is the sole instance in the poem of a Greek offering ransom.[85] Donna Wilson, in an examination of the implications of this singular passage, emphasizes the importance of the word choice —"ransom," not "recompense," for the slight to Achilles' honor—and argues convincingly that "Agamemnon has made an offer Achilleus cannot but refuse."[86] By contrast to gifts of compensation, she observes, "the system [of ransom] dictates that accepting ἄποινα should cost the victor none of his gains in τιμή [honor]." Wilson continues: "Instead of consolidating Achilleus' gains in τιμή, the ἄποινα conserve Agamemnon's τιμή by reason of his largess, and. . . . Several of the items [offered in the ransom] assert Agamemnon's position of superiority in relation to Achilleus."[87] Finally, she notes, ransoming takes place between enemies.[88]

Achilles is, in effect, holding himself hostage; it is his body that is being ransomed for use on the battlefield.[89] To give himself up and return to battle would involve, as Wilson points out, a massive loss of honor, because of the exhorbitant extent and nature of the payment, and would confirm Achilles' subordinate position. Nikias, in his almost perverse reconfiguring of a ransom exchange, offers to supply hostages, but in an exchange that likewise is way out of proportion. For Achilles to accept Agamemnon's offer of ransom would have virtually meant, from his perspective, a devaluing of his life because of the diminution of honor. For the Syracusans and Gylippos and his men to accept Nikias' offer would have equally constituted a de-

see also Allison (1997a), who documents the increased abundance of Homeric allusions at the end of the Sicilian narrative.

84. See Hainsworth 1985 ad loc.

85. Robbins 1990, 12.

86. Wilson 1999, 143. Note Nestor's reformulation of Agamemnon's ἄποινα after Agamemnon has concluded his list of possessions he will offer Achilles. Nestor reverts to his earlier characterization of what Agamemnon should give as "gifts"; as gifts, they are "not to be scorned" (δῶρα...οὐκέτ' ὀνοστά, 9.164).

87. Wilson 1999, 142. As Emmet Robbins has pointed out to me, this status imbalance is emphasized explicitly by Agamemnon in 9.160, where he refers to himself in relation to Achilles as βασιλεύτερος. This is not expressed to Achilles, but the implication is not lost on him, as he later refers to Agamemnon sarcastically as "more kingly than I" (ὅς βασιλεύτερος ἐστιν, 9.392).

88. Wilson 1999, 137–38.

89. Contra Wilson (1999, 141, 143), who states without argument that the ransom is to spare future Achaian lives. While this is possible, it seems to me to be blurring the consequences of the exchange, the anticipated saving of Achaian lives, with the immediate objects of exchange themselves, Achilles' body in return for the payment.

valuing of their honor, and an acceptance of their subordination to Nikias —victors and conquered would be exchanged. Nikias has made a critical mistake in judgment.

Thucydides makes clear that the Syracusans' desire to defeat the Athenians decisively, rather than simply to win, but at the cost of an Athenian retreat, has as much to do with their reputation in the Greek world as with how it will increase their power, and that they are concerned about their reputation not only among their contemporaries, but for all time. Should they "conquer the Athenians and their allies by land and by sea, the contest would appear to the Greeks noble for themselves" (καλὸν σφίσιν ἐς τοὺς Ἕλληνας τὸ ἀγώνισμα φανεῖσθαι), and they would be "greatly marveled at by other men [now] and by those in the future" (εἶναι ὑπό τε τῶν ἄλλων ἀνθρώπων καὶ ὑπὸ τῶν ἔπειτα πολὺ θαυμασθήσεσθαι, 7.56.2).[90]

Reading Nikias' offer and the Syracusans' blanket and immediate refusal against Agamemnon's offer and Achilles' unequivocal and likewise immediate refusal in the *Iliad* thus enhances the meaning of the narrative in the *History,* and suggests one further implication. At this stage of the war, the Athenians have been presented (most conspicuously in the Melian Dialogue) as having dispensed with the traditional values of honor and justice, viewing them as outmoded relics of the past, and have insisted that all that matters in this new world is sheer power, including the power of money. But the Syracusans' refusal, like that of Achilles, constitutes in part a triumph of these traditional values: honor and reputation win; those who hold the cards will not subordinate themselves even—or especially—for vast amounts of material possessions or money. In part, they want to see their enemy destroyed.

Additional ironies emerge from the presentation of Nikias within Thucydides' narrative. Recall that Nikias' prime argument against evacuation was, as Thucydides puts it, that the Athenians should not depart "defeated by money." But it is Nikias who is defeated by money in the end, when his offer of making the men hostages until an indemnity was raised is refused. In this final scene he is presented in a rather crude light: he thinks money will buy his way out of the catastrophe in which he has placed his men.[91] He overrates the importance of money at this stage in comparison with other factors; by thinking that money will talk, he reveals a lack of intelligent judg-

90. Cf. also 7.68.3: Gylippos' reference to "the noble contest" (καλὸς ὁ ἀγών, 7.71.1: during the final naval battle the Syracusan side is φιλονικῶν . . . περὶ τοῦ πλέονος ἤδη καλοῦ; and 7.86.2: after all the Athenians were captured, Gylippos thought that it would be a καλὸν τὸ ἀγώνισμα to hand the enemy generals over to the Spartans.

91. Cf. Plut. *Nik.* 28 and Diod. 13.19; but cf. also Plut. *Nik.* 10.1, where, according to Theophrastos, at the time of the Peace of Nikias, Nikias used bribery to fix the lot that would determine who had to restore possessions, Athens or Sparta.

ment.[92] By contrast, Demosthenes willingly gives up his men and their money for a guarantee of their safety: Demosthenes gauges the situation with greater intelligence and judgment than Nikias: he is thinking about the safety—the value—of his men. Demosthenes aimed to save men, not money; Nikias, whose intentions were similar, nevertheless loses lives as wealth.[93]

But surely the most conspicuous irony in the presentation of Nikias emerges when the victors debate the fate of Nikias and Demosthenes. Gylippos wanted to take the generals back to Sparta, thinking it a "noble achievement" (καλὸν τὸ ἀγώνισμα, 7.86.2). But Thucydides notes (with the qualifier "as it was said") that some of the Syracusans opposed letting them live, and most of all the Corinthians, who feared that Nikias would bribe his way out, "because he was rich,"[94] and stir up new trouble (86.4). So both generals were killed. Nikias' own money led directly to his own—and Demosthenes'—destruction.

On the public level, the larger interpretative layer of the Sicilian expedition, ignorance, finances, and leadership come together to undermine the city's power. On the personal level, private wealth and the perceptions and inferences of others based on it also lead to destruction. Alkibiades' extravagant expenditures were able to fuel widespread fear and suspicion against him and led to his elimination from Athens. But paradoxically, as we saw in chapter 1, Thucydides also implicitly makes the Athenians mimic Alkibiades' greed and lusts, and this led to their downfall. Nikias lost his life precisely because of his money.[95] It cannot be accidental that Thucydides highlights Alkibiades' wealth at the beginning of the Sicilian narrative, and Nikias' at the end.

CONCLUSION

Thucydides' presentation of the Sicilian expedition, long appreciated for its drama, passion, and tragedy, has as well a crucial methodological purpose: to impart lessons. For Thucydides the expedition provided the best test case

92. If, as Westlake (1968, 205) argues, the offer had been "carefully thought out" in advance and was not "the outcome of a sudden impulse," the criticism becomes even more pronounced.

93. In another irony, Nikias had offered to convert his men into wealth for the Syracusans; the latter, in the end, made the conversion themselves when they made Nikias' soldiers into public property (7.85).

94. ὅτι πλούσιος γάρ—"devastatingly casual three words," as Hornblower nicely puts it.

95. Indeed, to go back to an earlier point in the *History,* Thucydides' political fall and exile—as he himself chooses to put it—resulted indirectly from his own money: knowing of Thucydides' influence in the north with the Thracian chiefs because of his mining contracts there, Brasidas went especially quickly to Amphipolis and succeeded in getting the surrender of the city before Thucydides could arrive to save it (4.105–6, with *Money,* 172–75).

of the combination of *periousia chrematon, gnome,* and the ability to lead. That he had such an aim in writing the account is clear from the nature of the financial information he presents and its relationship to the larger narrative. From the outset of the expedition, in which he emphasizes the recovered financial strength of the Athenians, to the attention to financing that punctuates key moments of decision making and reaches an explicit climax at the end, to the narrative techniques he employs to keep the reader focused on money, Thucydides highlights the critical factor of *gnome,* in order to show it lacking. His presentation adds up to two central criticisms: first, the folly of not sending out a larger expedition initially and of not supporting adequately the one that the Athenians did send out, reinforcing it substantially only when it was too late. The Athenians collectively are implicated, to be sure, but the historian's lens is focused on the character of Nikias, who was particularly useful for Thucydides precisely because of his concern about, and presumed knowledge of, war finance, and his obsession with money. For Thucydides, Nikias was someone who appeared to have a grasp of the role of financial resources in war and power; yet because he made bad judgments and failed as a leader, he did even more damage to the city ultimately than might otherwise have been done. In short, in Thucydides' overall assessment of Athenian leadership, Nikias was the antithesis of Perikles.[96]

96. Bender (1938, 43–51) argues that the two men are presented as opposites when it comes to "knowing what is necessary" (γνῶναι τὰ δέοντα).

CHAPTER FIVE

The Financing of the Sicilian Expedition and the Economic Nature of the *Arche*

Thucydides and Inscriptions

In the preceding chapters my focus has been primarily literary and historiographical in order to establish how Thucydides was thinking about the usefulness of money as a theme in his work. I have argued that his treatment of the financial aspect of the Sicilian expedition is highly rhetorical, imbued with irony, and above all concerned to highlight the improper uses of wealth that result from a lack of proper leadership and a climate of irrationality. That is to say that Thucydides' presentation of the financial aspect parallels and enriches other themes in the Sicilian books: passion, irrationality, ignorance, and excess. The historiographical and rhetorical function of Thucydides' treatment of money makes his account more rather than less valuable for understanding the historical context. For one thing, the nature of Thucydides' treatment of financial resources in books 6 and 7 demonstrates how deeply interested he is in both the financing of the Sicilian expedition and Athens' management of its finances; even when, as we have seen, he is vague and impressionistic in his presentation of financial details, it is not because he is not interested in the subject, but rather because of his historiographical purpose. Above all, he wants to present a critique of Athenian leadership and democracy and to highlight the deadliness of the combination of money, greed, and emotion.

Given this focus, it makes sense that Thucydides' text should be of value in contributing to our knowledge both of the financing of the expedition and of the imperial economy. It should also be useful in assessing other evidence and perhaps in arriving at a fuller picture of the Sicilian expedition. In this chapter I shall examine Thucydides in relation to some of the central epigraphic documents with which his text has been linked or with which I shall propose it may be linked. I shall also consider the usefulness of his text for better understanding the changes in the economic administration of the *arche.*

THUCYDIDES AND THE DECREES RELATING TO THE SICILIAN EXPEDITION: *IG* I^3 93 (ML 78)

IG I^3 93 consists of eight fragments of fine, crystallized white marble that have been associated with one or more meetings of the assembly pertaining to the Sicilian expedition in 415.[1] None of the fragments joins, though there is a possible physical join in the case of fragments *d* and *g*. None of the fragments mentions Sicily, yet they have, since the publication of *IG* I^2, been attached to the decision to go to Sicily in 415, chiefly because of the belief that they accord neatly with Thucydides' narrative of the assemblies leading up to the launching of the expedition and, secondarily, because of three references to sixty ships, and the compatibility of the letter forms with a date of 415.[2] Only Rudi Thomsen and Harold Mattingly have dissented, although only in part; they too associate the fragments with the Sicilian expedition, preferring to assign them to 413, when reinforcements under Demosthenes were sent out.[3]

These inscriptions are important in their own right, for, although frag-

1. I examined all of the fragments, as well as *IG* I^3 94 (on which see note 2), on two separate occasions in 1996 and 1997. I am grateful to Dr. Charilambos Kritzas, Director of the Epigraphic Museum, for permission to examine the stones. I thank Mr. Stergios Tzanekas of the EM for confirming the similarity of the marble of each fragment. I also thank Robert Morstein-Marx and Ronald Stroud for examining the stones with me.

2. The eight fragments came to be grouped together in two stages. Frags. *a* through *e* were published as *IG* I 55. Kirchhoff noted the similarity of subject matter and physical resemblance but asserted that frags. *c* and *d* could not be joined "propter nimios eorum quae interciderunt hiatus." All five fragments were found on the Akropolis and published by Pittakys (in the *Ephemeris* or *L'ancienne Athènes*) or by Rangabé (*L'antiquités helléniques,* 1842), both of whom associated frags. *b* and *c*. *IG* I^2 98/99 includes those five fragments, with an additional three: *f* and *g*, added by Wilhelm; and *h*, under the heading *loci incerti* (but curiously Hiller does not mention who associated it with the others, nor does Kirchner refer to it in his commentary). The fragments have been variously placed. At different times, *a* and *f* have been thought to be from the same stele; *a, d,* and *g* placed under the heading *stela secunda?* and *e, f,* and *h* under *fragmenta incerti loci.* The current grouping in *IG* I^3 depends heavily on Dover's republication of the fragments in *HCT* 4. It should be noted that an additional fragment was apparently at one time thought to belong to the same group, since it has the same EM number as the others (6591); in *IG* I^2 100 (= *IG* I^3 94), Kirchner noted its similarity in lettering to the others. From the physical standpoint of the characteristics of the marble and measurements of thickness, there is, contra the standard view, no impediment to the hypothesis that all fragments could have come from the same stele. The differences in thickness noted by Dover are insignificant when considering variations in thickness of intact stelai, many of which tend to get thicker toward the bottom. This is not to say, it needs to be stressed, that the fragments do belong on the same stele.

3. Thomsen 1965, 174–75; Mattingly 1968, 453–54 [1996, 219–20].

mentary, they contain detailed information about military preparations and decision making that can enhance our knowledge of the functioning of the assembly. But if they do belong to the Sicilian preparations, they are also highly significant for assessing—in fact, they are damaging to—Thucydides' account of the Sicilian expedition.[4] Scholars have associated fragments *b* and *c* with the assembly meeting reported in 6.8.2, and *a* and *d/g* with the meeting held four days later, which is introduced in 6.8.3, where the speeches of Nikias and Alkibiades are also presented. How closely do the fragments correspond to what we find in the *History*?

Fragments b *and* c *and Thucydides 6.8.2*

We need to recall that prior to the meeting reported by Thucydides in 6.8.2, the Egestan envoys were in Athens urging the Athenians in repeated sessions of the assembly to help them in their war with the Selinountines (6.6.2–3). They promised to pay for the war, and in response the Athenians voted to send an embassy to Sicily to confirm the existence of the money and to assess the situation with Selinous. The embassy subsequently returned, accompanied by the Egestan envoys, who produced 60 talents of bullion (6.8.1), on the basis of which the Athenians voted to send sixty ships to Sicily and to appoint as generals with full powers (στρατηγοὶ αὐτοκράτορες) Alkibiades, Nikias, and Lamachos. Five days later a second assembly was held to consider the speediest means of equipping a fleet and to vote whatever else the generals might require for the expedition (6.8.3).

How well do the inscriptions fit this narrative outline? Fragment *b*, with portions of nine lines, concerns a decision about the number of generals ("whether one general," τὸν δε̃μ]ον αὐ̣τ̣ί̣κα μάλα εἴτε δοκεῖ hένα στρατ[εγόν], line 2[5]); we can infer from a later reference to ships (line 7) that it was a naval expedition. The decree also contains a reference to "the enemy as much as they are able" (τὸς πολεμίος hος ἂν δύνονται, line 4), to "allies" in the genitive (τõν χσυμμάχον, line 5), "to the boule," probably "cities to the boule" (π]όλες ἐς τὲμ βολέν, line 6)—the "cities" certainly referring to subjects of Athens—and to "sixty ships" in the genitive (h]ε̣χσέκοντα νεõν, line 7). Scholars commenting on this fragment have focused especially on the phrase "whether one general" and the possibility that only one general

4. Curiously, they have never received substantive, comprehensive scrutiny, and even Dover, who republished them in 1970 (*HCT* 4: 224–27) based on autopsy in 1963, did not consider in any depth the contents of the fragments. It is beyond the scope of this chapter to examine them as fully as they deserve; I hope to publish a more extensive epigraphical and historical discussion elsewhere.

5. For ease of reference I shall refer to the continuous series of line numbers as they appear in *IG* I[3] 93 and ML 78, rather than numbering each fragment separately.

might be appointed. Thus Dover comments: "The fact that a proposal to entrust an expedition of such magnitude and importance to a single general was seriously entertained is the most interesting contribution to our knowledge offered by any of these fragments."[6] This does not necessarily conflict with Thucydides; he gives no details about the nature of the proposals before, or the deliberations in, the assembly, only the final result. But one would have to suppose that farther along in the decree reference would be made to the decision about whether to appoint one general or more;[7] this information does not seem to have been recorded in this section of the decree, but there are parallels in which the decision appears both immediately after the εἴ[τε . . . εἴ]τε clause and farther on in a later part of a document.[8] Yet it is important to note that Dover is begging the question, since his comment is based on the assumption that the fragment belongs to the first assembly meeting recorded by Thucydides.

Apart from the references to sixty ships and "the enemy"—references that could of course apply to numerous situations, and have no necessary connection to the Sicilian expedition[9]—nothing in fragment *b* corresponds closely to Thucydides, and it is difficult to interpret the reference to π]όλες ἐς τὲμ βολὴν (line 6) in the light of his text. Adding fragment *c*, which Lewis in *IG* I^3 suggests was inscribed on the *stela prima* together with *b*, does not clarify the picture; Dover thought it most likely pertained to a later meeting, and, indeed, it has a different character from fragment *b*. Fragment *c* is concerned partly with the financial arrangements primarily, it seems, for a naval expedition: again there is a reference to "the sixty ships"[10] (line 13) and to the "expedition of the ships" (line 19). There is also a possible reference to taxation in the phrase ἀπὸ τõτιμέματος (line 11),[11] and to an "*eisphora*, whenever it is necessary" (ἐσφέρεν hόταν δεε, line 14), to "the city spending as much as" (τὲμ πόλιν ἀναλõν hόσον, line 12), a reference to "the gen-

6. *HCT* 4: 225; also Busolt 1904, 1277.

7. Frag. *c* mentions generals in the plural; if it comes from the same stele as frag. *b*, reference to the decision reached would have to intervene. But it is not even certain that if so, they necessarily refer to the same expedition.

8. Immediately after: Tod 2.123 (stele of Aristoteles); later on: *IG* I^3 61 (Methone).

9. Sixty ships seems a fairly standard number in naval operations: e.g., a detachment to Egypt, late 450s, from a larger fleet of 200 ships (Thuc. 1.112.3); to Samos, 440 (Thuc. 1.116.1; Diod. 12.27.4); again to Samos (Thuc. 1.116.3; Diod. 12.28.2); to Corinth, 427 (Thuc. 3.80.2); to Kythera, 424 (Thuc. 4.53.1; Diod. 12.65.8); against the Peloponnesian fleet, 411 (Diod. 13.38.7); to Samos, 406 (Diod. 13.97.1). Cf. non-Athenian operations: e.g., from Peloponnesian allies to help Corinth, 432 (Diod. 12.33.3); from Corcyra, 427 (Thuc. 3.77); from Sparta, 425 (Thuc. 4.2.3).

10. The definite article seems inevitable from the sigma before hεχσέκοντα ναῦς in line 4 of the fragment (line 13 in *IG* I^3 93).

11. One cannot rule out other kinds of payments or costs.

erals" in the dative plural (line 18) and "the rest of the crew" (τε̃ς ἄλλες hυπερεσίας, line 22), to "silver for a sacrifice" (ἀργυρίο ἐς καλλιέρεσιν, line 23), and to the number 1,600 (line 24).

These financial arrangements seem premature not only for a preliminary assembly, but also for the one held several days later (6.8.3); and far from corresponding to Thucydides' narrative, they conflict with it. Two points in particular tell against the correspondence. First, as demonstrated above, Thucydides is at some pains to bring out the fact that the Athenians had rebuilt their finances during the Peace of Nikias and were thus able to prepare easily and expeditiously for the operation;[12] therefore, the idea that the Athenians would have had recourse to such harsh measures as internal direct taxation, which was as a rule resorted to only in times of perceived pressing need, contradicts his narrative.[13] Second, Thucydides also makes clear that the Athenians fully believed the Egestans when they said that they had plenty of ready cash with which to pay for the expedition.

Moreover, as concerns the correlation with the first assembly, Nikias' second speech (6.20–23) suggests rather that neither the generals nor the Athenians had yet made any specific arrangements, including arrangements for the financing of the expedition. There are further difficulties. The decree refers to the holding of an assembly in or within ten days;[14] yet the next assembly after that in 6.8.2 was to be held in four days. There is also a reference to "correcting" something ([ἐ]πανορθο̃σθαι, lines 19–20), which is also odd in view of the preliminary nature of the matter before the assembly in 6.8.2. Of course, Thucydides makes clear that there were several meetings of the assembly at which the issue of an expedition to Sicily had arisen prior to that at which the Athenians voted to send sixty ships and appoint Alkibiades, Nikias, and Lamachos as generals (6.6.2); but the only decision they had made, as far as we know, was to send ambassadors to Sicily to investigate the truth of the Egestans' promise of money and to determine the state of the conflict with the Selinountines, and both of these instructions had been carried out.[15]

There is, then, very little to link either fragment *b* or *c* with the assembly

12. E.g., 6.26.2; cf. 6.12.1; above, chap. 1, p. 47; chap. 4, pp. 149–50.

13. As both Thomsen (1965, 174–75) and Mattingly (1968, 453–54 [1996, 219–20]) point out in their objections to assigning these decrees as a whole to 415 on the grounds that the Athenians were not in any dire need of money in 415 and would not yet have resorted to such an oppressive measure as an *eisphora.* On *eisphorai* in the war, see Dover 1950, 59; Thomsen 1964, 143–77; Mattingly 1968, 450–56 [1996, 215–22]; *Money,* 134–36.

14. ΛΕΣΙΑΝ ποιεσάντον δέκα hε is preserved in line 6; the restoration [ἐκκ]λεσίαν ποιεσάντον δέκα hε[μερο̃ν] seems inevitable.

15. At least we know they investigated—though that is putting it charitably (cf. Thuc. 6.46)—the financial situation, and can assume they looked into the state of the conflict.

reported in Thucydides 6.8.2, and there are difficulties as well in applying fragment *c* to the second assembly.[16] Now let us consider the other fragments in relation to the narrative.

Fragments a *and* d/g *and Thucydides 6.8.3–26.1*

Fragments *a* and *d/g* have been correlated with the meeting at which Nikias and Alkibiades spoke, which is reported in 6.9–23.[17] Recall that, according to Thucydides, after his second speech, Nikias was pressured into delivering details on the spot about the expedition's size and composition. Responding that he would have preferred to decide on the specific arrangements in private with his fellow generals, he nevertheless estimated that the Athenians should determine the number of troop transports, that they should bring no fewer than one hundred triremes, five thousand hoplites (Athenian and allied) and if possible more, and as to the rest of the preparation, it should be proportionate, including archers from Crete and slingers (6.25.2); he also noted that they should bring as much food and money as possible. The Athenians then voted immediately that the generals should have absolute authority both about the size of the army and about the expedition generally and should make decisions in the best interests of the Athenians (6.26.1).

Now the inscriptions. Fragment *a* contains a substantial amount of specific information relative to its preserved parts: in order, references to the number forty, to peltasts (restored but likely),[18] archers, four obols, the *kubernetai, tamiai,* trierarchs, the boule, and the enemy occur. What is striking about this fragment when read alongside Thucydides is that it does not match the impression created by the latter. I use "impression" deliberately, because, as argued above,[19] Thucydides constructs his account to emphasize the muddled and disorderly nature of the decision-making process in the assembly (recall that the result, the *paraskeue,* is described as ὀχλώδης, "crowdlike" in 6.24.2). In Thucydides the final decisions are left up to the generals, who are, after all, designated as having absolute authority (*autokratores*).[20] In the inscription, by contrast, details down to the specific rate of pay for certain individuals are laid out, none of them recognizable either

16. In addition to the difficulties in making the contents of the fragments mesh well with Thucydides, the etas are slightly different: in *c,* they are consistently narrow, as Tracy noted (1984, 282), whereas in *b* they tend to be somewhat wider, often the same size as a nu.

17. They are placed under *stela secunda* by Lewis in *IG* I^3, though under "Assembly C" by Dover. Cf. Tod (ad 1.77), who thinks the fit is precise.

18. Devine, in a review of the revised edition of Meiggs and Lewis (1988, 111), refers to this restoration as apparently the earliest epigraphic testimony of peltasts; but cf. *IG* I^3 60.17, which is undated but usually placed ca. 430.

19. Chap. 1, pp. 42–44.

20. I shall return to this point below.

from the part of Thucydides' account summarized above or from the narrative dealing with what the Athenians finally sent out in 6.31, apart from the number forty and reference to trierarchs, both of which could fit any number of contexts. Moreover, the only rate of pay Thucydides mentions is 1 drachma a day for the sailors (*nautai,* 6.31.3). If the oarsmen, the lowest of the naval crew, were being paid a drachma a day, it is difficult to see what group would be receiving a lesser amount.[21]

If we return to fragments *d/g,* near the top is a reference to "either guarding the [city or] the land" (ἒ φροροῦσι τὲ[μ πόλιν ἒ τὲ]ν χόραν, line 41), followed in the next line by mention of "whoever is not on patrol or receiving pay" (hὸς ἂν μὲ περιπο[λε̃ι μεδὲ μ]ισθοφορε̃[ι, line 42). There is reference to a voyage (line 43), to the boule (line 43), to liability to a penalty (line 44), to the prytaneis (line 44), to rescinding a decree (lines 44–45), and to the expedition of sixty ships (line 46). Finally, there is an apparent prohibition against using resources for other purposes (line 47). There is possibly a reference to either "three thousand" or "without the thousand" on the next line (ΡΙΣΧΙΛΙΟΝ is extant, line 48), followed by the likely formula "but if anyone proposes or puts to the vote" (ἐ[ὰν δέ τις εἴπει] ἒ ἐπιφσ[εφίσει], lines 48–49), and, finally, in the next line, most of the word for "set aside" (ΕΧΣΑΙΡ, line 49). Reference to rescinding an earlier decree would certainly fit the context of the assembly in Thucydides just summarized, for the expedition was expanding beyond the scope envisioned in 6.8.2. In that case, however, reference to "the sixty ships" is unclear, unless it belongs to the *psephisma* to be rescinded of the previous line, but it is a little farther removed on the stone than one would expect.[22]

What is to be made of ΡΙΣΧΙΛΙΟΝ? With the exception of Mattingly all commentators have accepted the restoration "three thousand" and have universally assumed that it is a reference to 3,000 talents, set aside for the expedition.[23] H. T. Wade-Gery initially expressed reservations about whether the figure was three thousand or one thousand, or even whether the fragment concerned the Sicilian expedition.[24] He apparently withdrew his doubts, for in *ATL,* it is stated as a fact that the expedition cost at least 3,420 talents, and the evidence for the 3,000 is this fragment.[25] Eugène Cavaignac estimated that the two-year expedition could not have cost less

21. But cf. Loomis (1998, 43), who questions whether the figure is a reference to pay but offers no alternative interpretation.

22. A possible explanation is that the increase in the fleet's size was put in terms of an increase of forty to the original sixty.

23. Mattingly 1968, 461 n. 2 [1996, 228 n. 50].

24. Wade-Gery 1931, 74 n. 69.

25. *ATL* 3: 357. See also Ferguson 1932, 160: "As a matter of fact we have in *IG* I^2 99 the mention of a sum of 3000 talents 'set aside' for the Sicilian Expedition."

than 3,000 talents,[26] but that the Athenians knew this in 415 is too neat a coincidence, and whether they earmarked 3,000 talents in 415 does not answer the question of what the expedition actually cost.[27]

There is, however, substantial evidence from Thucydides to vitiate the restoration of "3,000," understanding "talents," and the corresponding reconstruction that the Athenians were setting aside, in 415, 3,000 talents for the Sicilian expedition.[28] We need to recall that the Athenians believed that the Egestans were going to pay for the expedition. To be sure, the Athenians equipped the fleet with their own resources, as Thucydides makes clear in his extraordinary description in 6.31, and they anticipated, he tells us, a lengthy campaign (6.31.3); but it does not make sense that they would, in 415, regard the expedition to Sicily as something that would be so costly to them, given their expectation of local funding and provisioning, or that they would prepare for it financially in advance—even by taxing themselves—rather than authorizing money as need arose.

Despite Nikias' warning in his last speech before the expedition, that the Athenians should "especially bring as much money as possible," on the grounds of the disingenuousness of the Egestans' offer (6.22), the Athenians clearly did not believe him on this point. Moreover, in the following narrative, as we saw in chapter 2, both Nikias and Alkibiades implicitly refuted the notion that the Athenians had either authorized or taken with them 3,000 talents. After uncovering the Egestan deception, the three generals consulted on what to do under the circumstances. With the exception of Nikias, they were surprised—recall that Alkibiades and Lamachos did not "calculate" on this[29]—and all were dismayed. Their ensuing proposals dealt with how to get money. That is to say, they clearly had not brought "as much money as possible" with them but had expected the Egestans to pay, and now were short of cash. As we saw, the narrative of book 6 consistently draws attention to their financial need. Nikias' proposal was to "see if the Egestans would provide money for the whole force, but if not, at least to provision the sixty ships they had requested," and he concludes by noting the importance of not spending home resources (6.47). In fact, all three generals advocate ways of obtaining cash or *sitos* from Sicily itself, not from home. Finally, in his speech at Sparta, Alkibiades refers to the Athenians' in-

26. Cavaignac 1908, 144.

27. There is, furthermore, difficulty in explaining why the accounts of the treasury of Athena for 415 (*IG* I³ 370) bear no evidence of massive expenditure; the relevant line (51) ends with 3 dr., 1 obol; cf. the discussion in Ferguson 1932, 161. See also below.

28. Of course, as should be clear by now, if the fragment does not belong to the Sicilian expedition, there is no impediment to the restoration, though a different reconstruction would be necessary.

29. 6.46.2; see above, chap. 1, p. 70.

tention at the outset to procure *chremata* and *sitos* from newly conquered areas in Sicily, "without using our revenues at home" (6.90.4).

So much in the narrative militates against a sizable financial outlay of Athenian money designated for the expedition in 415, given the facts that, first, the figure 3,000 is not complete on the stone,[30] and, second, the number does not necessarily refer to talents. It is plainly cavalier to state as a fact that this inscription sets aside 3,000 talents for the Sicilian expedition.

Other sections of this combined fragment have important implications for its interpretation but have received less attention. How well does the reference to guarding the land, and "to whoever is not patrolling or receiving pay," fit the context of 415? It is still the period of the Peace of Nikias. The Athenians were under no direct threat at home from their enemies; yet this part of the inscription might suggest a state at war, whose borders were under threat. The injunction farther on in the fragment against, apparently, using resources for any other purpose than that for which the decree is concerned with, followed, most likely, by the clause "and if anyone proposes or puts to the vote using . . . ," only reinforces the idea that a serious threat is facing the Athenians; it cannot be said that the situation in 415 fits such a context.[31]

Finally, how does the reference to "the expedition of the sixty ships" fit the later assembly or assemblies concerned with preparing for the Sicilian expedition? In response to Nikias' advice the Athenians expanded the size of the naval contingent from sixty ships to one hundred.[32] It might be tempting to take the phrase directly with the instruction immediately preceding to rescind something; but the reference is to "the expedition of the sixty ships until" (τ]õ ἔκπλο τõν ἑχσέ[κοντα νεõ]ν hέος ἂν); therefore it is difficult to see how it could be connected with the previous section on repealing (a decree), since decrees are not repealed until a future time or situation.

30. It could be restored, as Mattingly suggests, χω]ρὶς χιλίον and as such be a possible reference to the 1,000-talent "Iron Reserve" that the Athenians set aside in 431 (Thuc. 2.24.1), which was still untouched. So ML, p. 240: "It is tempting to interpret ll. 10–11 as a prohibition on touching the reserve fund of 1,000 T established in 431 (Thuc. ii.24.1, viii.15.1)."

31. An instructive comparison for such language is the situation in the summer of 431, when the Peloponnesians under King Archidamos invaded Attica. It appeared that many Athenians did not expect that the Spartans would actually invade their land; such a thing had not happened since the Persian invasion of 480–479, and a Spartan threat to invade in the middle of the century never materialized (1.114.2). The invasion made the Athenians realize the seriousness of the conflict now begun, and in response, Thucydides tells us, they decided to set aside (ἐξαίρετα) 1,000 talents, placing it apart (χωρὶς θέσθαι) and not spending it, but to wage war from other funds: "And if anyone proposes or puts to the vote to put these moneys into use for other purposes . . . he shall be punished with death" (2.24.1).

32. Reference in frag. *f* to, likely, one hundred triremes does not mitigate the difficulty posed by frag. *d/g*, since it is completely uncertain to what stele frag. *f* belongs. See below, n. 37.

Whether we take these fragments individually or as a group, the extent to which the demos is considering and dealing with minute details about the arrangements of an expedition or expeditions becomes clear; is this compatible with Thucydides' presentation, in which it was left up to the generals as *autokratores* to decide what they needed? It is true that in 6.8.3 we are told that another assembly would meet in four days to vote on what the generals required,[33] but Nikias' second speech makes clear that the generals manifestly had not yet decided on specific arrangements; he is presented as coming up on the spot with estimates and figures. According to W. K. Pritchett, in the inscription [i.e., the fragments taken as a unit], though fragmentary, "enough is preserved to show that part at least was a probouleuma containing explicit instructions about rates of pay and enjoining strong penalties if some unrecoverable acts were not carried out."[34] He continues: "The existence of such a document is enough to show that αὐτοκράτωρ (Thuc. 6.8.2) must not be understood as meaning the possession of full powers to do anything one wished."[35]

If the fragments do, as Pritchett maintains, reflect a probouleuma, then we are even farther removed from the implications of Thucydides' account: namely, that the generals were to have full authority to decide on the arrangements. But is the conclusion drawn by Pritchett correct, that therefore *autokrator* does not mean what, on the face of it, it seems to mean? He assumes that the inscriptions were definitely fixed to the Sicilian expedition; they could accordingly be used as independent evidence with which to assess or correct Thucydides. But, as we have seen, the assumption that the inscriptions all belong together and pertain to the Sicilian expedition does not rest on solid ground. Methodologically we cannot use the inscriptions to prove that generals "with full authority" did not actually have full authority.

There are two possible conclusions to be drawn from this examination of the relationship between the epigraphic evidence and Thucydides: either the inscriptions do not in fact belong to the assemblies of 415 (and perhaps, additionally, are not to be associated with one another), or, if they do, then, far from complementing Thucydides, they suggest that the historian is presenting a seriously misleading account of the proceedings, whether because he is misinformed or because he is making a deliberate attempt to rewrite the events and speeches concerned with the authorization and preparation of the expedition to Sicily. Certainly Thucydides is writing a carefully crafted account designed to lead readers to infer the insufficiency of the right kind

33. Strictly speaking, we are told simply that an assembly was held four days later, but its timing would likely have been arranged at the earlier meeting.

34. Pritchett 1974, 30.

35. Ibid. See also Hamel 1998, 201–2.

of preparations and expectations, especially in the area of financing; but, as it stands, there is no good evidence to disprove it. Given the facts that the fragments are undated, their association is uncertain: in particular, recall the uncertainty over which fragments might belong to the same stele and pertain to which assembly meeting recorded by Thucydides, the generic nature of much of the information that they yield, and, above all, the absence of any mention of Sicily. The burden of proof falls squarely on the epigraphic material, not on Thucydides.[36]

If some of the fragments do indeed belong together—and it should be stressed that this is an arbitrary assumption—and pertain to the Sicilian expedition, the contents, as Mattingly argues, fit the context of 413 much better, since reinforcements were sent out under Demosthenes in that year. By this point, the Spartans had fortified Dekeleia, and the decision to remain in Sicily rendered the city in financial and military need; hence the references to guarding the city or the land, to internal taxation, to spending as much money as possible, and to injunctions against using funds for other purposes more relevant to that situation.[37] On the other hand, there are details that do not find concurrence in Thucydides' narrative of the decision to send reinforcements; agnosticism is ultimately in order.

THUCYDIDES AND THE INVENTORIES OF ATHENA

A major conclusion to emerge from the analysis in chapter 2 was that Thucydides was writing his account with the aim of showing how little of their own money the Athenians actually spent in Sicily, despite the renewed accumulation of funds (6.26.2); they had the resources to spend, could have brought a larger expedition and paid for it adequately, but did not. Regrettably for the modern historian, Thucydides' treatment of the financing of

36. Meritt's own caution in the case of a decree with similar problems, the inscription that had been associated with the Athenian expedition to Melos in 416 (now *IG* I^3 60), is salutary. The inscription contains ship numbers but no mention of Melos. Meritt (1953, 300) comments: "The points of agreement lie in the number of Athenian ships which participated in the expedition (30), in the number of Athenian hoplites (1200), and in the number of bowmen (300). Interesting as these coincidences are, the figures indicate nothing more than a routine expedition of thirty ships, and the fact that Athens sent 30 ships to Melos does not warrant the identification of them with the 30 ships of this inscription. . . . The differences between the inscription and the text of Thucydides, V, 84, are fundamentally more significant than the agreements." As we have seen, the points of agreement between *IG* I^3 93 and Thucydides are even fewer.

37. I do not see the isolated, tiny frag. *f,* which has ατον τριερε̣, restored as hεκ]ατὸν τριέρε̣[ς, as carrying such sufficient weight against a date of 413 as did Lewis in *IG,* given its lack of physical join with any of the other fragments, and the undeniable possibility that it does not belong with the group (a point that applies to the others that do not join, as well).

the expedition results in less than satisfying answers to the question, how much exactly of their public financial resources did the Athenians spend on the expedition? Thucydides does not reveal the specific amount of public money sent out in 415, saying only that if anyone had calculated, they would have discovered that *polla talanta* had been removed from the city;[38] he gives just one specific piece of information, namely, that the sailors were paid 1 drachma a day. Other than that he offers precise figures only twice, 300 talents in the spring of 414 (6.94.5) and 120 talents in the summer of 413, sent out with Eurymedon in advance of the main reinforcements (7.16.2). He plainly does not supply enough details to make his account useful; but the implicit thread running through the account is itself an important piece of evidence: a deeply interested contemporary to the event found the level of the Athenians' financial commitment to the expedition wanting.

What light does the epigraphic evidence shed? As we saw in examining *IG* I³ 93, it is not valid—and indeed is irresponsible—to argue that the epigraphic evidence authorizes 3,000 talents for the expedition. On the basis of comparisons with war financing in the Archidamian War, we should expect to find evidence of actual expenditures in the inventories of Athena. The fragments of the accounts for the years 418–414 (*IG* I³ 370) reveal four payments to the generals in Sicily: in three entries for 416/15, the treasury paid out an unknown amount ending in 3 dr., 1 ob., 30 T and 14 T, 1,000 dr. (lines 51, 52–53, 54–55). In the record for 415/14, 300 T, and an additional 4 T, 2,000 dr. were paid out for traveling expenses for the reinforcing voyage (lines 73–76). The account of 414/13 (*IG* I³ 371) contains a reference to payments for Sicily (line 10), but the figure is not preserved.[39]

The difficulty with these accounts should be obvious. Despite their highly fragmentary nature, scholars have long been troubled by the fact that there is nevertheless no sign of any massive payments, and they have explained this in two ways. On one side, the editors of *ATL* argue that if we had complete inventories for the years 415–413, the record would contain large expenditures.[40] In part they are objecting to William Ferguson's contention that the extant figures for the year 415, when the financial outlay should have been especially great, do not allow for large withdrawals. He concluded that Athena's treasury accounted for only a small portion of the city's expenditure on the expedition, and argued for the existence of a separate, secular fund created during the Peace of Nikias from which moneys for the

38. It is possible that he could have consulted the inventories of Athena, but, given his attention to the expenditure of private wealth, his reference to *polla talanta* likely includes private as well as public wealth.

39. One hundred twenty talents have been restored on the basis of Thuc. 7.16.2.

40. *ATL* 3: 357.

expedition were drawn.[41] However, not a scrap of evidence exists for such a fund, and the suggestion of its existence raises its own problems: for example, if it did exist, why did Athena's treasury make any payments for the expedition, both as much as 300 T and as paltry as some of the others?[42]

One major assumption clearly underlies the concern about the inventories—namely, that the Athenians *did* pay huge sums from their treasuries to the force in Sicily. Yet it is worth keeping in mind that if the counterevidence from Thucydides is accepted, we may be on the wrong track to search for amounts of extraordinary magnitude. It bears repeating that Thucydides shows an army and navy in need, plainly without—until perhaps the very end[43]—the financial resources to allow them to strike hard and fast, and generals expecting to rely on local financial and other resources, again and again finding them insufficient to sustain a large force. Thus it is not clear that we should be looking for huge sums in the inventories of Athena or elsewhere—which is not to deny that the record is woefully incomplete. But we ought to keep in mind that the magic figure of 3,000 talents, which scholars have felt it necessary to find or account for, is itself something of a mirage, drawn largely from the restoration of *IG* I^3 93.[44]

It is often the case that Thucydides and epigraphic documents do not speak to each other as much as scholars would like, as an examination of the alleged Sicilian expedition decrees shows. In this case, however, there is an intriguing correspondence: we cannot find any evidence of major funding from Athens for the expedition, and Thucydides' narrative tells against it, instead suggesting the insufficiency of funding from home.[45] The state of the record notwithstanding, Thucydides' suggestion of inadequate financing and the absence in the epigraphic record of anything that points to massive expenditures from state treasuries certainly may warrant a revision of our thinking about the financing of the expedition and its implications.

THE *EIKOSTE*

As I argued in chapter 3 from an examination of the *eikoste* in its narrative context (7.27–28), Thucydides' inclusion of the decision seems above all to

41. Ferguson 1932, 160.

42. The inscription *IG* I^3 99, which records in 410 repayments to Athena's treasury, is also relevant. Although the Athenians' financial condition had changed by then, it seems to risk special pleading to assume that this was because the secular treasury had run out of money and the Athenians had gone back to borrowing from Athena.

43. See chap. 4, p. 158.

44. It is also, more reasonably, based on analogy with other sieges and campaigns; cf. *ATL* 3: 357.

45. See chap. 2 for full argument.

have been guided by a desire to illustrate a negative result of what he presents as the Athenians' irrational state in 413. If this reading of the text has validity, it is important that we are able to determine how one contemporary Athenian at least judged the elimination of tribute and the imposition of the tax; yet even more than in the case of the financing of the Sicilian expedition, we lack anything concrete, in Thucydides or elsewhere, that gives us explicit information about the tax. Indeed, the *eikoste* has received remarkably little scholarly attention, and that is no doubt due to the paucity of information about it; still, it is surprising that it often receives mention merely in passing, and one does not get the sense that it has any special significance. Consider the comments of Russell Meiggs: "[By 413] the Athenians decided to change the system of tribute and replace fixed assessments by a 5 per cent levy on imports and exports in the harbours of the allies. It is possible that the Athenians thought that this change would be popular among the allies, since it would relate tribute more directly to the benefits of sea-power, but the main motive, according to Thucydides, was to raise more money. . . . More important and more significant is Athenian policy toward Persia."[46]

Yet it must be acknowledged that this two-part decision, to abolish tribute and to impose the *eikoste,* is nothing short of extraordinary in the history of the *arche,* representing a major overhaul of its financial and economic basis with far-reaching implications for the Athenians' changing conception of their rule—regardless of whether the measure was successful.[47] I shall argue, first, that it suggests the culmination of a shift in the Athenians' conception of their *arche* from a political system to more of an economic system; and, second, it may be connected to another benchmark in Athenian imperial history, namely, the decision to impose uniform coinage, weights, and measures throughout the *arche,* reflected in the "Standards Decree" (*IG* I^3 1453).[48]

46. Meiggs 1972, 349; see also McGregor 1987, 158.

47. The elimination of tribute had to have symbolic and religious significance as well, since if the allies were no longer paying tribute, it is a reasonable assumption that they were also no longer dedicating the *aparche* to Athena; therefore, it is important to explore the implications of this decision for the question of Athena's patronage of the *arche,* and which deity, if any, might now have been privileged. See also below, p. 217.

48. My purpose in examining the *eikoste* will be to consider a number of issues concerned with the tax that can help to enhance our understanding of the historical context of Thucydides' reference. A comprehensive study of the *eikoste* would be ideal in this regard, but it is too vast a subject to be treated in the context of this book. Thus my treatment must be regarded as preliminary and incomplete; I shall be raising questions more than answering them. Issues such as the exact kind of tax (Thucydides says only "of the things by sea," but is this is an import/export tax, a harbor tax, or some other kind of tax?) and its relation to other existing taxes (e.g., 1- and 2-percent taxes, the *dekate*) await further discussion. I shall raise further issues below. A full study of maritime taxation is badly needed.

Before considering the decision's implications and its possible connection to the "Standards Decree," we must establish what can be reasonably assumed as the motivation behind the decision. First, as pointed out earlier, the Athenians were by no means bankrupt in 414/13.[49] If one considers the nuances of *dunamis*-related words and phrases in Thucydides, the negative expression *adunatoi chrematon* means not "no money at all," but literally "lacking power in money." Power in and through money, as Thucydides has demonstrated implicitly throughout his work, is not simply money in the form of revenue to be immediately expended; it is *periousia chrematon,* reserves continually replenished by revenue, which allow sizable and immediate expenditure to maintain power, in a continuous cycle.[50] It is this cycle that has been interrupted: as we saw, Thucydides is explicit that "[the Athenians'] revenues were perishing" (7.28.4).[51] It is significant, though, that Thucydides applies the judgment "unpowerful in money" to a rather early point in the period of the "two wars," the δύο πόλεμοι: that is, not long after Dekeleia was occupied in 413.[52] Thus the phrase may point to a projected shortfall; such a perspective would not be surprising if what Thucydides claims in 28.4 is true: namely, that the Athenians recognized that income was no longer (going to be?) offsetting expenditure.[53] This in turn may suggest that the Athenians normally planned as far as possible to finance operations through revenue, and not to dip into the reserve. But when it became clear that the two wars would take a large bite out of the reserve —their *periousia chrematon*—they decided to experiment (in the context of imperial fiscal administration) with a different kind of revenue device, the 5-percent tax.[54]

49. See above, chap. 3, p. 130. Unfortunately, reconstruction of the amount of the reserve at this time is hampered by the fragmentary state of the inventories and expense records; by the assumption, on the basis of *IG* I³ 93, that the Athenians spent over 3,000 talents on the Sicilian expedition—an assumption which, as we have seen, is untenable; and by taking Thuc. 8.1 at face value.

50. See *Money,* s.v. *periousia chrematon* in the index.

51. Dover (*HCT* 4, ad loc.) assumes the revenue referred to is domestic: "There was nothing to interfere with external revenue until the fleet had been lost in Sicily." Yet I would counter that simply because revolts had not yet occurred, there is no reason to restrict Thucydides' comment to Attic revenue; for one thing, even though the Athenians had not abandoned other operations within their *arche* (cf. the expenditures from the treasury of Athens, *IG* I³ 370; also Matthaiou and Pikoulas 1989, 122–23, on a routine expedition to Lemnos in 415/14), the allies, observing that the Athenians were well occupied far away to the west, likely saw their opportunity to renege on their obligation or tried to get away with smaller payments.

52. For the chronology, see Dover, *HCT* 4, ad loc.

53. In that case, the verb ἀπώλλυντο in 7.28.4 might carry ingressive force: "Their revenues were beginning to perish."

54. Thucydides' statement about the Athenians' thinking—"for their expenditures were not the same as before, but they were far greater, inasmuch as the war too was greater; on the

In one respect, the *eikoste* is part of a larger, and unsurprising, pattern in the war, one of increased difficulties extracting revenue from the *arche* and, correspondingly, of steps taken to improve collection, though with questionable success.[55] There are various indications of this development, ranging from epigraphic and literary evidence attesting to a concern over falling revenue and improved collection methods, to actual recourse to alternatives to extracting the wealth of the Aegean through tribute, like cleruchies, revenue from mines, and, I have argued, state-authorized raids.[56] The *eikoste* is the most radical development in this trend. It also strengthens the argument that measures like the 425 reassessment decree, which called for an increase in the amount of tribute for most states, were largely ineffective, though, undeniably, the level of military expenditures had dramatically increased as a result of the "two wars," as Thucydides makes clear.[57]

There is an intriguing parallel between 7.28.4 and 1.4, which concerns Minos and his thalassocracy. Thucydides introduces Minos as the earliest "thalassocrat": he was both ruler and oikist of (most of) the Kyklades and had expelled the Karians and established his own sons as rulers. Then Thucydides comments: "It is likely that Minos set about ridding the sea of piracy as much as he could, to ensure the flow of revenue instead to himself" (τό τε λῃστικόν, ὡς εἰκός, καθῄρει ἐκ τῆς θαλάσσης ἐφ' ὅσον ἐδύνατο, τοῦ τὰς προσόδους μᾶλλον ἰέναι αὐτῷ) and continues with a discussion of piracy and attitudes toward pirates (1.5). Now consider 7.28.4: the Athenians instituted the *eikoste* instead of tribute, "thinking that more money would thereby come into their hands" (πλείω νομίζοντες ἂν σφίσι χρήματα οὕτω προσιέναι).[58] As mentioned in chapter 3 above, it is explicit that their purpose is to collect more money, and the clear implication is that tribute had proved inadequate—though perhaps only for the requirements of the two wars.

Both Minos and the Athenians already have sea power before they under-

---

other hand, their revenues were perishing" (αἱ μὲν γὰρ δαπάναι οὐχ ὁμοίως καὶ πρίν, ἀλλὰ πολλῷ μείζους καθέστασαν, ὅσῳ καὶ μείζων ὁ πόλεμος ἦν· αἱ δὲ πρόσοδοι ἀπώλλυντο, 28.4)—is an important qualifier to the standard assumption that the Greeks (and Romans) had no concept of a budget because they lacked a double-entry bookkeeping system (de Ste. Croix 1956; Macve 1985). Thucydides' comment clearly shows an awareness of the income-expenditure ratio and of future expenditures, not merely emergency measures for a present need. Theoretically the *eikoste* could have been imposed as a short-term measure, but its radical nature and the changes it would have necessitated in administrative structure suggest not.

55. Cf. *IG* I³ 60, 68, 71.

56. See *Money*, 198–201.

57. In 424, the Athenians faced serious revolts among their important northern Aegean holdings, such as Amphipolis; these events may have been a factor in the ineffectiveness of the 425 reassessment decree. For further discussion of the decree and its significance, see *Money*, 164–70, 190–94.

58. See above, chap. 3, pp. 137–39, on the nuances of this statement.

take to exploit the profits of the Aegean more effectively;[59] and both take measures to extract more from the Aegean. The thinking Thucydides attributes to Minos may well come from his observations about the financial motives of *arche* among the Athenians, as well as reflect common assumptions about what thalassocrats did. The decision to replace tribute with the *eikoste* also implies that, contrary to our impression of Athens' virtually absolute control of the Aegean—the "Athenian lake"—there were substantial profits to be had from maritime trade that did not reach the city, despite its naval *arche*.[60]

At the same time that the tax is part of a pattern of revenue-enhancing measures, it also reflects a long-term interest in profits from trade.[61] The Athenians had shown a consistent interest in, and a hard-nosed attitude toward, Aegean trade since the early days of the Delian League. A clear example is their dispute with Thasos over the latter's *emporia* (and control of mines) on the mainland opposite the island in the early to mid-460s, which led to the island's revolt (1.100). Evidence like the Methone decree (*IG* I³ 61) reveals Athenian control of the grain trade from the Black Sea. This interest can be linked up with other indications that suggest a trend, culminating in the Peloponnesian War at the latest, in which the *arche* was becoming increasingly economic in nature and purpose. Which is to say that the Athenians came to regard their system of control more and more as a revenue-generating mechanism rather than *strictly* a means of military/

59. Starr (1984, 217), in alluding to the purpose of thalassocracy, comments: "Thucydides suggests that Minos tried to regularize his revenues, which is a possible hypothesis but for which there is no evidence." That even Thucydides suggests "regularizing" revenues goes beyond the text, as attractive an idea as it is.

60. Cf. Dover (*HCT* 4: 408): "The Athenians estimated that the annual value of the seaborne traffic on which they would hope to collect the tax exceeded 18,000 talents"; he bases this figure on the assumption that the yield of a 5-percent tax would have to be higher than the 900 talents that he infers Athens collected annually in this period from tribute. Isager and Hansen (1975, 52) estimate at least 2,300 talents in seaborne traffic in the Peiraieus in 401/00 on the basis of calculations stemming from inferences from Andok. 1.33. But cf. Andreades (1933, 298), who rightly notes that "Thucydides does not say that [the Athenians] hoped to collect more than what had been theoretically fixed as the tribute, but simply more than what they would actually have taken in at this time." Related to this are the issues of whether tribute was a full measure of prosperity, and the sources of tribute; most scholars assume that tribute can be used to gauge accurately the wealth of the polis; see, for example, Nixon and Price 1990; Figueira 1998, 52 with n. 15. This assumption is highly problematic, failing as it does to take account of nontributary revenues and literary evidence that jars with the assumption. Meiggs (1972, 265 with n. 3) cites examples pointing to the great wealth of a city or district whose tribute was low (Thuc. 8.28.3; cf. also below, chap. 6, p. 252; Xen. *Hell.* 1.4.8–9 reports Alkibiades in 407 collecting 100 talents from the Ceramic Gulf in Caria; cf. also Thuc. 3.31.1, with *Money*, 140–43). As for the sources of tribute, see below.

61. See Pébarthe 1999 for a suggestive treatment of the Athenians' interest in *emporia* and maritime taxation in the *arche*.

political rule over other Greeks. This is nothing short of a radical reorientation of the *arche.*

The indications of this change are subtle but together they suggest a shift in thinking that is fundamental. For example, after Nikias' capture of Kythera in 424, the Peloponnesian island was assessed 4 talents of tribute but was not brought into the empire, thus setting a precedent for the detachment of what had been symbiotically attached, *phoros* and *arche.*[62] Similarly, under the terms of the Peace of Nikias in 421, the northern poleis of Argilos, Stageiros, Akanthos, Skolos, Olynthos, and Spartolos, which the Spartans were to hand over to the Athenians, were to pay tribute but have political independence (αὐτονόμους); moreover, they were to be neutral, unless they wished to be allies (ξυμμάχους) of the Athenians.[63] Irrelevant here is the question of whether it would have been in these cities' best interests of survival to be allies of Athens rather than neutrals;[64] what is noteworthy is the detachment of tribute from the issue of political control over subjects.[65]

The decision to abolish tribute entirely and impose the *eikoste* marks the culmination of this development: the Athenians are willingly eliminating a primary signifier of their political hold over the allies and restructuring the fiscal administration of the *arche* to be, so they hope, a more effective revenue-generating instrument. This shift has some important implications for our understanding of the development of the economic sphere as well as of the cohesion of empire. The measure suggests that the Athenians' self-interest in their empire in the course of the Peloponnesian War has come to have to do with money above all—not power over allies per se, as signified by the practical but also symbolic collection of tribute, or honor or any of the justificatory claims cited in the past.[66] Therefore one can begin to speak of money as the primary motivation for the ensured continuation of the union of poleis; the Athenian thinking, in short, is not how to gain a stronger hold on their subjects but how to extract more revenue from the Aegean.

The preceding discussion might seem the dry analysis of an economically oriented explanation of a historical development. Yet, in the framework of the *History,* the implications of such a development are anything but detached or neutral. On the contrary, as we have seen, Thucydides depicts the

62. Thuc. 4.57.4; see *Money,* 159–60.

63. 5.18.5. Hornblower (1996, ad loc.) notes that the Spartans likely had a hand in this stipulation, but even if so, the fact remains that this was an acceptable term to the Athenians.

64. See Bauslaugh 1991, 70–83 on the tenuous position of neutrals; see also Figueira 1993, 255–92.

65. *Money,* 182.

66. It therefore ties in with the emphasis on self-interest over other considerations in the Melian Dialogue.

majority of Athenians as desiring conquest for money, an idea fueled by Alkibiades, as they prepare to sail off to Sicily (6.24.3);[67] the portrayal is inscribed with censure, the development, through the inversion of means and end, a perversion of goals. As the narrative proceeds, Thucydides offers further examples of the trend through the telling detail: individual soldiers and traders who set out on the expedition with their own money, brought for the purpose of exchange (6.31.5); sailors who had been enticed into the navy by pay who desert their posts and become traders, paying slaves to take their place at the oars, and causing the navy to deteriorate (7.13.2). This last illustration, a remarkable piece of information that Thucydides includes in Nikias' letter, emblematizes the development. Profit-seeking for its own sake will contribute to the destruction of the city. The *eikoste* is, as situated in the narrative, but another example of misplaced motivations (as well as of economic impracticality) that foreshadows the dangers of the love of money.

The Economic Effect on Cities and Individuals

Of obvious importance in assessing the impact of the tax in comparison to tribute is the source of tribute in the cities. This is a crucial issue for understanding the *arche,* and unfortunately any answer can only be speculative, for we lack direct evidence. Most scholars believe that tribute assessments were based on land and that the burden fell primarily on the wealthy landowners in the cities.[68] Some assume that tribute would have been collected largely from maritime taxation.[69] It is surely unwarranted to assume that the assessments of poleis and islands were based on identical criteria in all cases, since at the very least we can imagine that a bustling trading center might arrive at its tribute through maritime taxes of various kinds (including harbor dues, import and export taxes, taxes on passengers), while an inland community would be assessed on the basis of land; and there would doubtless be many who drew their revenue from a combination of sources. But the few inferences we can draw from the scraps of indirect evidence suggest that land was certainly an important criterion in the assessment process. First, Artaphernes' assessment, based on land, for Persian taxation of the Ionian cities after the Ionian revolt was put down in 494 may have formed the basis of Aristeides' assessment of tribute in 478.[70] Second, the extant fragment of An-

67. 8.18; see chap. 1, pp. 40–42.

68. This underlies the argument of de Ste. Croix 1954/1955. Cf. Tenger (1995), who argues, on the basis of a study of eighteen cities in the Troad, that the Athenians took a much more complex approach to tribute assessments, basing them on much broader economic factors than agriculture based on area.

69. Figueira 1998, 106, 298–99, for example; see Brock 1996.

70. Artaphernes' assessment: Hdt. 6.42; see Murray 1966.

tiphon's speech *On the Tribute of the Samothrakians,* revealingly, contains explicit reference to the extent of uncultivable land in relation to the size of the island[71]—for this to be relevant the Samothrakians' assessment must have been based largely on land. In addition, the settlement imposed on Lesbos after its revolt in 427, in which the island was converted into a cleruchy in lieu of tribute (Thuc. 3.50.1), may suggest that tribute had been assessed on the basis of the criterion of land. In these cases, the change from tribute to tax would have been dramatic: communities whose tribute was based on land income and who were not exporters of agricultural produce would have been unaffected by the *arche,* and their wealth would have remained at home; those who did export agricultural produce would have been affected. On the other hand, in cases where tribute came in part or entirely from maritime taxes, the *eikoste* could affect a polis' ability to enhance its public treasuries, for the Athenians were assuming the role that the individual poleis would have played, and by doing so would eliminate the cities' potential to derive state profit off trade.[72]

One crucial aspect of the change from tribute to tax, which provides an additional indication of this developing economic conception of the *arche,* is that the imperial revenue would likely for the first time have officially (from the Athenian standpoint) affected noncitizens in the communities,[73] the *xenoi,* or metics who primarily, though not exclusively, would have been engaged in trade. This marks a further step away from the connection between money and the political hold on the allies: metics, as noncitizens in subject cities, would in an important respect have stood outside of the subject-master relationship, when the relations between Athens and the poleis had been defined primarily in political terms. They would, however, have played a direct part in trade that may have been a revenue source for a city's

71. Antiphon frag. A.1 (Blass). This supports the argument of Tenger 1995 that the Athenians were concerned with the quality, not merely the area, of arable land of an allied state in assessing tribute.

72. I see no reason, however, to assume, with Meritt (1945), Mattingly (1979, 320 [1996, 158]), and Walbank (1978, 322), that allies would have had to cease levying their own maritime taxes once the *eikoste* went into place, given that concurrent taxes were common, as MacDonald 1981 points out. For Athens, cf., for example, Ar. *Wasps* 656ff., with reference to the "many 1-percents." Nor is Hasebroek (1933, 162) convincing that the Athenians merely took over a local tax in place, simply raising the rate. He cites Thuc. 7.28.4 as evidence for a "substitution," not an "imposition," but, as Thucydides himself puts it, the Athenians "created" (ἐποίησαν) the *eikoste.*

73. I find unpersuasive Foucart's thesis (1877), followed and adjusted by Gauthier (1971), that in *IG* I³ 40 Athens is instructing foreigners residing in Chalcis to pay tribute to Athens. See Whitehead 1976. It is of course possible that metics were forced to contribute revenue toward tribute, but even where this may have been so, they would not have been officially involved from the standpoint of the Athenian state.

tribute; there is no indication, however, that the Athenians made any direct or formal stipulations concerning foreigners in cities. (For further discussion of this point, see below.)

The change to a maritime tax also had this extraordinary implication: with some exceptions, communities in the *arche* without major trading ports, not to mention inland communities without a coastal *emporion,*[74] would now evidently have had little or no financial burden.[75] Furthermore, a crucial difference between tribute and the tax was that payment of the latter would have been a private matter, not state business, handled through tax collectors and levied on private individuals involved in commerce.[76]

A final point that bears on the economic impact and nature of the *eikoste* is that presumably it would have affected those outside the *arche:* when they traded in ports within the *arche,* they would have been subject to the tax as well. This is another indication that the Athenians were thinking about their *arche* in much broader terms than as a purely political instrument of control over subjects.[77]

74. The list is long; a brief sampling from around the *arche* includes Maiandrios, Kolophon, Miletoteichitai, Pythopolis, Skepsis, Thymbra, Petra, Kolonai, Palaiperkote, Zeleia, Spartolos, Stolos, Berge, Pergamoteichitai, and Trailos. It may be significant that virtually all inland sites, except those in the Thrace-ward region, are minor poleis. The fact that the Athenians are now, with the *eikoste,* in a sense letting them go, and focusing on the major economic centers, contributes to the argument that what matters most is revenue, not rule over as great an area as possible.

75. The exceptions would be cases where the Athenians would presumably still have been extracting revenue by other traditional means, for example, through cleruchies, rents on sacred land, and so on; see *Money,* 160–64, 200–202. Countering this, however, would be that some other cities, like Smyrna, for example, which apparently had not paid tribute, would now be affected by the tax, although, again, the burden for collecting the tax would not fall on the state.

76. It would be useful to know the precise relationship between the *eikostologoi* and the tax farmers who would have obtained the contract, whether they were Athenian or local, and where the auction for the collection of the *eikoste* would have been held. It is beyond the scope of this chapter to pursue these questions in detail, crucial though they are for understanding the tax fully, given the focus of this book. But I would suggest here, regarding the issue of the residence of the tax collectors, that since the tax was to be collected throughout the *arche,* likely not just Athenians but locals will have been included among those who bid for the right to collect the tax. Without the cooperation of wealthy locals, *xenoi* and citizens alike, it is difficult to see how such a widespread tax would have effectively been collected (on the potential problems of collection, see Meiggs 1972, 369; Andrewes 1992, 458). This will have provided a profit incentive for those in the communities to aid Athens in the collection of the *eikoste,* a point that accords with Thucydides' "collaborative" theory of power and empire (see *Money,* 8–9, 27). No such incentive for local individuals would have existed when the tributary system was in place. For discussion of the *eikoste* elsewhere than Athens, see Gauthier 1989, 33–36; see also Velissaropoulos (1980, 212), who mentions only the *eikostologoi* in the context of collection.

77. I shall return to this point below in connection with the "Standards Decree" and the "First Fruits Decree."

The Reception of the Eikoste

What political implications would the end of the tributary era and the institution of a maritime tax have had for the allies? First and most obviously a tax on maritime trade would not have had the negative associations of the *phoros* in both name and practice.[78] By this period, as is clear from our sources, tribute symbolized, above all, the subject status of the allies who paid it; those who paid tribute were referred to as "subjects" (ὑπήκοοι). More than mere symbol, the tribute quota lists, inscribed on large, imposing stelai set up in front of the Parthenon, were a striking visual reminder of the subject status of the allies, which greeted them every time they ascended the Akropolis in their enforced participation in the Panathenaic procession, bearing cow and panoply as dedications to Athena. One possible scenario, then, is that the elimination of tribute may have been accompanied by widespread relief.[79] At the same time, it is important to acknowledge that the Athenians had an economic goal in relieving the allies of this marker of political oppression: namely, the expectation of greater wealth flowing into Athens as a result of decreased hostility.

In addition to relief, the elimination of tribute may have produced skepticism. We should not look at this measure naively, as the allies may not have. The fact remained that the Athenians were not disbanding their *arche;* they were only getting rid of tribute.[80] The measure may also have created considerable uncertainty about the Athenians' motives and about the implications for the allies' de facto status. Many may have reacted in all three ways (or others), and it is important to keep in mind that the allies would have reacted not only to the political implications of the tax but also to its economic impact: that is, its effect on on their ability to make a profit off trade.

The radical nature of the *eikoste* and its implications for the economies of the cities should be clear. Now let us examine the implications of the context of the *eikoste,* both as portrayed by Thucydides and from a practical standpoint, recalling first that, according to Thucydides, the tax was to increase revenue for military expenditure, and, second, that the taxes would be com-

78. Thucydides implicitly draws attention to the power of names in 1.96.2 in describing the use of the word *phoros* in 478: "For that is what the cash payment was named," to distinguish it, as Murray (1966) has argued, from *dasmos.* See Whitehead's (1998) discussion of the significance of Thucydides' phraseology.

79. Cf. the fragment from the Middle Comedy poet Heniochos (frag. 5 Kock). In response to the question "What are the cities doing at Olympia?" comes the answer "They have come to sacrifice for freedom, since they have just been freed from tribute (*phoros*)."

80. Thucydides, perhaps cynically, refers to the allies as "subjects" in 28.4 in the same breath that he notes the elimination of tribute and the substitution of the *eikoste.* Cf. also 7.57.3, 4, 5; 7.63.3; 8.2.2.

ing in regularly, not once a year like tribute. Given these requirements, the efficiency not only of collecting the revenue but also of making it immediately usable would have been of prime concern. It is here that the famous "Standards Decree" comes into our discussion.

THE "STANDARDS DECREE" AND THE *EIKOSTE*

In recent years there has been renewed and vigorous interest in the date and purpose of the so-called Standards Decree, an Athenian decree concerned with coinage, weights, and measures. Interest in the decree's date has grown chiefly as a result of the redating of the Egesta decree to 418 by M. H. Chambers et al.[81] That decree contains a three-barred sigma, a letter form that orthodoxy held went out of fashion by mid-century. But its redating has bolstered the arguments of scholars like Mattingly, who want to downdate a series of floating inscriptions, among them, the "Standards Decree," in which in the Kos fragment published by Mario Segre,[82] a three-barred sigma is used.[83] Regardless of the dates proposed, however, whether the mid-fifth century or the 420s (the two most popular periods in which to locate the decree),[84] scholars have overwhelmingly sought to connect the decree with the collection of tribute,[85] with most regarding it as a heavy-handed political measure reflecting the height of Athenian imperialism.[86]

I would like to suggest the possibility, however, that the decree to impose standard coinage, weights, and measures on Athens' subjects in the empire was connected not with tribute but rather with the decision to *abolish* tribute and to impose the *eikoste* in its place. Proof is impossible; my aim here,

81. Chambers, Gallucci, and Spanos 1990; see also Chambers 1992/1993, 1993, and 1994.

82. Segre 1938.

83. Most of Mattingly's formidable output of articles are conveniently collected in Mattingly 1996. I am accepting for the sake of discussion here the standard hypothesis that the fragments comprise a composite decree, but should make clear that this is by no means a certainty.

84. The vast majority place the decree in mid-century, only a few in the 420s, beginning with Hiller and Klaffenbach 1924/1925, 11; more recently, Mattingly 1996; Erxleben 1971, 159–61; Vickers 1996; see the valuable survey of Figueira 1998, 4–9 and 431–63.

85. E.g., Cavaignac 1953; *ATL* 3: 281; Schuller 1974, 216; Martin 1985, 201–3; Figueira (1998) offers the most comprehensive argument for the close association of the decree with tribute.

86. E.g., Finley 1999, 168–69: "The political element is unmistakable. . . . Athens was now able and willing to demonstrate who was master within the empire by denying the subject-states the traditional symbol of autonomy, their own coins"; *ATL* 3: 281: "The Monetary Decree (D14, the Decree of Klearchos) and the Kleinias Decree (D7) completed the subjugation of the allies again to the will of Athens"; Austin and Vidal-Naquet 1977, 326: "It is better to see the decree as one further instrument among others of Athens' crushing political domination." For general discussion, see Figueira 1998, 4–9.

in what is necessarily a speculative discussion, is to demonstrate a plausible connection between the decree and the *eikoste* and to explore the implications of the connection.

Arguments that the decree was closely connected with the tributary system have always run up against two major stumbling blocks: first, attempts to discern any widespread impact of the decree in the numismatic record have failed, and, second, the decree concerns not only silver coinage but also weights and measures. In regard to the numismatic record one can always resort to an argument that the decree was ineffective.[87] The second stumbling block, however, is, in my view, almost insurmountable. In general, scholars have downplayed the importance of this aspect of the decree[88] and have privileged the sections concerned with coinage,[89] no doubt because of their conviction that one of the purposes of the decree was to enhance the collection of tribute, or, alternatively, that it reflects a heavy-handed imperialism that is consistent with other measures known to be directed toward tribute.[90] Thus Thomas Figueira justifies his reference to the document as the "Coinage Decree" (as opposed to the "Standards Decree") by pointing out that the chief focus in the extant fragments is coinage.[91] As we shall see below, however, this emphasis does not weaken the significance of the decree's inclusion of the Athenian metrological system. The objection made above about the fragments connected with the Sicilian expedition—that there is no mention of Sicily in any of the fragments—applies here as well. Nothing in the extant fragments of the decree refers directly to tribute, though much in the document(s) is compatible with it, most obviously the emphasis on silver coinage, as well as references to the Hellenotamiai.

Figueira gives great weight to the appearance of the Hellenotamiai as an argument in favor of the decree's implicit concern with tribute;[92] but how strong is the argument? It is highly significant that after tribute was abolished and the tax imposed on the empire, the board of the Hellenotamiai, far from being disbanded, was enlarged as part of an apparent restructuring in 411. Then the *kolakretai* disappear and the Hellenotamiai seem to take

87. I am not unsympathetic to this objection per se (see below), but it does not help us to understand the reasoning behind and purpose of the decree.

88. Mattingly did shift discussion to weights and measures in his study of the capacity of Chian amphorae but recently retracted his case; Mattingly 1981, 78–80 [1996, 435–41]; cf. Mattingly 1996, 521. See also Martin 1985, 203–4; Lewis 1986, 61–62. Figueira 1998 has a chapter devoted to the metrological aspect, but it is premised on the assumption that commercial taxes were the source of tribute in the allied cities; see, for example, p. 313.

89. There is no better reflection of this than the fact that the decree is almost universally referred to as the "Coinage Decree."

90. E.g., the 425 reassessment decree, *IG* I^3 71; Kleonymos' decree, *IG* I^3 68.

91. Figueira 1998, 3 n. 6.

92. Ibid., 265–66, 333.

over their functions, administering secular funds (τὰ ὅσια) while sacred funds (τὰ ἱερά) fall under the purview of the Treasurers of Athena.[93] It *is* possible—though, as we shall see, by no means certain—that tribute was restored in 410. However, even if it was, the Hellenotamiai had much broader oversight by then, as is reflected in their increased number. Moreover, given the fact that the Athenians received considerable revenue from the empire aside from tribute while the tributary system was in place, the Hellenotamiai would have been overseeing the collection and distribution of nontributary income all along. In short, the presence of the Hellenotamiai is not a compelling argument in favor of a tributary context for the "Standards Decree."[94]

As mentioned above, the extant fragments pay far more attention to coinage than to weights and measures. Assuming for the sake of argument that the decree did not, in non-extant fragments, deal further with weights and measures, there is a good reason for this imbalance that does not require the traditional association between the decree and tribute collection, or the privileging of coinage. Simply put, conversion into a common Athenian coinage is a far more complex procedure than the standardization of weights and measures and would therefore have required fuller details than the conversion to Athenian weights and measures. The Athenian state had to be involved, and the procedure had to be carried out in Athens, at Athenian mints. By contrast, Athenian weights and measures would have been well-known from trade and available in the Aegean communities, and conversion to them would have required neither travel to Athens nor the intervention of the state (beyond the instruction to use them). It would not even have been necessary to produce Athenian weights;[95] makeweights could have

93. Ferguson 1932, 3.

94. Figueira (1998, 336–40) also derives support from the restoration ἐσα[γόντων] in the beginning of section 2, which he then connects with the board of *Eisagogeis* known from *IG* I³ 71.7, who oversaw cases concerned with tribute. Yet neither is the restoration assured nor the particular board involved (as Figueira himself notes, "various boards are possible for the officials directed to bring these cases" [338]), nor is there any reason why a board of *Eisagogeis* could not handle the adjudication of cases arising from disputes about coinage, weights, and measures.

95. But cf. Olympia, where weights on the traditional (105 dr.) Athenian standard have been found (Hitzl 1996, 52–62, 105–20, 142–45). These weights (class 2) were introduced alongside older weights on the (100 dr.) Aeginetan standard (class 1) sometime in the second half of the fifth century, arguably as a result of the "Standards Decree," as Kroll (1998) suggests in his useful review. Hitzl proposed that the "Standards Decree" was responsible for replacing the class 1 and 2 weights with typologically distinct weights on a new 110 dr. standard (class 3) in the 420s, but Kroll observes that the 110 dr. standard is unknown in Attica. Moreover, if the class 2 weights were introduced as a result of the "Standards Decree," it follows that the class 3 standard would not have been begun until some later time (Kroll thinks probably not until the fourth century).

been used, and in the case of standards, at issue was volume, not the container used.

Thus nothing in the fragments per se compels, or even warrants, a tributary connection or impetus; and such an impetus fails to explain the metrological concern. It is telling that attempts, at least those in the last half-century, to explain the order for the allies to use standard weights and measures as well as coinage invariably fall back on the sphere of trade, though most leave it with only a brief mention.[96] Thomas Martin has done this aspect of the decree the most justice; his discussion, while necessarily cursory, given its purpose as a *comparandum* in a larger argument against coinage as a symbol of sovereignty, is far more balanced than other treatments in according to weights and measures their importance in the inscription and in explaining their desirability. While he, like Figueira, notes that "the explicit concern of the decree with silver coinage also suggests a direct connection with the assessment and collection of the tribute from the cities of the empire" (referring back to Finley),[97] he explains the concern with standard weights and measures as a means to facilitate the collection of taxes on trade: "This concern with revenue can also explain the inclusion of weights and measures in the decree (apart from the direct link between coins and weights as units of weight). The Athenians levied taxes on goods in order to raise revenue from import/export traffic, and these taxes were set at a certain percentage of the value of the goods involved. It was obviously necessary to know the exact weight . . . or volume . . . of the goods in a shipment if the tax was to be levied and collected accurately."[98]

Martin then provides a hypothetical example of the difficulty that could arise from needing to determine the value of and to convert foreign weights and measures, and discusses the corresponding ease of collection on a single standard. A chief advantage in a uniform standard is the potential to deal with greater volume in an expeditious fashion. As he notes, "many more shipments of foreign goods could be processed in the same amount of time

96. As Schoenhammer (1995, 352) notes.

97. Martin 1985, 201. The facilitating factor of uniform coinage in administrative and military payments has been widely acknowledged; cf. Finley 1999, 168–69; Starr 1970, 69–70; Will 1972, 207–10.

98. Martin 1985, 203. Cf. also Gardner 1974, 230. One can object to Martin's blanket insistence on exactitude. For example, in the case of a tax on cargo in transit, it seems unlikely that the ship would be unloaded and all its contents carefully weighed. Estimating may have been common; but even in such cases, any appeals by ship captains would have necessitated exact weighing. This applies to taxing by container, not exact weight or volume, as well. Lawall (2000, 74) points out that "literary and papyrological sources [suggest] that the concern portside was primarily with numbers of jars and not the specific quantity of contents of any one jar" (see additional bibliography in his n. 104). Yet, again, should there have been a dispute, it would have been necessary to know exact weight or volume.

and with far greater accuracy (i.e. full collection of the duty owed) if it was necessary to refer only to one universal set of weights and measures. Since the Athenians in the later fifth century enjoyed the benefits of a very large foreign trade in all sorts of goods in great quantities, these practical considerations were far from minor."[99] Martin sees the decree as a "revenue enhancement act" whose aim was identical to the Athenians' intent in imposing the *eikoste:* "an eminently practical concern to increase revenue."[100]

I would like to consider the possibility of situating the "Standards Decree" at the time when the Athenians decided to abolish tribute and exploit the empire's commercial profits more directly, and then explore the implications of both a strong financial motivation for the decree and the clear commercial context of the order to use standard weights and measures as well as uniform coinage. We should start by recalling two key considerations: first, the expediency of, and thus greater profit achieved by, uniform coinage, weights, and measures—a practical and economic concern for the ancient Greeks and Romans as much as for moderns (and those in between)[101]—and, second, the large-scale military context in which, according to our sole source, the *eikoste* was to be put to immediate use. The Athenians had had ample experience of a central fact in the waging of naval war and the exercise of naval power: the need for access to an immediately usable reserve supplemented by revenue. Thus when they came to consider substituting a tax on trade for tribute, an inevitable topic of discussion would have been the potential for delay, confusion, and losses inherent in levying such a widespread tax on goods from throughout the large empire, especially if the value and weight of those goods were measured according to different standards, and the tax upon them could be paid in different coinages that would have to be melted down and restruck before use in the field.[102] Thus I suggest that an impetus for the "Standards Decree" may well have been a point at which the polis was envisioning receiving the great bulk of its imperial revenue through a monetary tax on trade. Unlike tribute, revenue from such a tax would come in more frequently than once a year.[103] Indeed,

99. Martin 1985, 204.

100. Ibid., 206.

101. An excellent reference to the expense and inconvenience involved in converting foreign coinage is found in *IG* XII 5.817 (end of third/beginning of second century B.C.), which thanks the banker Timon of Delos for exchanging Tenian currency rejected by the grain dealers on Delos without charging a fee; see Bogaert 1968,176–78; Reger 1994, 12–13. For the adoption of the Athenian standard, see *IG* XII 2.161 A4–5; and Hackens in Bruneau and Ducat 1983, 107–11. Cf. also Xen. *Poroi* 3.2 on the rejection of foreign currency (except Athenian) outside of home ports throughout the Greek world, with Gauthier 1976 ad loc.

102. This of course applies to tribute as well, but the process would happen only once a year.

103. How often is of course unknown. In the fourth century B.C. the tax farmer of the 2-percent tax deposited his collections every prytany ([Dem.] 50.27). *Ath.Pol.* 47.3 refers to

this may have been a large part of its appeal: the Athenians could get their hands on cash more often and more quickly, especially if, on the analogy of other taxes, tax farmers made a down payment (προκαταβολή) on acceptance of their bid.[104]

Is there anything specific in the "Standards Decree" that buttresses the interpretation suggested here? First and foremost is the threefold concern with uniform coinage, weights, and measures. But further support may come from a section of the decree that has especially troubled commentators. In section 3 of the composite text as printed and restored in *IG* I³ 1453 the decree reads: "if any . . . of the archons in the cities does not act in accordance with the decrees (?) (concerning) either the citizens or the foreigners, let him be deprived of citizenship" (ἐὰν δέ [τις . . . τ]ῶν ἀρχόν[των ἐν ταῖ]σι πόλεσι μὴ ποιῆι κα[τὰ τὰ ἐψηφισ]μένα ἢ τῶν [πολι]τῶν ἢ τῶν ξένων, [ἄτ]ιμος ἔστω). This provision has given rise to much controversy, especially over the references to the ἄρχοντες ἐν ταῖσι πόλεσι, the ξένοι and πολῖται (if that is the correct restoration, as seems virtually certain from epigraphic *comparanda*).[105] Figueira is surely correct in thinking that the ἄρχοντες are Athenian officials in the local cities, because of the contrast between them and the officials cited in the following clause,[106] and he convincingly regards the two genitives, τῶν [πολι]τῶν and τῶν ξένων, as dependent on the likely participial phrase largely restored before them, κα[τὰ τὰ ἐψηφισ]μένα, suggesting κα[τὰ τὰ συγκεί]μενα, "compacts" or "agreements."[107] Thus he translates the section as follows: "If some other one of the archons in the cities not act in accordance with the engagements either with the citizens or with the foreigners, let him be deprived of civic rights and let his property be expropriated and a tithe belong to the goddess."[108]

---

the requirements of tax farmers to pay their installments every prytany, three times a year, or once a year. On this passage, see Rhodes 1981 ad loc. See also Stroud 1998, 61–62.

104. On the analogy of other taxes, perhaps at the end of each prytany; see Rhodes 1981, 555–56; Stroud 1998, 61–64, 110–15, for arrangements concerning the auction connected with the grain-tax law of 374/73.

105. The disagreement concerns the identity of the archons as Athenian or local officials, and the identity of the "foreigners" and "citizens" and their relationship. See Figueira 1998, 340–9.

106. [καὶ εἰ μ]ὴ ἄρχοντες Ἀθηναίων . . . , section 4. So also Erxleben 1969, 104–6. Cf. Gomme (*HCT* 1: 381–83) and Leppin (1992), who think that they are local officials.

107. Figueira 1998, 344. The distance between the genitives ἢ τῶν [πολι]τῶν ἢ τῶν ξένων and the τ]ῶν ἀρχόν[των makes it unlikely that the former set is dependent on the latter, or on whatever nominative (most likely τις) is to be restored on which τ]ῶν ἀρχόν[των is dependent. I take the genitives τῶν [πολι]τῶν and τῶν ξένων as objective genitives with the preceding participle.

108. Figueira 1998, 349. I do not understand his substitution of the word "engagements" in the translation in preference to "agreements" or "compacts." The ἄλλος restored after τις,

For our purposes here it is unnecessary to engage in the numerous complexities of this provision and, rather, simply ask, who are the *politai* and the *xenoi?* Explanations of the presence of these persons, especially the *xenoi* in the inscription, have in my view been awkward at best. Figueira and P. Gauthier have explained the *politai* as citizens of states outside of Athens, and the *xenoi* as citizens of still other states; the vantage point is thus that of an allied city, which may have had agreements with other cities.[109] Thus, in Figueira's restoration and interpretation, Athenian officials in the allied cities were to hold to prior agreements, whether between allies (πολῖται) and the Athenians or allies and others (ξένοι).[110]

The notion that the *xenoi* are citizens of other poleis entirely seems highly improbable. In such a context as Figueira reconstructs, agreements between states, not individuals, are at issue, and the reference to third parties would normally be expressed in terms of the city.[111] This objection applies to earlier interpretations as well. Using *xenoi* as an Athenian designation for the allies would be highly unusual, as Figueira notes.[112] If we understand the context of the decree as pertaining to trade and taxation entirely, however, the reference to the *xenoi* becomes intelligible. The decree directs certain officials in the cities not to interfere with what has been voted? (or agreed upon?) in connection with "citizens" and "foreigners." It seems most natural to take these two groups as residing in the same polis, and not as a reference to relations between or among poleis.[113] While the reference to "foreigners" makes no apparent sense in the context of tribute,[114] since that requirement concerned only citizens (from the Athenian standpoint), if the decree is concerned with the realm of trade, the reference to *xenoi* not only makes sense but is necessary. The decision to abolish tribute and impose the *eikoste* had direct ramifications for the population of foreigners in the cities,

---

accepted by Figueira, is difficult to make sense of, but alternative restorations are unsatisfying as well.

109. Gauthier 1971; Figueira 1998, 343. 110. Figueira 1998, 343.

111. E.g., *IG* II^2 24, frag. b, line 5 (alliance between Athens and Thasos): καὶ τὰ[ς ἄλλ]ας πόλ[ες.

112. Figueira 1998, 343. Cf. also Whitehead 1976, 254; Leppin 1992. Gauthier's view (1971.55–56) that the *xenoi* are citizens of allied states and cannot be resident aliens is unconvincing, partly because it stems from the assumption that the *xenoi* themselves would be liable to the punishment referred to in this section of the decree—namely, loss of citizenship and confiscation of property.

113. So Whitehead 1976, 254; Koch 1991, 616 n. 6; Schoenhammer 1995, 45–46. The distinction between citizens (πολῖται) and foreigners (ξένοι) within a city is well attested epigraphically: e.g., *IG* II^2 1270.6–7; *Syll.*^{3} 193.5; 495.115; 708.15; 714.25; 729; 900.20.

114. Contra Foucart 1877 and Gauthier 1971. As mentioned above, foreigners may have been indirectly involved in tribute, but I would draw a distinction between direct and indirect concern.

who would be most heavily involved in the commercial life of the polis and, most important, with whom the Athenians now are to be directly and for the first time concerned in an empire-wide way.[115]

The clause dealing with the addition to the bouleutic oath (which reads: "If anyone (ἐάν τις) mints coinage in the cities and does not use Athenian coinage, weights, and measures," etc., section 12) may also support viewing the decree within a context of trade. The focus on the individual in the cities rather than on the cities themselves, while not impossible to account for in the usual association of the decree with tribute, does suggest a context in which private individuals would be using local standards. This same context has relevance for section 13 of the decree, represented only by the lost Smyrna fragment, reported to contain the following: [———c. 26———] αι τὸ ξενικὸν ἀργύριον [———c. 29———ὅ]ταμ βόληται· τὴν δὲ πό-[λιν———c. 28———]· αὐτὸν δὲ τὰ [ἑ]αυτõ ἕκαστ[ον———c. 23——— τὸ ἀργυ]ροκόπιον. While restorations have varied, they have the same thrust, because of the presence of ὅ]ταμ βόληται and αὐτὸν δὲ τὰ [ἑ]αυτõ ἕκαστ[ον: namely, that the Athenians are extending to private individuals the option of exchanging foreign for Athenian silver.[116]

Figueira presents a number of objections to the view that this part of the decree is concerned with private individuals (outside the *arche,* as interpreted in *ATL*), beginning with this telling remark: "It is hard to imagine a rationale for an Athenian interest in the monetary holdings of persons who lived outside their alliance, *since that use of money did not affect tribute collection* and disbursement of funds."[117] This interpretation is not necessarily correct, but Figueira's objection carries no weight, since it is based on the elevation to the status of fact what is only a hypothesis about the tributary context and purpose of the decree. It is true that *if* the decree's concern is with tribute collection, then the interpretation makes little sense. But if the decree relates to trade and the *eikoste,* then reference to individuals makes considerable sense: whether pertaining to those outside (who might be affected through trade with Athens' allies) or those within the *arche,* the Athenians would be offering an opportunity to facilitate their exchanges as well.

A final consideration may be adduced in support of the compatibility of the "Standards Decree" and the *eikoste.* Both deal with a decentralized situation: whereas under the tributary system the *phoros* was brought to Athens

115. Cf. *IG* I³ 40, lines 53f., however, which is also giving instructions for the *xenoi* in Chalcis.

116. E.g., Erxleben 1969, 127: [τὸς δὲ ἰδιώτας ἐν τῆι πόλει ἀποδõν]αι τὸ ξενικὸν ἀργύριον [ὃ ἂν ἔχωσιν, ἐπὶ καταλλαγῆι ἕκαστον ὅ]ταμ βόληται; cf. *ATL* 2: 66.

117. Figueira 1998, 412 (my emphasis).

by the allies, the tax would have been collected in the ports throughout the empire and then presumably brought to Athens by the tax farmers. If Athenian coinage becomes the standard medium of exchange for commercial purposes throughout the empire, then this measure in theory would have facilitated the exchange of goods and money outside of Attica. The "Standards Decree" requires that poleis in the *arche* use Athenian silver coinage and weights and measures in their communities; but nothing in the decree (apparently) requires them to come to Athens itself to carry out these instructions beyond a one-time exchange of foreign coinage currently in circulation.[118] Neither the "Standards Decree" nor the *eikoste* seems to warrant the supposition that Athens was out to gain a commercial advantage by requiring traders to come to the Peiraieus;[119] both measures, taken together as complementary, provide for the facilitation of commercial exchange and taxation in local ports.

The Significance of the "Standards Decree" and the Eikoste

There has been a recent tendency to see the decree not in political terms but rather largely as an administrative mechanism. Martin and Figueira rightly note that no fourth-century orator cites the decree in the context of recounting fifth-century imperial excesses, nor is it alluded to in injunctions against former oppressive practices in the Stele of Aristoteles, which concerns the formation of the Second Athenian League in 378/77. This absence suggests that we may be looking at the Standards Decree from the wrong angle by interpreting it largely as a political measure that reflects the oppressive exploitation of the allies by the imperial city.[120] The interpretation advanced here is sympathetic with the inclination to give the decree greater administrative than political weight. If the "Standards Decree" was

118. There are two extant references to a mint, one in section 5 of the composite decree, [ἐν δὲ τῶ]ι ἀργυροκοπίωι τὸ ἀργύρ[ιον . . . , and the other in section 8, where the order is given for the decree to be set up in the agora of each city and in front of τὸ ἀργυριοκοπίον. Both of these references are taken to refer to the mint at Athens. In section 8, the only instance relevant to the question of the procedure of conversion to Attic silver coinage, and the crucial passage for understanding the procedure envisaged, most scholars have argued that the Athenians are ordering the allies to bring all their silver money to the Athenian mint for conversion to Athenian coinage (e.g., Finley 1965, 22; Lacroix 1969, 172–73; Starr 1970, 69; Schuller 1974, 46; Martin 1985, 200–201). Figueira (1998, 353–63), on the other hand, restores this section as an order for Athenian officials to coin money that is already present in the mint.

119. Contra Segre 1938, 151–78; Sutherland 1943 sees this as a more general motive of Athens not explicitly connected to the decree.

120. Martin 1985, 206–7; Figueira 1998, 201–3. On the other hand, if the measure was short-lived and ineffective—as may well have been the case (see below)—future recollection might not have carried much rhetorical force.

promulgated in connection with the collection of a tax on trade, it loses much of its putative politically motivated significance as a measure demonstrating (above all) the Athenians' oppressiveness. The decree does of course suggest the projection of enormous power, but its purpose would not have been to encroach further on political autonomy as a way of strengthening the hold of the imperial city over its subjects. Thus it is far from being "one further instrument among others of Athens' crushing political domination."[121]

On the other hand, both Martin and Figueira argue that the Athenians did not intend a total ban on local coinage, only the use of such coinage for tribute payments to Athens. For both this is a hypothesis of necessity, given the failure of the numismatic record to reveal any trace of an empire-wide break in minting.[122] There may be, however, a significant obstacle to the argument in the decree itself. Section 10 concerns an addition to the bouleutic oath: "The secretary of the boule should add to the bouleutic oath . . . the following: if anyone mints silver coinage in the cities and does not use Athenian coinage or weights or measures but (uses) foreign coinage, weights, and measures. . . . according to the previous decree of Klearchos" (προσγράψαι δὲ πρὸς τὸν ὅρκον [τ]ὸν τῆς βολῆς τὸν γραμματέα τὸν τῆς [βολῆς - - - c. 10 - - - τα]δί· ἐάν τις κόπτηι νόμισ[μα] ἀργυρίο ἐν τῆσι πό[λεσι] καὶ μὴ χρῆται νομ[ίσμασιν τοῖς] Ἀθη[να]ίων ἢ σταθμοῖς ἢ μέτ[ροις ἀλλὰ ξενικοῖς νομίσμασι]ν καὶ σταθμοῖς καὶ [μ]έτροις, [——— c. 6——— 14———]τ[———κατὰ τὸ πρότε]ρον ψήφισμα ὃ Κλέαρχ[ος εἶπεν———c. 19———?]). There are numerous complexities in the consideration of this oath, its restoration, and the reference to the decree of Klearchos. Here, however, we need only to focus on one implication that arises from Figueira's understanding of the ἐάν clause. According to his interpretation the clause refers to two coordinate activities by the same group, those who mint, who also do not use Athenian coinage, weights, and measures. Drawing attention to the καί, as opposed to ἤ, he concludes that "there is nothing here that on superficial reading mandates the *exclusive* use of Athenian standards."[123]

In his interpretation, the *bouleutai* are to be held responsible *only* for noncompliance by minting cities, and this is where, in my view, the difficulty lies. Whenever one dates the decree, the number of minters is but a fraction of the cities in the *arche;*[124] that is, the vast majority of allied poleis did not

121. Austin and Vidal-Naquet 1977, 326. So Figueira 1998, 556: the decree was not a "watershed in the movement from alliance to empire."

122. Martin 1985, 199: the ban was only on silver coinage, not coins in other metals; Figueira 1998, 395.

123. Figueira 1998, 395. This necessitates his rejection of the traditional restoration of the subsequent stipulation, [ἀλλὰ ξενικοῖς νομίσμασι]ν καὶ σταθμοῖς καὶ [μ]έτροις, in favor of [καθάπερ ἑαυτõ νομίσμασι]ν.

124. See Figueira's appendix (1998.563–98).

fall into the category of those whose compliance the members of the *boule* were to be held accountable for. On Figueira's reading, local coinage would continue to be minted and to circulate, and not necessarily only internally,[125] and local weights and measures would continue to be used. Should any non-minting city use non-Athenian coins, weights, or measures in dealings with Athens, it would have been of no concern to the members of the boule. Moreover, the emphasis on the minters alone makes the reference to weights and measures seem tagged on, with no clear relevance, especially, again, given that the majority of allies are unaffected by bouleutic authority. Furthermore, the first clause referring to the activity of minting local coinage is completely redundant: the sole issue for the Athenians is the use of Athenian coinage, weights, and measures, not that local cities (continue to) mint. The final consideration is that, if we are to envisage two activities, one positive—minting local coinage—and the other negative—not using Athenian coinage, weights, and measures—then a single penalty for both situations would make no sense, nor would we obviously want a penalty to be expressed for the first. But the construction of the Greek on Figueira's interpretation necessitates a single penalty applied to both cases.

These considerations, in my view, militate against Figueira's interpretation; it makes little sense that the boule would be concerned with enforcing the compliance of a tiny minority instead of that of all within the *arche*. While ideally we would want to have "or" rather than "and" separating the components of the *if*-clause, it is preferable to read the clause as understanding a second ἐάν τις than to omit from the purview of the *bouleutai* most of the empire.[126] The second group of potential infractors, those who do not use Athenian coinage, weights, and measures, would thus include minters but also comprise the rest of those in the *arche*.

If, then, we have returned to the traditional view, that the Athenians were in fact decreeing a general prohibition on local minting, we are, nevertheless, not obliged to revert to the traditional interpretation of the significance of the decree as a politically heavy-handed act of oppression.[127] It may

125. This would be the case especially with cities whose coinage had "international" value: for example, Abdera; given the commercial function of coinage, both its use as a commodity and as a medium of exchange, it would be difficult to insure that local coinage remained in the cities and did not find its way to other cities, including Athens.

126. There is not enough room in the clause for a further protasis dealing with those cities: the Siphnos fragment is continuous and allows for ca. 20 letter spaces at most between the ἐάν τις . . . clause and καὶ κατὰ τὸν πρότε]ρον ψήφισμα (even if one restored differently before ψήφισμα there would still need to be a phrase attached to ψήφισμα).

127. Nor do we need to suppose a necessarily harsh punishment to be administered to noncompliers by the *boule* in the missing section of the decree in the Siphnos fragment that would have stated the penalty, restored variously by commentators; cf., for example, the proposals in Erxleben 1969, 125–26 (ἐσαγγελέσθω ἐς] τ[ὴν βολὴν . . .); Koch 1991, 398–

still be seen above all as a measure designed purely to facilitate exchange and transactions in the commercial realm. Figueira has demonstrated that there was a gradual reduction in local minting in the fifth century, likely due to the practical value of using a uniform coinage.[128] This means that allies—most of whom were not minters anyway—might not have regarded as oppressive the formalization of a process that was already well under way (except insofar as they might dislike being told what to do by the imperial city). In the case of the use of Athenian weights and measures, likewise, there would have been obvious commercial advantages.[129]

A practical consideration emerges from linking the two measures, which relates to the economic, not the political, context. Assuming that cities would not have stopped the practice of exacting their own maritime taxes after the imposition of the *eikoste,* one can imagine the confusion in local harbors if, in accordance with Figueira's view that local coinage would continue to be used in local contexts, foreign coinages (and standards) continued to be used in transactions at the same time that the Athenians were insisting on the exclusive use of Athenian coinage for the tax that was to end up in Athens. Moreover, if we link the "Standards Decree" with the *eikoste,* collection by the tax farmers themselves would have been simplified, allowing them to get their own profits more expeditiously as well as turn over revenue to the Athenian polis.[130]

Above all, the "Standards Decree", as well as the *eikoste,* needs to be located properly and appreciated in its economic context and for its economic significance. Both measures, viewed together, suggest a large-scale attempt by Athens to create a closed economic system for the purposes of enhancing and facilitating their revenue collection, a system that in a sense replicates normal practice within the polis empire-wide. Indeed, in this light Athens is regarding the *arche* in effect more as an extension of the polis of Athens

---

99 (καταγνώσομαι καὶ] τ[ιμήσω . . .); and Figueira 1998, 402–3 (αὐτὸν οὐκ ἐάσω κα]ὶ ζ[ημιώσω . . .). Note, however, that Figueira's suggestion involves rejecting Erxleben's reading of tau instead of iota zeta in between the brackets, a reading accepted by Lewis in *IG* I[3]. For the death penalty as part of an entrenchment clause, and therefore not directed at the allies for noncompliance with the decree itself, see Lewis 1974; Mattingly 1974 [1996, 347–51]; Figueira 1998, 375–79.

128. His work is less helpful for the period under consideration here, since he dates the decree to the mid-century.

129. This is a separate issue from the political issue of whether allies liked to be told what to do.

130. One wonders about the economic effect of the "Standards Decree" on poleis with silver mines under their control, akin to the situation in Attica with the Laureion mines, as was especially the case in the northern Aegean cities. If they were forced to stop minting, or for that matter if they had reduced minting production voluntarily over the course of the fifth century, the polis would not make a profit on minting but of course could have exported bullion as a commodity.

rather than as a larger, extra-polis sphere over which it has political control. It is now applying to the *arche* a system that every polis naturally applied within its borders, imposing taxes within its ports as a regular means of obtaining revenue for the city, and using its own money and metrological standards as a normal means of transaction and exchange within its borders.

The development explored here, in which the Athenians treat the *arche* as an extension of the polis, fits into a larger pattern that can be observed in the intertwining of the religious and political spheres, in which, for example, as mentioned above, the "allies" participated in the Greater Panathenaia and received cults of Athena from Athens in their territories.[131] Such requirements brought economic benefit to Athens. But the Athenians also aimed at benefiting economically from those outside the *arche*. Recall that the *eikoste* would possibly have affected those not in the *arche* who traded at ports in the *arche*, and that the "Standards Decree" may have contained a provision for those outside the empire to bring their coinage to Athens and convert it to Athenian coinage. It is intriguing that the Eleusinian "First Fruits Decree" includes a similar clause inviting those outside the *arche* to participate in sending dedications to Demeter, since the decree, although undated, may have been passed around this time.[132] These attempts to draw in outsiders, in areas that brought economic benefit to Athens, would be further important signs of the changing nature of the Athenians' attitude toward their rule—one that would ultimately transform the nature of that rule.

Thus, the Athenians, in this reconstruction, impose the "Standards Decree" and the *eikoste* in order to standardize and facilitate an economic system and to generate more revenue. These economically motivated acts would have been expected (by the Athenians) to have political benefits: willingness to accept "membership" in the *arche*, and fewer revolts. It is even possible that both measures may have been designed to send a signal that the Athenians were lightening their hold on their allies, in a departure from the old imperial model of political alliance. That, at least, would have been the Athenian perspective; the "allies" may have had quite another, as noted above.

131. See Smarczyk 1990, 58–154; Parker 1994; Parker 1996, 142–51. Dismissing those as propaganda does not lessen the significance of the act, for they are still manifestations of a trend toward regarding the allies as part of Athens, whether for propagandistic or other purposes; cf. also the increase in exploitation of the Ion myth; Parker 1987, 206–7.

132. *IG* I[3] 78 (ML 73, lines 30–36). It is tempting to connect the decree with the abolition of tribute, the *eikoste*, and the "Standards Decree," given the replacement of tribute with a tax on commodities that would have included agricultural products, and the likelihood that just as the Athenians had shifted the divine patronage of the *arche* from Apollo to Athena (though by no means ignoring Apollo), they might well have viewed Demeter as a valuable divinity to associate with the *arche* at this time. The religious significance of the change from tribute to *eikoste*, as it affected Athena, is a subject that warrants further attention.

The Date of the Eikoste *and the "Standards Decree"*

We have been exploring a connection between the "Standards Decree" and the *eikoste,* and the implications of such a conjunction. Since the "Standards Decree" is an internally undated (composite) document, and Thucydides does not locate the *eikoste* precisely in time, we need to consider the chronological pegs we have. Early in the twentieth century the favored date for the decree was ca. 414, since Aristophanes' *Birds* was produced in the spring of that year and contains an allusion to a "new decree" that sounds strikingly similar to the "Standards Decree."[133] If the allusion in the *Birds* is indeed a reference to the "Standards Decree," as I think it is, then the latter should not postdate the spring of 414,[134] the year in which some have placed the *eikoste.*[135] Both decrees could, then, have been passed at around the same time, in 414. Thucydides' narrative, however, implies a date of 413, but his account is not without difficulties. In contrast to other sections of the *History* where he has related financial information with chronological precision —for example, 1.95–96, which he describes meticulously the steps leading to the institution of tribute in 478, or 3.19, where he mentions the collec-

133. χρῆσθαι Νεφελοκκυγιᾶς τοῖσδε τοῖς μέτροισι καὶ σταθμοῖσι καὶ ψηφίσμασι καθάπερ Ὀλοφύξιοι, line 1041. See, for example, Johnston 1932; Weil 1906, 1910; Gardner 1913. Weil and Gardner put the decree of Klearchos in that year, the "Standards Decree" a little later. Wilamowitz (1880, 30–310) famously inferred from the passage in *Birds* the existence of the "Standards Decree" before any fragments were recognized (Mattingly [1977, 83 n. 1] points out that the Smyrna fragment had been published in 1855, "but [was] not recognized."). Likewise, Bergk (1857, ad loc.) noted that νομίσμασι would have been the expected word in place of ψηφίσμασι, a suggestion adopted by Blaydes (1882, ad loc). Yet, as Dunbar (1995, ad loc.) comments, "applying prosaic logic removes Ar.'s joke; when the audience is expecting to hear νομίσμασι, the Decree-seller slips in ψηφίσμασι instead, thus representing his decrees as imposed on the new city by the sovereign Athenian Assembly no less than his weights and measures"; cf., alternatively, Sommerstein (1987, ad loc.): "The decree-seller may have deliberately 'adjusted' the text of the decree in order to make his 'customers' believe that it was compulsory for them to purchase his wares!"

134. Although given the fact that the proposal leading up to the passage of the decree must have been accompanied by a good deal of discussion and thus have been a popular subject, the allusion could be to a decree that was in the process of being approved by the assembly (and was therefore extremely new). Alternatively, and also necessarily speculatively, if Klearchos' decree (alluded to in section 12) was earlier and was concerned with the same subject matter as the "Standards Decree," then one could place the former in 414 and the latter in 413, as Weil and Gardner suggested (see previous note). The possibility has to be conceded that the joke in the phrase "new laws" (1037) lies in its very old nature, as is the view necessarily taken by those who prefer a mid-century date (e.g., Pouilloux 1953, 39 n. 5; 1954, 118 n.3; Figueira 1998, 209), just as it has to be conceded that proof about the date is impossible; but I find the idea that the Decree Seller is selling well-worn or obsolete laws no more persuasive than that the laws are "hot off the press," given the propensity for topicality in Aristophanes' plays.

135. Mattingly 1979, 320 [1996, 158]; Dover, *HCT* 4, ad loc.

tion of the first *eisphora* in 428—in this passage Thucydides is conspicuously vague about the timing of the *eikoste,* saying only "around that time (ὑπὸ τοῦτον τὸν χρόνον, 7.28.4). He does, however, imply strongly that it post-dates the fortification of Dekeleia, since he embeds his reference to the decision to abolish tribute and impose the tax in a digression on Athens' economic state as a result, chiefly, of the fortification, and following his discussion of the Athenians' decision, despite the fortification, to remain in Sicily. This points to a date of 413, following the fortification of Dekeleia in the early spring of that year (Thuc. 7.19).[136]

One could argue that an unrealistically tight chronology results. It is unclear, especially given the number of events throughout the war that were contrary to expectation,[137] whether the Athenians could have predicted immediately the heavy economic toll that Dekeleia would exact or could have realized that the Spartans were in fact setting up a permanent fort; this is an instance in which it is particularly important to resist hindsight. One could therefore argue for a reconstruction that would allow time for the economic and fiscal consequences of Dekeleia to be felt. This would place the actual proposal to be voted on in the assembly at the earliest in the following year, 412, by which point the Athenians were back from Sicily—in other words, they were no longer fighting two wars, though by then they were in serious financial straits. It seems a priori highly unlikely that in 412 and the years following, once the war had resumed in the Aegean and it was clear that the Spartans were finally moving toward naval war, the Athenians would have considered a tax on maritime trade a likelier means of raising revenue than tribute, no matter how unsatisfactory tribute may have become as an adequate source of revenue.[138]

136. Also suggestive of a post-414 date is Thuc. 6.91.7. Alkibiades, speaking at Sparta, refers to the chief advantage of fortifying Dekeleia as disrupting the revenue coming into Athens from the allies: μάλιστα δὲ τῆς ἀπὸ τῶν ξυμμάχων προσόδου ἧσσον διαφορουμένης. The passage is not conclusive as a reference to tribute as opposed to a tax, but it seems likely that Alkibiades is referring to tribute. On the other hand, the reference in the "catalogue of ships" in 7.57.4 to "tributary allies," that is, in the spring of 413, may not be a strong indication that the allies were in fact still paying tribute. Thucydides is listing the participants, among other objects, to illustrate and characterize the power relationships through the presence of advantage or compulsion. This motive may underlie his categorizing of those on the Athenian side as "tributary subjects," among other kinds of relationships. Also, there are literary reasons for placing the catalogue where it is, a consideration that makes it unwise to put too much temporal weight on the reference. Perhaps the same applies to a reference to "tributary allies" in a speech by Nikias (7.63.3) also in 413, but it also has to remain open whether the *eikoste* had as yet been imposed.

137. E.g., the first Spartan invasion (2.21.1–2), and the anticipated length of the war (5.14).

138. Contra Gauthier (1989, 35), who places the *eikoste* after the disaster in Sicily, but without discussion.

One might also think that the paired decision to abolish tribute and impose a tax, with its far-reaching implications for the *arche,* as well as for the city's fiscal structure and administration, would have involved much discussion and debate. It is indeed a decision of a decidedly different character from the standard measures for raising revenue in the midst of war, for example, by levying *eisphorai,* as in 428/27 (Thuc. 3.19.1). On the face of it, then, the decision to impose the maritime tax might seem to be one that would have taken considerable time to reach, involving careful research into the commercial yield of the ports within the *arche,* calculations and estimates about the volume and expected profits of trade, fixing of the percentage to be taxed, how the tax was to be auctioned, and who was eligible to bid and other details concerning the means of collection, and the restructuring of the tributary bureaucracy, which may have entailed decisions of its own about eliminating officials or redirecting administrative personnel and machinery to the new revenue system.

Yet Thucydides is at some pains to represent the decision as one made not in a calm, rational setting, and he implies that it was made in 413, and it did not involve painstaking investigation or lengthy deliberation about the likelihood of its success at the time. Despite our lack of knowledge about the actual workings of maritime taxation throughout the empire—even for Athens, our best-documented polis—we can assume a system for collecting harbor taxes of 1 to 2 percent already in place in the local harbors, as it was in Athens, with local tax-farming and collection officials (e.g., the *pentekostologoi,* the collectors of the 2-percent harbor tax in Athens), who would have kept records of the volume of trade and the tax collected.[139] Moreover, if some cities were assessed partially on the basis of revenue from harbor taxes, the Athenians would already have possessed such records. All of this is speculation, of course, but it is useful for suggesting a possible scenario in which such a decision might have been reached relatively quickly.

However, we need to distinguish between two issues: (1) the research, knowledge, and time necessary to achieve these measures, and (2) discussion in the assembly and persuasive efforts to get them adopted. Undeniably, the tax, like all taxes then and now, would have looked far simpler "on paper" than it would have been in reality.[140] It would have been advertised as an easy way in which massively to increase the revenues flowing into Athens, precisely because Athens, like other poleis, was already accustomed to think of harbor taxes as a normal and, importantly, dependable and lucrative form of revenue. Yet we also need to recall the radical and sweeping na-

139. Cf., for instance, Dem. 34.7 (cited by Böckh 1842, 314).

140. Cf. Ar. *Ekkl.* 823ff., which lists decisions concerning taxes and coinage that turned out to be disasters; the implication is that they looked advantageous in theory and seemed like good ideas at the time. I shall return to this passage below.

ture of this change, of a nature unprecedented in the *arche*'s long history. Considerations of the date of enactment of a measure tend to ignore the preceding decision-making context, but this fuller context must be appreciated, especially in the case of far-reaching decisions like this one that affected the entire structure of the *arche*. It makes sense that the adoption of the *eikoste* and the elimination of tribute may well have taken considerable persuasion, and perhaps have come up a number of times, only to be tabled.

The following reconstruction of the chronological context of the "Standards Decree" and the *eikoste* allows a connection between the two without their having to have been actually passed at exactly the same time; indeed, there are good reasons for placing the "Standards Decree" before the *eikoste*. Let us begin with the hypothesis, reasonable given Athens' ongoing concern with the dependability of its wartime revenue, and not prohibited by Thucydides' narrative, that an idea like the *eikoste* did not emerge for the first time in 413 but had arisen in discussions previously, along with, we may suppose, other proposals for making tribute more effective or considerations of other means of raising revenue. Indeed, it is possible that talk of a measure like the *eikoste* may well have begun during the Peace of Nikias. The year 421 had brought peace, but it is vital to appreciate that the Peace was unlikely to be understood as anything more than a time to recoup; after all the battle of Mantineia had taken place already in 418, and the Athenians were clearly planning to expand on a large scale: the actual decision to invade Sicily may have been prompted by the Egestan appeals in Athens in 416, but the idea did not come out of the blue.[141]

The period of relative calm during the Peace will inevitably have stimulated trade within the regions of the empire and will have increased revenues disrupted in varying degrees during the Archidamian War. Peacetime provides a likely context for a polis like Athens to begin to reflect on the merits of trade versus tribute as a revenue-generating system; the Athenians would certainly have seen the potential for profits from trade at such a time. Moreover, when they began to discuss returning to Sicily they must have had their financial capability to undertake the expedition at the forefront of their minds.[142] It is highly significant that when Thucydides, for example, mentions the Athenians' aims in Sicily in his account of the first expedition in 427 and the second in 415, he explicitly draws attention to the island's wealth. Regarding the first expedition, he cites as the Athenians' "real reason" for accepting an appeal for help the desire both to prevent the export of grain from Sicily to the Peloponnese and to test out the possibility of con-

141. It is important to keep in mind their earlier expedition of 427.

142. There is an instructive parallel in Philip V's activities in 185. According to Livy (39.24), in anticipation of attacking the Romans, still in a time of peace he increased revenues from harbor taxes and agricultural products.

quering the island (3.86). In his fuller narrative concerned with the expedition of 415 he again emphasizes the Athenians' desire for the wealth of the island (6.24.3). According to the hypothetical scenario proposed here, as they debated substituting an *eikoste* for *phoros* the Athenians' knowledge of the inherent wealth and commercial prosperity of Sicily might have led them to consider the profits to be had if Sicily were within their *arche.* For one thing, as they must have known, the prospects of collecting tribute from a place so far away would be minimal, whereas a tax collected locally in Sicilian harbors would be far more practical and profitable.

Such discussion may have come up, then, and research may already have been undertaken, but the radical nature of the *eikoste* may have precluded easy passage, until the situation of the "two wars" made the arguments for eliminating tribute and imposing the port tax more compelling. Thus the measure passed only when the Athenians had decided to remain in Sicily and knew that they would require substantially greater financial resources, and resources that were available for immediate use. The "Standards Decree", on the other hand, may have been easier to pass. At least insofar as coinage is concerned, as mentioned, it would have formalized a process already under way and concerned directly very few cities: the minters, for the most part. Moreover, such a measure, according to the interpretation adopted here, would have lacked the symbolic overtones and implications that the *eikoste* would have had in its role as a replacement for tribute. As concerns weights and measures, the city itself would not have had to put into place any new arrangement, especially if it formalized an increasingly common situation in the *arche.* Furthermore, in this reconstruction, the "Standards Decree" would have needed to be in place prior to the instruction to the allies to cease paying tribute and the order to those residing in the *arche* (a broader group including noncitizen metics in the cities) to pay a maritime tax to Athens. Cities and individuals would need time to bring whatever local currency remained to Athens for conversion into Athenian denominations.

Obviously this scenario is speculative; its purpose, motivated by the appeal of a connection between the *eikoste* and the "Standards Decree," has been to suggest a possibility that takes into account a likely historical context as well as the evidence of Thucydides. One final issue remains before we return to Thucydides.

The Success of the Eikoste *and the "Standards Decree"*

How successful was the 5 percent tax? Unfortunately, as Antony Andrewes has noted, "there is no direct evidence of the working of the new system."[143]

143. Andrewes 1992, 458. There is a possible allusion to the *eikoste* in Antiphon *Herodes* 77 (ca. 421–411), in which the speaker, Euxitheos, refers to the τέλη duly paid by his father, a Mytilenaian; the correspondence is suggested by Wade-Gery (p. 214 of the Loeb translation).

Most scholars believe that tribute was reinstated in the summer of 410, which would imply that the tax was a failure.[144] Adduced in support of the revival of tribute are five fragments assumed to be of a tribute reassessment published by Benjamin Meritt in 1936.[145] The fragments, none of which join, are undated but likely were inscribed toward the end of the fifth century. The evidence placing the assessment in 410 is entirely circumstantial: the place-name Miletoteichos (partially restored)[146] appears in one fragment, and since it lies a good distance inland from Kyzikos, its presence is associated with the great victory there in 410; Krateros cites an assessment in his ninth book, which includes a section on Antiphon's trial in 411–410; finally, Xenophon states that after the city of Kalchedon surrendered to the Athenians in 410, it was to pay the tribute to the Athenians that it had been accustomed to pay (ὑποτελεῖν τὸν φόρον Καλχηδονίους Ἀθηναίοις ὅσονπερ εἰώθεσαν).[147] Against the 410 date stands a reference in Aristophanes' *Frogs*, produced in 405, to an *eikostologos* operating on Aigina (363). Only Mattingly has dissented, preferring to date the fragments to 418.[148]

It is necessary to stress that the evidence in support of the reinstatement of tribute in 410 cannot be treated as a fact, as it generally is. It is not that the reference in the *Frogs* militates against the restoration of tribute: since Aigina never paid tribute, the allusion could easily accommodate a situation in which cities affected by the *eikoste* but which were not tributary members of the League continued to be required to pay the maritime tax. Not only does the lack of a date prohibit certainty, but even the Kalchedon reference in Xenophon's *Hellenika* can be used equally to refer to a specific, particular case as a punishment, and not to a general reimposition.[149] In short, none of the evidence compels. This is not to deny the possibility that tribute was reimposed but rather to caution against its status as fact when so much is tenuous and uncertain. In any case, even if tribute was reinstated, we cannot be sure, as Meritt, Wade-Gery, and McGregor note, that the tax did not continue to be collected,[150] which would mean that the *eikoste* might not have been a failure, only that the Athenians by then needed to collect even more revenue. Certainly Xenophon suggests that by 411 the Athenians faced a

144. See Meiggs 1972, 438–39, for a useful summary; see also Lewis in *IG* I³ 291. Mattingly (1967, 13–15 [1996, 205–8]; 1979, 320–21 [1996, 158–60]) is an exception, at least insofar as he rejects the idea that tribute was reintroduced in 410.

145. Meritt 1936, 386–89.

146. Note that in *ATL* 1: 159 (A13) the restoration is Μιλητο[πολῖται], line 5.

147. Xen. *Hell.* 1.3.9.

148. See Mattingly 1979, 321 [1996, 159].

149. Underhill (1984 [1906], ad loc.) notes, among several alternative explanations, the possibility of a "special arrangement," though another interpretation suggested, that Xenophon is referring to the *eikoste*, is clearly untenable. Krentz (1989, ad loc.) also sees a special case as possible.

150. *ATL* 3: 148.

severe financial crisis, at least in operating the fleet off Asia Minor and the Hellespont.[151]

As for Thucydides, in one respect he is of no help here, because his *History* breaks off before the suggested date of reimposition; but it is not clear that he would have mentioned it anyway, because in mentioning the *eikoste* at all he is guided more by historiographical aims than the desire to provide a record of Athenian economic and fiscal policy per se. In another respect, however, as argued above, the evidence he provides is useful, because he implies strongly that the decision was a grand mistake. Indeed, it may be relevant that his narrative subsequent to the decision to eliminate tribute and impose the maritime tax provides no clear sense of the changed economic situation of the allies; it gives the impression rather of a continuation of the status quo.[152]

A passage from Aristophanes' *Ekkleziazousai,* referred to earlier,[153] ridiculing economic measures of the past, which no doubt looked good "on paper" but turned out to be fiascos, provides important evidence by analogy not only of the kind of context in which the decision to try an *eikoste* was likely reached, but also the pattern of failure of the Athenians' attempts to regulate their economy (and by extension the larger sphere of the *arche* as well). The Dissident and the Citizen are discussing the decree by which the women order the men to turn in their property to the state. The Citizen recalls other absurd decrees voted recently that turned out to be disasters. He notes the "salt decree," the decree about the copper coinage, and the 2.5 percent tax proposed just recently by Euripides: "Weren't we all swearing that it would bring in three million drachmas? And then we looked into it and found out, as usual, that it would not work" (823ff., trans. Sommerstein). What is intriguing about this comic reference is that every measure held up as foolhardy and unworkable by the Citizen is economic in nature. Obviously this tells us nothing directly about the *eikoste,* but it suggests a pattern of ineffective economic decisions made by the Athenians as they struggled to recover their financial position after the Peloponnesian War. Such attempts sound strikingly similar to the context in which Thucydides places the *eikoste.*

Whether a failure by design, the *eikoste* was likely to fail in practice simply because of the military and political situation in which the Athenians found themselves following the Sicilian expedition. Even under the best of cir-

151. *Hell.* 1.1.8–22, including the dispatch of many ships to collect money, Alkibiades' comment that they had no money, and the imposition of a *dekate* on grain ships traveling through the Hellespont. It may be significant that Xenophon chooses to emphasize financial difficulties to the extent that he does, in a part of his work continuing Thucydides.

152. E.g., 8.5, 8.6, 8.45.5; cf. 8.2.2 (allies referred to as ὑπήκοοι).

153. N. 139, above.

cumstances, evasion of this kind of tax, levied in hundreds of ports likely in many cases without a strong official presence, would have been much easier than evasion of tribute, of which the Athenians had to keep track only once a year. The same can be said of the "Standards Decree": though those in the *arche* may well have been transacting business in Athenian coinage increasingly anyway without it, local minting, where it occurred, did not cease, given that the Athenians would not have been in a position to enforce the total ban on local coinage or the use of Athenian metrological standards. Both measures may well have flopped.[154]

CONCLUSION

In conclusion let us return to Thucydides. The hypothetical scenario I have been considering places the "Standards Decree" and the *eikoste* together in a context of large-scale economic reorganization or systemization. Yet there is not a shred of evidence in the *History* that the Athenians are rethinking their *arche* in practical, economic terms. It would be easy to resort to the explanation that ancient elite authors abjured writing about the commercial realm, but this would justifiably risk a charge of special pleading. For one thing, Thucydides has demonstrated an acute interest in the revenue basis of Athens' *arche* and has provided much of the evidence for the argument presented here about the increasingly economic nature of the *arche;* moreover, we have seen his interest in the financial backing (or lack thereof) of the Sicilian expedition. He does mention the *eikoste,* which, in the context of Athenian imperial history, was a crucial development because of its role as a replacement of the tributary system, which had political, as well as financial and economic, significance. On the other hand, the "Standards Decree," if it had the effect of formalizing an economic process that had gradually been taking place, to facilitate revenue acquisition for Athens, may have been far less dramatic than it appears to us (and so for Thucydides would not have warranted explicit mention).

There may, however, be other reasons, one of which has been intimated already, for Thucydides' decision to mention the *eikoste* in the manner he

154. I have, with others, stressed the greater facility of making commercial transactions using uniform standards; thus one might ask, on the assumption that this was widely recognized, why the allies, not viewing the decree as an infringement on autonomy, would not have gone along with the decree despite Athens' weakness, given its advantages to their own commercial interests? Yet it is important to keep in mind that whatever the perceived impact of the "Standards Decree," it was nonetheless still a measure imposed on the allies by the imperial city, and therefore not likely to be embraced if one could get away with continuing local practice (which may have included the use of Athenian coinage anyway).

does, and to omit reference to the "Standards Decree." Both likely, as suggested above, were, after all, essentially dead letters. At the same time, we need to recall the narrative context of the reference to the *eikoste,* which encourages the reader to criticize its conception. The "Standards Decree," in the interpretation offered here, was neither unreasonable nor, according to the suggested chronology, passed at exactly the same time as the *eikoste.* These considerations also offer an explanation for Thucydides' treatment and omissions.

CHAPTER SIX

The Problem of Money in the Ionian War

Book 8 is "unfinished, dull and spiritless. . . . The historian seems to grope his way like a man without a clue."[1] "Book 8 is in its final form."[2] No other book of Thucydides has provoked such wide-ranging assessments.[3] That one can find plausible arguments to buttress both of these opposing judgments is a compelling indication that the inclination to categorize the book as finished or unfinished and to reach conclusions on the basis of such an identification is flawed. The results of scholars' close examination of this final section of the *History* also suggest a third possibility: the book has some undeniable rough spots and curious features that may be best explained by the hypothesis that Thucydides had not entirely polished it to his final satisfaction, *and* the book has a narrative and thematic coherence and an intimate connection with the rest of the *History*. These characterizations of book 8 are mutually contradictory only if one forces the narrative into either the "unfinished" or the "polished" category.

There is no doubt that book 8 differs in flavor and structure from the

1. Cornford 1971 [1907], 244.

2. Patwell 1978, 330.

3. The bibliography is extensive. For the "unfinished" position Wilamowitz 1908 has been fundamental; see also, for example, Holzapfel 1893; Schwartz 1919, 72–91; Brunt 1952; de Romilly 1963, 224–26; Lewis 1977, 85; Andrewes, *HCT* 5: 1–4; Rawlings 1981, 176–77; Westlake 1969, 35; 1989, 176; Allison 1997b, 95; Cawkwell 1997, 135 at n. 15. Those who emphasize the finished, even polished nature of the book from the standpoint of thematic unity and narrative structure include Delebecque 1965, 1967; Patwell 1978; Pouncey 1980; Macleod 1983, 141 (implied); Erbse 1989b; Forde 1989, 117 n. 2; Rood 1998, 251–84; Gribble 1998, 65–66; Rood's (1998, 251–84) treatment of book 8 is especially good and complements the examination here. See also, for a general survey of opinions, Luschnat, *RE* Suppl. 12.1112–21; Weil and de Romilly (Budé edition), xi–xv.

earlier books of the *History*. Among other differences, the shifting arenas, lack of direct speeches, and less abstract language set it apart. However, the fragmentation that scholars on both sides have observed and used to support their positions has a simpler explanation: the character of the war has changed, and Thucydides must deal with a complicated series of events in a number of arenas.[4] Indeed, the book's fragmentation might even be seen as contributing to a kind of thematic unity.[5]

Carolyn Dewald has argued cogently that despite a rather chaotic appearance, book 8 possesses a narrative unity. She observes that, in contrast to the paratactic nature of books 2 through 5 (at least as far as 5.24), the structure and nature of units of action, or scenes, in book 8 have a hypotactic arrangement, in which apparently disjointed scenes are in fact "linked together to form a continuous, ongoing story"; and notes further that "the scenes which follow each other in book viii are aspects of a single question: will the Peloponnesian or the Athenian fleet dominate the eastern Mediterranean?"[6] In its narrative arrangement, Dewald argues, book 8 bears a close connection with the Sicilian books and comprises a unit, in sharp contrast to the earlier books of the *History*. Yet she also contrasts book 8 and the Sicilian books: "Book viii thus resembles the Sicilian account in the extent to which scenes which succeed each other take up the same few foci repeatedly. Yet in another respect the two accounts still appear to be very different. The Sicilian account is understandable on a level that book viii lacks; we know in books vi and vii what Thucydides thinks about the events unfolding as well as what occurred. Thucydides has not revealed, in the portion we have, his interpretation of the Aegean War."[7]

Yet I suggest that Thucydides does in fact construct a larger, coherent interpretative layer in book 8, using its hypotactic narrative arrangement to achieve emphasis and development. The theme of money and naval financing not only pervades the book but often serves as a linking device between seemingly disconnected episodes. As in the treatment of this theme earlier, the nature and context of the details provided in book 8 reveal a larger historiographical agenda to which the information is put to use, thus giving the theme greater significance in the book than it might otherwise have.

A quick look at some statistics will illustrate immediately the prominence of the theme just from the preponderance of financial vocabulary in book 8.

4. As Westlake (1989, 113), Connor (1984, 217–18), Rood (1998, 253), and others have noted.

5. Pouncey (1980, esp. 142–43) sees him as deliberately constructing the narrative to achieve fragmentation, as part of his larger historiographical purpose of highlighting moral and social fragmentation.

6. Dewald 1975, 193, 194.

7. Ibid., 195.

The word *chremata* occurs thirty-five times in book 1, drops off dramatically over the next four books, and picks up again in book 6 with twenty-seven instances, nineteen in book 7, and twenty-five in book 8. *Misthos* occurs ten times in books 1 through 5, eight times in books 6 through 7, and eleven in book 8. The most interesting case is the use of *trophe*. There are only six occurrences in books 1 through 4 (three of which mean "food"), four in books 6 through 7, but an impressive seventeen in book 8. I shall examine Thucydides' use of this terminology in the appendix; the terms are cited here to highlight the centrality of the theme of money in this narrative of the final stage of the war, which itself constitutes yet another beginning.[8] As we will see, just as Thucydides introduces and develops the importance of the money/power link, and in particular, the necessity of *periousia chrematon* at length in book 1 and the beginning of book 2, and in books 6 through 7 focuses on the failure to apply *gnome* to *periousia chrematon,* in book 8 he carefully charts and tracks the difficulties of cash flow facing both sides, and the corrosive consequences of attempting to fight naval war without *periousia chrematon*.

Book 8 is linked to the account of the Sicilian expedition not only in similarities of narrative arrangement but also through the embedding of Herodotos' account of the Ionian revolt (examined in chapter 2) and, at the end of book 8, the use of the Persian Wars, as an interpretative tool. We have seen that the Ionian revolt narrative is especially germane to book 8, since a chief concern is the cities in Ionia under Athens' control that attempt another Ionian revolt. There are many ironic twists: the Ionian cities seek freedom from Athens, not Persia; Persia, indeed, can be said to be aiding their revolts through its funding of the Spartan navy (though insufficiently and sporadically at this stage); Alkibiades and Tissaphernes alternate in an Aristagoras-type role, with Tissaphernes as an unreliable paymaster and Alkibiades a middleman between Greeks and Persians; Alkibiades is as out for himself as Aristagoras was; in the "Ionian revolt" that will close the century, Sparta is now assisting the Ionians as firmly as Kleomenes had refused to do so in the revolt that opened the century.[9]

Not only does the narrative arrangment of book 8 resemble that of the Sicilian books, as Dewald has argued, but its opening chapters link it closely with what has preceded thematically as well. As Allison points out, "the most notable stylistic feature [of book 8] is the recurrence of words and phrases which intimately connect this section with the Sicilian narrative. . . . [Their]

8. As he will make explicit in 8.5.1. See Allison 1997b, 85; Rood 1998, 252–53. Similarly, as we saw in chapter 1, the beginnings of the Sicilian expedition are presented as a kind of new beginning as well and are meant to be contrasted, in this case, with the beginning of book 2.

9. See also chap. 2, pp. 95–97, for discussion.

repetition is a rhetorical enhancement and suggest[s] that it functions to convey concepts over narrative so that they can be summoned anew."[10] Indeed, familiar themes—money, passion, and hope—quickly emerge, and are powerful links to the earlier narrative.

5.103–4 AND 8.1.1

Book 8 opens with a vivid description of the reaction in Athens to the news of the expedition's total failure, a reaction that proceeds in stages from disbelief to anger, and, finally, to terror and panic: "They were distressed in all ways and in every quarter and because of what had happened they were seized by the most extraordinary fear and panic" (πάντα δὲ πανταχόθεν αὐτοὺς ἐλύπει τε καὶ περιεστήκει ἐπὶ τῷ γεγενημένῳ φόβος τε καὶ κατάπληξις μεγίστη δή, 8.1.2). The book comprises what will be, in its own way, as remarkable a chapter in the final stage of the war, and as intriguing a narrative as books 6 and 7, from the standpoint of the themes being explored.

The thematic links appear immediately. For example, Thucydides refers sarcastically to the Athenians' collective anger at the orators "who shared their zeal for the expedition" (τοῖς ξυμπροθυμηθεῖσι τῶν ῥητόρων), intensifying his censure by adding: "just as if they had not themselves voted for it" (ὥσπερ οὐκ αὐτοὶ ψηφισάμενοι).[11] This judgment readily recalls the impressive stream of vocabulary of passion and zeal used to describe the Athenians' mood in 6.24 after Nikias' second speech and Thucydides' emphatic statement that they all felt this way;[12] now the shared zeal, *prothumia,* shifts to the Lakedaimonian allies (ξυμπροθυμηθέντες, 8.2.1).[13]

The opening of book 8 also evokes the Melian Dialogue, in a way that helps illuminate further Thucydides' interpretation of the Sicilian expedition. Let us return to a chapter examined at the beginning of this study, 5.103, the warning to the Melians about hope in relation to financial resources:

> Ἐλπὶς δὲ κινδύνῳ παραμύθιον οὖσα τοὺς μὲν ἀπὸ περιουσίας χρωμένους αὐτῇ, κἂν βλάψῃ, οὐ καθεῖλεν· τοῖς δ' ἐς ἅπαν τὸ ὑπάρχον ἀναρριπτοῦσι (δάπανος γὰρ φύσει) ἅμα τε γιγνώσκεται σφαλέντων καὶ ἐν ὅτῳ ἔτι φυλάξεταί τις αὐτὴν γνωρισθεῖσαν οὐκ ἐλλείπει. ὃ ὑμεῖς ἀσθενεῖς τε καὶ ἐπὶ ῥοπῆς μιᾶς ὄντες μὴ βούλεσθε παθεῖν μηδὲ ὁμοιωθῆναι τοῖς πολλοῖς, οἷς

10. Allison 1997b, 87, concentrating on the word παντοχόθεν (88–91); see also Rood 1998, 255. Patwell (1978, 225) also sees book 8 as a "true continuation of the books on the Sicilian Expedition."

11. Cf. the almost snide tone of the comment in 6.46.5 (above, chap. 1, pp. 78–79).

12. τὸ ἐπιθυμοῦν, πολὺ δὲ μᾶλλον ὥρμηντο, ἔρως ἐνέπεσε τοῖς πᾶσιν ὁμοίως ἐκπλεῦσαι; πόθῳ; ἄγαν ἐπιθυμίαν, 6.24.2–4. Cf. also the irony in the juxtaposition of those emotions with the idea of safety (6.23.3, 24.1, 24.2).

13. Cf. also the striking correspondences with 7.64.1, noted by Luschnat (1942, 92).

παρὸν ἀνθρωπείως ἔτι σώζεσθαι, ἐπειδὰν πιεζομένους αὐτοὺς ἐπιλίπωσιν αἱ φανεραὶ ἐλπίδες, ἐπὶ τὰς ἀφανεῖς καθίστανται μαντικήν τε καὶ χρησμοὺς καὶ ὅσα τοιαῦτα μετ' ἐλπίδων λυμαίνεται. (5.103)

Hope, that inciter to danger, does not utterly ruin, even if it harms, those who use it from a position of abundance. But for those who gamble their existing resources entirely on it—for it is expensive in nature—they see it for what it is only when they are destroyed, and it does not fail as long as there is a chance that someone will guard against it after recognizing it for what it is. This is what you, being weak and at the mercy of a single balancing of the scale, do not want to suffer, nor want to become like the many, who, when it is in their human power still to be saved, whenever manifest hopes fail them when they are hard pressed, they fall for invisible ones, prophecy and oracles and all that nonsense that causes ruin when accompanying hopes.

Ἐς δὲ τὰς Ἀθήνας ἐπειδὴ ἠγγέλθη, ἐπὶ πολὺ μὲν ἠπίστουν καὶ τοῖς πάνυ τῶν στρατιωτῶν ἐξ αὐτοῦ τοῦ ἔργου διαπεφευγόσι καὶ σαφῶς ἀγγέλλουσι, μὴ οὕτω γε ἄγαν πανσυδὶ διεφθάρθαι· ἐπειδὴ δὲ ἔγνωσαν, χαλεποὶ μὲν ἦσαν τοῖς ξυμπροθυμηθεῖσι τῶν ῥητόρων τὸν ἔκπλουν, ὥσπερ οὐκ αὐτοὶ ψηφισάμενοι, ὠργίζοντο δὲ καὶ τοῖς χρησμολόγοις τε καὶ μάντεσι καὶ ὁπόσοι τι τότε αὐτοὺς θειάσαντες ἐπήλπισαν ὡς λήψονται Σικελίαν . . . ἅμα μὲν γὰρ στερόμενοι καὶ ἰδίᾳ ἕκαστος καὶ ἡ πόλις ὁπλιτῶν τε πολλῶν καὶ ἱππέων καὶ ἡλικίας οἵαν οὐχ ἑτέραν ἑώρων ὑπάρχουσαν ἐβαρύνοντο· ἅμα δὲ ναῦς οὐχ ὁρῶντες ἐν τοῖς νεωσοίκοις ἱκανὰς οὐδὲ χρήματα ἐν τῷ κοινῷ οὐδ' ὑπηρεσίας ταῖς ναυσὶν ἀνέλπιστοι ἦσαν ἐν τῷ παρόντι σωθήσεσθαι, κτλ. (8.1.1–2)

When the news was reported in Athens, for a long while the Athenians disbelieved even the most credible of the soldiers who had themselves escaped from the action and had given an accurate report, that [the expedition] had been so utterly wiped out. But when they accepted it, they were angry at those of the orators who, together with themselves, had so passionately advocated the expedition, as if they had not themselves voted for it, as well as at the oraclemongers and soothsayers and as many other oracle readers who had caused them to hope that they would conquer Sicily. . . . At the same time the city and each individual felt oppressed at being robbed of many hoplites and horses and young men and not seeing any others to replace them; but at the same time not seeing sufficient ships in the shipyards or money in the treasury or crews for the ships made them feel hopeless at the prospect of survival at the present time, etc.

The similarities are too close to be unintentional: the emphasis on hope as dangerous, having the potential to drive men to ruin; "the many"/the Athenians who place trust, in deadly combination with hope, in the soothsayers and oraclemongers;[14] the utter destruction that can result; the role

14. Wassermann (1947, 34) notes that the attack on the belief in oracles in 5.103 "is not called forth by any previous mention on the part of the Melians," and he explains it with reference to the late fifth-century "spirit of sceptical enlightenment." But that explanation still

of resources and implied loss; the relationship between hope and present survival.

As noted in the prelude, scholars have long observed the thematic reversal that takes place between the Melian Dialogue and the account of the Sicilian expedition as the Athenians suffer the fate against which they warn the Melians.[15] The additional echoes noted above support such an interpretation yet also make clear that it is only half the picture. Thucydides' portrayal of the Athenians overall is considerably more complex; indeed, he is representing the Athenians in and after the Sicilian expedition as embodying both positions that they laid out in 5.103. On the one hand, the Athenians are like those who "stake their all on hope" and are destroyed, those who, by implication, do not act from a *periousia,* an abundance of resources, for we have seen that the Athenians in Sicily manifestly did not possess abundant resources in the field but were in continual need of reinforcement and unable to ensure the regular provisioning needed from local sources; moreover, as has been noted, they relied on hope in attacking the island (e.g., 6.24.3, 6.31.6) and in the end had only hope left, which soon changed to hopelessness. When hope became the chief resource, the expedition was utterly destroyed (πανωλεθρία, 7.87.6; οὕτω γε ἄγαν πανσυδὶ διεφθάρθαι, 8.1.1).

On the other hand, as noted previously, the Athenians at home were not destroyed.[16] As we saw in chapter 1, Thucydides represents the expedition in Sicily implicitly and explicitly as another Athenian polis.[17] The idea becomes more pronounced and explicit only when disaster is imminent, that is, in the narrative of the end of the expedition. The idea is implicit in Nikias' allusion to the Athenian force as the "besieged" (7.11.4), and it becomes explicit in the general's final, wrenching speech to his men, when he asserts: "You are a polis wherever you choose to sit down"; "For men make the polis, not walls or ships empty of men" (7.77.4, 7). In addition, in describing the pathetic state of the army, Thucydides himself refers to the "starved-out city" of 40,000 men (7.75.5).

The concept of the divided city serves several functions, one of which connects to Thucydides' argument about the importance of unity for military success, made first in the Archaeology and reiterated implicitly in the Thracian digression in book 2.[18] It allows him to set up the expectation, and

---

does not account for why the statement comes out of the blue. A better explanation, I suggest, is that Thucydides was deliberately linking 5.103 to 8.1, just as in his Trojan analysis of 1.11, which also in a sense comes out of the blue but is explicable if he was thinking about the Sicilian expedition when he came to analyze the Trojan expedition.

15. See the prelude, p. 15.

16. Liebeschuetz 1968a, 75; Pouncey 1980, 91; see the prelude, p. 15.

17. Avery 1973, 8–10; and above, chap. 1, p. 25.

18. 1.3; 2.97.6.

provide an explanation, of failure. It is also an idea he will develop in book 8 in treating the Athenian city in Athens and that on Samos (e.g., 8.76). But in the case of the Sicilian expedition, it also allows a nuanced reading of the expedition itself, and the Athenians' situation in its aftermath. The "polis" in Sicily, without the resources to allow them to withstand defeat, relied chiefly on hope and was utterly destroyed (οὕτω γε ἄγαν πανσυδὶ διεφθάρθαι 8.1.1); future hopes were transformed into present destruction.

The polis in Athens, however, had embarked on the expedition with financial strength (6.26.2); and, therefore, following the premise of 5.103, in 413 they were harmed but not utterly destroyed. Thucydides also makes this clear in the narrative that immediately follows. There—rather astonishingly given his emphasis on the fear and terror on all sides[19]—he represents the Athenians as able, on the heels of the Sicilian disaster, to rebuild their fleet, and this presupposes either financial reserves or the capability to extract wealth from the empire. Thus 5.103 helps to elucidate 8.1, and vice versa.

There is also a close interplay between 8.1 and 6.31, the important passage from the account of the Sicilian expedition (already examined in depth above, in chapter 1) that describes the launching of the fleet.

8.1 AND 6.31

As I argued, Thucydides composes 6.31 in such a way as to echo and contrast ironically with 2.13 as concerns the focus on wealth to be used on the war, first in 431 and then in the second "beginning," in 415. Likewise, the historian emphasizes sight, costliness, the appearance of the ships, and the expensiveness of the crew (the *huperesiai,* 6.31.3). Consider again the construction of 8.1. After stressing the fear and panic of the Athenians, Thucydides explains:

> ἅμα μὲν γὰρ στερόμενοι καὶ ἰδίᾳ ἕκαστος καὶ ἡ πόλις ὁπλιτῶν τε πολλῶν καὶ ἱππέων καὶ ἡλικίας οἵαν οὐχ ἑτέραν ἑώρων ὑπάρχουσαν ἐβαρύνοντο· ἅμα δὲ ναῦς οὐχ ὁρῶντες ἐν τοῖς νεωσοίκοις ἱκανὰς οὐδὲ χρήματα ἐν τῷ κοινῷ οὐδ' ὑπηρεσίας ταῖς ναυσὶν ἀνέλπιστοι ἦσαν ἐν τῷ παρόντι σωθήσεσθαι. . . (8.1.2)
>
> For being deprived individually and as a polis of many hoplites and cavalry and men of an age they did not see anymore present they felt oppressed. But at the same time not seeing sufficient ships in the shipyards or money in the treasury or crews on the ships, they became bereft of hope of survival. . .

Thucydides' choice of verb is immediately conspicuous. The Athenians were despondent not because they did not *have* men, ships, or money, but because they did not *see* (ἑώρων; ὁρῶντες) them.[20] Thucydides thus continues to focus the reader's attention on sight and perception as it relates to

19. See Allison 1997b, 87–91.

20. Connor 1985, 14.

signs of power, as he did most conspicuously in 6.31 at the beginning of the expedition and in 7.71 and 7.75 to mark its end; but the obvious difference here is that the Athenians are in a negative state of seeing. Thucydides' choice of vocabulary especially recalls 6.31. Besides words of sight, the reference to the *huperesiai* may also be a prompt, since the word, a rarity in the *History*, occurs twice in 6.31 (31.3) and subsequently only in 8.1.2. Moreover, Thucydides emphasizes the costliness of the expedition in 6.31 with the adjective *poluteles*, used twice (31.1, 3); in 8.1.3 he refers to the Athenians' intention, after the disaster, to economize, employing the word *euteleia*, then repeating it in 8.4. Finally, he notes that the Athenians embarked on the expedition with the "greatest hopes for the future compared to their present resources" (ἐπὶ μεγίστῃ ἐλπίδι τῶν μελλόντων πρὸς τὰ ὑπάρχοντα, 31.6); by contrast, in 8.1.2, they are bereft of hope (ἀνέλπιστοι) when they look at what is present (ὑπάρχουσαν ἐν τῷ παρόντι).

The parallels between 6.31 and 8.1 enhance the reading of the latter chiefly through irony. Hope, extravagance, and the misinterpretation of what one sees have all resulted in negatives: the Athenians lack hope, they do not see. The irony is intensified by the fact that in 415 the Athenians had the greatest hopes for what they could not see and were bolstered by what they did see. They mistake what real resources are and count on nonexistent ones. In 413 they are no longer under the illusions that compromised their earlier judgment; they see nothing, and they see it clearly.[21] They are also clouded by emotion: Thucydides notes explicitly that they were in the throes of "the greatest possible fear and terror" (φόβος τε καὶ κατάπληξις μεγίστη δή), both irrational fears.[22] As Connor observes, 8.1 is "full of descriptions of feelings"; it is concerned with mood.[23] The implication is that the Athenians may be just as susceptible to misinterpretation of the absence of seeing as of its presence earlier; and this is borne out by the narrative.[24]

THE ATHENIANS: PERCEPTION AND REALITY

The nature and context of Thucydides' attention to the Athenians' emotional perception of their lot upon news of the disaster in Sicily—in 8.1 itself and in its links to 5.103 and 6.31—reveal that the historian is not pro-

21. This again recalls 5.103.

22. On the distinction between irrational fear (φόβος) and rational, grounded fear (δέος), see de Romilly 1956; Huart 1968, 337–44.

23. Connor 1985, 14.

24. By contrast, as argued in chap. 4, in 7.71 and 7.75 they see *opsis* for what it is: their feeling of hopelessness about the prospect of survival (71.7) was based on what they saw and it ominously proved correct.

viding factual information about Athens' finances and general condition;[25] he is, rather, bringing out how, in their irrational state, they have a distorted sense of their situation that is characterized in extreme terms (e.g., no money, no men); this is confirmed by the narrative that follows. Connor notes the effect of Thucydides' presentation: "The narrative creates in the reader the feeling of being directly present at an episode of the war."[26] Thus we participate in the mood of the Athenians, and the reality unfolds for us as it does for the Athenians. Yet Thucydides also composed the narrative to relate to the larger theme of the interplay of emotion and decision making, as well as the ambiguity of *opsis* that he has been developing.

However, although he has been implicitly critical of decisions made in an emotional climate and of the dangers of false perceptions (e.g., 6.24, 46; 7.28), here his treatment changes. The Athenians do not, in their current mood, make rash, regrettable decisions; quite the contrary, as Thucydides tells it: "Nevertheless, the Athenians decided to resist according to their means,[27] and to provide a fleet, procuring timber from wherever they could, and money, and to keep their alliance secure and especially Euboia, and to manage the city prudently with a view toward economy and to elect a board of elders who would advise them as the occasion arose" (8.1.3).

In contrast to the description of the panicked state of hopelessness with which book 8 opened, in what follows Thucydides presents—rather extraordinarily—a scene not only of resilience, as has often been noted,[28] but also of calm and rationality as the Athenians prepare for renewed war with Sparta, and he offers no suggestion that they are incapable of dealing with the present situation and in particular the need to rebuild a fleet. Indeed, it immediately becomes clear that the fear and panic were unjustified and did not infect decision making. This picture is accomplished partly by its juxtaposition to the Spartan preparations. Thucydides first describes at length

25. As Connor (1985, 14) notes about 8.1.2–3 in general (against Meiggs [1972, 351] and others, who take this passage as a statement of fact and then observe that the narrative does not bear it out): "Thucydides says that the Athenians did not *see* the resources to deal with the present situation; he does not say there were no resources to see." The passage is often taken by historians of Athenian finance as evidence that the treasury was empty: e.g., Cavaignac 1908, 146; but this would make impossible the Athenians' clear ability to recover, and inexplicable that they did not use the "Iron Reserve."

26. Connor 1985, 15.

27. The translation of the phrase ὡς ἐκ τῶν ὑπαρχόντων, is controversial. Jowett, for instance, translates it as "[still they determined] under any circumstances"; Tucker rejects this and gives "[to hold out] as far as circumstances (or resources) is concerned." Classen-Steup cite 7.76 (as does Krüger) and translate "so gut es nach Lage der Dinge möglich war"; LSJ s.v. ὑπάρχω include this passage under the translation "under the circumstances," "according to one's means" (B.IV.1).

28. E.g., Pouncey 1980, 91; Rood 1998, 257–58.

King Agis' measures to outfit and finance a fleet and to acquire more allies.[29] The historian then describes the Athenians' preparations, but much more briefly:

> The Athenians also started to make preparations, just as they had intended, for shipbuilding, getting timber, and fortifying Sounion, in order to insure safe passage of the grain ships around it, and they abandoned the fort in Lakonia, which they had built when they were engaged in Sicily, and in other respects, if they thought they were incurring any unnecessary expenses, they eliminated them for economy (καὶ τἆλλα, εἴ πού τι ἐδόκει ἀχρεῖον ἀναλίσκεσθαι, ξυστελλόμενοι ἐς εὐτέλειαν), and they kept a special watch on the allies to prevent them from revolting. (8.4)

The description of Athenian preparations is shorter in part because in 8.1 Thucydides has already related some of the measures the Athenians implemented. But the preparations mentioned first concerned the recovery from the Sicilian expedition, rather than the engagement with Sparta specifically, with which 8.4 is specifically concerned.[30]

At first sight the absence of any mention of ways to raise money in the description of the Athenian preparations is astonishing: the Athenians are concerned instead with *economizing* and not wasting money, but that presupposes resources to conserve. By omission, then, Thucydides implies the existence of a reserve adequate enough to purchase timber and build ships, the ability to generate revenue, and generally prepare for renewed war with Sparta. The repetition of *euteleia,* "economy," which occurs first in 8.1 (combined with the phrase ὥσπερ διενοήθησαν), need not signal lack of revision, improper book divisions, or later, clumsy insertion; rather, it is necessary and serves a function where it appears. In the first passage, it signals a dramatic change from the extravagant spending on the initial fleet. In the second, it draws attention to the contrast between Athens' and Sparta's resources: the Spartans need to raise money for they are about to incur huge expenses on a navy, for which they will need financial resources, while the Athenians need to reduce their expenses.

What is the explanation for the remarkable transformation in Thucydides' portrait of the Athenians from panicked with a sense of utter hopelessness into a collective rationally and calmly meeting a crisis? It may not be an accident that the sense of calm that pervades the narrative immediately after 8.1.2—in which it almost becomes possible to forget already the chaotic,

29. 8.3.1–2; I shall return to this passage below.

30. Thus I do not see this as an exact (and therefore problematic) doublet that needs explanation; rather, Thucydides wants to emphasize by repetition the financial preparations. Those who are troubled by it include Momigliano (1930, 17–18) and Wilamowitz (1908, 578–81); cf. also Andrewes *HCT* 5, on 8.4; Rood 1998, 255.

emotional portrait of the Athenians, both in Sicily and at home—appears in conjunction with the arrival of the *probouloi,* the "board of elders who would advise them about their present circumstances as need arose" (8.1.3). While Thucydides does not expressly refer to the financial purview of the *probouloi,* his presentation suggests a connection: the Athenians decided "to manage the city more prudently (σωφρονίσαι) with regard to economy and to elect a board of elders to provide advice." The verb of moderation, *sophronisai,* as mentioned earlier, serves to underscore that Athenian "tyrannical" excessiveness will now be reined in.[31] Thus the implication is that the Athenians have *gnome* working for them in the presence of the *probouloi,* who will, among other things, help them properly use their *chremata,* which, although no longer a *periousia,* is not entirely insufficient. It is as if they are back on track, obeying the Periklean dictum about intelligent judgment and money in a strategy of consolidation.

The narrative, then, gives the impression that the Athenians are far from being in a dire financial crisis, and this is borne out by the facts. First, they have not yet touched the "Iron Reserve" of 1,000 talents and will not do so until the summer of 412 (8.15.1), significantly in another irrational state of fear[32]—that is, not even then with a total lack of funds.[33] Second, the dedications in the sacred treasuries remained untouched as a source of money.[34] The Athenians' success in using their financial resources to rebuild a navy is confirmed in 8.8. Thucydides tells us that the Peloponnesians, reflecting on their adversary's condition in the aftermath of the Sicilian expedition, at the point when they were intending to dispatch an initial fleet to help the Chian revolt, were unconcerned about keeping it a secret from the Athenians, "having contempt for their impotence (*adunasia*), on the grounds that they did not yet appear to have a fleet worth anything" (8.8.4).[35] Yet as the narrative proceeds it becomes clear that this perception was incorrect: the Athenians intercept the Peloponnesian fleet, first facing them with an equal

31. See chap. 1, pp. 79–82.

32. In considering the state of Athens' finances during the Sicilian expedition as it bears on the city's fiscal condition in 413, it is relevant to note Lewis' discussion (1966) of the sale of the confiscated property of the Hermokopidai, in which he estimates that the total of the property might well have neared 1,000 talents.

33. Two qualifying pieces of information are important for putting in perspective the rhetorical formulations of financial crisis in Thucydides for the period of the aftermath of the Sicilian expedition: first, *IG* I[3] 99, an inscription that records a decision to repay borrowed monies from Athena in 410; and the resumption of work on the Erechtheion; see Harris 1991, 78; also the following note.

34. In 412 the dedications in the Pronaos, for example, were at their height; see Harris 1995, 77 and her book generally for the contents of the Parthenon and the Erechtheion.

35. καταφρονήσαντες τῶν Ἀθηναίων ἀδυνασίαν, ὅτι ναυτικὸν οὐδὲν αὐτῶν πολύ πω ἐφαίνετο.

contingent of twenty-one ships (including seven Chian ships), and then, having excused the Chians, manned a total of thirty-seven ships and defeated the Spartans (8.10).[36]

THE TRANSFORMATION OF THE SPARTANS

Thucydides' presentation of the Spartans at the beginning of book 8 fits into the broader theme of reversal and transformation developed in the course of the Sicilian narrative. The Spartans now throw themselves into the war and are transformed into quasi-Athenians,[37] emboldened by the passionate eagerness both of their allies to see the struggle to its end and of Athens' subjects to revolt, "even beyond their power" (8.2.2). At the same time Thucydides makes explicit that what especially energized the Spartans was the expected addition to their forces of a Sicilian navy: they were especially emboldened by the likelihood (ὡς εἰκὸς) that they would be joined in the spring by their Sicilian allies in great force, who had recently been compelled (κατ' ἀνάγκην) to increase (προσγεγενημένου, or "improve"), their navy (8.2.3). The references in this comment to compulsion and probability are noteworthy: the Sicilian allies of Sparta, although instructed to send a naval contingent to the Spartan side at the beginning of the war (2.7.2), never did so; thus the ὡς εἰκός has a sting to it.[38]

But the remark may also be a less-than-subtle reminder that the Spartans

36. The presentation is similar to that in 3.15–16, where the Peloponnesians are persuaded by the Mytilenaians that Athens' power was weak, the Peloponnesians act on that basis, and the Athenians promptly demonstrate the invalidity of the claim. See also Rood 1998, 257–58 on the use of ὅμως (8.1.3, 8.6.4) to signify resilience.

37. Recall the transferred verb ξυμπροθυμέομαι, 8.1.1, 2.1. Thucydides also refers to them —uniquely—as "the polis of the Lakedaimonians" (ἡ δὲ τῶν Λακεδαιμονίων πόλις), which "is emboldened" (ἐθάρσει) now to prosecute the war with vigor (8.2.3). Why refer to the Spartans in this way? Andrewes (*HCT* 5, ad loc.) does not comment on the formulation; Classen-Steup, only that it refers to "die gesamte Bürgerschaft." It is not that the phrase itself is unique (cf., for example, 1.10.2), but rather that only here does he use the abstract formulation to refer to agents who think and act. The singular nature of this form of reference, in which the abstract polis feels and acts, cannot be casual. It is likely that Thucydides speaks of the Spartans in this way to stress their new collective resolve; they are like the Athenians at the beginning of the war, united, and emboldened (e.g., 2.13.2); by contrast, Thucydides has presented the Athenians as increasingly fragmented—in Sicily and Athens, soon in Samos and Athens, but also within the polis of Athens. On the other hand, while this, as noted above, fits into Thucydides' argument about unity and military success, the conception of the Spartan polis acting aggressively in unison will quickly break down as the narrative proceeds.

38. See *HCT* 5, ad loc. Cf. also *HCT* 5: 10: the number 500 that Thucydides reports the Spartans requesting in 2.7.2 reflects the intended total on the Peloponnesian side, not just the Sicilian contingent (against Brunt 1965, 261; I retract my tacit acceptance of Brunt in *Money*, 87 with n. 42).

had failed all these years of war to get naval power on their side, and that only now were they about—so they expected, and for a change, it turned out, rightly—to receive significant naval support, but from elsewhere. The comment, however, is also highly ironic. The Spartans only now were likely to get help because the Syracusans had been forced (κατ' ἀνάγκην) to develop their navy because of Athens.[39] The implication is that the Syracusans now, as in 431, might not otherwise have complied.

Let us return to what the Spartans did in their emboldened state. King Agis of Sparta immediately (εὐθύς) set about preparing for war that winter (413/12):

> Εὐθὺς οὖν Ἆγις μὲν ὁ βασιλεὺς αὐτῶν ἐν τῷ χειμῶνι τούτῳ ὁρμηθεὶς στρατῷ τινὶ ἐκ Δεκελείας τά τε τῶν ξυμμάχων ἠργυρολόγησεν ἐς τὸ ναυτικὸν καὶ τραπόμενος ἐπὶ τοῦ Μηλιῶς κόλπου Οἰταίων τε κατὰ τὴν παλαιὰν ἔχθραν τῆς λείας τὴν πολλὴν ἀπολαβὼν χρήματα ἐπράξατο, καὶ Ἀχαιοὺς τοὺς Φθιώτας καὶ τοὺς ἄλλους τοὺς ταύτῃ Θεσσαλῶν ὑπηκόους μεμφομένων καὶ ἀκόντων τῶν Θεσσαλῶν ὁμήρους τέ τινας ἠνάγκασε δοῦναι καὶ χρήματα. . . . Λακεδαιμόνιοι δὲ τὴν πρόσταξιν ταῖς πόλεσιν ἑκατὸν νεῶν τῆς ναυπηγίας ἐποιοῦντο . . . (8.3)
>
> Agis immediately in that same winter set out from Dekeleia and collected money from the allies for the fleet and, turning toward the Malian Gulf, exacted money from the Oitaians, taking much plunder on account of their ancient enmity, and, despite the objections of the Thessalians, compelled the Phthiotic Achaians and the other subjects of the Thessalians there to give money and hostages. . . . And the Spartans ordered the cities to build a hundred ships. . .

Thucydides then lists the contributors and the number of ships demanded of them and then concludes the section on the Spartans' preparations by noting that they did everything to make sure that they would be ready immediately (εὐθύς) in the spring (8.3.2).

Thucydides intends a comparison to be drawn between this new beginning, in which the Athenians and Spartans prepare for renewed war with each other, and the first beginning in 432, since he comments that "both sides were as intent upon preparing for the war as they had been at the outset" (8.5.1).[40] Indeed, the emphasis on the speed with which Agis moves into action recalls Thucydides' description of the Spartans' preparations for

39. So Arnold ad loc., but he does not note the irony; the irony is enhanced further when read against 7.21.3: Hermokrates, in trying to get his countrymen to fight the Athenians at sea, asserts that the Athenians had been mainlanders more than the Syracusans and only became a naval power when compelled (ἀναγκασθέντας) by the Persians.

40. Allison (1997b, 85), in discussing the sense of a new beginning that Thucydides writes into the narrative here, cites 1.1, the opening of the book; cf. also the passages listed in her n. 72.

war in 432. There, the historian remarks that "it seemed impossible to the Spartans to attack immediately (εὐθύς), given their lack of preparedness; nevertheless, they undertook to make the necessary preparations and less than a year passed before they invaded Attica and declared open war" (1.125.2).[41] The Spartans in 432, Thucydides tells us, immediately prepared for war; yet their actual preparations did not involve insuring naval power. Thus when they began war, they had neither a navy nor money to pose any serious threat to Athenian power, nor did they seem really to grasp that they needed these to beat Athens.[42] Moreover, not until the expedition of Brasidas did they make any concerted attempt to help revolts.[43] Only now, finally, in their new emboldened and collective state, nearly two decades into the war, do they take the proper steps to prepare.

In addition, Thucydides' greater attention to the Spartans' preparations forms part of the reversal narrative that layers books 6 through 8. In relating the nature and extent of the power of the Athenians and Spartans on the eve of war, Thucydides describes and analyzes in detail the development of Athenian power but devotes only a sentence or two to Sparta's basis of power (1.89–117 and 1.19, respectively). The disparity is explained partly by the fact that the traditional basis and nature of Spartan power were well known, while Athenian power, which relied on money and ships, was something new that required explanation.[44] In the case of the respective preparations in 413, Thucydides' greater attention to Spartan preparations at that time is not casual or incidental; he could simply have noted that Agis went around collecting money and ships, but instead he provides much greater detail. Why?

I suggest that Thucydides aims to show that the Spartans have finally grasped the connection between money and power, though it is significant that, as in the case of Brasidas, he stresses the importance of individuals—in this case, Agis—in taking the correct action.[45] Thucydides says that Agis "collected money *for the fleet*" (ἠργυρολόγησεν ἐς τὸ ναυτικόν), making the point as explicit as possible. By contrast, where he mentions "money collect-

41. See *Money,* 91–93.

42. Nor, apparently, did others; cf. 7.28.3 for the expectation at the beginning of the war that if the Spartans invaded Attica, they would win in two or three years.

43. On the contrary, Thucydides stresses their incompetence; see *Money,* 139–40 on Alkidas.

44. In addition, it was Athenian power that caused the fear that led to the outbreak of war, and thus Thucydides needed to explain the basis of the Spartans' fear by documenting the nature and growth of Athenian power.

45. Brasidas was acting in accordance with a Spartan decision, but he requested a force to take north on his own initiative (4.81.1); Thucydides makes the explicit point in 8.5.3 that Agis had the authority to act without consulting the Spartans at home.

ing" elsewhere, he is referring to the Athenians and no mention of purpose —"for the navy"—is included.[46] The Athenians in Thucydides, from the beginning of the Delian League on, knew well that money was needed for naval power; the qualifier "for the fleet" in reference to their activities would have been superfluous, even otiose. In 8.5, however, it is necessary: Thucydides wants to make the implicit point that the Spartans had finally recognized the money/power link. He also wants to demonstrate that the Spartans are actually acting upon their knowledge, in contrast to 432, when they issue instructions but do not follow them up.

However, the detail also resonates negatively with an earlier part of the *History*. The description of the Spartans' coercive practice represents in a sense an analysis of the development of Spartan naval power that contrasts sharply with Thucydides' earlier analysis of the origins of Athenian naval power. In 1.95–99, Thucydides presents the methods and stages by which the Athenians gained power, focusing on their brilliantly skillful methods of both getting money and exercising control over others, the latter actually including a high degree of voluntary participation by the allies. Even the account of the conversion of ship contributors to tributary members (1.99), though it refers to the Athenians "applying compulsions," also remarkably conveys a sense that the Athenians have developed a neat solution to the allies' distaste for naval service.[47] They do not apply force in the case of those who have not revolted, but offer them the alternative of payment for service, the decisive factor in the increase of Athenian naval power.[48] When these two passages are considered together, it is clear that the Spartans are relatively heavy-handed at this kind of military financing and warfare.[49]

Perhaps most important, however, for understanding the larger narrative of book 8 is Thucydides' emphasis of a central problem that will plague both sides at this final stage of the war. Surplus cash (*periousia chrematon*), not cash alone, brings power and wins wars. As Perikles puts it in his first

46. On the money-collecting ships, see 2.69, 3.19, 4.50, 4.75, and *Money*, 160–64, 200–202. 8.5.1 is a critical passage for demonstrating that ἀργυρολογέω and Thucydides' use of it refer to the collection of money generally, not tribute specifically.

47. Ostwald (1988, 12) sees 8.3.1 and 1.99.1 as similar examples of compulsion, and it is true that both cases reflect power and show a superior power exerting force on a weaker state; but I think there is a subtle difference between the two as regards the means and success of developing naval power.

48. So Plut. *Kim.* 11.2.

49. I am distinguishing "heavy-handedness" from the often ruthless but skillful methods of oppression employed by the Athenians. Agis' extortions also suggest the unwillingness of Greeks even at this stage of the war actively to help Sparta against Athens. Westlake (1989, 113–53) notes the lack of ardor that many Ionians exhibited toward the Spartans during the Ionian War.

speech to the Athenians in book 1, "financial reserves (*periousiai*) rather than forced taxes maintain wars."[50] Thus the Spartans may be raising cash for a temporary, current need—as they will attempt to do, mostly unsuccessfully, throughout book 8—but this method will not, in the Periklean/Thucydidean analysis, successfully maintain naval power and win wars. Thus 8.3 is emblematic and programmatic of the larger narrative of book 8, as Thucydides describes with a systematic relentlessness both the continual efforts of the Spartans to obtain money for the fleet and Athenian concerns about their own financial condition. Accordingly, Thucydides, in this new beginning, sets the stage for the narrative of the aftermath of the Sicilian expedition by making financial concerns prominent on both Spartan and Athenian sides, but especially, as we have seen, in the case of Sparta.

SPARTA AND PERSIA

In both the description of Spartan preparations for this final stage of the war, and the account of the entry of the Persians, the key themes that will unify the book as a whole are clearly laid out for the reader in the narrative: the Spartan need for money and the role of the Persians as financiers. In developing these themes in the chapters that follow, with the exception of the Athenian decision to rescind the decree barring the use of the "Iron Reserve" (8.15.1), Thucydides focuses exclusively on the Spartans, and this is significant for understanding the nature of his interest in money and financing.

Key factors and players appear in the narrative after his discussion of the preparations for war. Thucydides notes that the Athenian allies were eager for revolt and introduces the Persians.[51] The issue of money comes immedi-

50. αἱ δὲ περιουσίαι τοὺς πολέμους μᾶλλον ἢ αἱ βίαιαι ἐσφοραὶ ἀνέχουσιν, 1.141.5.

51. The treatment of the entry of the Persians into the war in 5.4–5 has been regarded as highly problematic, chiefly because of the number of elements unexplained fully either here or earlier (e.g., the date of King Dareios' accession, mention of Amorges) and Tissaphernes' administrative position in the Persian empire. Thucydides describes him first as "general" (στρατηγός) of Dareios in the maritime district (by which we should understand Ionia), but the subsequent reference to his *arche,* and his responsibility for collecting tribute, suggest that he is a satrap, which is how I shall refer to him (cf. 1.129.1 and Hornblower 1991a, ad loc.); for full discussion see Andrewes, *HCT* 5, ad loc. On Dareios' accession, the point is not so trivial, since Thucydides refers twice to arrears in tribute, which accumulate only so long as a current King reigns; the slate is wiped clean with the accession of each new King (Hdt. 6.59). Most notorious is the reference to Amorges, who, it becomes clear later on, was being supported in his revolt by the Athenians, 8.54; cf. also Andok. 3.29; Lewis 1977, 85–87. On this detail, perhaps crucial for accounting for the timing of Dareios' commands, Thucydides is mute; cf. Lewis 1977, 87 n. 25. It is also possible that Dareios learned that the Athenians had abolished the tribute in 413 (7.28.2) and thought that this might work to his advantage. It is possible, however, to see why this section is as it is, without resorting, at least entirely, to the "unfinished the-

ately to the fore as Thucydides relates the visit of an envoy from Tissaphernes, satrap of Ionia, and some Chians, and Erythraians, to the Spartans: "Tissaphernes invited the Peloponnesians to come over, and he promised to provide support (*trophe*). For he happened to have been pressed recently by the King for the tributes (*tous phorous*) from his own province, tributes he still owed, unable to collect them from the Hellenic cities, because of the Athenians; so he thought he would be better able to collect the tributes were he to harm the Athenians, and simultaneously he would make the Lakedaimonians allies of the King and, also by the King's orders, take alive or dead Amorges, the bastard son of Pissouthnes, who was in revolt in Karia" (8.5.5).

This passage, like 8.3 on the Spartan preparations, is crucial for introducing central themes of book 8: the role of the Persians, competition among the satraps, and their ulterior motives; the importance of money as a motivating factor (on both sides); and, as was the case earlier, others' responsibility for both moving the Spartans to the arena where they can harm the Athenians and providing the resources for them to do so.[52] But perhaps most immediately intriguing is Thucydides' focus on Tissaphernes' private thinking, a perspective that dominates his portrayal of the satrap throughout.[53] Significantly, the thinking and motivations ascribed to Tissaphernes concern money: namely, his need to produce tribute for the King from the Ionian cities, and his consequent desire to use the Spartans for his own ends.[54] There is no qualifier, no nod to probability; Thucydides states plainly: "Tissaphernes thought" (ἐνόμισε). None of his motives for urging Spartan participation in the eastern Aegean would have been publicly expressed at

---

sis," the ready answer to explain any unsatisfactory (to us) parts of book 8. These pieces of information comprise the reasoning that led Tissaphernes to seek help from the Spartans; that is, as has been noted (e.g., Lewis 1977, 87), there is nothing to suggest that the King directly or indirectly sent Tissaphernes to make an alliance on his behalf with the Spartans. Thucydides is explaining Tissaphernes' thinking (ἐνόμισε). He had two instructions from the King: first, to collect tribute arrears (possibly not the first time he had been ordered to do such a thing); and, second, to capture Amorges. Tissaphernes himself thought that he could accomplish both of these assignments, plus author a Persian/Spartan alliance, if he could persuade the Spartans to come over to Asia Minor. The narrative context, therefore, is one in which these details about Tissaphernes' orders, Dareios II, and Amorges are presented in this section not as part of the chronological, historical narrative, but rather as descriptions of someone's thinking, and as explanations of someone's decision to do something. In such a context, Thucydides would either have had to insert epexegetical comments or leave it as is, the most simply to relate this part of the larger episode without cumbersome detail, since the point of this section is to explain why Tissaphernes sent an envoy to Sparta.

52. Lewis (1977, 88), however, is right to point out that Agis evidently thought he was capable of helping the intended revolt in Lesbos or Euboia on his own resources.

53. See Patwell 1978, 256–305; Westlake 1989, 166–80; Cawkwell (1997, 47) is especially skeptical of Thucydides' ascription of motives and treatment of character. I agree with him that Tissaphernes is indeed "inscrutable."

54. As Patwell (1978, 268) notes with reference to Thucydides' treatment of Alkibiades.

Sparta, since they are presented as ulterior designs. We are given Tissaphernes' mental process as a statement of fact.

The actual fact—that Tissaphernes had been pressed by the King to recover tribute that the Athenians prevented him from obtaining for himself—allows for readings of both weakness and strength. It suggests weakness when read as a comment on the Athenians' changed situation as a result of Sicily: the King considers the Athenians diminished in strength and can thus take advantage of the situation by recovering revenue for himself. But it also enables Thucydides to make the point that at the time the Athenians still were successfully extracting revenue for themselves; that is, they still possessed *dunamis.*[55] Thus the statement conveys a sense of ambiguity in the Athenians' position. Moreover, Thucydides' insertion of Tissaphernes' thinking, which is extremely detailed concerning the issue of tribute, and much less so about getting Spartan help to suppress the revolt of Amorges, establishes his interest in the theme of money at this stage of the war as well.

Thucydides' attention to Tissaphernes' promise to fund the Spartan navy, and his ulterior motives, immediately conveys an ominous sense of déjà vu. We recall the Egestans' false promise of funding in book 6 and Aristagoras' ulterior motives as outlined in Herodotos. Here, as in those examples, Thucydides endows the reader with omniscience, and the inter- and intratextual resonances have the pronounced effect of making the reader suspect that Tissaphernes may prove unreliable; the suspicion will be abundantly borne out in the subsequent narrative.

The Chians, then, and Tissaphernes were jointly after the same goal (8.6.1). But so were others, as noted above: around this time, Thucydides writes, Kalligeitos the Megarian and Timagoras the Kyzikene, both exiles from their own countries and living at the court of Pharnabazos (satrap of Daskylion in northern Asia Minor), also came to Sparta, wanting the Spartans to send ships to the Hellespont: " [Pharnabazos] himself wanted, if he were able, to accomplish the very thing that Tissaphernes was after: namely, to effect the revolts of Athenian cities in his own region *because of the tributes* and engineer an alliance between the King and the Spartans" (8.6.1). This is a cryptic account compared with the treatment of Tissaphernes' envoys and is conspicuous because of an omission and because of narrative delay: Thucydides says nothing, as noted above, about payment for the Spartan fleet, but then in 8.8.1, in remarking on the departure of the envoys, he writes: "They left . . . without giving the 25 talents they had brought with them to help dispatch a force."

The result is that when Thucydides then states that "a great contest broke

55. This passage is clearly relevant, as noted in chap. 5, to the issue of the effectiveness of the *eikoste* and the source of Athenian tribute, but it is not clear what interpretation to give; is the implication that the Athenians have gone back to tribute by this time?

out among those in Sparta, over who could persuade the Spartans to send ships and men first, on the one side, to Ionia and Tissaphernes, and, on the other, to the Hellespont," we concentrate on Tissaphernes, especially since the historian conspicuously omits Pharnabazos' name, saying merely "to the Hellespont." Most intriguing is Thucydides' use of the word ἅμιλλα—"contest" or "competition"—the very word that he used to describe the race to Aigina of the ships setting out to Sicily, and a word that, as argued earlier, was intended to recall Herodotos' description of the race of Xerxes' fleet off Abydos.[56]

Further similarities emerge. Thucydides exploits additional resonances with the Egestan episode, this time with a different slant. The Lakedaimonians decidedly favor the requests of the Chians and Tissaphernes, which Alkibiades was also supporting, there as the guest-friend of the ephor Endios.[57] "Nevertheless," Thucydides notes, "the Spartans first sent Phrynis, one of the Perioikoi, to Chios, to investigate whether the Chians had as many ships as they said they had, and especially to see if the city was as large as it was reputed to be, and when he reported back to them that what they had heard was actually true, they immediately made the Chians and Erythraians allies and voted to send forty ships to them, since there were no less than sixty there according to what the Chians said they had" (8.6.3–4). This passage closely resembles 6.6. Recall that there the Egestans' offered to provide "sufficient money" (χρήματα ἱκανά, 6.6.2) for the war in Sicily, in response to which the Athenians voted "first to send envoys to Egesta to investigate whether the money existed, as the Egestans said." (6.6.3); also noteworthy is the emphasis there on believing that it was true.

The similarities in expression and substance suggest that Thucydides meant to evoke the earlier episode, as well as Herodotos, when he was composing this part of book 8. There is the initial request by the Chians for help, a contest (in a completely different context, but ἅμιλλα is the significant resonance), a vote for an investigation to be made first into whether the respective reports were true,[58] and, once it was ascertained that they were, a vote to send help to the requesting party.[59] From the purpose of the inves-

56. Thuc. 6.31.3, 32.2 (ἁμιλληθεν, ἅμιλλα); Hdt. 7.44; cf. also 7.71.3; see above, chap. 1, p. 54, and chap. 2, p. 86, also chap. 4, pp. 164–65.

57. Andrewes (*HCT* 5, on 8.6.3) comments that the Spartans made the better choice.

58. οἱ Ἀθηναῖοι . . . ἐψηφίσαντο πρέσβεις πέμψαι πρῶτον ἐς τὴν Ἔγεσταν περί τε τῶν χρημάτων σκεψομένους εἰ ὑπάρχει, ὥσπερ φασίν . . . , 6.6.3; οἱ Λακεδαιμόνιοι πρῶτον κατάσκοπον ἐς τὴν Χίον πέμψαντες Φρῦνιν . . . εἰ αἵ τε νῆες αὐτοῖς εἰσὶν ὅσασπερ ἔλεγον καὶ τἆλλα εἰ ἡ πόλις ἱκανή ἐστι πρὸς τὴν λεγομένην δόξαν, 8.6.4.

59. οἱ Ἀθηναῖοι ἐκκλησίαν ποιήσαντες καὶ ἀκούσαντες τῶν τε Ἐγεσταίων καὶ τῶν σφετέρων πρέσβεων τά τε ἄλλα ἐπαγωγὰ καὶ οὐκ ἀληθῆ καὶ περὶ τῶν χρημάτων ὡς εἴη ἑτοῖμα . . . ἐψηφίσαντο ναῦς ἑξήκοντα πέμπειν ἐς Σικελίαν, 6.8.2; ἀπαγγείλαντος αὐτοῖς ὡς εἴη ταῦτα ἀληθῆ ἅπερ ἤκουον . . . τεσσαράκοντα ναῦς ἐψηφίσαντο αὐτοῖς πέμπειν, 8.6.4.

tigation—to see if the ships promised were really there—we can assume a Chian offer to provide ships, even though Thucydides does not mention in its place (when the Chians arrive in Sparta) their offer to supply sixty ships.[60]

The similarities are certainly striking, but the differences equally so. First, whereas the Athenians were presented as gullible and the Egestans as liars, so that the latter (and the Athenian envoys) tell the assembly untrue things in response to which the Athenians vote to send aid, the Chians' apparent offer of ships, and their reputation, turn out to be true, in response to which the Spartans vote to send aid. Second, whereas the Egestans lacked the resources they promised for their war, the Chians possess them and in fact initiate the revolt on their own.

Let us pull together the results of the preceding discussion in order to assess Thucydides' presentation of the Spartans. The Spartans finally seem to grasp the connection between money and ships. At the same time, they appear less as aggressive agents than as pawns, and as those in need of others to suggest a course of action that will harm the Athenians; they are used by Tissaphernes, and they do not go out inciting revolts but rather respond to requests. Yet even their response is sluggish and uncertain. The narrative encourages condemnation of their failure to respond quickly and decisively where they could have done substantial harm to Athens but also reaped greater resources for themselves—in the Chian revolt; Thucydides' emphasis on the Chians' strength and prosperity drives the point home (8.24). In addition, echoes of the Egestans' offer lend considerable irony to the narrative. The Egestans lie about their resources, yet the Athenians send help promptly; the Chians tell the truth to the Spartans, but the Spartans are unable or unwilling to respond swiftly and effectively. The Chians raise the revolt by themselves.[61]

THE REVOLT OF CHIOS AND THE "IRON RESERVE"

When news reached the Athenians of the Chians' revolt, Thucydides relates,

> καὶ νομίσαντες μέγαν ἤδη καὶ σαφῆ τὸν κίνδυνον σφᾶς περιεστάναι, καὶ τοὺς λοιποὺς ξυμμάχους οὐκ ἐθελήσειν τῆς μεγίστης πόλεως μεθεστηκυίας ἡσυχάζειν, τά τε χίλια τάλαντα, ὧν διὰ παντὸς τοῦ πολέμου ἐγλίχοντο μὴ ἅψασθαι, εὐθὺς ἔλυσαν τὰς ἐπικειμένας ζημίας τῷ εἰπόντι ἢ ἐπιψηφίσαντι ὑπὸ τῆς παρούσης ἐκπλήξεως, καὶ ἐψηφίσαντο κινεῖν καὶ ναῦς πληροῦν οὐκ ὀλίγας. . . (8.15.1)
>
> they considered the danger that threatened them great and true, and they thought that the rest of the allies would not want to remain quiet when the

60. It is impossible to be certain that the absence of this reflects the unfinished state of the work.

61. Cf. the parallel with the Mytilenaian revolt in the first half of book 3 (esp. 3.2, 25–29).

largest polis had revolted; so in their present terror they immediately rescinded the penalty for using the 1,000 talents, which they had been striving not to use through the entire war, in the case of anyone proposing or putting to the vote the use of the 1,000-talent reserve, and voted to use the money and to man many ships. . .

Grammatically difficult, with what Andrewes calls a "bold structure,"[62] this passage is pregnant with nuances and resonances with earlier passages. Commenting on the passage's repetition of information provided in the narrative when the original decision was made to set aside money and ships (2.24.1), Andrewes observes that "from the amount of detail he repeats here it looks as if Thucydides did not expect his readers to have the earlier passage all in mind."[63] On the contrary, the repetition and choice of words here are prompts designed to lead the reader to draw contrasts between their original context, in which the decision to create the "Iron Reserve" was made —to face the ultimate emergency of an enemy attack on Athens by sea—and that in which the Athenians were now moved to rescind the decree and use the 1,000 talents. Thucydides is not saying: "I know you readers will not remember, so let me remind you for the sake of information"; but rather: "I expect you to recall and reflect on the contrasts with the earlier situation and the rationale for the reserve."

In 2.24.1, Thucydides comments: "After the Peloponnesians withdrew [from Attica], the Athenians established guards by land and sea, just as, indeed, they had intended to for the duration of the war. And they also decided to set aside 1,000 talents from the moneys on the Akropolis, and not to spend it, but to fight the war from the rest of the funds. And if anyone proposed or put to the vote to use (*kinein*) this money for any other purpose than in defense of an enemy attack by sea, he would be punished by death." The account relays a sense of calm and suggests the application of rationality to a financial decision at a critical moment, that is, when the reality of the first Spartan invasion hit the Athenians. In fact, as Thucydides makes clear, the Athenians had been in a highly agitated state just before this, upon hearing of the Peloponnesian invasion, and they felt anger (*orge*) at Perikles for preventing them from defending their land (2.21.3). Yet the historian chooses to separate their highly emotional state from the decision to set aside the "Iron Reserve," inserting between them, first, a discussion of Perikles' refusal to call any assembly meetings precisely because they might make a decision on the basis of anger (*orge*) and not intelligent judgment (*gnome*, 2.22.1),[64] and, second, a description of the events culminating in the Peloponnesians' withdrawal from Attica (2.22.2–23). The narrative distancing

62. *HCT* 5, ad loc.

63. Ibid.

64. The antithesis between *orge* and *gnome* is fundamental in the *History;* see Huart 1968, 56–57; Mittelstadt 1977, 52–53.

removes the initial, highly charged, emotional reaction from the subsequent decision, once calm and rationality had been restored, to conserve resources for the ultimate emergency, a Spartan attack by sea.[65]

By contrast, the decision to cancel the ban on using the money—the same verb as in 2.24.1, *kinein,* is used here—was made in the throes of an irrational state of terror (ὑπὸ τῆς παρούσης ἐκπλήξεως, 8.15.1). The juxtaposition of the Athenians' emotional state and their immediate (εὐθύς) decision—linked causally—to lift the ban on using the money drives home the contrast: a rational decision to set aside the money is now canceled because of irrational fear upon learning of the revolt of Chios; this was not a direct threat to Athens itself. The emotional context in which Thucydides embeds the decision suggests criticism of it, as does the pointed use of the verb *kinein,* instead of the more neutral *chresthai,* since when he employed it earlier in a financial context it was to suggest an improper appropriation of money.[66] Likewise, the reference to their "present" terror suggests that it would pass, and that they should have waited until it passed to decide what to do. Thucydides further emphasizes—and implicitly criticizes—the decision by explictly noting that the Athenians "had been striving (ἐγλίχοντο) not to use [the money] through the entire war (διὰ παντὸς τοῦ πολέμου)." As Rood notes, "the word 'striving' (ἐγλίχοντο, the only use of the verb in Th.) is forceful."[67] Indeed, by including this comment Thucydides intends the reader to recall the numerous occasions over the past two decades on which the Athenians had suffered tremendous, grave setbacks and nevertheless had not rescinded the decree.

One obvious recent example of loss fresh in the reader's mind is the immediate aftermath of the Sicilian disaster, when the Athenians likewise were in an enormously heightened and emotional state of terror (φόβος τε καὶ κατάπληξις μεγίστη δή, 8.1.2) and feared an attack by sea—exactly the legitimate circumstance (though an actual attack, not merely fear of one) envisioned when the decision to set aside the money and ships was made in 431; yet, rather than use the money, they calmed down and took rational, prudent steps to deal with the effects of the disaster on their financial and military condition. The ensuing narrative then confirms an impression not only of extraordinary resilience, but also of success: recall, among other things, that the Athenians confounded the Spartans' expectation of their *adunasia,* "powerlessness," thus suggesting their renewed power.

With its explicit context of allied revolt and Athenian fear, this passage

65. I am not suggesting that these events did not intervene. But Thucydides, had he wanted, could have noted the decision to set aside the "Iron Reserve" when he was writing the Athenian section of 2.20, and not have waited until he had related other events. See Rood 1998, 109–30, on temporal manipulation in the narrative generally.

66. E.g., 1.143.1; and see *Money,* 95.

67. Rood 1998, 254 n. 14.

also revives other occasions in the reader's mind: specificially, the revolts of Lesbos and Amphipolis.[68] In the former case, the Athenians initially disbelieved the Lesbians' intention to revolt (cf. 8.1.1); but when they realized that it was true, in fear (δείσαντες), they immediately dispatched forty-two ships to deal with the situation (3.3.1–4). Their initial reaction stemmed from the fact that they were still suffering from the plague, and the war was in full swing. The subsequent action they took was based on the seriousness of the threat posed by the potential addition of the Lesbian fleet and full power (δύναμιν ἀκέραιον) to their enemy's resources (3.3.1). The resonances are clear: the Athenians are presented in a state of great distress and alarm; their fear has to do with the loss of resources. Yet their state of mind is described with the participle *deisantes*—reflecting a rational ground for concern, not irrational terror—and they take immediate (ἐξαπιναίως) steps, sending ships to stop the revolt. The passage was clearly written to emphasize the Athenians' suffering, fear, and action, and to encourage comparison.[69]

In the case of Amphipolis, which fell into Brasidas' hands in 424, Thucydides describes the Athenians' emotional state and response after learning that they had lost their colony to the Spartans. They were in a state of great fear (μέγα δέος κατέστησαν), which stemmed from the loss of resources of money and timber (ξύλων τε ναυπηγησίμων πομπῇ καὶ χρημάτων προσόδῳ, 4.108.1). Yet, as in the account of the Athenian reaction to the Lesbian revolt, their fear is described as grounded, rational alarm—*deos*. The Athenian response is active and rational: they immediately sent garrisons to the area to prevent further revolts (4.108.6).

An additional pattern is reflected in 8.15. It cannot be accidental that the two most critical financial decisions undertaken in the war are presented in Thucydides' narrative in causal connection with an irrational collective state of mind. In 7.28 (examined in chapter 3) we saw that Thucydides carefully constructed the narrative surrounding the decision to end tribute and institute the *eikoste* to emphasize the Athenians' highly impassioned and "diseased" state "around the time" of the decision. Recall that he includes their reasoning for it—"thinking (νομίζοντες) that they would get more money that way" (7.28.4)—which, I argue, likely has a critical overtone.[70] Likewise in 8.15.1, Thucydides writes that the Athenians, "thinking that the dan-

68. I omit Poteidaia from this context simply because its revolt began before the outbreak of war, in 432 (1.56ff.)

69. Rawlings (1981, 181–215) presents a thorough and compelling analysis of the similarities in the larger narrative of the two revolts, constructed by Thucydides to evoke a contrast, not only as pertains to the Athenians, but to the Spartans as well. He rightly stresses the Spartans' greater effectiveness in 412 in contrast to 427 but perhaps exaggerates their successful role in 412.

70. Chap. 3, pp. 137–39.

ger was now great and clear" (καὶ νομίσαντες μέγαν ἤδη καὶ σαφῆ τὸν κίνδυνον σφᾶς περιεστάναι), voted to rescind the decree. Thucydides supplies the thought process in both cases alongside the irrationality, but he does not endorse it. Rather, the use of the participle *nomizontes* has the effect of distancing the historian from his subjects' thought processes; he could have written "since the danger was now manifestly great and clear" or "since this would bring in more revenue" but instead makes clear that the thinking was theirs and did not necessarily reflect his own view.

Thucydides' linkage of money and emotion leads the reader toward the conclusion that the Athenians were not exercising *gnome* with respect to their finances and indeed were irresponsible in making decisions in the heat of the moment about finances, an area critical to their power, and thus survival. Thucydides is making the point that the Athenians' emotional state had significant, serious consequences for their collective ability to know how to use their money and fight the war. These moments in the narrative are intended to reveal in emphatic terms the folly of the Athenians at this stage, with financial strength at their disposal in comparison to their foe, and thus the undoing, not so much through loss of money as loss of political leadership and rationality, of that strength whose foundations were laid by the founders of the Delian League and by Perikles.[71]

SPARTA AND PERSIA AGAIN: PAYMENTS AND TREATIES

The narrative now returns to the Spartans. Alkibiades and Chalkideos, the Spartan commander, help bring about a number of revolts from Athens—in Chios, Klazomenai, Miletos, and elsewhere—yet Thucydides attributes their success more to persuasion and disinformation than to naval strength (8.12.1, 14.2). Then the historian introduces the first of three treaties between the Persians and the Lakedaimonians and their allies. It looks like the tide is turning decisively in the Spartans' favor. However, the narrative suggests that the Spartans are merely filling the role of Persian pawns, an impression the reader readily accepts after Thucydides' lengthy description of Tissaphernes' motives in offering to assist the Spartans. As the story unfolds we see the Spartans doing what the satrap wants for his own ends[72]—namely, effecting revolts. The treaty presented does nothing to mitigate the sense that the Persians, not the Spartans, intend to gain by the arrangement, for the treaty, which Andrewes calls "no more than a preliminary working arrangement," worked to the advantage of Tissaphernes, not to that of the Spartans.[73]

71. E.g., 1.96, 99; 2.24.

72. See also below, pp. 251–53, on the capture of Iasos.

73. *HCT* 5, on 8.17.4. Cf. also Cawkwell (1997, 47 and 135 n. 15), who regards the first two treaties as drafts and only the third as a genuine treaty.

Moreover, there is no reference to the promise Tissaphernes made in 8.5.5 to pay for the fleet.[74] The Spartans' acceptance of the treaty obliquely implies criticism of them in not demanding inclusion of this.[75] But there is special reference to "money and anything else" that the cities traditionally under Persian control had been giving to Athens: the Lakedaimonians and their allies and the King were jointly to prevent "money and anything else" from going to the Athenians (8.18.1). The phrases χρήματα ἢ ἄλλο τι and χρήματα . . . μήτε ἄλλο μηδέν make clear that *chremata* refers to money specifically, whereas goods or supplies would be encompassed by the reference to "anything else." The clause acknowledges the chief usefulness of these cities—that is, their resources—but the treaty refers simply to preventing the flow of resources to the Athenians, and it is silent on who will benefit instead, the Lakedaimonians or the King. The implication, when one considers the reason Thucydides gives for Tissaphernes' desire to bring in the Spartans (8.5.4–5), is that the revenues will go to the Persians.[76] Hence it reinforces the impression that the Spartans fail to recognize the value of their appropriation of the Greeks' money for their own ends, to conquer the Athenians. Yet comparison with the second treaty (on which, see below) seems to reveal that the Persians at least had concerns about the lack of specificity in this clause.

Thucydides then returns to the revolt of Miletos and a land battle that ensued between the Athenians and Argives and the Peloponnesians, Tissaphernes, and his cavalry (8.25), the description of which, as argued in chapter 2, is intended to evoke the Ionian revolt. The Peloponnesians were badly defeated; yet immediately afterwards they received substantial naval reinforcements—fifty-five ships from the Peloponnese and Sicily (8.26.1)—and resolved to relieve Miletos. But the Athenian commander, Phrynichos, having learned of their arrival, persuaded the Athenians not to fight at sea, and thus when the Peloponnesians arrived, the Athenians were gone (8.27). Yet rather than take the initiative and, with their advantage, pursue the Athenians, the Spartans allowed themselves to be persuaded by Tissaphernes to sail to Iasos to capture Amorges (8.28.2). Thucydides suggests criticism of the Spartans. By endorsing the correctness of Phyrnichos' proposal (8.27.5), he implies that the Spartans might well have achieved an important naval victory over the Athenians. Moreover, the attack on Iasos was for Tissaphernes' benefit, not the Spartans' in their war against Athens: Tissaphernes was once again using the Spartans for his own ends, in order to

74. As Andrewes notes (*HCT* 5, ad loc.).

75. Thucydides delays a reference to the Spartans' dissatisfaction with the omission until 8.26.2, the effect of which suggests that they came only gradually to realize the problem.

76. Lewis 1977, 91: "That the cities should stop paying Athens tribute is an essential of the Spartan war against her . . . ; for Tissaphernes it is an essential preliminary to their starting to pay him, a point on which the treaty has nothing to say."

fulfill the King's instructions (8.5.5). And at this juncture Thucydides again focuses on money and financing.

He notes that the Peloponnesians captured Amorges and sacked the city, which was full of booty (*chremata panu polla*), and then comments that the land had been wealthy from of old (παλαιόπλουτον γὰρ ἦν τὸ χωρίον, 8.28.3). He then describes the fate of the captured. In an arrangement with Tissaphernes, the Peloponnesians handed over all the captives at a price of 1 Daric stater each (28.4). Thucydides' focus on the financial consequences of the Spartans' submission to Tissaphernes' plans reflects more than mere matter-of-fact reporting of the events. He troubled to inquire about the financial implications of the capture of Iasos and to record them, providing two details: the large quantity of booty, and the price of the captives. But while we are meant to be impressed by the booty, it remains a vague impression, while the one quantified detail in the chapter—the figure of 1 Daric stater per head—undercuts the positive assessment of what the Spartans got out of sacking the city. Thucydides focuses attention on this detail by his specificity and strict accuracy—he does not report the amount as translated into Attic units. The precision makes the reader wonder about the amount: did the Spartans get a good price? In fact, they appear to have been duped, for as David Lewis dryly comments, the amount, which is equivalent to 20 Attic drachmas, is "hardly commercial value."[77] Indeed, if one uses ransom sums as a rough parallel, the Spartans received significantly less than might have been expected.[78]

Thucydides' description of Iasos and reference to the large quantity of booty are intriguing details as well. Thucydides calls the site "wealthy of old" (παλαιόπλουτον); Strabo, writing in the first century B.C.E., described the land as "poor in soil" (παράλυπρος).[79] Andrewes comments that Iasos "might have been a more substantial place in the Classical period, but hardly so rich as this sentence implies; its annual tribute to Athens was one talent before the war, later raised to three. It looks as if Thucydides had been misinformed; perhaps the bulk of the money (cf. 36.1) was booty taken from Amorges."[80] Yet this conclusion is unsatisfying for several reasons. First, in chapter 28 and the following one, Thucydides' interest is above all financial. He did careful research, inquiring extensively into the details of the result of Amorges' capture, and into the terms of Tissaphernes' pay to the Peloponnesians in the next chapter. Second, the reference to Iasos as not just wealthy but "wealthy of old" implies a tradition, which, if true, suggests some-

77. Lewis 1977, 91. Andrewes (*HCT* 5, ad loc.) cites Xen. *An.* 1.7.18, for the equivalence in Athenian coinage, which works out to 20 dr. per stater.

78. See Pritchett 1991, 247–48; the lowest price recorded is 1 mina.

79. Strab. 14.2.21.

80. *HCT* 5, on 8.28.3.

thing more widely known than a specific piece of information received from an individual pertaining to a specific period of time. Third, Thucydides offers the statement about Iasos' long-standing wealth as an explanation for the quantity of booty; it therefore does damage to the text to suggest that the booty came from Amorges, and not from the area. Finally, the objection to Thucydides' report is ultimately based on the assumption that tribute reflects the total prosperity of a community, an assumption that is highly suspect, for among other reasons it fails to take into account that the Athenians were extracting wealth from their *arche* in ways other than tribute.[81] To use an assumption correlating tribute and prosperity to reject Thucydides is methodologically unsound.

Thucydides continues to focus on money and financing as the narrative continues, using the subject as a link among seemingly distinct arenas of action. Dewald selects 8.29–43 as illustrative of the historian's technique of constructing scenes so as to blur the boundaries between them, rather than to form separate, unrelated segments. The arenas and topics shift in the eleven scenes Dewald counts, yet, as she observes, "not only is there a blending of subject within the individual scene; the same topics are repeatedly introduced throughout the passage, which further serves to break down any remaining sense of boundary between scenes." She continues: "The elements shared by any two scenes constantly change: sometimes it is setting, sometimes actor, sometimes activity. . . . The scenes in viii.29–43 are thus interdependent to an extent unknown in the earlier narrative of the *History*."[82] Topics change, yet one that remains remarkably consistent is the issue of pay for the Spartan fleet.

According to Thucydides, Tissaphernes met up with the Peloponnesians at Miletos and

> distributed a month's subsistence (μηνὸς τροφήν) to the whole fleet as he had promised at Sparta, at the rate of 1 Attic drachma a day for each man. But in future he wished to give no more than 3 obols until consulting the King; if the King consented, he would pay the full drachma. But Hermokrates, the general of the Syracusans, objected to this arrangement, for since Therimenes was not commander but was sailing along to hand the ships over to Astyochos, he yielded [literally: was soft] about the pay, and an agreement was reached according to which Tissaphernes would add a total of five ships' pay distributed among the crew. Thus Tissaphernes was going to pay 30 talents a month for fifty-five ships, and beyond that number, at the same rate. (8.29)

81. See *Money*, 198–202. Meiggs (1972, 265 with n. 3) cites this passage and Xen. *Hell.* 1.4.8–9, which relates Alkibiades' collection of 100 talents from the Keramic Gulf in 407, to demonstrate that cities and regions could be substantially wealthier than their tribute assessment implies.

82. Dewald 1975, 191–92.

The complexity of the arrangement, the meaning of the Greek (e.g., παρὰ πέντε ναῦς). and the accuracy of the numbers in this passage are in much dispute,[83] but what is important to appreciate here is the denseness of the passage and the extraordinarily precise detail with which Thucydides describes the funding of the Peloponnesian navy; the impact of its extent is unaffected by the emendations proposed or problems of interpretations. In fact, beginning with the successful capture of Iasos, there is a remarkable clustering of financial details: we are told (1) that the booty collected from Iasos was great; (2) why it was great; (3) the price per head, expressed in Persian coinage, for the captives turned over to Tissaphernes; (4) the precise amount of Tissaphernes' distribution of pay to the fleet; (5) the precise amount of its reduction in subsequent months; (6) that the King could instruct him to give the full drachma rate; (7) Hermokrates' objection to the arrangement; (8) why it was Hermokrates and not Therimenes who cared about the rate of pay; and (9) the new agreement with Tissaphernes for payment.

The detail, precise and complicated, reflects Thucydides' interest in the financing of the Ionian stage of the war; and it makes clear that he made exceptionally detailed inquiries about this occasion, the first payments made by Tissaphernes to the Peloponnesian navy. Many of these items of information might be regarded as mundane or minor in the grand overall scheme of the war between the Peloponnesians and the Athenians, but Thucydides lists them all and includes explanatory comments to account for some of them (e.g., why a large quantity of booty was collected from Iasos; why Therimenes did not care about the rate of pay to the Peloponnesians but Hermokrates did). Their inclusion and density demonstrates clearly that Thucydides did not consider them marginal or incidental details. Like his treatment of money in general, these details have a purpose; they are not recorded merely for their own sake.

What, then, is the function of this information? Above all, the episode

83. Thompson (1965), following Arnold and Jowett, retains the manuscript reading of τρια and takes παρὰ πέντε ναῦς in the sense of "according to units of five ships." Pearson (1985) in response defends τριάκοντα, but his interpretation of the compromise arrangement is wildly improbable; he argues that the extra money would not have been pay for the sailors but, rather, was insurance money, a "commission," to the ship captains; in his view, the reason that Thucydides allows the conclusion that the money is to go to the crew is because of his prudish reluctance, typical of the time, to mention bribery, despite the fact that Thucydides and other Greek authors have no difficulty noting cases of palm greasing. Equally improbable is Perneé's (1980) proposal, in retaining the manuscript reading, that Thucydides is referring to weights when he mentions talents, which seems to be an anachronistic attempt to see the passage in a Homeric light. See also Andrewes, *HCT* 5, ad loc., for a good discussion of the problems and the solutions proposed. The difference in the total of the money offered in the compromise agreement in the various hypotheses is not significant.

marks the appearance of a new factor in the prosecution of the war, a factor that Thucydides regards as instrumental in the Spartans' eventual success over the Athenians (cf. 2.65.13): Persian financing. Thus, as revealed already in his treatment of the visit of Tissaphernes' envoys to Sparta (8.5.1), Thucydides has a special interest in analyzing the details of this new and crucial development that relates directly to his broader concern with money and power in the *History*. In recounting the episode in such precise detail he draws the reader into the various facets of and problems inherent in the new relationship between Sparta and Persia, which will be developed in detail in the rest of the narrative. Tissaphernes' reliability is called into question by his announcement of a future reduction in pay unless the King directs him otherwise. Moreover, it is Hermokrates, a Syracusan, who objects to the arrangement, not Therimenes, a Spartan, and Thucydides finds it necessary to step in to explain why a Spartan did not speak out: Therimines was not *nauarch;*[84] yet in the absence of any Peloponnesian of higher rank on the spot, it would have been appropriate for him to raise concerns.

Thucydides' emphasis on Therimenes' authority later in the narrative, at a point when his superior, Astyochos, was on the spot, suggests that he is criticizing Therimenes' acquiescence here.[85] In introducing the second treaty between the Persians and the Peloponnesians at Miletos, when Astyochos had just arrived, the historian specifies merely that it was made "while Therimenes was still present" (36.2); twice later, however, he refers to the treaty as "the treaty of Therimenes."[86] Thus when the reader comes to those later passages, the implicit criticism of Therimenes becomes clear: if Therimenes is credited with authority as an undersigner of a treaty when Astyochos was present, then his failure to assert himself earlier in the absence of any overranking official is damning. The allusion to his inferior position, then, is either dismissive, if Thucydides is providing an explanatory detail of his own or is intended to highlight the unsatisfactory nature of the justification for remaining quiet, if this was a reason given by Therimenes.[87] In either case, the simple statement "For Therimenes was not nauarch" is hardly neutral.[88] Thus the effect is to render the Spartans passive in this financial context—the harsh adjective *malakos,* which is used to describe Therimenes'

84. Thucydides does not give him a title but makes clear he was subordinate in rank to Astyochos.

85. Westlake (1968, 296 n. 2) thinks Astyochos did not arrive until after the treaty was concluded.

86. 8.43.3, 8.52 (σπονδαὶ Θεριμένους). See Andrewes, *HCT* 5, on 8.36.2, for a discussion of the problem with that allusion; see also Lewis 1977, 93 on *spondai;* and see below, pp. 256–58.

87. I find it difficult to be certain from the Greek.

88. Westlake (1968, 296) thinks that the statement "implies some criticism of Astyochus for having delayed so long," but I think the emphasis is on criticism of Therimenes.

reticence, is striking[89]—just as the narrative relating the price for the captives from Iasos, examined above, suggests that the Spartans had received a paltry sum apparently without objection.[90]

Above all, the passage creates the impression that these measures are a far cry from the systematic arrangements of the Athenians to finance their fleet. There is, rather, a kind of amateurishness to the arrangements made here, behind which is a lack of clarification between the parties over something as vital and critical to success as money: we recall that the details about financing the fleet apparently were omitted from the first treaty between the Spartans and Tissaphernes.

In fact, during the same winter, a second treaty was concluded. Thucydides' introductory comments make clear his interpretation of cause and effect (8.36). He notes that the Peloponnesians were adequately funded (καὶ γὰρ μισθὸς ἐδίδοτο ἀρκούντως),[91] the soldiers still had plenty of booty from Iasos (μεγάλα χρήματα), and the Milesians were contributing eagerly to the war (οἵ τε Μιλήσιοι προθύμως τά τοῦ πολέμου ἔφερον, 36.1),[92] and then continues: "Nevertheless, the Peloponnesians found the first treaty made by Chalkideos with Tissaphernes wanting (ἐνδεεῖς) and to Tissaphernes' advantage, and so concluded another" (36.2). The way that Thucydides introduces the second treaty represents the key issue troubling the Spartans as financial. Andrewes observes that the word ἐνδεεῖς, "wanting," has a political not a financial sense, since the first treaty said nothing about pay.[93] Yet ὅμως, "nevertheless," suggests rather that the concern was financial and that it is precisely because the first treaty was silent on the financial aspect that it would have been found wanting. Despite their adequate funding at that time, the Spartans had good reason to want to have assurances about future pay, given Tissaphernes' response thus far.

The introduction to the second treaty, in which Thucydides notes that

89. Thucydides will criticize Astyochos similarly (μαλακωτέρως) in connection with pay in 8.50.3, where Astyochos is "soft" about Persian pay; see below, p. 264.

90. Thucydides wants to make a point as much about Hermokrates as Therimenes. As Bender (1938, 102) has observed, passages concerned with Hermokrates in book 8 tend to focus on character and reflect Thucydides' admiration of the Syracusan. It is therefore noteworthy that such references to Hermokrates (cf. also 8.45.3, below) link him with financial concerns and considerations.

91. Holzapfel (1893, 436) rejected this statement because it contradicts 8.29, where Tissaphernes reduces the pay from 1 drachma to something more than 3 obols a day per individual; yet this view fails to take into account that Tissaphernes had initially distributed the full drachma rate for a month, and that he was not yet paying irregularly, as he would subsequently upon advice from Alkibiades (cf. 8.45.2, 46.5). Cf. below on 8.45–46.

92. Andrewes (*HCT* 5, ad loc.) sees this as a reference to provisioning, including perhaps money.

93. *HCT* 5, ad loc.

the Spartans found the first more advantageous to Tissaphernes than to themselves, carries the implication that this second treaty would be more in their (financial) interests. Yet its second clause, which dictates that the Lakedaimonians and their allies should not exact tribute from the cities and territories belonging traditionally to the Persian King (8.37.2), undermines this conclusion. And while there is now a provision that specifically notes that the King is to bear the expense (δαπάνη) of the war (8.37.4), a rate is conspicuously absent.

Thucydides' allusion to the treaty as Therimenes' has been regarded as itself problematic. Wilamowitz questioned the historicity of Therimenes' role and suggested that the treaty had actually been concluded by Astyochos, who, when it was subsequently found disadvantageous to the Spartans, removed responsibility from himself by blaming Therimenes; this version, he argued, found its way into Thucydides' narrative.[94] Yet E. Lévy objects that if Thucydides had access to the complete text of the treaty, as seems to have been the case, then he would also have seen the names of the contracting individuals; and his objection is not with merit.[95] In any case, what is important is that Thucydides has chosen to highlight Therimenes' authority while he is in the same subordinate position as he was in 8.29,[96] and in connection with an arrangement that is to the disadvantage of the Spartans.

The historian-narrator does not offer commentary on the treaty's contents; he lets it speak for itself, implying its inadequacy from the Spartan perspective, but also a continuation of the Spartans' passivity and acquiescence. Only later in the narrative (8.43.2) do eleven Spartan advisors appear on the scene and find fault with both treaties. In particular, one of them —Lichas—objected to the Persian King's claim to land formerly ruled by himself or his advisors, and said that they would not receive pay from Tissaphernes under these conditions. But what does Thucydides want us to conclude without the knowledge of this later exegesis? The first clause in the initial treaty, which refers to both sides hindering the Athenians from extracting money or anything else from the Asian cities, is replaced by a clause prohibiting the Peloponnesians and their allies from extracting tribute from the cities, on the grounds that they belong to the King.[97] Thus the Spartans

94. Wilamowitz 1908, 598; Andrewes (*HCT* 5, on 8.36.2) finds this plausible.

95. Lévy 1983, 223 n. 22.

96. Lewis (1977, 95) describes him as "Astyochos' temporary predecessor."

97. Goldstein (1974, 163) comments: "Clearly a disagreement concerning tribute had arisen after the negotiation of the first treaty. The primary reason for the drafting of the second treaty was the dissatisfaction of the Lacedaemonians, who had apparently demanded a guarantee for provisions in Asia Minor and received satisfaction in the fourth and sixth clauses of the second treaty. In return, the question of tribute was settled in the King's favor." This interpretation makes the Spartans more active participants in the drafting of the terms than does

relinquish a substantial source of financing—tribute from the Greek cities. To have exacted tribute would, admittedly, be at odds with their role as liberators, but the very fact of its mention raises the possibility and, fitting as it does into Thucydides' larger narrative, it confirms that the Spartans will be completely reliant on Persian subsidies. Yet in the clause in which financing arises, as mentioned, no rate of pay is given; the Spartans are basically back where they were. Thus even with the second treaty, considerable uncertainty about the financing of the Peloponnesian fleet remains.[98]

Thucydides develops this impression as the narrative proceeds. It eventually becomes clear to the Spartans that Persian financial assistance might be problematic, as their next move reveals. They sail to Rhodes on the invitation of individuals there, to assist in the island's revolt. Thucydides supplies their thinking: they considered the land and sea strength of the Rhodians, and "at the same time they believed themselves to be powerful (enough) from their existing alliance not to have to ask Tissaphernes to pay for their fleet" (8.44.1). The result was that they "levied 32 talents from the Rhodians, hauled their ships ashore, and remained inactive for eighty days" (8.44.4).[99]

This narrative description offers insight into the points that Thucydides wants to make about the Spartans, money, and their ability to use it properly. On the one hand, their recognition of the uncertainties of relying on Tissaphernes and the Persians reflects a correct appraisal of the situation and foreshadows the subsequent narrative once Alkibiades arrives on the scene and begins to work with the satrap. On the other hand, their expectation that they can fund their navy adequately without Persian assistance shows their failure to understand how much money is involved in fighting

---

Thucydides' narrative, which stresses by implication and silence the absence of clout. In addition, it fails to take into account the absence of a specified amount of support, which is surprising, given the disagreement over pay in 8.29, if the treaty were really the product of negotiation and compromise.

98. Thucydides also gives the impression that the Spartans do not yet really know how to fight effectively at sea, even when they have the resources to equip a fleet. They are portrayed as amateurs, already once (8.11), when in the battle off Epidauros they did not know how to protect their ships, and now, when Lakedaimonian ships sailing from the Peloponnese and meeting up with some Athenian ships at Melos decide to sail to Crete, fearing the Athenians on Samos would be alerted to their arrival (8.39.3); but cf. Westlake 1989, 149 n. 82: "Evidence on the quality of the rival fleets suggests that the Peloponnesians were somewhat more effective than the Athenians when receiving adequate payment from the Persians."

99. Lévy (1983, 233) raises the question whether this would have contravened the second treaty, and suggests a distinction between "theory" (i.e., technically it did) and practice (i.e., Tissaphernes allowed the Spartans to extract money from territory belonging to the King under the terms of the treaty). Yet it is not clear that Tissaphernes was *allowing* the Lakedaimonians to extract money, or whether they just did it; it is important that by this point they were distrustful of Tissaphernes and not working closely with him. Nor is there reason to think that Rhodes was claimed by the King.

naval war.[100] As Andrewes notes, "the payment of 32T to the Peloponnesians was well within [the Rhodians'] means, but even at the 3-obol rate (1/2T per ship per month) this would not pay ninety-four ships for a month, much less for eighty days."[101] Moreover, the second treaty expressly excludes the Spartans from access to money from the region claimed by the King; their thinking, then, rather than reflecting initiative and resourcefulness, reveals, by contrast, as Thucydides explains it, their shortsightedness.

Perhaps most damning is Thucydides' allusion to what they do when they get money: they then remain inactive for eighty days.[102] It is significant, that is, that he chooses to specify the number of days and their action—or rather inaction—once they levy money on their own. Admittedly it is winter; yet naval activity had been carried out in winter consistently in that very year,[103] and the narrative juxtaposition of the two pieces of information, the collecting of the 32 talents and the decision to remain inactive, is deliberate. Thus up to this point in the narrative of book 8, Thucydides has inserted the role of money and financing conspicuously and prominently and he has portrayed the Spartans as amateurs at military/naval financing, accepting what Tissaphernes throws their way without clear and specific assurances, or, conversely, thinking they do not need his assistance at all.

ENTER ALKIBIADES

The picture changes dramatically as Alkibiades now takes center stage, with the role of money continuing to form a linking theme. Alkibiades had become persona non grata at Sparta, with orders given to Astyochos to put him to death. But Alkibiades went over to Tissaphernes and, with the intent of harming Sparta, "became his instructor in every matter" (διδάσκαλος πάντων, 8.45.1). Then begins a lengthy description of Alkibiades' advice in 8.45–46. With the same meticulous and detailed reporting that was so prominent in 8.29, Thucydides relates the precise measures recommended

100. Cawkwell (1975, 64) implies that not until Lysander appeared on the scene did the Spartans appreciate this fact.

101. *HCT* 5, ad loc.

102. 8.44.4. See *HCT* 5: 147–49 for discussion of attempts to emend the figure of eighty days, on the grounds that the chronology does not conform to Thucydides' *termini* of winter. Yet, as Andrewes comments, "it must be remembered that they are proposed not to resolve an acknowledged factual difficulty, but in defence of a theory about Thucydides' chronological system which is by no means uncontested" (147). But even if the correct figure is a smaller number—for example, forty—on Pritchett's suggestion (1965, 260), my argument about the effect of relating Peloponnesian inactivity for a precise number of days immediately after noting their receipt of money still should bear weight.

103. E.g., 8.30–44.

by Alkibiades in a passage marked by its "extreme density," in which "every word is laden with meaning."[104] It will be helpful to quote the passage in full.

> He cut down the pay from an Attic drachma to 3 obols a day, and even this not paid regularly. And he urged Tissaphernes to say to the Peloponnesians that the Athenians, who had after all possessed a navy for a long time and were knowledgeable in this area, paid their crew only 3 obols a day per man, not so much because of poverty as of not wanting the sailors to act outrageously because of having too much money, and weakening their bodies by spending money on such pursuits that would enervate them; and that they paid their crews irregularly as a security against desertion, on the grounds that the crew would not leave owed money behind. Alkibiades also instructed Tissaphernes to bribe the trierarchs and generals of the cities to get their complicity, which worked in every case but that of the Syracusans, for Hermokrates refused on behalf of all their alliance.
>
> Next Alkibiades sent away the cities asking for money, replying in the name of Tissaphernes that, first of all, the Chians were shameless in asking for money, as they were the richest of the Greeks, and nevertheless thinking it right that they should be aided by others who were jeopardizing both bodies and money on behalf of their freedom. As for the other cities that had paid money to Athens before they revolted, they could not justly be unwilling to contribute as much or even more on behalf of themselves. He also pointed out that Tissaphernes was at present justly economizing, since he was paying for the war out of his own pocket, and if he ever received remittance from the King, he would give them their pay in full, and reasonably be of material use to the cities.
>
> Alkibiades further advised Tissaphernes not to be in such a hurry to end the war or to let himself be persuaded to bring up the Phoenician fleet that he was equipping or to provide pay for more Hellenes, and thus put the power by land and sea into the same hands; but to leave each of the contending parties in possession of one element, thus enabling the King when he found one troublesome to call in the other. For if the command of the sea and land were united in one hand, he would not know where to turn for help to overthrow the dominant power; unless he at last chose to stand up himself, and go through the struggle at great expense and hazard. The cheapest plan was to let the Hellenes wear each other out, at a small share of the expense and without risk to himself. (8.45.2–46.2)

Thucydides has introduced this section by noting that Alkibiades became Tissaphernes' "instructor in every matter" (διδάσκαλος πάντων). Thus in Thucydides' detailed description of what Alkibiades instructed it is significant that "every matter" bears on money and financing. Scholars have long

104. "On est frappé par l'extrême densité du chapitre: Thucydide analyse toute une politique nouvelle et en condense les traits essentiels en suivant un ordre principalement logique; chaque mot, qu'il soit de Thucydide ou Alcibiade, est lourd de sens" (Delebecque 1964, 43–44). See also Rood's discussion (1998, 262–65) of Thucydides' narrative techniques and the questions they raise in this passage.

objected to the first section, in which Alkibiades reduces the daily rate of pay from 1 drachma to 3 obols, on the grounds that it is a doublet of 8.29, in which the rate began at 1 drachma a day but then was reduced to slightly more than 3 obols.[105] Yet as Andrewes notes, the doublet is not exact in the case of the rate of reduction and of Hermokrates' role—he objects in 8.29 to a reduction as well as to irregular pay, and in 8.45 to the irregularity of pay. Indeed, there are further points to be made against a doublet. It is important to bear in mind that in 8.29 Tissaphernes did in fact distribute a month's pay at the daily rate of 1 drachma; he then threatened a reduction *for the future,*[106] to which Hermokrates objected, and the compromise was struck. But we are to understand that the fleet had received ample pay for the first installment, which accords with Thucydides' statement in 8.36.1 that the fleet had received "adequate pay." The two chapters do not mesh entirely when taken as two separate stages, one later than the first; the overlap, however, and consequent difficulties from assuming an overlap, have been overstated.

Perhaps most interesting about this section from a narrative standpoint is Thucydides' inclusion of the elaborate explanation Alkibiades supplies to Tissaphernes for the reduction.[107] His teacher in words as well as action, Alkibiades instructs Tissaphernes to say to the Peloponnesians that 3 obols was the normal rate of pay that the Athenians gave to their sailors, and, in order to give the statement greater authority, to tell them that the Athenians had long experience at this sort of thing, and then to reveal the reason for the low rate, namely, to keep the men from becoming corrupted by having too much pocket money. Finally, he was to tell them that the Athenians also paid their crews irregularly, the rationale, although somewhat paradoxical, being that this would prevent the men from deserting, since they would not leave without their arrears.[108] What insights does this information afford the reader? Above all the reader is likely to conclude that the Spartans are ignorant about naval financing: they need an explanation for a certain rate of pay over another and why it should be paid irregularly. This impression of their ignorance is heightened by Thucydides' emphasis on the sham nature of the explanation, confirmed by the fact that the ship captains from the

105. See Andrewes, *HCT* 5, ad loc., for discussion of the perceived problem. See also Rood 1998, 264–65.

106. In that context the imperfects ἐδίδου and ἐδίδοτο must be conative, or possibly iterative (so Pernée 1980, 116).

107. Cf. 8.83, where this is precisely what happened; see below, p. 273.

108. For discussion of his source(s) here, and in the following narrative, see, for example, Delebecque 1965, 77–126; Westlake 1989, 154–65; Erbse 1989b, 75–82. I side with those who think that Alkibiades (Delebecque) or someone close to him (Westlake) was his source. Likewise, Thucydides got close to Tissaphernes, either talking to the satrap himself or to someone who knew him well.

cities—who had previous experience in Athens' navy—were to be bribed because they would see through it.

It needs to be stressed that in relating this turn of events Thucydides would not have provided such detail and elaboration on the thinking involved were he not acutely interested in the financing of the Spartan navy and in making the topic a central feature of his narrative. He could simply have stated that on Alkibiades' advice Tissaphernes reduced the rate of pay and made pay irregular. His interest in this subject is manifest throughout these two chapters, for as he goes on to relate Alkibiades' advice and thinking, he continuously focuses on financial factors, including—remarkably—ways for the King to achieve his own ends most economically.[109] Of course he is as interested in Alkibiades himself as in financing proper, but this raises another fundamental point, that in his narrative about Alkibiades in book 8, money is also consistently present. The connection forged here between Alkibiades and finances—and this is not the first time Thucydides has made it (cf. 6.15)—has the effect of once again reminding the reader of the seriousness of the loss of Alkibiades from the Athenian side (and the danger to them even when he is on their side).

Tissaphernes took Alkibiades' advice and treated him as a confidant.[110] Alkibiades, for his part, counseled Tissaphernes as he did because he believed it to be the best strategy, but also because he wanted to leave open a chance for his own restoration to Athens and figured that the best means would be to convince the Athenians that he had Tissaphernes' ear (8.47.1). His plan worked: the Athenians at Samos saw that Alkibiades was close to Tissaphernes and, Thucydides notes, Alkibiades himself sent word to the most powerful among them that if they changed the government, he would be glad to return and use his influence with Tissaphernes to help the Athenians.

THE COUP OF 411 AND PERSIAN FINANCING OF THE WAR

As Thucydides moves from the narrative of Alkibiades and Tissaphernes to that of the revolutionary coup begun on Samos, he foregrounds the subject of money but also shifts the focus from the Spartans to the Athenians. From the start the narrative makes clear that the financing of the war was, in an important sense, a linchpin of the coup that began among Athenians at Samos; the ostensible purpose of subverting the democracy at Athens was, from the point of view of the Athenians involved, to obtain money from Per-

109. Cf. 8.87.5, Thucydides' own thinking, presented as remarkably similar to the remarks given here to Alkibiades. See below, pp. 274–77.

110. Gribble (1999, 196–204) emphasizes Alkibiades' persuasive powers but also the "unreality of [his] influence" (200) over Tissaphernes. This serves to underscore the Athenians' gullibility; see also below.

sia (via Tissaphernes), and so to overcome the Spartans.[111] Indeed, Thucydides tells us, when the "powerful men" (δυνατοί) among the Athenians presented the plan to the fleet at Samos, "they said openly that the King would be their friend and give them money (χρήματα) if they restored Alkibiades and did not live under a democracy. And the crowd, if at first they were somewhat disturbed by these plans, nevertheless kept silent because of the abundance of hope of pay (τὸ εὔπορον τῆς ἐλπίδος τοῦ μισθοῦ) from the King" (8.48.2–3).[112]

The presentation of the "crowd" (ὄχλος) in this chapter accords with Thucydides' account of the various motives of Athenians for desiring the Sicilian expedition. In the case of the common people (ὁ δὲ πολὺς ὅμιλος καὶ στρατιώτης, 6.24.3) the goal in conquering Sicily was money for the present and everlasting pay for the future. Moreover, Alkibiades fools the Athenians as easily as the Egestans did—and as Aristagoras did their ancestors in the 490s; they have not learned at all. But the portrayal also chimes with Thucydides' "theory of collaboration"—that weaker and stronger parties collaborate toward an end that is to the greater advantage of the stronger —which explains an apparent paradox: namely, how and why would weaker parties *willingly* submit to a situation that will work to their ultimate disadvantage? The answer: for financial gain.[113] Now the Athenians have become the weaker group and for the sake of financial gain we see them submitting to the previously unthinkable—a change in government—which would, if it lasted, make them worse off than before. Indeed, as Thucydides portrays it, their desire for money outweighed their fear of the potential for damage and danger within the polis if Alkibiades were restored. It was "the people" who, at the beginning of the Sicilian expedition, thought Alkibiades might be aiming at tyranny (6.15.3–4), yet their desire for profit led them to accept his arguments for the Sicilian expedition; and the suspicion of Alkibiades on the part of the fleet at Samos is evident as well in their allegiance to Phrynichos instead of Alkibiades (8.51).[114] Thus Thucydides casts in the

111. Cf. *ATL* 3: 359: "The political revolution in 411 came in the midst of a financial crisis." I would put it rather that the political revolution was fueled and facilitated by a financial crisis. Yet the flat statement (358) that "all financial resources were exhausted" by 411 does not carry the certainty supposed, for it is based on a comment in a speech made at the assembly called by the soldiers at Samos (8.76.6; see below)—that is, not on any factual evidence. It is not necessary to assume on the basis of a reference to loans made by the treasurers of Athena "from the annual [revenue]" (*IG* I^3 375.3–4) that Athens had no reserve; the reference could indicate that the Athenians were determined to preserve what remained of the reserve.

112. The phrase "abundance of hope of pay" is a nice touch: hope will be all that is abundant, not pay.

113. Thuc. 1.8.3, 99.3; see *Money,* 8–9, 26–27, 61–62.

114. See Gribble 1999, 202: "The aim of the narrator in describing the strategic self-projections of Alcibiades in 411 B.C. is to expose the truth behind the illusion (characteristic

highest relief possible here the hold that money had on the Athenian collective mentality.

After the plan was communicated to the sailors, the chief men discussed Alkibiades' plans among themselves. The only one to object was Phrynichos, asserting that Alkibiades cared no more for oligarchy than democracy and wanted a change only so that he would be restored by his comrades; Thucydides registers agreement with the phrase ὅπερ καὶ ἦν (8.48 4). Phrynichos made a number of other objections to Alkibiades' proposal in which he emphasized the unreliability of Tissaphernes' supposed allegiance to Athens, and the unsoundness of the view that a change in government in the allied cities would make them more likely to come to terms and cease their revolts (8.48.5–7).

Phrynichos' objections were not shared by the others, and so, fearing that if Alkibiades were restored to Athens he would then take revenge because Phyrnichos had spoken against the plan, he wrote a letter revealing all to Astyochos, the Spartan commander (8.50.1–2). But the effect of the letter was the opposite of what was intended, for Astyochos did not go after Alkibiades, as Phrynichos had desired, but instead went to Alkibiades and Tissaphernes and turned informer. What is especially interesting about this section is that Thucydides produces an accusation whose veracity he does not confirm—he says: "as the story went" (ὡς ἐλέγετο, 8.50.3)—yet then builds an argument on it that concerns money: Astyochos informed for money (ἐπὶ ἰδίοις κέρδεσι), and "this is the very reason why Astyochos was weak about the pay not being given in full" (διόπερ καὶ [περὶ] τῆς μισθοφορᾶς οὐκ ἐντελοῦς οὔσης μαλακωτέρως, 50.3). The choice of the adverb μαλακώτερως is surely meant to recall Therimines' "softness" in 8.29; and in both cases, Thucydides chooses to supply the reason for the lack of response; and in both, as well, word choice and explanation imply strong criticism.[115] That he inserts this comment, which concerns an issue not directly relevant to the specific context, attests not only to his focus on the financial aspect of the war at this stage, but also his emphasis on the continuing intrusion of private motives of greed into the public arena.

The narrative of the origins of the revolution of 411 is significant because it makes clear that the Persians were now expected to be the Athenians' financiers. When Peisander, a ringleader of the imminent coup, addressed the assembly in Athens, he put the situation the Athenians faced like this: the Spartans have parity in ships, more cities in alliance with them, and the King and Tissaphernes to supply them with money, of which the Athenians

---

is the use of the focalization through Phrynichus . . . to provide a 'realistic' commentary on Alcibiades and his plans)."

115. See above, pp. 255–56.

had none (σφίσι τε οὐκέτι ὄντων, 8.53.2).[116] Therefore they must change their government, that being the only way to win Persia over to the Athenian side through Alkibiades' connection with Tissaphernes. Thus, Thucydides intends us to understand as readers that, at this stage of the war, success or failure is presented as depending almost entirely on Persian financial help; yet it also emerges clearly that while money is an essential factor in the war, it is not the only factor. Thucydides breaks the account concerning the Athenians and Tissaphernes with a description of an Athenian attack on Rhodes, in which we learn that the Spartans are still idle, their ships on shore. Thus far, the focus on money throughout makes it easy to recall that although receiving "sufficient pay" and considerable booty, the Peloponnesians failed to prosecute the war and instead remained inactive; their money has been spent for nothing. This provides the backdrop and the transition for Thucydides to renew the narrative concerned with Tissaphernes and the Spartans. In other words, Thucydides has used the theme of money, along with the role of Alkibiades and Tissaphernes, as a linking device between the two narrative sections. Thucydides highlights the Athenians' gullibility in expecting Persian support by juxtaposing the account of the Athenians' willingness to change their government, with their "abundance of hope of pay," with Tissaphernes' renewed (but still unreliable) commitment to the Spartans (8.57.1).

THE THIRD TREATY WITH THE PELOPONNESIANS

Thucydides relates the abandonment of the Athenians by Tissaphernes, achieved through Alkibiades' treachery, and his decision to return to the Spartans, which culminates in a third treaty (8.58). As he has made a point of doing before, Thucydides delves into Tissaphernes' thinking and characteristically focuses on money. The satrap decided to treat again with the Peloponnesians

> to supply them with pay, making a new treaty upon such terms as he could get, in order not to bring matters to an absolute breach between them. He was afraid that if many of their ships were left without pay (*trophe*), they would be forced to fight and be defeated, or that their ships being left emptied of men, the Athenians would achieve their goals without his help. Still more he feared that the Peloponnesians might ravage the land in search of *trophe*. Having cal-

116. In the reverse direction, cf. Ar. *Lys.* 173–74, produced around this time (for the date, see Henderson 1987, xv–xxv): Lampito refers to the Athenians' "bottomless source of money," and the specific aim of the women's seizure of the Akropolis is to keep Athens' financial resources from the Athenian men; the premise is therefore that the Athenians are not out of money. Of course, one can no more use this as a statement of fact than the highly rhetorical assertions in Thucydides' speeches. Both are exaggerations. See also below, p. 290.

culated and considered all this, in accordance with his plan of keeping the two sides equal, he now sent for the Peloponnesians and paid them and concluded a third treaty. (8.57)

In this passage Thucydides illustrates the problems that can arise in a naval war that lacks adequate financial resources behind it (as well as making clear Tissaphernes' self-interested aims). He focuses on the minor as well as major details of funding and provisioning rather than simply on the results of battles. Here, finally, we see a heightened expression of a concern that has been present but not always so immediately explicit—Thucydides' complete awareness of the financial aspects of naval war. Throughout the work, he has probed into the establishment and development of naval power, but here he expressly illustrates the consequences of the lack of a substantial reserve: the war could come to a halt. The issue of *how* both sides are going to be able to fight is still a new problem for the Spartans, used to fighting on land without the need of money. Thucydides illumines this by focusing on the nuts and bolts of financing a fleet.

The treaty contains the fullest details of financing yet, as outlined in sections 5–6: "Tissaphernes shall pay for the ships currently present in accordance with the agreement until the ships of the King arrive. When the King's ships have come, the Lakedaimonians and their allies may pay for their own ships if they wish, but if they wish to receive pay from Tissaphernes, Tissaphernes shall provide it, and the Lakedaimonians and their allies shall repay the money borrowed at the end of the war" (8.58.5–6).[117] Which agreement is mentioned in the treaty is unclear, but it implies that the King had fixed a rate of pay, and that he would provide the pay to be disbursed by Tissaphernes.[118] The assumption has been that the money will come from the King, whereas before Tissaphernes was apparently paying out of his own purse, but this is nowhere explicitly stated in the agreement, nor is the rate.[119] Indeed, as Lewis has well brought out, this treaty is even less advantageous to the Spartans than the second one.[120] The King promises to pay only the ships then present, not any reinforcements. Moreover, both the reference to the King's fleet and the clause providing for the Peloponnesians to pay for their own ships after its arrival, or to treat any further money paid as a loan, not a gift, demonstrates that the King now regards the Peloponnesian

117. τροφὴν δὲ ταῖς ναυσὶ ταῖς νῦν παρούσαις Τισσαφέρνην παρέχειν κατὰ τὰ ξυγκείμενα μέχρι ἂν αἱ νῆες αἱ βασιλέως ἔλθωσιν.

118. Andrewes, *HCT* 5, ad loc.

119. See Andrewes, *HCT* 5, ad loc. It should be noted, however, that the second treaty did specify that the King would bear the expense of the Peloponnesians and their allies in his land (8.37.4). Yet, as Andrewes notes, Tissaphernes was still paying for the force in 45.6.

120. Lewis 1977, 103–4; see also Lévy 1983, 224.

fleet as dispensable.[121] The reason is clear: the expectation is that the arrival of the Phoenician fleet will diminish the usefulness of the Spartans, with corresponding impact on their ability to obtain adequate funding from the Persians for their war against Athens.

The prospects for Persian financing for the Spartans are grim. As he has done before, Thucydides juxtaposes financial discussions with Spartan naval actions, stressing consistently their inability to aid Athens' allies in their revolts effectively—that is, to know how to use what money they get effectively. Thus in 8.60–61 he relates events at Chios, which is still attempting to revolt from the Athenians, and he specifically notes the Spartans' desire to help the Chians in preference to the Eretrians, who are planning the revolt of Euboia (8.60.2). What follows, however, is Astyochos' utter inability to provide help to the Chians (ὁ Ἀστύοχος ἠπόρει ὅπως βοηθήσοι, 8.61.1), reinforcing the point that money and expertise go hand in hand—Thucydides is stressing Spartan incompetence at sea along with their financial difficulties. It might seem then that the Athenians could easily gain the upper hand, but at this point Thucydides turns back to the Athenian situation to make clear why their strength is weakening: financial problems are only exacerbated by the fact that the city and its resources are divided.

ATHENS: THE DIVIDED CITY

Thucydides resumes his account of the coup when he relates the failure of the Athenians on Samos to sail out against Astyochos and his ships; the reason was that the Athenians were divided among themselves and suspicious of one another (8.63.2). With this point Thucydides then begins a lengthy section dealing with the coup itself. First, the historian relates what transpired on Samos and then at Athens. Peisander and the other envoys returned to Samos after their visit to Tissaphernes, determined to strengthen the army and to make the chief men on Samos change the government to an oligarchy, although they had recently worked to prevent that very change.[122] In addition, they determined not to treat with Alkibiades, since he did not want to join them and was in any case, Thucydides adds, unsuitable for an oligarchy. They would do their best to preserve their cause and to carry on the war, contributing money without stint from their private estates, since they now had only themselves to toil away for (8.63.4).[123]

121. See Andrewes *HCT* 5, on 8.58.6, on the phrase τρέφειν ἐφ' ἑαυτοῖς and its implications.

122. On the nature of Thucydides' terminology in treating this episode, see Sealey 1973, 286–87.

123. αὐτοὺς δὲ ἐπὶ σφῶν αὐτῶν, ὡς ἤδη καὶ κινδυνεύοντας, ὁρᾶν ὅτῳ τρόπῳ μὴ ἀνεθήσεται τὰ πράγματα, καὶ τὰ τοῦ πολέμου ἅμα ἀντέχειν καὶ ἐσφέρειν αὐτοὺς ἐκ τῶν ἰδίων οἴκων προθύμως χρήματα καὶ ἤν τι ἄλλο δέῃ, ὡς ἢ σφίσιν αὐτοῖς ταλαιπωροῦντας.

This passage has fascinating verbal and thematic parallels with Herodotos 5.78, which deals with the effect on the Athenians of the expulsion of the tyrants. As often, the Thucydidean "version" of Herodotos makes use of inversion and irony to draw comparisons and contrasts. In Herodotos, following the expulsion of the tyrants, the Athenians, now under the condition of *isegoria*—literally, "freedom of speech"—were able to increase in strength. Under tyranny, he comments, they were no better than their neighbors at military achievements, but afterward they became preeminent. As he puts it, "when they were held down, they were cowards, since they exerted themselves for a master, but after they were freed, each one himself exerted himself to achieve for himself."[124] The emphasis on men exerting themselves wholeheartedly on their own behalf is especially striking.[125] In Herodotos, it is the democracy that spawns zeal to achieve for oneself.[126] In Thucydides the democracy has made the revolutionaries sluggish in exerting themselves; their corollary would be that they were oppressed by "master Demos." In both, interestingly, the context is military strength—in Herodotos, the context seems to be actual fighting, and in Thucydides, financial backing of war is at issue.

Comparison between the passages and broader contexts suggests further ironies. Herodotos prefaces the passage with the remark "Thus, then, the Athenians increased in strength" (ηὔξηντο). The result, of course, was the Athenian *arche*. Thucydides, in his analysis of the increase in Athenian power in book 1, notes the connection between the allies' unwillingness to "suffer hardships"—ταλαιπωρεῖν, the same verb used for the Four Hundred in 8.64.3—that were not on behalf of themselves but the Athenians, increasingly looking like their masters; the result was that they became tributary and the Athenian navy "was increased" (ηὔξετο) by the expense the allies bore (1.99.1–3).

In his treatment of the destruction of the democracy, Thucydides neatly brings together both Herodotean resonances and echoes of book 1, not only in 8.64, but also a little further on, in 8.68.4. In commenting that it was not easy for the demos to give up its freedom, Thucydides notes that it had been "about one hundred years since they had put down the tyrants, and not only were they not subject, but over half that time they had been used to ruling others." The choice of expression, not dating their freedom to the

---

Cf. also another parallel in connection with the coup, 8.89.3 with Hdt. 3.82.3, on the struggles for ascendency in oligarchies; Hornblower 1996, 145.

124. κατεχόμενοι μὲν ἐθελοκάκεον ὡς δεσπότῃ ἐργαζόμενοι, ἐλευθερωθέντων δὲ αὐτὸς ἕκαστος ἑωυτῷ προεθυμέετο κατεργάζεσθαι.

125. Hdt.: αὐτὸς ἕκαστος ἑωυτῷ προεθυμέετο; Thuc.: προθύμως, ὡς ἢ σφίσιν αὐτοῖς ταλαιπωροῦντας.

126. I am taking this for the purposes here as being implied by the term *isegoria*.

beginnings of democracy—the issue in 411—but rather to the end of tyranny, may be designed again to evoke Herodotos, then in an ironic touch alluding to the Athenians' rule over others.[127]

Let us return to the account of the coup. When Peisander and the others arrived in Athens, they quickly held an assembly and voted to elect ten men with full powers to determine how best to run the city; when this was done, the assembly would meet and the Ten would present their proposal. They insured success by holding the assembly at Kolonos in the sanctuary of Poseidon, which was small and outside of Athens (8.67.2). Thucydides draws attention to the intellectual powers of leading men in the coup—Antiphon, Phrynichos, and Theramenes (8.68)—partly to account for the (temporary) success of the conspirators; for, he continues, it was a grave matter to deprive the demos of its freedom after so long a time, even of ruling others (8.68.4).

The reign of terror imposed by the Four Hundred was carried out in the city. The narrative that follows continues to develop the story of the revolution alongside that of the larger war, in treating which, the narrative alternates between the funding difficulties each side (the Athenian and the Spartan) is encountering, in such a way as to crystallize the consequences of the lack of *periousia chrematon,* and to heighten the sense of a situation unraveling. The themes of money as a motivating factor, the relationship of size and resources, and the inevitable weakening of power caused by disunity inform the narrative. Let us now see how these themes are developed.

The account moves to Samos, and Thucydides comments: "The struggle was now between the army trying to force a democracy on the city, and the Four Hundred, an oligarchy on the camp" (8.76.1). The soldiers called an assembly, deposed former generals and any trierarchs of whom they were suspicious, and chose new ones in addition to Thrasyboulos and Thrasyllos. Then they encouraged each other with various arguments; significantly, Thucydides again focuses on the financial ones: "Standing up, they made various exhortations, among which they urged [the men] not to lose heart because the city [of Athens] had revolted from them; they were more numerous and better equipped in resources, for they had the whole navy, and they could force the other cities they ruled to give them money (*chremata*) as if they were based there [i.e., in Athens]. . . . Moreover, they had lost nothing in losing those who no longer had money to send—which the sol-

127. A further similarity, also loaded with irony, that may have stimulated Thucydides to think about Herodotos here, is that as soon as the Athenians changed their government from tyranny to democracy, they attacked and overwhelmingly defeated the Chalcidians on Euboia (5.77, the great military victory that prompted him to digress on the effects of *isegoria*); as soon as the Athenians changed their government for the first time since the overthrow of tyranny, Euboia revolted (for the conclusion, see 8.95–96).

diers now had to provide for themselves—or good counsel, which gives a city power to lead an army" (8.76.3–4, 6). The connection between financing and good judgment is by now a thoroughly familiar and therefore obvious point that serves as a reminder in the midst of a narrative much concerned with the difficulties faced by both Athens and Sparta, and by the divided Athenians among themselves. In addition, the notion of the transferable polis recalls the Athenians in Sicily, a significant association that has to do with the transfer of resources outside of Athens itself, though the twist in this case is that, unlike in 415–413, the city at home now had few resources to give, and the other city on Samos was likewise bereft of money. Indeed, in a sense the halving of Athens has resulted in an inevitable weakening of power precisely because the polis was divided. Yet the city on Samos had an advantage, the soldiers note, in having a navy, whose usefulness, Thucydides explicitly records, they express not in terms of winning against Sparta but of extorting money from their subjects. The historian's focus on the financial arguments—recall his privileging of the financial component of their various exhortations—reveals his intention of keeping the reader firmly focused on this area above all others.[128]

SPARTA AND ATHENS

The narrative now proceeds to alternate between events on the Spartan and Athenian sides, and once again, money provides a link between the preceding narrative and this next stage. The historian first takes up the Peloponnesians' problems in maintaining and using their fleet. There was tremendous suspicion of Astyochos and Tissaphernes. Astyochos had kept the fleet inactive, despite the Peloponnesians' numerical advantage over the Athenians and their risk of wasting away (διατρίβειν—here, "being expended") awaiting the arrival of the King's fleet, whose existence, Thucydides continues to imply, was illusory. Meanwhile Tissaphernes was paying them erratically and thus harming their navy. They thought that they must attempt a naval battle soon and not delay anymore. Thucydides comments that the Syracusans were particularly zealous in pushing this (8.78), making the implicit point that it is still non-Spartans who need to push the Spartans into naval action. They put out from Miletos with 110 ships and sailed to Samos, but the Athenians had received advance warning and refused to engage the Spartan fleet because of their numerical disadvantage: they had only 82 ships and were awaiting reinforcements. The Spartan fleet encamped at Mykale and intended to sail against Samos the following day but when they learned that the Athenian side had received reinforcements, they imme-

128. Cf. also 2.13.3–9; 6.8.2; 8.45, 76.6, 82.1, and below.

diately sailed back to Miletos. The Athenians, now fortified to a total of 108 ships, sailed against Miletos but returned to Samos when no one came out to meet them.

This sequence of events, in the light of the omnipresent problems of financing and following on the description of both the Athenians' and the Peloponnesians' reflections, suggests wasted resources. Thucydides shapes the narrative to juxtapose attempts to get money for a navy with examples of the entirely ineffective use of the navy once financed, as for instance, in 8.44.4, where he emphasizes the Peloponnesians' (temporary) *periousia chrematon* with their subsequent inaction and failure to press their advantage. He develops the theme of money and expense in his *History* to show the two-headed nature of *dapane,* "expense." Depending on the context, it is indispensable to power, yet in other circumstances it can corrode if not cripple power if not put to correct use. Moreover, by also making clear the lack of *periousia chrematon* on both sides, as well as the difficulty of getting financial help from the Persians, who do possess the resources, and the use of precious resources on the kind of hunt-and-hide, start-and-stall actions that he relates in 8.78, Thucydides underlines the inadequacy of naval operations without financial power on both sides. The Athenians have squandered theirs in Sicily, and the Spartans, lacking them in the first place, are at the mercy of those who do not have them.

The point is sharpened in 8.80. Throughout book 8, the Spartans have been concerned to enlarge their fleet in order to match the Athenians. But now that they possess so many ships, they are at a loss over where to look for money for such a large number, especially given Tissaphernes' unreliability as a paymaster (8.80.1). Thucydides thus pinpoints the obvious problem: greater numbers demand greater financial resources. The Spartans have stumbled badly in failing to understand that, given their difficulties in funding a smaller navy, they will only exacerbate the problem by increasing the navy's size.[129] Like the Athenians in Sicily, they lack the judgment to recognize that size alone cannot accomplish their aims; *periousia chrematon* has to be present. In desperate need of money, the Spartans accept Pharnabazos' offer of pay (*trophe,* 8.80.1–2). Yet we are told only that Pharnabazos was "ready to provide pay," and there is no indication in the subsequent narrative that he actually did so; indeed, when Thucydides returns to the Spartans in 8.83, they are impatiently tapping their fingers waiting for *Tissaphernes* to pay them.

Meanwhile the Athenians at Samos continue to be concerned about how

129. The Athenians, however, are impressed by the mere report of the Peloponnesians' greater numbers and thus do not become involved, nor wait to see the forces; cf. Hermokrates' comment in 6.34.7 on the effect merely of hearing about numbers: "We should be reported as more numerous than we are, for men's minds are affected by things said."

to fund their fleet. Alkibiades seizes the opportunity. He knows the right button to press: "Boasting, he held out to the army such extravagant promises as these, that Tissaphernes had genuinely given him to understand that while he had anything left of his own to give, if he could trust the Athenians, they would never want for pay, not even if he had to convert his silver couch to money, and that he would bring the Phoenician fleet to the Athenians, not the Spartans" (8.81.3). The condition was Alkibiades' recall. Thucydides continues: "After hearing this and much more besides, the Athenians immediately elected him general and put all their affairs into his hands" (82.1). Thus the promise of money fuels and facilitates the trickery of Alkibiades, who dissuaded the Athenians from sailing to the Peiraieus and attacking the Four Hundred, as well as from vigorously prosecuting the war with Sparta.

As in 8.76, where the Athenians encouraged themselves with financial arguments, "among other things," in this passage too Thucydides has chosen to present the part of the *logos* that focuses on money and finances, and he makes clear that he is doing so by explicitly including the phrase "much more besides." By isolating and showcasing the issue of money, he not only continues to develop his historiographical agenda and to keep the theme before the reader but also allows not a little irony to emerge. The Athenians are represented in an important respect as more gullible than the Spartans about the reality of Persian money. Unlike the Spartans and the reader, they are apparently unaware of Tissaphernes' utter unreliability and are willing to be fooled because of their desire and need for money, whereas the Spartans are coming to recognize it but are so desperate they continue to hold out hope that the satrap will come through and have apparently abandoned their expectation of acquiring ample funds from Greeks.[130] Such gullibility about money recalls the Athenians in Egesta who were shown glittering precious metal objects instead of money (6.46), an allusion enhanced by the reference to Tissaphernes' silver couch. The point should have sparked concern about the overall financial resources at Tissaphernes' ready disposal, just as the Athenians should have been suspicious of being shown only silver dedications at Eryx and fancy cups in private houses.

When Thucydides returns to the Spartan side, he concentrates on their financial difficulties. The narrative is surprising in one respect, since they are in the midst of complaining about Tissaphernes; when Thucydides last treated the Spartans, they had accepted Pharnabazos' offer. They had heard of Alkibiades' recall and, already distrusting Tissaphernes, their disgust at his treatment of them only increased as he became even slacker about his

130. As mentioned in chap. 2, p. 92, Herodotos' comment on the greater gullibility of the Athenians as compared with that of the Spartans (5.97.2) is apposite.

payments. Thucydides relates how the soldiery and even some of the more notable Spartans began to calculate how they had never received their pay in full (*misthon entele*); that what they did receive was small in quantity and not even regular; and unless they fought a decisive naval battle or went to some place where they could find *trophe,* the men would desert the ships. They held Astyochos responsible for their crisis, on the grounds that he had been humoring Tissaphernes for his own private gain (8.83.3). Some of the sailors even tried to attack Astyochos after demanding pay (*misthon*) and being threatened by him (8.84.2).

Thus the issue of pay spawns a threat of violence and contributes greatly to the sense that the situation is unraveling. Indeed, the presentation of the Spartans parallels in an important respect the linkage between money and violence that Thucydides developed in his account of the origins of the revolutionary coup in Athens: the lack of money in the military sphere leads to violence, which itself parallels the destructive effect of the misuse of money in the Sicilian narrative.

The presentation of the Spartans in this narrative is also noteworthy. Only now do the fact and the consequence of Tissaphernes' irregular and incomplete payments to the fleet appear to sink in. As Thucydides puts it, they "began to calculate" (ἀνελογίζοντο, 8.83.3)—something they should have done long before; in addition, their fear that without regular pay the sailors would desert is deeply ironic in light of the rationale for irregular payment that Alkibiades instructed Tissaphernes to give to the Peloponnesians (8.45)—namely, that it would *prevent* desertions.

In the midst of the considerable discontent surrounding Astyochos and Tissaphernes, the Spartan Mindaros arrived to succeed Astyochos, who was now sent home. He was accompanied by Hermokrates, among others, who intended to accuse Tissaphernes of joining with Alkibiades to harm the Peloponnesians and of playing a double game (8.85.2). But Thucydides makes a point of adding that Hermokrates was Tissaphernes' enemy over the issue of back pay, commenting that after Hermokrates had been exiled from Syracuse, Tissaphernes kept making accusations against him, including the charge that Hermokrates had once asked for money from Tissaphernes and then spread it around that he was his enemy for failing to provide it (8.85.3). Westlake notes the unusual anecdotal nature of this passage.[131] Whether the anecdote is proleptic because Hermokrates could not yet have been exiled, or correctly placed chronologically,[132] its very presence is revealing. Thucydides inserts into the narrative a story that concerns Her-

131. Westlake 1969, 193–94 at n. 38; 1989, 173, 179 n. 32.

132. For the controversy, see Westlake 1969, 193–94 n. 38 (proleptic) and Andrewes, *HCT* 5, ad loc. (not proleptic). For our purposes the issue is not crucial.

mokrates and money, and recalls 8.29.[133] One effect is to keep alive the theme of the role of money in disagreements and behavior during this stage of the war.

Thucydides continues the alternation and juxtaposition of Spartan and Athenian affairs by interweaving the theme of money as he switches briefly to Samos, where envoys of the Four Hundred have arrived to talk to the soldiers and ease their minds. The war might have ended soon after had Alkibiades not been able to dissuade the Athenians on Samos from sailing to the Peiraieus, leaving Ionia and the Hellespont able to revolt; indeed, Thucydides asserts that "no one else could have persuaded the fleet," an extraordinary testament not only to Alkibiades' influence (8.86.5) but also to his inherent dangerousness. At the same time he called for the dissolution of the Four Hundred and accepted the idea of the Five Thousand, but also wanted the Council of Five Hundred to be reinstated. And he praised any efforts to cut back spending in the interests of economizing so that the soldiery might better be able to be paid (86.6). Thus the historian keeps before the reader the issue of pay as a fundamental part of the political crisis, an argument for support or resistance, depending on the outcome.

TISSAPHERNES' MOTIVES (8.87)

Thucydides returns to the Spartans in a unique chapter that focuses on interpretations of Tissaphernes' behavior. Tissaphernes realized the extent of the Spartans' discontent with him and their (unfounded) concern that he now favored the Athenians. Thucydides recounts what he did next: "Wishing, so it certainly seemed, to acquit himself of the charges against him, he prepared to get the King's fleet at Aspendos and invited Lichas to accompany him; meanwhile he left Tamos in charge of providing pay for the men in his absence" (8.87.1). In other words, Thucydides puts Tissaphernes' actions immediately in the negative context of an attempt simply to get back in the Spartans' good graces (and thereby the Persian King's). But the clause "so it certainly seemed" (ὡς ἐδόκει δή) reflects not Thucydides' own opinion —for he would have written δόκει, not used the imperfect—but that of others at the time.[134] His own views about Tissaphernes emerge as he continues:

> Reports differ, making it difficult to know with what intention he went to Aspendos and did not bring the fleet after all. That 147 Phoenician ships came

133. See above, pp. 253–55.

134. Lateiner (1976, 270) remarks: "Thucydides hedges this assertion of motive with an ironic—or desperate—'so, at least, it seemed (87.1).'" It certainly carries irony (so Tucker; Denniston 1934, 236). Cf. Westlake 1989, 178 n. 17: "The phrase ὡς ἐδόκει δή does not denote uncertainty on the part of Thucydides, as some editors and translators have imagined. It is correctly interpreted by Tucker, n. *ad loc*, 'as he would have them believe.'"

> as far as Aspendos is clear enough, but why they did not come beyond is a matter of much conjecture. Some say that he went away in order to waste the resources of the Peloponnesians, which was part of his plan—the evidence being that Tamos was not a better but a worse paymaster than Tissaphernes. Others think that he meant to exact money from the Phoenicians for their discharge, the idea being that he never intended to use them. But still others claim that it was because of the outcry at Sparta, so that it could be said that he was not to blame, because he had clearly gone to get ships actually manned. To me, however, it seems most likely that he did not bring the fleet because he wanted to wear out and bring to a halt the Peloponnesian fleet, that is, to cripple them further by the time he spent going to Aspendos and delaying there, and to make the enemy fleets more equal by not making either side stronger than the other. For if he had really wanted to, he could have ended the war, at least if we suppose that the appearance of the fleet was not at all doubtful. If he had brought it up, he would have very probably given the Lakedaimonians the victory, whose fleet, even as it was, was more equal than inferior to the Athenians'. But what especially reveals him in the act [of lying] is the excuse he gave for not bringing up the ships: he claimed that the ships that were gathered there were fewer than the King had ordered. But surely he would have gained even greater credit by spending little of the King's money and accomplishing the same purpose at lesser cost. In any case, whatever his intention, he went to Aspendos and came to the Phoenicians; and at his instructions the Peloponnesians sent a Lakedaimonian named Philip with two triremes to fetch the ships. (8.87.2–6)

This passage is one of the most intriguing in the *History* and not surprisingly has received considerable attention.[135] As Andrewes points out, "it is rare for Thucydides to refer in any detail to the difficulties he had in gathering information (vii.44.1n.); here however the next sentence shows that he was in no doubt about the facts, only about the interpretation."[136] The passage is not only almost Herodotean in its inclusion of variant versions side by side, concluding with the author's own judgment; its greatest value lies in the unparalleled insight it provides into Thucydides' mind and interests, because Thucydides is explicit—for once—about his views and interpretation, and we see firsthand how he is thinking and what kinds of deductions he makes. That he lets us into his thoughts in this way in a context that features money and financing above all is especially revealing.

Consider the language Thucydides uses and the elaboration with which he supports his opinion. First, he comments that Tissaphernes "most clearly,

135. E.g., Lateiner 1976; Patwell 1978. For objections to Thucydides' sole emphasis on one interpretation, see Hatzfeld 1951, 251–53; Lewis 1958, adducing contemporary Egyptian evidence of a revolt occurring at the same time, which diverted Tissaphernes' fleet from the Ionian War. It should be noted that Lewis leaves open the question of Tissaphernes' intentions vis à vis the Ionian War.

136. *HCT* 5: 289–90.

it seems to me" (ἐμοὶ μέντοι δοκεῖ σαφέστατον εἶναι), did not bring up the fleet in order to waste away (διατριβῆς ἕνεκα) and paralyze the Hellenic fleets. Then he finds it necessary to explain what he means: "That is, by causing their destruction (φθορᾶς) during the time that he was away and delayed, and keeping them equal, by not making one side stronger" (87.4).[137] The last element in the elaboration reminds the reader that Tissaphernes is following the strategy of Alkibiades. The vocabulary in the first part is especially illuminating, for the word for "destruction," φθορά, is the very word used in the economic digression preceding the massacre of Mykalessos with reference to the Athenians' wealth and itself has a medical resonance through which Thucydides connected money and disease.[138] What Thucydides is referring to through the use of and linkage between διατριβή and φθορά is above all a financial situation: the wasting away is literally a "spending down," since the destruction comes as a result of the lack of funds to operate the navy. Tissaphernes intended, in Thucydides' view, to make the Peloponnesians spend money on a fleet at rest. Moreover, here he also states explicitly an argument and theme that is implicit earlier in book 8: namely, that resources, hard acquired and without *periousia chrematon* behind their expenditure, have been greatly wasted by inaction. Thus, through the use of rare, carefully placed vocabulary, as in the case of φθορά earlier, Thucydides illuminates negatively the now-paradoxical relationship between spending and power that pervades the last books of the *History:* spending can actually corrode power; the medical resonance of φθορά neatly captures the sense of a debilitating disease that gradually eats away naval strength.

Let us move on to Thucydides' deductive trump card: "What especially reveals him in the act of lying (καταφωρᾷ) was his reason for not bringing up the fleet. For he said that it was smaller than what the King had ordered. But he surely would have earned still greater credit with the King than otherwise had he spent little of the King's money (οὔτ' ἀναλώσας πολλὰ τῶν βασιλέως) and accomplished his aims for less" (8.87.5). There is no better window into Thucydides' interest in money and financing and the linkage between money and naval power than this statement. It reveals his own view that *(a)* bigger is not necessarily better—especially if the fleet could not be financed properly; and *(b)* it is important to conserve, not waste, resources, a remarkable argument, since it is expressed as a concern of the Persian

137. The sentence is grammatically difficult, but there is no justification for Schwartz's proposal to delete the entire clause; cf. Classen-Steup ad loc.; Andrewes, *HCT* 5, ad loc. The complexity reflects the desire to provide exegesis and elaboration, which often results in a complexity of construction.

138. 7.27.3; cf. 2.47.3. As I noted in chap. 3, p. 131, Thucydides unusually applies the word to inanimate destruction. Thucydides uses the word only in these three instances.

King, whose riches were vast.[139] The argument fits neatly into that made implicitly from book 6 on and is conspicuous for the shift it marks from arguments in the early books of the *History* that spending more brings power, that *dapane* is good. Most of all it shows us that as Thucydides analyzes words and deeds he is above all thinking about and assessing them from the standpoint of financial considerations, in particular the nuts and bolts of financing a naval war.

A passage at the end of book 8 sheds light on Thucydides' interpretation of Tissaphernes' true motives in this section. In 8.109, the final chapter of the book as we have it, Tissaphernes has learned that Pharnabazos has finally persuaded the Peloponnesian fleet to come to him in the Hellespont, and is miffed. The reason for his irritation is that Pharnabazos "should receive the Peloponnesians and in less time and expense perhaps succeed better against Athens than he had." Thucydides continues by noting that Tissaphernes sped to the Hellespont to do damage control. The similarity between this passage and Thucydides' most damning criticism of Tissaphernes is instructive. The later passage suggests that behind Tissaphernes' earlier reaction was clearly the thought, obvious if unexpressed, that Pharnabazos would earn greater credit than he from the King for spending less money (and time) in achieving his aims, aims that were after all, as the beginning of book 8 made clear, to be accomplished in the interest of the King. This passage deepens our understanding of Thucydides' "most damning criticism" of Tissaphernes in 8.87: Tissaphernes must not have been telling the truth when he claimed that the King's fleet was too small and therefore unusable, since if he had used it he could have spent less of the King's money, ended the war at the same time, and upstaged his rival Pharnabazos. If we had the conclusion of book 8, we might well find an even more elegant closure: the book begins with Tissaphernes and Pharnabazos competing for Spartan support for their cause, and as the book (as we have it) ends we find the two featured again in a final phase of their rivalry, in which the payment of money is featured.

THE FINAL PHASE

Up to this point it should be apparent that, far from being disjointed, the narrative possesses a certain rhythm. Thucydides alternates between examples and demonstrations of Athenian and Spartan attempts and failures in financing their respective sides, giving the sense that both sides were

139. It is also an especially interesting comment in light of the argument, implicitly developed in the Sicilian narrative, that the Athenians, given the numbers on the campaign, should have spent more money. Cf. 8.45, where Thucydides presents Alkibiades' arguments along similar lines.

on the verge of being crippled at sea, almost entirely because of a lack of funds.[140] The rhythm breaks in the remaining narrative, for two reasons: first, Thucydides now treats the revolution of the Four Hundred in greater detail; and, second, when he returns to the events in the eastern Aegean, military action intensifies. In some respects the narrative thus far is similar to the narrative of the final stages of the Archidamian War. There, too, the historian alternated between the responses of the respective sides, naval and land, and the conflict was brought to an end only by the Peace of Nikias. To this point in book 8 the prevailing impression of events has been stalemate, which, as Thucydides has constructed his narrative, has come about mainly because of the absence of *periousia chrematon,* and the inability of the Spartans to know what to do with a navy.[141] But Thucydides has also stressed implicitly the gradual weakness of Athens as a divided city and the effects of the revolution of the Four Hundred on its power. Now, in 8.89–90 he pays closer attention to the political situation in Athens under the coup, in the midst of which the revolt of Euboia occurs. By setting the island's revolt against the narrative of events in the eastern Aegean as well as the revolution in Athens, Thucydides constructs the narrative to diminish the Spartans' first spectacular success.

On the Euboians' invitation, forty-two ships, including some from Sicily and Italy, arrived from the Peloponnese and effected the revolt of the island before the Athenians, who had been misinformed about the ships' destination, could sail against them (8.91). The success of the revolt was clearly due partly to the fact that the Athenians were in the midst of a violent coup; one impact on the reader of the account of the fractured and disturbed state of Athens is to diminish the Spartans' role. At the same time, however, it is difficult not to contrast the Spartans' achievement in this arena with that in the eastern Aegean, where they had expected to have the greatest success with the help of Persian financing. This episode, then, serves to highlight by contrast the problems, addressed above, that the Spartans had in maintaining and using their navy in the Ionian war.

Not that Thucydides is now praising the Spartans, as he makes clear in a lengthy discussion of the situation following the revolt. He comments on the reception of the news in Athens: "When the Athenians heard the news about what had happened to Euboia, the response was the greatest panic ever in the course of the war (ἔκπληξις μεγίστη δὴ τῶν πρὶν παρέστη).

140. I say "almost entirely" because he has also stressed the inability of both sides to act when they could have.

141. Cf., on the opening stage of the Ionian War, Westlake (1989, 130), who stresses other factors inhibiting the Spartans: e.g., difficulties of communication, of determining the enemy's position, and foul weather.

Not even the disaster in Sicily, although it seemed to be so severe at the time, nor any other had so thrown them into such a state of fright" (ἐφόβησεν, 8.96.1). Thucydides elaborates on the concurrence of a variety of debilitating factors—the camp in Samos in revolt, the lack of ships and men, discord among themselves about to erupt, and on top of that the loss of Euboia. The Athenians' immediate concern, according to Thucydides, was that the Spartans might sail into the Peiraieus, and they would have no ships with which to defend the city. He continues: "This might easily have happened if the Spartans had been a little more courageous." He then lists the rewards that would have come to them, including the entire Athenian empire (96.4) and remarks: "But this was not the first time that the Spartans had shown that they were the most convenient people by far to be at war with; they had demonstrated this on numerous earlier occasions. The great difference between their respective characters, the Athenians who were quick in contrast to the Spartans who were slow, the enterprise of the former and the lack of daring of the latter, proved to be most helpful, especially for a naval empire like Athens. This is demonstrated by the Syracusans, who were most like the Athenians and most successful in combating them" (96.5).

This scathing judgment, a highly compressed version of the Corinthians' fuller portrait of the contrast in book 1 (1.68–71), is meant to emphasize that the Athenians were not facing a worthy opponent, and it implies that if the Athenians had not made so many mistakes and errors of judgment—nor been ruled by emotion—they could easily have beaten the Spartans at sea (cf. 2.65.11); thus the commentary implicitly censures the Athenians as well. Thucydides' disgust is almost palpable. In a sense, the Athenians were being beaten by themselves, since they had divided and decentralized themselves and their financial resources allowed a violent coup, and were as gullible from hope of money now as they were in 415 when they sailed to Sicily. Insult is added to injury when Thucydides moves back to the eastern arena, picking up the thread where he left off, with the Spartans' inability to get money (*trophe*) from Tissaphernes (8.99), a pointed reminder of Spartan sluggishness and inadequacy.

Thus Thucydides emphasizes that the Spartans in the eastern Aegean were back where they had been throughout almost the entire narrative: they are in need of money, still expecting and not receiving pay (*trophe*) from Tissaphernes' agents, still vainly awaiting the Phoenician fleet. Meanwhile Pharnabazos invited them to come to the Hellespont, eager to get their fleet and cause the revolts of subject cities of Athens in his region, just like Tissaphernes. Mindaros finally yielded to his appeals (8.99). This information is odd given that we had been informed in 8.80 of the Spartans' previous response to his invitation, when they sent forty ships to him, though only ten actually arrived. Financial details punctuate this final stage of the narrative infrequently; curiously, at first glance the relative absence of financial details coincides with the escalation of naval activity on both Spartan and Athenian sides, as Mindaros and the Peloponnesians set out from Miletos toward the Hellespont.

Thucydides does make a point of mentioning that before it continued on its way, the Peloponnesian fleet, which had put in at Chios, received provisions (ἐπισιτισάμενοι) for two days, and "τρεῖς τεσσαρακοσταί for each man" from the Chians, and then sailed out (8.101.1). What the standard of the "three fortieths" is is not absolutely certain, but it is now generally agreed that it is a reference to coinage,[142] and, according to the most persuasive estimate it is likely a modest amount.[143] As Andrewes explains, "Mindaros needed only to tide over till he could receive his subsidies from Pharnabazos."[144] Yet the point of Thucydides' inclusion of this piece of information may be rather to suggest its paltriness, given his emphasis on the Spartans' inability either to recognize or obtain the level of money necessary not merely for short-term survival but for longer-term naval success. We thus follow the Spartans on their journey to the Hellespont, eking out pay and, given the narrative emphasis on the unreliability of Persian financial support, wondering whether Pharnabazos will be any more forthcoming than Tissaphernes.

The Athenians under Thrasyllos and Thrasyboulos made their way to the Hellespont as well and fought a major sea battle off Kynossema, in which, despite the Peloponnesians' numerical advantage—eighty-six ships to the Athenians' seventy-six—the Athenians gain a decisive victory (8.104); the specific numbers underscore that the Peloponnesian force's increased size would not necessarily bring success. Following their victory, the Athenians recovered Kyzikos, which had been in revolt, and "levied money" (χρήματα ἀνέπραξαν, 8.107.1). Then Thucydides writes that Alkibiades returned to Samos from Kaunos and Phaselis and levied a great deal of money from the Halikarnassians (πολλὰ χρήματα ἐξέπραξε, 8.108.2). It is worthy of note that Thucydides does not give precise figures for the levies; did he not know how much was collected? In any case, an important effect of this information, following so soon after mention of the small sum of money that the

142. For discussion see Andrewes, *HCT* 5, ad loc.

143. Thompson (1971a, 323) calculated an equivalence of approximately 26 talents, but on the basis of the most comprehensive survey of Chian coinage, Hardwick (1996) has argued persuasively that the amount was significantly less, under 4.5 talents. He proposes that the Chian silver stater of 2.6 g is 1/40 of a Persian gold daric (64–65). To determine how many days' pay for each sailor there would have been he assumes a normal pay of 3 obols beginning in 413 (down from 1 drachma); while this is not at all certain, nevertheless the amount would have covered only the short term.

144. *HCT* 5, on 8.101.1.

Spartans obtained, is to contrast Athenian success in naval financing with Spartan inadequacy.

Tissaphernes now comes back into the picture, learns that the Peloponnesians are with Pharnabazos, and heads for the Hellespont (8.109). Here, book 8 ends. As mentioned above, there are two conspicuous features of these final chapters of the book. One is the increase in naval activity, which stands in sharp contrast to the sense of inactivity, the delaying, and the cat-and-mouse episodes between Athens and Sparta that characterize most of the book. The other is the curious reduction in financial details. There is reason to correlate these features, for it is apparent from the examination above that Thucydides is most of all interested in documenting the problems of financing and their consequences. Once the fleets are actively engaged he reduces his attention to this theme, because money is no longer the central problem in the war's prosecution. As I suggested above, it is tempting to speculate that book 8 might have ended with a description of Tissaphernes' appearance along with Pharnabazos and the Spartans at the Hellespont, forming a ring with the beginning of book 8, where Thucydides describes the—as it turns out—momentous event of the Persian envoys' visit to Sparta offering money in return for their support. But even without such an episode, 8.109 heightens the lessons and ironies of the book as it has unfolded, as Thucydides has meticulously detailed the consequences of a lack of *periousia chrematon,* presenting the Spartans as literally and emphatically at sea when it comes to knowing how to obtain and then use money in naval war, and portraying the Athenians as having poorly learned the lesson of Sicily when they once again create a divided and hence weakened city and display the same gullibility as before about offers of money, with equally momentous effects.

CONCLUSIONS AND SPECULATIONS

Both the Athenians and the Spartans were impeded in the Ionian war by a lack of money, and by a failure to press any advantages when money does not (temporarily) seem to be the chief problem. The problem of money, then, is twofold: its absence causes obvious difficulties, but when it is present, neither side effectively exploits it. To draw attention once again to the connection between the breakdown of power and a lack of funds and the issue of size in relation to money, Thucydides highlights the unsatisfactory nature of ad hoc financing over the years 412–411, with the graphic illustration of the perils of relying on Persia for financial support. This narrative scheme has been characteristic of book 8 in general, and the nature of the narrative as it concerns financing demonstrates unequivocally that Thucydides had been continually asking his informants about the financial element of the war at this stage. One important indicator of his intense interest in the financing of the war is, as we saw above in the case of 8.87, his authorial intervention in the narrative in precisely those parts of the *History* where he is focusing on money and finances; another is his privileging of financial issues when relating indirect speeches, and explicitly letting the reader know that that is what he is doing through variations on the formula "among other things they said."

As we have seen, book 8 has a close thematic connection with the account of the Sicilian expedition, with its emphasis on the link between money and passion, and money and *gnome,* and the continued underlay of Herodotos' account of the Ionian revolt as well as the Persian Wars. Book 8, intriguingly, provides a fitting conclusion to the *History* as a whole.[145] It forms a rather elegant closing frame to the opening of the *History* if we consider the relationship from the standpoint of the dovetailing purposes to which the theme of money is put.[146] Beginning in the Archaeology in book 1, Thucydides lays out systematically and thoroughly the lesson or argument that naval *dunamis* is predicated on *periousia chrematon.* The Athenians' power was so great and its potential unlimited precisely because they built up a financial surplus, not merely money for the short term.[147] Thucydides also emphasizes the importance of unity, revealing his understanding of its crucial role partly through negative statements about the lack of power that comes from its absence in the Archaeology. Equally systematically and thoroughly, in book 8 Thucydides lays out the counterlesson, showing in detail what happens to power without *periousia chrematon.* Characteristically, he complicates the analysis by putting other factors into the mix: the breakdown of unity through internal discord and the consequent weakening of power, as well as the ignorance and sluggishness of the Spartans.

It is far-fetched to believe that Thucydides did not intend to write a history of the entire war.[148] The arguments presented above, about the way in which book 8 complements book 1, and marks a fitting culmination of the decline of power through the lack of *periousia chrematon,* help us to see the intensely organic narrative connections that make of what we have an intellectually coherent whole. Another aspect of the end of the book is also suggestive as a powerful element of at least intellectual closure. Book 8 may well

145. See Dewald 1975, 199: "Book viii . . . most fully demonstrates in action the proud claim of i.1.2: κίνησις γὰρ αὕτη μεγίστη δὴ τοῖς Ἕλλησιν ἐγένετο καὶ μέρει τινὶ τῶν βαρβάρων, ὡς δὲ εἰπεῖν καὶ ἐπὶ πλεῖστον ἀνθρώπων."

146. By a frame I mean not a rigid structural kind of composition but one structurally loose but framing the work thematically.

147. The argument culminates in 2.65.13.

148. As does Konishi 1987. See the variants of Wettergreen (1980) and Munn (2000, 323–27), both of whom argue, for different reasons, that Thucydides intended to end where he did.

have ended (shortly after it breaks off) with an episode featuring Tissaphernes, Pharnabazos, and the Spartans at the Hellespont—an elegant frame to the opening of the book, where the narrative focuses on the Persian envoys' visit to Sparta. It is suggestive that book 8 ends at the Hellespont, and that places like Abydos, Sestos, and Elaious, with its sanctuary of Protesilaos—the very places that are prominent at the end of Herodotos' *History*—are featured in the narrative.[149] Both works close with action at the Hellespont. In Herodotos, the Athenians besiege Sestos, but Herodotos pauses to tell the story of Artayktes' removal of the property of Protesilaos from Elaious to Sestos.[150] In Thucydides, the Athenians are the besieged at Elaious, and Thucydides bothers to mention that one Athenian ship was captured near the sanctuary of Protesilaos (8.102.3). Is this merely a fascinating coincidence? Thucydides, of course, mentions these places because in fact the war had moved to them; yet given the intertextual play with Herodotos embedded in these last books of the *History,* there may be a final intentional mapping onto Herodotos, as well as to Homer and the Trojan War—especially if one considers the unnecessary nature of the reference to Protesilaos and the minor detail of the one captured ship.

Looking at the end of book 8 in this light enhances irony and meaning. If Thucydides was evoking Herodotos' account of the end of the Persian Wars in writing about events that led to the downfall of Athens, it shows that one contemporary at least read Herodotos' Persian Wars as a warning to Athens. Moreover, when read against Herodotos' narrative, the end of book 8 rings ironically as yet another reversal: the Spartans are in the position the Athenians were in in 479, while the Athenians are in the earlier position of the Persians. But might it also look ahead ironically to Sparta's future? At the end of the Persian Wars, after the fleet of the Hellenic League had sailed to Abydos and discovered that the bridges the Persians had used to cross the Hellespont had already been destroyed, the Spartans refused to remain with the Athenians and the Ionians in the Hellenic League to besiege Sestos, desiring to return home and be rid of the naval war in Asia (9.114.1). Now in 412, the Spartans have finally, for the first time, moved to the Hellespont and are eager, like the Athenians of 479, to remain in the area and fight. One outcome of this war, whose conclusion was decided at the Hellespont with the battle of Aigospotamoi, followed by the movement of the fleet to Athens (which mirrors in reverse the movement of the Greek fleet in 479 from Athens to the Hellespont via Mykale), was Sparta's attempt to become the new Athens. If Thucydides lived into the mid-390s,[151] he would have

149. The parallel is cited by Hornblower 1996, 145. On the ending of Herodotos and the ambivalences built into the endings of works of narrative histories, see Dewald 1997.

150. See Boedeker 1988 on the significance of this episode for Herodotos.

151. Pouilloux and Salviat 1983.

seen enough to arrive at this conclusion. He may have decided to complete book 8 in such a way as to echo Herodotos, in order to foretell and foreshadow the outcome, illustrating yet again his view of the historical process and the utility of history, expressed in book 1 (1.22.4).

It is not only the ending, but also the ways in which Thucydides treats the subject of money in his work, perhaps especially in book 8, that reveal the extent to which money, for him, is a crucial factor in history itself. To expand his own formulation in 1.22.4, all historical events will be found to share (among other things) the following factor: success or failure as a city depends on how effectively financial reserves are used (presupposing their accumulation and replenishment). The Sicilian expedition offered a prime example of the failure of proper and sufficient use; the analysis in book 8 demonstrates the consequences of misuse. The treatment in book 8 also shows how acutely interested Thucydides was in the minute details of naval financing, as well as revealing the extent of his own knowledge about naval financing. This is not surprising, given that he commanded a fleet himself for at least one year,[152] but it is important to bear in mind, for in this case, the biographical information enhances our understanding of the significance he attributes to money in his *History,* and helps our assessment of the quality and importance of the information he supplies, as well as of the interpretation.[153]

152. 424/3 (Thuc. 4.104.4). His knowledge about money and his attitudes about its value and use were surely enhanced by his mining concessions in Thrace, which he also finds it important to mention (4.105). These rare autobiographical details can be read as establishing his credentials, in a sense, to write about money as he does. On these passages, see also *Money,* 174–75.

153. Moreover, it is an important corrective to the commonly held view that financial acumen among the city's elite was a phenomenon that had to await the fourth century.

CONCLUSION

Method, Theme, and the Historical Process

"Plainly," observes Colin Macleod, " . . . Thucydides meant to impress and to move his readers, but he does so because it is his considered opinion that the Peloponnesian War really was the greatest and most terrible of all time. Thus the rhetorical emphasis is a proper part of his historical apparatus; it simply brings out what the facts were, for 'the facts' are felt and endured and enacted experiences."[1] Intended as an explanation of the historian's use of superlatives to describe the subject of his *History,* Macleod's observations also apply more broadly to Thucydides' aim and methods in approaching his subject generally. They help specifically to illuminate his treatment of the role of money in Athenian political life, and attitudes toward money, as they relate to the *arche* and the war, and to the practical issue of financing navies on both sides at the beginning of the final stage of the war.

Thucydides employs a variety of methods to develop and illuminate the themes of money and war financing and to relate them to broader issues and themes in the work. Among his strategies, temporal displacement, anticipation, negative presentation, anecdote, metaphor, intertextuality, and, in book 8, the frequent, exclusive concentration on financial issues in reporting indirect speeches, which privileges the theme of financing, not only serve to maintain the reader's attention on the financial aspect of the war but also are designed to guide the reader to draw conclusions about the proper and improper uses of money in a military context and to understand the larger meaning of events. At the same time, such methods elegantly highlight irony and ambiguity, which form an essential part of Thucydides' approach to the themes of money and finance.

1. Macleod 1983, 141.

The aim of engaging the reader as closely as possible in the issues of the meaning of history, the relationship of contemporary events to past events, and of the particular to the general, explains the extraordinary multiple layering in the text and the historian's diverse narrative approaches. Metaphor and intertextuality are especially useful historiographical tools with which to insinuate multiple meanings into the text, hallmarks, above all, of his fondness for the implicit method of making arguments and encouraging interpretations.[2]

One argument of this examination was the importance to Thucydides of Herodotos and Homer in illuminating the Sicilian expedition and its aftermath. These texts serve a crucial function in Thucydides' view of the historical process. He embeds accounts of earlier events, such as the Ionian revolt, in his text, to encourage the reader to think about comparisons and contrasts both on a broad, structural level and through focusing on particular individuals and their roles. One has only to recall Thucydides' programmatic statement in 1.22.4. He does not leave it to the reader to wait and see if the utility he ascribes to his *History* is actually borne out by later events; he sets out to prove it and show its truth within the *History*. Intertextuality, then, is evidence of a fundamental kind. It is a method of showing that the facts and events are not just "enacted experiences," as Macleod puts it, but re-enacted experiences.

Yet Thucydides does not employ Herodotos and Homer in a slavish or derivative way to make the point that a history repeats itself. Rather, he consistently has a variant take, a contrast, a different emphasis, that demonstrates similarity (given human nature), not uniformity of experience. Within general patterns, in which individuals act—for example, the Ionian revolt and the Sicilian expedition—there are also important differences of detail and the intrusion of additional factors in his analysis.[3]

THE THEME OF MONEY IN THE *HISTORY* AS A WHOLE

From a broader narrative standpoint, the pervasiveness of the theme of money and financing, and the contrasts between Thucydides' treatment of money in roughly the first half of the *History* and in books 6 through 8, relate intriguingly to Dewald's demonstration that books 6 through 8 have not only a fundamentally different narrative arrangement from books 2 through

2. See Strasburger 1966: Thucydides' "geübten Technik, durch literarische Komposition geschichtliche Sinndeutung ohne Wörte sichtbar zu machen." This purpose is related to Thucydides' narrative methods designed to illuminate differing perspectives and choices, well brought out by Rood 1998.

3. A good example is the greater criticism of the collective Athenians in being fooled by the Egestans in Thucydides than Maiandrios in the story of Oroites and Polykrates in Herodotos; see above, chap. 1, p. 75.

5.24 but also a shared narrative structure. In Dewald's words, "the whole account has become a single, unified development, and all actions are described as part of that development"; she notes further that "Thucydides has in a sense made the entire narrative in these books into a single unit."[4]

This investigation complements Dewald's thesis in suggesting a close interrelationship between narrative and thematic organization. Thucydides' approach in these books helps the reader focus on the larger picture and see the relationship between particular passages and items of information, and thus the broader consequences of, for example, the privileging and misreading of display and the insidious combination of the passions and money. It further enables the reader to adopt a highly critical stance toward the ability of the city's leaders and generals to exercise *gnome* in the use of the city's resources in military engagements. One conclusion Thucydides makes patent is that money is not everything; at issue ultimately is its proper use.

Books 6 through 8 have a character all their own, but they also have a close thematic relation to the early books of the *History*. A survey of the broader narrative and thematic structure of the last three books shows that in the context of military finance Thucydides combines money with different factors to show in what circumstances it will have a particular consequence. With the exception of the very beginning of book 8, where the assessment of the Athenians' ability to use what financial resources they have to rebuild naval power has a slightly positive cast,[5] the combinations of money with other factors are fundamentally negative. Thucydides demonstrates what happens when money is combined with an emphasis on display and appearance, with passion, without *gnome,* and with the absence of *periousia chrematon.*[6] The earlier parts of the *History,* especially the first two books, reveal positive corollaries to these negative combinations.[7] Thus in the first half of the *History periousia chrematon* and naval power and *periousia chrematon* and *gnome* are positive groupings. The early books also highlight the absence of passion or, alternatively, portray passion as a positive force to be harnessed for power, they also emphasize the use, rather than the display, of money.[8]

Thus the contrasts themselves comprise a thematic unity in the *History* as a whole, as the early part of the work serves as a foil for the final books. Thucydides' historiographical approach has two major implications for understanding his treatment of money in the public/military sphere. First, it sug-

4. Dewald 1975, 203, 204.

5. 8.1.3–8.4.

6. See esp. chaps. 1, 3, 4, and 6, above, respectively.

7. I am using the terms "positive" and "negative" not in a moral sense, but within the framework of the successful acquisition and exercise of *dunamis.* Thus even if one sees irony underlying the Funeral Oration (e.g., Flashar 1969), for example, it is the factors that contribute to military success and polis power that are important, whether or not that success and power are seen as good or bad.

8. E.g., book 1 passim; 2.13, 40.1, 43.1.

gests that underlying these groupings there is a practical and didactic function. Thucydides combines money and public finance with various factors to demonstrate the consequences of the groupings, implying that it is possible to avoid a negative result from a particular combination. Thus his treatment of money in the context of public finance is similar in nature to his treatment of the role of ignorance and knowledge in public life, as constructed in the first half of book 6 in the early narrative of the expedition and the Peisistratid digression, which not only shows the dangers of ignorance for public life but also how one sets about learning the truth, again with the suggestion that knowledge has a practical, political function.

Second, the historian's approach reveals a conception of money as something intrinsically morally neutral, an idea that runs counter to much Greek thought.[9] By inserting money in a variety of circumstances to show where it has a positive or, conversely, a pernicious and destructive value, Thucydides demonstrates that even the accumulation of vast amounts of money need not be a source of danger, but rather can be a source of success and power. Thucydides is ultimately concerned with the polis as a whole, with how the Athenians collectively acquire, use, and regard money in relation to the power of the polis. He shows how the potential for the destruction of the polis is enormous when money is an object of individual desire and when it is combined with the negative factors he lays out, including passion and the misinterpretation of objects of wealth. In demonstrating and illustrating the destructive results of the use of money in conjunction with dangerous factors, Thucydides is, significantly, focused on human life—recall how he indirectly connects money and the slaughter at Mykalessos, or how at the end of book 7, money is associated with the vast destruction of human life, part of the *panolethria* of the Sicilian expedition. Thus Thucydides explicitly shows that the misuse of money and dangerous attitudes toward it in the larger political sphere of the polis can have disastrous human consequences.

INDIVIDUALS AND HISTORICAL CAUSATION

Thucydides' arguments about incorrect uses of money and the role of individual greed and passion related to money in infecting public life shed light on a broader issue. The historian's emphasis on individuals at this stage of the war has elicited much discussion, stemming in particular from Westlake's thesis that the greater prominence accorded to individuals later in the *History* shows that Thucydides had changed his mind about historical causation as the war progressed and has done so chiefly because of Alkibiades.[10] West-

9. Cf., for example, Soph. *Ant.* 295–300; cf. also, on archaic thought about money and its dangers (as well as its blessings), Figueira 1995.

10. Westlake 1968; Hornblower 1994b, 145–46.

lake sees this as a composition issue: that is, Thucydides wrote the later books at a separate, later stage. The logical implication of this thesis is that if Thucydides had composed the early books after witnessing Alkibiades' impact on history, he would have conceived of them differently, ascribing a greater prominence to individuals. David Gribble has argued convincingly against this view. Drawing on Thucydides' analysis of leaders after Perikles, he notes that "the story of Athens after the fall of Pericles was no longer that of a unified and consistent policy directed by one man, but of individual Athenians and individual competing politicians. The increasing importance of private interests brought a plurality of individual historical actors increasingly into prominence."[11]

This study supports Gribble's critique. One has only to examine the causal factors that Thucydides sees operating in the later books and how they relate to the themes he stresses to understand that it is not the case that Thucydides changed, but rather that he wanted to illustrate and demonstrate the change of history in the post-Periklean period itself. Thucydides made the importance of individuals like Themistokles and Perikles abundantly clear early on (e.g., 1.90–93, 2.65). His emphasis increases and shifts to a negative portrayal because he wants to show how private motives intruded onto the public stage in disastrous ways—the collective (led by Perikles) no longer acts in the interest of the state; individuals act in behalf of themselves. Hence the role of their emotions, an all but inevitable corollary of an emphasis on human individuals. Thucydides reveals this not only as it relates to Alkibiades but to Nikias and to the Athenian citizenry at large—recall his emphasis on Nikias' privileging of private over public in his first speech, and the private motives of the Athenians for wanting the expedition.

This emphasis also ties into the larger causal role Thucydides ascribes to human nature, which brings us back not only to 1.22.4, but to his analysis of human behavior in stasis (especially 3.82). Thucydides' examination of both the downward spiral in human behavior and the increase in individual motivations caused by stasis and war at the expense of any allegiance to the state likewise necessitates an increased narrative emphasis on individuals. For Thucydides, understanding the importance of individual decisions and actions at this stage of the war is an important part of the meaning in history itself.

THUCYDIDES ON ATHENS' FINANCES

There is ample evidence in the *History* that Thucydides was consistently focused on both the specific, detailed level of nuts-and-bolts financing and on the more general level of policy and management. Understanding Thucyd-

11. Gribble 1999, 171.

ides' narrative methods and historiographical aims in treating the subject of money and Athenian finance is a necessary preliminary to our ability to assess both individual items of information, and his overall view of the relationship between the treasury and the war. In general, in his account of the Archidamian War, Thucydides emphasizes the Athenians' naval strength through their expenditures, though at times he suggests a collective anxiety about finances, which led the Athenians to collect emergency revenue (e.g., 3.19.1). As I argued, there is no indication that Athens' financial resources were in any direct way connected to the desire for an armistice and finally the Peace of Nikias.[12]

In his account of the Sicilian expedition, Thucydides draws attention to the wasteful destruction of money and lives but at the same time gives no hint, with the exception of his account of the consequences of the "double war" of Dekeleia and Sicily, of the dangerously low level of the treasury. Only when the city becomes divided, with accordingly divided resources, do significant problems emerge, first in the case of the two cities of Athens and Sicily, and second in that of the two cities of Athens and Samos. Finally, in his treatment of the war carried on in the wake of the Sicilian disaster, the Athenians appear at first surprisingly resilient but then, increasingly, limp along in tandem with the Spartans, who never had the financial strength and even now when they possessed a navy as large as Athens' could not pay for it and did not know what to do with it. Yet as we also saw, the only statements of desperate financial circumstances come from nonfactual contexts: reports of what Athenians believed or saw; rhetorical comments in indirect speech; significantly, never in the voice of the historian himself. Similarly, decisions to obtain more money, like the *eikoste* or the application of the "Iron Reserve," are situated in narrative contexts that suggest their emotional, not rational, impetus.

Thucydides' treatment and larger interpretation are not contradicted by other evidence; it is unfortunate, however, that we lack the end of his intended *History* to test the validity of this reading of his text, for the Athenians finally did run out of money and resorted to melting down dedications. Thucydides' argument, that the Athenians were never completely out of money and that the critical problem was their inability to know how best to get it and use it (as well as how to make other important political decisions), constitutes a development and elaboration of the argument in his account of the Archidamian War following the death of Perikles. The implication is that the Athenians had the resources to win the war if they had had a leader with *gnome* at the helm, at least until the Persians systematically funneled money into the Spartan fleet, during the last stage of the war. Thus Thu-

12. *Money*, 179–80.

cydides' narrative as a whole confirms and supports his comment in book 2, following his discussion of the aftermath of Sicily and the problems the Athenians faced, including the financing of the Spartan fleet by Cyrus: "So abundant were the resources then [in 431], based on which Perikles predicted that the city would easily prevail over the Peloponnesians alone" (2.65.13).

Finally, the attention the historian gives to the Athenians' desire for more money, and to the means by which they attempt to obtain it, combined with other evidence, suggests a fundamental transformation in the purpose of the *arche* from the standpoint of the Athenians. Power increasingly becomes a means to an economic end; the Athenians transform their system of control into an economic *arche*—a development not without irony, given the accompanying emphasis in Thucydides on the Athenians' underlying failure to know how to use their economic power properly. They attempt to generate resources that they themselves are unable to handle. It is this development, moreover, that receives implicit censure from the historian.

DISPLAY, WEALTH, AND POWER

Thucydides' treatment of money constitutes a vigorous polemic, against traditional and contemporary ideologies of the value and power of wealth, and about what kind of wealth constitutes power. His view therefore is not reactionary but revolutionary and operates on both symbolic and practical levels, which together help to explain his definition of *dunamis.*

On the symbolic level, precious metal objects, the display of wealth, private expenditure on display that is applied to a civic context, and public monuments are all both called up in the narrative and then devalued, or in some cases denied any value at all. Thucydides does not make a blanket statement, of course: his concern is above all with the military sphere; but he himself widens the lens to include the notion of polis power more generally, in order to reconfigure its meaning. Alkibiades' speech to the Athenian assembly lays out the traditional view: his private displays at Olympia enhanced the power of the city in the eyes of other Greeks (6.16.1). Spectators at the launching of the fleet marveled at the power of the city, inferred from the fleet's lavish and costly appearance of it (6.31); likewise the Athenians at Egesta inferred power from gazing at the misleading appearance of precious metal objects (6.46).

These three examples reveal Thucydides' strategy: he lets others arrive at these interpretations and then complicates them so that they become open to doubt. His emphasis on *opsis* in relation to judging power in 6.31 and 6.46, conditioned by 1.10 and the Funeral Oration, aims to undermine these traditional ways of thinking about power. The argument is simple: objects and displays are irrelevant and illusory symbols. Thus, in particular, when private wealth is on display, one learns nothing about the power of the city—

a notion that rubs against conventional and long-enduring attitudes and ideologies. Nor does one learn anything about the power of the city from examining monuments, as 1.10 makes clear. In a sense, then, Thucydides is also devaluing the importance of reputation and fame, if it is based on the display of great wealth; in this respect, there goes Homer in one stroke. Perikles speaks of the city's fame on the basis of its power, not its appearance; and the *dunamis* he is talking about comes from military action, which brought forth the *arche.* Yet in all this, Thucydides and Herodotos are on common ground—think, for example, of Croesus' misreading of his wealth.

Therefore, in denying validity to belief in a city's power on the basis of image and appearance, Thucydides also formulates a narrow conception of polis power that privileges the military realm. This brings us to the practical sphere in which his critique operates. As in the case of the symbolic level, it requires appreciation of the specific framework within which Thucydides sets the terms of discussion—namely, the military. When we move from display and expenditure for display to efficient use in the military sphere, precious metal objects occupy a fundamentally ambiguous position in relation to money in his analysis, but one in which I think his views are clear.

Such objects constitute an important form of sacred and (elite) household wealth and have transactional value as well as being a measure of value. They can be used in the military sphere—in his list of the usable wealth available to the Athenians at the beginning of the war, Perikles includes non-monetary sacred wealth (2.13.4, 5)—but they have transactional value only once they have been melted down and coined; they are too bulky for transport on the needed scale, cannot be divided, nor can they be used to pay soldiers.[13] But in Thucydides' (and Perikles') hierarchy of forms of wealth, they are at the bottom.[14] There is more to the issue than simply time, inconvenience, and loss of metal involved in coining; of concern to him is the meaning and significance of precious metal objects in a military context. In Thucydides' analysis, put polemically, they signify the absence of power: if a city is expending precious objects, then ipso facto it lacks money (coined or uncoined); if it lacks money, it lacks *dunamis.* By the end of the Peloponnesian War, the Athenians' recourse to melting down dedications is itself a sign that their *dunamis* had vanished.

Thus objects can be used in the military sphere, but their use reflects the absence of money. As the response of actors in the *History* shows, however, Thucydides' argument was neither self-evident nor widely shared. Indeed,

13. For an almost comic example, cf. 8.81.3 (Tissaphernes' silver couch).

14. Cf. the different perspective on the relationship between precious metallic wealth and coined money argued for by Kurke (1999, esp. chaps. 1 and 8) in reference to archaic poleis (and not in military contexts).

as regards the theme of money, the *History* is significant not only on account of its vigorous rejection of the traditional ideology of wealth as symbol, but because of Thucydides' configuration of a new kind of negative symbolic meaning of objects: they can express the absence of money and, accordingly, the absence, or at least uncertainty, of power.

THE UNITY AND COMPOSITION OF THE *HISTORY*

I have argued, following Dewald, that books 6 through 8 possess a character and structure all their own, and together they contrast sharply with the rest of the *History* from the perspective of Thucydides' treatment of money and finance. At the same time, however, this contrast contributes to the unity of the work as a whole, inasmuch as the later books form a neat, negative reflection of the earlier books. Moreover, within the contrasting/unifying structure, book 8 closes the *History* in a thematic ring with the opening book; books 1 (and 2 through 2.13) and 8 chart the rise and fall of power, respectively, with special emphasis on the role of *periousia chrematon*. Whether or not Thucydides would have gone on farther to deepen his analysis, by showing in a ninth book what happened to an Athens increasingly without money, I have tried here to show the profound correspondences between books 1 and 8 that give the *History* as we have it a powerful thematic unity of its own.

This conclusion may have implications for Thucydides' composition of the *History*, a topic for which I confess to have little enthusiasm, simply because of the speed with which one reaches a dead end. This examination cannot prove anything. It is tempting to suppose a late date for the early books on the basis of the close connection between the two halves of the *History* in both themes and word usage. For the most part, however, Thucydides could have written the later books to complement the themes of the earlier books; he would not have needed to know what happened to Athens in order to write about money in the way that he did in the first part of the *History*. All that can fairly be said is that one extended portion of the work influenced and helped to shape the writing of the other. There can be no doubt, however, that some parts of the Archaeology (i.e., 1.4, concerned with Minos; and 1.10–11, the Trojan analysis) were composed after the Sicilian expedition took place, though again that need not imply that Thucydides *wrote* the Sicilian narrative first. Yet one could argue alternatively that because Thucydides' subject had changed in character, so did his narrative style and presentation, as a strategy aimed at enhancing meaning and understanding (a notion with which Dewald is sympathetic).[15] In the end,

15. 1975, 204–6.

what matters most is not exactly when Thucydides wrote what and in what order, but that the results of this two-part examination of Thucydides' treatment of money in the *History* support the position of the fundamental unity of the work and perhaps go a step farther, to support the argument that book 8 connects and relates closely with not only the Sicilian narrative in books 6 and 7 but the *History* as a whole.

APPENDIX

τροφή, μισθός, and χρήματα in Book 8

In counterpoint to book 1, where he demonstrated how the presence of *periousia chrematon* creates and enables naval power, Thucydides, I argued in chapter 6, develops another aspect of the theme of financial resources in book 8—the rapid deterioration of naval strength when *periousia chrematon* is absent—and through detailed repetition of references to money and pay emphasizes the hand-to-mouth financing that characterized this stage of the war. As has already been pointed out, the sheer quantity of financial vocabulary in book 8, and in particular the striking frequency of the use of the word *trophe,* are remarkable when compared to occurrences in the rest of the work. Thucydides' narrative approach and underlying argument may help us understand better an important issue of terminology that has been the subject of controversy: namely, the usages of *trophe, misthos,* and *chremata* in the fifth century, the primary text for which is Thucydides.

The immediate question is the relationship of *trophe* to *misthos* and *chremata.* In his study of Thucydides' terminology W. K. Pritchett concluded that the historian uses the words interchangeably, thus showing that they were mere synonyms and that the distinction between pay and rations that is found in the fourth century and later did not yet exist. *Trophe* and *misthos* both refer to ration-money.[1] William T. Loomis agrees on the synonymity of *trophe* and *misthos* but reaches the opposite conclusion—namely, that the two terms refer to rations plus pay.[2] Loomis makes two main points. First, he

1. Pritchett 1971, 3–6; cf. also 23–24, 27–28, accepted by Will 1975. On the other hand, Pritchett's statement that *trophe* and *misthos* referred to a soldier's "entire monetary allowance"(4–5) seems to me somewhat ambiguous.

2. Loomis 1998, 34–36.

maintains that daily rations could be procured for less than 1 drachma, the rate of pay for sailors and soldiers at times during the Peloponnesian War (e.g., at Poteidaia, Thuc. 3.17.3; in Sicily, Thuc. 6.31.3) as well as for mercenaries (e.g., Thracian mercenaries, Thuc. 7.27.2). Second, he argues that mercenaries would have to have been enticed into service with a promise of more than mere subsistence pay. Both points are valid, though it is not clear that the second, while a reasonable assumption, is a necessary one.

The very fact that Pritchett and Loomis, while agreeing on the synonymity of *trophe* and *misthos,* arrive at opposite conclusions about their meaning, should alert us to the problematic nature of the evidence of Thucydides, and the difficulty of forcing his terminology into strict synomyms with a consistent meaning, whether "ration-money" or "full pay." For example, given that a rate of pay less than 1 drachma can be documented for military and state service,[3] then a priori 1 drachma should exceed what was merely necessary for daily food. On the other hand, we cannot be certain that the procurement of food in the field was not more expensive, requiring a higher monetary allotment.[4] At the same time, Thucydides' usage of *trophe* in 1.11 seems to provide an obstacle to Loomis' position that in Thucydides *trophe* consistently refers to daily rations plus pay, for in that passage, the analysis of the Trojan expedition, the idea that more than "money" for rations is at issue strains reason. The concern of that section of the text is clearly subsistence, since Thucydides notes that the Greeks were forced to turn to farming (and piracy) to support themselves. The logic of his argument depends on their need for food, not on a situation in which the Greeks were plundering and farming for surplus money.

Thus, as far as concerns the evidence of Thucydides, one can adduce counterarguments for each of the positions taken. In fact, there are examples in the *History* in which *trophe, misthos,* and *chremata* appear to be used synonymously, and others where the historian seems to be drawing a distinction. Book 8 provides an excellent testing ground for Thucydides' usage of these terms because the three terms appear side by side more frequently here than in any other book of the *History.* I shall examine Thucydides' usage of the terms more comprehensively below; first I would like to consider his usage in the book generally and its significance in relation to the theme and argument about finances examined in chapter 6.

That Thucydides uses *trophe* with great frequency in book 8 and hardly at all in the rest of the *History* should be an important clue to his usage. This

3. See the examples cited in Loomis 1998, 35.

4. So Pritchett 1971, 23 with reference to Poteidaia and Syracuse. Loomis' response (1998, 35) that food should have been cheaper in those cases does not seem to me to carry the necessary weight, since one could easily imagine that the market value may have increased prices given the necessity of the demand.

statistical peculiarity immediately implies that Thucydides is distinguishing *trophe* from both *misthos* and *chremata;* otherwise why hasn't he used the words interchangeably elsewhere in the narrative? Given, however, the frequency of financial vocabulary in general in book 8, we need to ask whether mere *variatio* offers an explanation. This cannot be absolutely ruled out, but there are several arguments against it. First, certain passages in book 8 make it clear that the historian has no problem repeating the same word in close proximity. The best example is 8.57, a relatively short chapter in which in the space of thirteen OCT lines Thucydides uses the word *trophe* four times. Second, if *variatio* were the key to his usage in books where there is an abundance of financial vocabulary, then it is surprising that we do not find *trophe* —or *misthos*—more frequently in books 1, 6, and 7. Finally, *trophe* occurs almost always in connection with the Spartans in Thucydides. This association is not adequately explained by the great amount of attention Thucydides pays to Spartan problems in funding their navy, for when he alludes to Athenian financial difficulties with military financing, he consistently employs other vocabulary: *misthos* or *chremata.*

SPARTA

Thucydides' use of *trophe* in the context of his account of the financing of the Peloponnesian navy provides, I suggest, an important clue to the word's meaning, for his focus on the Spartan side is deliberate, and his vocabulary has an important narrative function. Indeed, previous attempts to deduce the meaning of Thucydides' vocabulary for pay have taken references largely out of context as if they can be used as straightforward, objective facts; yet the narrative context of these passages is essential to an understanding of the historian's usage, a point that obviously applies to any piece of information he supplies in his *History.* As already argued above, one of Thucydides' aims in constructing the narrative of book 8 is to provide detail in a systematic fashion in order to highlight the Spartans' lack of *periousia chrematon* and their continued ignorance about financing a fleet (they are aware that money is intimately involved but are represented as ignorant about rates of pay, overall sums of money needed, and the consequences of expanding their fleet without proportionally greater financial resources), both of which have resulted in their scrambling for even minimal funding now that they have taken to the sea in earnest in the Ionian War. The Spartans do not have a *periousia chrematon,* indeed they have never had one, and thus they would be operating from the expectation of mere subsistence, in which the notion of receiving regular pay for rations may have been regarded as desirable enough. If there is a distinction between *trophe* and *misthos* in Thucydides' usage, this may explain the use of *trophe* in 8.5.5, where, in an attempt to bring the Spartans over to the Persians, Tissaphernes promised the

Spartans *trophe;* for if *misthos* had sounded better to them, one might have expected Thucydides to have used that word to enhance irony.[5] The Athenians, on the other hand, would have approached their lack of *periousia chrematon* from the opposite perspective. They would have been thinking in grander terms about the need for an abundance of resources. It is important to bear in mind that the Spartans had not been exposed to the idea of pay to anywhere near the extent that the Athenians had, given the role of money in Athenian domestic as well as military life; accordingly the former would arguably expect that the primary use of money in the support of manpower would be for their rations.

This difference in perspective is important background for understanding the issue of funding the Spartan navy in a historical (as opposed to historiographical) sense. But if we return to Thucydides' narrative purpose, his exaggerated use of *trophe* in connection with the Spartans has the effect of contributing to the argument that the Spartans are concerned above all with hand-to-mouth existence. It is not that there is always a clear and consistent distinction between terms—there are certainly places in the narrative where Thucydides uses *trophe* or *misthos* but could well have substituted one term for the other (e.g., 8.46.1, 5)—but rather that the concentration of occurrences of *trophe* in the discussion of Spartan financing, along with Thucydides' clear narrative aim of revealing the range of difficulties that the Spartans' lack of money was creating for them, suggests that the use of this word in preference to *misthos* is deliberate.

An interesting passage in which Thucydides does apply the term *misthos* to the Spartan side may be significant. In 8.29.1, Thucydides notes that Tissaphernes distributed a month's *trophe* to the fleet, at the rate of 1 drachma per man. Right before this distribution, the Peloponnesians had attacked Iasos, where they obtained *chremata panu polla* in booty (8.28.3). Shortly after, in 8.36.1, Thucydides refers to their financial condition as follows: "The Peloponnesian fleet was still plentifully supplied (οἱ Πελοποννήσιοι εὐπόρως ἔτι εἶχον ἅπαντα τὰ κατὰ τὸ στρατόπεδον), for sufficient (ἀρκούντως) *misthos* had been provided and the soldiers still had *megala chremata* from Iasos." It may be significant that the one occasion when Thucydides, in his own voice, refers to what the Spartans actually have received as *misthos* suggests relative abundance. Indeed, this is the one instance in the entire book in which Thucydides lets us know in the narrative that the Peloponnesian fleet had been paid in full; as argued in chapter 6, a likely reason for the inclusion of this information is to set up a contrast with the

5. At the same time, we have no way of knowing whether Thucydides knew that this was the word Tissaphernes used, but this does not weaken the point, since it also accords with Thucydides' presentation of the Spartans as not thoroughly understanding the use and quantity of money necessary for waging naval war.

Spartans' subsequent inaction in order to highlight their inability to use financial resources effectively once they obtain them.

When Thucydides refers to actual payments to the Peloponnesian side, he consistently uses *trophe* in preference to *misthos.* When he occasionally uses *misthos* in connection with the Peloponnesian side, it is in a hypothetical or prospective context in which the question of sufficient pay is at issue. Thus, for example, in 8.29.1, where Tissaphernes distributes *trophe* at the promised 1-drachma rate but then proposes a reduced rate after the first month, Thucydides relates the objections to the arrangement made by Hermokrates and then, rather strikingly, goes to the trouble of explaining why the Spartan Therimenes did not make trouble over *misthos.* Here, the issue of adequate future pay occasions the use of *misthos.* In 8.45.2 Alkibiades is instructing Tissaphernes to tell the Peloponnesians to explain the reduction in pay on the grounds that the Athenians paid their sailors only 3 obols to prevent their spending on indulgences, and also to pay the Peloponnesian crew irregularly "so that the men would not desert through the *misthos* in arrears left behind." Here again the context is a theoretical reflection, and the issue is *sufficient* pay. The passage at 8.83.2–3 is similar. Here, the Peloponnesians have heard about Alkibiades' recall and become more disgusted with Tissaphernes, who had grown slacker and slacker with the *misthodosia.* Gathering together, they begin to calculate how they have not yet received their pay in full—*misthon entele*—or regularly, and might have to go someplace where they can obtain *trophe.* Here there does seem to be a contrast between a theoretical plenty (*misthon entele*) and mere subsistence (*trophe*). Consider the slight shift in 8.78, where Thucydides writes that Astyochos kept the Peloponnesians waiting for Tissaphernes to bring in the Phoenician fleet: "But Tissaphernes not only did not bring up the fleet, but was ruining the navy by not paying *trophe* regularly or fully (*entele*)." Thucydides in his own voice is referring to the irregular and incomplete pay as *trophe,* perhaps in order to stress the insufficiency, and because *trophe* is the word he consistently uses when referring to what Tissaphernes actually provided to the Peloponnesians.

As mentioned above, there is not a neat consistency in Thucydides' use of *trophe* and *misthos,* but it is important to recognize that it is a question of choice and that the contexts in which *trophe* is preferred and the few occasions in which *misthos* does occur in passages concerning the Spartans give a decided impression that Thucydides uses *trophe* as a kind of subcategory of *misthos,* to connote mere subsistence, the sense in which he seemed to be using the term in 6.93.4, to convey the inadequacy of the Athenian reinforcement of the Sicilian expedition.[6] This term's appearance in book 6 in

6. Cf. above, chap. 2, p. 108; cf. also 6.47.

association with the Athenians raises a question: how does Thucydides use the term in reference to the Athenians in book 8?

THE ATHENIANS

In book 8 Thucydides uses *trophe* twice to refer to Athenian pay (8.81.3, 86.6), and on both occasions Alkibiades is speaking. In the first passage, Alkibiades, "making extravagant boasts, promised that Tissaphernes had assured him that if he could only trust the Athenians, they would never want for *trophe,* not even if he had to coin his silver couch." At first sight this would seem to run counter to what I have been suggesting about the lesser nature of *trophe* compared to *misthos,* since, according to Thucydides, Alkibiades is making excessive promises. Yet it may be significant that this is Thucydides writing what Alkibiades said Tissaphernes said to him; there may be irony here. The reference to Tissaphernes coining his silver couch is intended, on the one hand, to illustrate his support in extremities, but it also creates the impression that Tissaphernes may well have difficulty providing full *trophe;* thus the passage overall carries an overtone of need and inadequacy. The second passage more explicitly reflects a condition of need. Alkibiades urges the Athenians to disband the Four Hundred and institute the government of the Five Thousand, and he approves fiscal retrenchment so that the army might receive *trophe.*

Except for these two instances, Thucydides routinely uses the word *misthos* or *chremata* when referring to the Athenian side. For example, the Athenian crowd at Samos kept quiet when the question of a change to oligarchy arose out of hope for ready *misthos* from the King (8.48.3). Just before, they had been told by representatives of the Four Hundred that the King would be their friend and provide *chremata* if they changed their government (48.2). In a non-military context, the Four Hundred told the members of the Council of Five Hundred to take their *misthos* and be gone (8.69.4), and, similarly in 8.97.1, under the regime of the Four Hundred, it is set out that "no one should receive *misthos* for any office." Comparison with terminology and usage in reference to the Peloponnesians and Spartans suggests that the Athenians are more used to the idea of money beyond mere subsistence for the fleet and more used to thinking about *chremata* in general.

Although the terms do not always conform to precise distinctions, the terminology as used in book 8 (as elsewhere in the *History*) leans toward a typology in which *misthos* is a term for fuller pay than is suggested by *trophe,* and *chremata* is used in a more general, or generic, sense and can subsume both *misthos* and *trophe,* although it is often used where *trophe* or *misthos* would be inappropriate.[7] It will be useful to lay out Thucydides' usage more com-

7. 8.1.2, 1.3, 3.1, 5.3, 18.1, 28.3, 36.1, 44.2, 45.3, 45.4, 45.6, 58.6, 63.4, 65.3, 107, 108.2.

prehensively and schematically in the following tables with brief comment where appropriate. Passages appear in the left column, with comment in the right column. In some cases a passage will be relevant to both Sparta and Athens but will be listed only once.

SPARTA

8.3.1: Agis levied *chremata* . . . and compelled the Thessalians to give *chremata*.

8.5.3: Agis had the authority to levy troops and levy *chremata*.

8.5.5: Tissaphernes invited the Peloponnesians to come over and promised to provide *trophe*.

8.8.1: Kalligeitos and Timagoras did not join the [Spartan] expedition to Chios, nor did they give the *chremata* of 25 talents that they had brought for the expedition.

8.28.3: Tissaphernes and the Peloponnesians sacked Iasos, captured Amorges, and took *chremata panu polla*.

8.29.1: Tissaphernes distributed *trophe* for a month at the rate of 1 drachma a day for each man; but for the future he was intending to give them 3 obols, unless the King ordered him to give the drachma rate. On protest from the Syracusan Hermokrates (as [the Spartan] Therimenes was not nauarch he was soft on the question of *ho misthos*) Tissaphernes agreed to give five ships' worth of men more than 3 obols for each man, and gave 30 talants a month for fifty-five ships.

8.36.1: The Peloponnesian camp was still plentifully supplied, for sufficient (*arkountos*) *misthos* had been given and the soldiers still had *megala chremata* from Iasos.

8.43.4: Lichas, rejecting the treaties, invited Tissaphernes to conclude a better treaty, as the Spartans certainly would not recognize those existing and did not want any of his *trophe* upon such conditions.

8.44.1: The Peloponnesians sailed to Rhodes, thinking that they would be able to maintain (*trephein*) their fleet without asking for *chremata* from Tissaphernes

Here *chremata* does seem interchangeable with *trophe* (as implied in the verb *trephein*). On the other hand, Thucydides may have chosen *chremata* to mesh with the logical use of *chremata* to refer to the Rhodian levy; *trophe* (or *misthos*) would not have been appropriate in that connection, and he certainly wants to imply an equivalence between the money levied from the Rhodians and that from Tissaphernes.

8.44.4: They levied 32 talents of *chremata* from the Rhodians.

8.45.1–2: Alkibiades, as advisor to Tissaphernes, cut down the *misthophoran* from an Attic drachma to 3 obols. He also instructed Tissaphernes to pay the men irregularly in order to prevent desertions from the *misthos* left behind in arrears.

8.45.3: Alkibiades urged Tissaphernes to bribe (*donta chremata*) the captains on the Peloponnesian side to cooperate in the insufficient and irregular pay scam.

8.45.4: Alkibiades sent away the cities (in revolt) asking for *chremata,* and told the Chians that they, the richest of all Greeks, should not expect others to risk not only lives but also *chremata.*

8.45.6: Alkibiades pointed out that Tissaphernes was carrying on the war with *ta idia chremata* and had good cause for being sparing (*opheilomenon*); but whenever he received *trophe* from the King he would give them their full *misthos.*

Here, could *chremata* have been used instead of *trophe,* but not *misthos? Trophe* implies "money for pay," whereas *misthos* would imply that Tissaphernes was himself the recipient of pay, rather than the recipient of money for pay for others.

8.46.1: Alkibiades persuaded Tissaphernes not to provide *misthos* for more Greeks and thus to put the power (*to kratos*) by land and sea into the same hands.

8.46.5: Tissaphernes approved of Alkibiades' plans and kept the Peloponnesians short of *trophe.*

In these two passages (46.1, 5) at first it seems that *misthos* and *trophe* are being used synonymously. But a closer inspection of the context suggests a subtle difference. In the first, *misthos* appears in a theoretical context of potential power (*kratos*). In the second, a reference to what Tissaphernes actually paid to the Peloponnesians, the context is clearly insufficiency of money, and *trophe* is used.

8.53.2: The representatives of the Four Hundred at Athens said that in view of the fact that the King and Tissaphernes were supplying *chremata* to the Peloponnesians and they had none (*sphisi te ouketi onton*), they should change their government.

Here *chremata* may be used with reference to the Peloponnesians because Thucydides is using the word appropriately also to refer to the Athenians' general lack of money and wants to draw an equivalence; the issue, that is, is money generally.

8.57: Tissaphernes desired to bring the Peloponnesian fleet

Note here the repetition of *trophe* in close proximity. The con-

back to Miletos and to supply the Lakedaimonians with *trophe.* He was afraid that if many of their ships left without *trophe,* they would be compelled to engage and be defeated . . . and still more he feared that they might ravage the inland in search of *trophe.* He now sent for the Peloponnesians and gave them their *trophe.*	text is clearly mere subsistence, made clear by the third reference.
8.58.5–6: (Third treaty between the Persians and the Peloponnesians) Tissaphernes shall provide *trophe* for the ships now present, but after the arrival of the King's fleet, the Lakedaimonians and their allies may support (*trephein*) their own fleet; if, however, they wish to receive *trophe* from Tissaphernes, Tissaphernes will furnish it, but the Lakedaimonians and their allies shall repay *ta chremata* at the end of the war.	Here *ta chremata* logically is substituted for *trophe,* since the money changes function in the two exchanges, shifting from money for pay to money not for a specific purpose for the recipient but as a repayment of a loan.
8.78: Astyochos kept the Peloponnesians waiting for Tissaphernes to bring the Phoenician fleet. But Tissaphernes not only did not bring up the fleet but was ruining the [Peloponnesian] navy by not paying *trophe* regularly or fully (*entele*).	
8.80.1–2: The Peloponnesians refused to fight with their united fleet, since they did not think themselves a match for the enemy and were at a loss (*aporesantes*) where they could find *chremata* for so many ships, especially as Tissaphernes gave it badly, so they sent	Here *trophe* and *chremata* appear to be used interchangeably; but it may be significant that *chremata* is used in connection with a concern for an especially large quantity—"so many ships"—and may be used to underscore the dilemma that the Peloponnesians now have

to Pharnabazos, since he had invited them and was prepared to provide *trophe.*

a substantial fleet, which will in turn require an abundance of money. It should be emphasized that *variatio* is an unlikely explanation for the varied terminology, given Thucydides' repetition of the same term in close proximity elsewhere.

8.83.2–3: The Peloponnesians heard of the recall of Alkibiades and were disgusted at Tissaphernes, who had grown slacker and slacker with the *misthodosia.* Gathering together, they began to calculate (*anelogizonto*) how they had not yet received their *misthon entele.*

8.84.2: The Syracusans were demanding their *misthos* from Astyochos.

Is it significant that when non-Spartans in the Peloponnesian fleet complain about pay Thucydides uses *misthos* instead of *trophe?*

8.85.3: Astyochos was sent home to Sparta, and with him Hermokrates, who intended to accuse Tissaphernes of ruining the Peloponnesian cause along with Alkibiades. In particular, Hermokrates had always been at enmity with Tissaphernes over the fact that *ho misthos* was not given in full (*entele*) and had been accused of having asked for *chremata.* And finally, after Hermokrates had been exiled . . . Tissaphernes pressed harder than ever and among other charges accused him of having once asked him for *chremata* . . . and failed to obtain it.

8.87.1–2: Tissaphernes, wanting to clear himself with the Peloponnesians, said he would appoint Tamos to give *trophe* to the army. . . . Some said he went away in order to waste away (*diatribein*) Peloponnesian resources . . . for Tamos provided *trophe* worse, not better.

8.99: The Peloponnesians in Miletos were not receiving *trophe* from anyone from Tissaphernes.

ATHENS

8.1.2: The Athenians, seeing that they did not have *chremata* in the treasury. . .

8.1.3: Nevertheless, the Athenians determined to provide a fleet and *chremata.*

8.18.1: (First treaty between Tissaphernes and the Peloponnesians) Whatever came to the Athenians from the King's cities, either *chremata* or anything else, the King and the Spartans will jointly hinder the Athenians from receiving *chremata* or anything else.

8.48.2: The representatives of the Four Hundred at Samos told the Athenian army that the King would be their friend and provide *chremata* if they would only change their government.

Here the context seems to be money for the war generally.

8.48.3: The Athenian crowd kept quiet out of hope for ready *misthos* from the King.

8.63.4: (The Four Hundred addressing the Athenians) The Athenians should be willing to contribute *chremata* and all else required from their private estates.

8.65.3: (The Four Hundred addressing the Athenians) There shall be no *misthophora* for anyone serving the state; those most able should serve the state with their *chremata* and their bodies.

8.69.4: The Four Hundred told the *bouleutai* to take their *misthos* and be gone.

8.76.4–6: The Athenian camp on Samos speaks of their advantage over the city in Athens. They had the whole fleet with which to compel the other cities that they ruled to give them *chremata*. . . . Indeed, with the fleet in their hands, they could better provide themselves with the necessary provisions (*ta epitedeia*) than the Athenians at home . . . , and they had lost nothing in losing those who no longer could provide *argurion* or good counsel (*bouleuma chreston*), through which a city can control an army.

8.81.3: Alkibiades held out to the Athenians on Samos extravagant promises, that Tissaphernes had assured him that if he could only trust the Athenians they would not be at a loss for (*aporesein*) *trophe*, even if he had to coin his silver couch.

8.86.6: Alkibiades prevented the

[Athenian] fleet from sailing into the Peiraieus. He said the Four Hundred should be disbanded, the Five Thousand reinstated, and meanwhile he approved any economizing measures (*euteleia*) so that the army might receive *trophe*.

8.97.1: The Four Hundred proclaimed that no one should receive *misthos* for any office.

8.107.1: The Athenians at Kyzikos levied *chremata* from the Kyzikenes.

8.108.2: Alkibiades levied *polla chremata* from the Halikarnassians.

BIBLIOGRAPHY

Allison, June W. 1989. *Power and Preparedness in Thucydides.* Baltimore and London: Johns Hopkins University Press.

———. 1997a. "Homeric Allusions at the Close of Thucydides' Sicilian Narrative." *AJP* 118: 499–516.

———. 1997b. *Word and Concept in Thucydides.* Atlanta: Scholars Press.

Alty, J. H. M. 1982. "Dorians and Ionians." *JHS* 102: 1–14.

Amit, M. 1970. "Hostages in Ancient Greece." *RFIC* 98: 129–47.

Ampolo, Carmine. 1984. "La ricchezze dei Selinuntini: Tucidide vi, 20, 4 e l'izcrizione del Tempio G di Selinunte." *PP* 39: 81–89.

Amyx, D. A. 1958. "The Attic Stelai, 3: Vases and Other Containers." *Hesperia* 27: 163–310.

Andreades, A. M. 1933. *A History of Greek Public Finance.* Translated by Carroll N. Brown. Cambridge, Mass.: Harvard University Press.

Andrewes, Antony. 1960. "The Melian Dialogue and Perikles' Last Speech (Thucydides V, 84–113; II, 60–4)." *PCPS* n.s. 6: 1–10.

———. 1992. "The Peace of Nicias and the Sicilian Expedition." In *The Cambridge Ancient History,* vol. 5². Cambridge: Cambridge University Press.

Andrews, James A. 1994. "Cleon's Ethopoetics." *CQ* 44: 26–39.

Archibald, Z. H. 1998. *The Odrysian Kingdom of Thrace: Orpheus Unmasked.* Oxford: Clarendon Press.

Arnold-Biucchi, C., L. Beer-Tobey, and N. M. Waggoner. 1988. "A Greek Archaic Silver Hoard from Selinus." *MN* 33: 1–35.

Arrowsmith, William. 1973. "Aristophanes' *Birds:* The Fantasy Politics of *Eros.*" *Arion* n.s. 1: 119–67.

Austin, M. M., and P. Vidal-Naquet. 1977. *Economic and Social History of Ancient Greece.* Berkeley and Los Angeles: University of California Press.

Avery, H. C. 1973. "Themes in Thucydides' Account of the Sicilian Expedition." *Hermes* 101: 1–13.

Badian, Ernst. 1993. *From Plataea to Potidaea: Studies in the History and Historiography of the Pentecontaetia.* Baltimore: Johns Hopkins University Press.

Bal, Mieke. 1981. "Notes on Narrative Embedding." *Poetics Today* 2: 41–59.

———. 1990. "The Point of Narratology." *Poetics Today* 11: 727–54.

———. 1997. *Narratology: Introduction to the Theory of Narrative.* 2d ed. Toronto: University of Toronto Press.

Banfield, Ann. 1973. "Narrative Style and the Grammar of Direct and Indirect Speech." *Foundations of Language* 10: 1–39.

———. 1978. "Where Epistemology, Style, Grammar Meet Literary History: Represented Speech and Thought." *New Literary History* 9: 415–54.

Bartoletti, V. 1937. "Potenza della Sicilia e ardore degli Ateniesi in Tucidide." *SFIC* 14: 227–35.

———. 1939. "Il dialogo degli Ateniesi e dei Meliee nella storia di Tucidide." *RFIC* 17: 301–18.

Bauslaugh, Robert A. 1991. *The Concept of Neutrality in Ancient Greece.* Berkeley and Los Angeles: University of California Press.

Bender, Georg Friedrich. 1938. *Der Begriff des Staatsmannes bei Thukydides.* Würzburg: Konrad Triltsch.

Bender, John, and David E. Wellbery. 1990. *The Ends of Rhetoric: History, Theory, Practice.* Stanford: Stanford University Press.

Bergk, Theodorus, ed. 1857. *Aristophanis Comoediae.* 2d ed. Leipzig: B. G. Teubner.

Blaydes, Frederick H. M., ed. 1882. *Aristophanis Aves.* Vol. 4. Halle: Orphanotrophei Libraria.

Bloedow, Edmund. 1990. "Not the Son of Achilles, But Achilles Himself: Alcibiades' Entry on the Political Stage of Athens, II." *Historia* 39: 1–19.

———. 1992. "Alcibiades 'Brilliant' or 'Intelligent'?" *Historia* 41: 139–57.

———. 1996. "The Speeches of Hermocrates and Athenagoras at Syracuse in 415 BC: Difficulties in Syracuse and in Thucydides." *Historia* 45: 141–58.

Blyth, P. H. 1982. "The Structure of a Hoplite Shield in the Museo Gregoriano Etrusco." *Bolletino dei musei e gallerie Pontifice* 3: 5–21.

Böckh, Augustus. 1842. *The Public Economy of Athens.* Translated by G. C. Lewis. London: John W. Parker.

Boedeker, Deborah. 1988. "Protesilaos and the End of Herodotus' *Histories.*" *CA* 7: 30–48.

———. 1998. "Presenting the Past in Fifth-Century Athens." In Boedeker and Raaflaub 1998, 185–202.Boedeker, Deborah, and Kurt Raaflaub, eds. 1998. *Democracy, Empire, and the Arts in Fifth-Century Athens.* Cambridge, Mass.: Harvard University Press.

Bogaert, Raymond. 1968. *Banques et banquiers dans les cités grecques.* Leiden: A. W. Sijthoff.

Bolla, Peter de. 1996. "The Visibility of Visuality." In Brennan and Jay 1996, 63–82.

Booth, Wayne C. 1974. *A Rhetoric of Irony.* Chicago and London: University of Chicago Press.

Bosworth, Brian. 1993. "The Humanitarian Aspect of the Melian Dialogue." *JHS* 113: 30–44.

Bowie, A. M. 1993. "Homer, Herodotus, and the Beginnings of Thucydides' *History.*"

In *Tria Lustra: Essays and Notes Presented to John Pinsent,* edited by H. D. Jocelyn, 141–47. Liverpool Classical Papers, vol. 3. Liverpool: Liverpool Classical Monthly.

Branigan, Keith. 1981. "Minoan Colonization." *BSA* 76: 23–33.

Bremmer, Jan N. 1994. *Greek Religion.* Greece & Rome, New Surveys in the Classics, vol. 24. Oxford: Oxford University Press.

Brennan, Theresa. 1996. "'The Contexts of Vision' from a Specific Standpoint." In Brennan and Jay 1996, 219–30.

Brennan, Theresa, and Martin Jay, eds. 1996. *Vision in Context: Historical and Contemporary Perspectives on Sight.* New York and London: Routledge.

Brock, Roger. 1996. "The Tribute of Karystos." *ECM* n.s. 15: 357–70.

Bronzwaer, W. 1981. "Mieke Bal's Concept of Focalization: A Critical Note." *Poetics Today* 2: 193–201.

Bruneau, Philippe, and Jean Ducat. 1983. *Guide de Delos.* 3d ed. Paris: Éditions E. de Boccard.

Brunt, Peter. 1952. "Thucydides and Alcibiades." *REG* 65: 59–96 (= pp. 17–46 of *Studies in Greek History and Thought* [Oxford: Oxford University Press, 1993]).

———. 1965. "Spartan Policy and Strategy in the Archidamian War." *Phoenix* 19: 255–80.

Buck, Robert. 1988. "The Sicilian Expedition." *AHB* 2: 73–79.

Busolt, Georg. 1904. *Griechische Geschichte.* Vol. 3, Pt. 2. Gotha: F. A. Perthes.

Cavaignac, Eugène. 1908. *Études sur l'histoire financière d'Athènes au Ve siècle.* Paris: Albert Fointemoing.

———. 1953. "Le décret dit de Kléarkhos." *RN* 15: 1–7.

Cawkwell, George. 1975. "Thucydides' Judgment of Periclean Strategy." *YCS* 24: 53–70.

———. 1997. *Thucydides and the Peloponnesian War.* London and New York: Routledge.

Chambers, M. H. 1992/1993. "Photographic Enhancement and a Greek Inscription." *CJ* 88.: 25–31.

———. 1993. "The Archon's Name in the Athens-Egesta Alliance (IG I^3 11)." *ZPE* 98: 171–74.

———. 1994. "Reading Illegible Inscriptions: Athens and Egesta." *Thetis: Mannheimer Beiträge zur klassischen Archäologie und Geschichte Griechenlands und Zyperns* 1: 49–52, pl. 5.

Chambers, M. H., R. Gallucci, and P. Spanos. 1990. "Athens' Alliance with Egesta in the Year of Antiphon." *ZPE* 83: 38–63.

Chatman, Seymour. 1986. "Characters and Narrators: Filter, Center, Slant, and Interest-Focus." *Poetics Today* 2: 193–201.

Cogan, Marc. 1981. *The Human Thing: The Speeches and Principles of Thucydides' History.* Chicago and London: University of Chicago Press.

Compernolle, R. van. 1950/1951. "Ségeste et l'hellénisme, I." *Phoibos* 5: 183–228.

Connor, W. Robert. 1984. *Thucydides.* Princeton: Princeton University Press.

———. 1985. "Narrative Discourse in Thucydides." In *The Greek Historians: Literature and History: Papers Presented to A. E. Raubitschek,* 1–17. Saratoga, Calif.: Anma Libri.

Conte, Gian Biagio. 1986. *The Rhetoric of Imitation: Genre and Poetic Memory in Virgil and Other Latin Poets.* Ithaca, N.Y.: Cornell University Press.

Cornford, Francis M. 1971 [1907]. *Thucydides Mythistoricus*. Philadelphia: University of Pennsylvania Press.

Crane, Gregory. 1996. *The Blinded Eye: Thucydides and the New Written Word*. Lanham, Md.: Rowan & Littlefield.

———. 1998. *Thucydides and the Ancient Simplicity*. Berkeley and Los Angeles: University of California Press.

Croally, N. T. 1994. *Euripidean Polemic: The* Trojan Women *and the Function of Tragedy*. Cambridge: Cambridge University Press.

Davidson, James. 1997. *Courtesans and Fishcakes: The Consuming Passions of Classical Athens*. London: Harper Collins.

Delebecque, Édouard. 1964. "Sur deux phrases de Thucydide." *REG* 77: 34–49.

———. 1965. *Thucydide et Alcibiade*. Aix-en Provence: Éditions Ophrys.

———. 1967. *Thucydide: Livre VIII*. Gap: Éditions Ophrys.

Denniston, J. D. 1934. *The Greek Particles*. 2d ed. Oxford: Clarendon Press.

Devine, A. M. 1988. Review of *A Selection of Greek Historical Inscriptions to the End of the Fifth Century B.C.* (rev. ed.), by R. Meiggs and D. M. Lewis. *CB* 64: 110–11.

Dewald, Carolyn. 1975. "Taxis: The Organization of Thucydides' History, Books ii–viii." Ph.D. diss., University of California, Berkeley.

———. 1985. "Practical Knowledge and the Historian's Role in Herodotus and Thucydides." In *The Greek Historians: Literature and History: Papers Presented to A. E. Raubitschek*, 47–63. Saratoga, Calif.: Anma Libri.

———. 1987. "Narrative Surface and Authorial Voice in Herodotus' *Histories*." *Arethusa* 20: 147–70.

———. 1993. "Reading the World: The Interpretation of Objects in Herodotus' *Histories*." In Nomodeiktes: *Greek Studies in Honor of Martin Ostwald*, edited by Ralph M. Rosen and Joseph Farrell, 55–70. Ann Arbor: University of Michigan Press.

———. 1997. "Wanton Kings, Pickled Heroes, and Gnomic Founding Fathers: Strategies of Meaning at the End of Herodotus's *Histories*." In *Classical Closure: Reading the End in Greek and Latin Literature*, edited by Deborah H. Roberts, Francis M. Dunn, and Don Fowler, 62–82. Princeton: Princeton University Press.

Dickie, Matthew J. 1976. "Thucydides, not Philistus." *GRBS* 17: 217–19.

Donini, G. 1964. "Thucydides 7.42.3: Does Thucydides Agree with Demosthenes' View?" *Hermes* 92: 116–119.

Dover, K. J. 1950. "The Chronology of Antiphon's Speeches." *CQ* 44: 44–60.

———. 1953. "La colonizzazione della Sicilia in Tucidide." *Maia* 6: 1–20.

———. 1954/1955. "Problems in Thucydides VI and VII." *PcPhS* 183: 4–10.

———. 1965. *Thucydides: Book VI*. Oxford: Clarendon Press.

———. 1973. *Thucydides*. Greece & Rome, New Surveys in the Classics, vol. 7. Oxford: Clarendon Press.

———. 1988. "Thucydides' Historical Judgment: Athens and Sicily." In *The Greeks and Their Legacy*, 74–82. Oxford: Oxford University Press [*PRIA* 81 (1981), sect. C: 231–38].

Ducrey, Pierre. 1968. *Le traitement des prisonniers de guerre dans la Grèce antique*. Paris: Éditions E. de Boccard.

Dunbar, Nan, ed. 1995. *Aristophanes'* Birds. Oxford: Clarendon Press.

Eberhardt, W. 1959. "Der Melierdialog und die Inschriften ATL A 9 (*IG* I^2 63 + und *IG* I^2 97 +." *Historia* 8: 284–314.

Edmunds, Lowell. 1975. *Chance and Intelligence in Thucydides*. Cambridge, Mass.: Harvard University Press.

———. 1995. "Intertextuality Today." *Lexis* 13: 3–22.

Ellis, J. R. 1979. "Characters in the Sicilian Expedition." *QS* 5: 39–69.

Engeman, T. S. 1974. "Homeric Honor and Thucydidean Necessity." *Interpretation* 4: 65–78.

Erbse, Hartmut. 1953. "Über eine Eigenheit der Thukydideischen Geschichtsbetrachtung." *RhM* 96: 38–46.

———. 1961. "Zur Geschichtsbetrachtung des Thukydides." *Antike und Abendland* 10: 19–34.

———. 1989a. "Thukydides und Alkibiades." In *Festschrift für Nikolaus Himmelmann*, edited by Hans-Ulrich Cain, Hanns Gabelmann, and Dieter Salzmann, 231–35. Mainz on Rhein: Philipp von Zabern.

———. 1989b. *Thukydides-Interpretationen*. Berlin and New York: Walter de Gruyter.

Erxleben, E. 1969. "Das Münzgesetz des delisch-attischen Seebundes." *AfP* 19: 91–139.

———. 1971. "Das Münzgesetz des delisch-attischen Seebundes." *AfP* 21: 145–62.

Fantasia, U. 1973. "Una particolarita del lessico attico sui tipi di proprieta." *ASNP* 3: 787–96.

Faraone, Christopher. 1999. *Ancient Greek Love Magic*. Cambridge, Mass.: Harvard University Press.

Feldherr, Andrew. 1998. *Spectacle and Society in Livy's* History. Berkeley, Los Angeles, and London: University of California Press.

Ferguson, William Scott. 1932. *The Treasurers of Athena*. Cambridge, Mass.: Harvard University Press.

Figueira, Thomas. 1993. *Excursions in Epichoric History: Aiginetan Essays*. Lanham, Md.: Rowman & Littlefield.

———. 1995. "*KREMATA:* Acquisition and Possession in Archaic Greece." In *Social Justice in the Ancient World*, edited by K. D. Irani and Morris Silver, 41–60. Westport, Conn. and London: Greenwood Press.

———. 1998. *The Power of Money: Coinage and Politics in the Athenian Empire*. Philadelphia: University of Pennsylvania Press.

Fine, J. V. A. 1951. Horoi: *Studies in Mortgage, Real Security and Land Tenure in Ancient Athens*. Hesperia Suppl. 9. Princeton: American School of Classical Studies at Athens.

Finley, John H., Jr. 1942. *Thucydides*. Cambridge, Mass.: Harvard University Press.

———. 1967. *Three Essays on Thucydides*. Cambridge, Mass.: Harvard University Press.

Finley, M. I., ed. 1965. *Deuxième conférence internationale d'histoire économique: Aix-en-Provence, 1962*. Aix-en-Provence: École Pratique des Hautes Études and Mouton.

———. 1982. *Economy and Society in Ancient Greece*. New York: Viking Press.

———. 1986. *Ancient History: Evidence and Models*. New York: Viking Press.

———. 1999. *The Ancient Economy*. Updated ed. Berkeley: University of California Press.

Flashar, Hellmut. 1969. *Der Epitaphios des Perikles: Seine Funktion im Geschichtswerk des Thukydides*. Sitzungsberichte der Heidelberger Akademie. Phil-Hist. Klasses, 1. Abhandlung. Heidelberg: Carl Winter Universitätsverlag.

Flory, Stewart. 1978. "Laughter, Tears, and Wisdom in Herodotus." *AJP* 99: 145–53.

———. 1988. "Thucydides' Hypotheses about the Peloponnesian War." *TAPA* 118: 43–56.

Forde, Steven. 1989. *The Ambition to Rule: Alcibiades and the Politics of Imperialism in Thucydides.* Ithaca, N.Y., and London: Cornell University Press.

Foucart, P. 1877. "Décret des Athéniens relatif à la ville de Chalcis." *Rev.Arch.* 33: 242–62.

Frangoulidis, Stavros A. 1993. "A Pattern from Homer's *Odyssey* in the Sicilian Narrative of Thucydides." *QUCC* 44: 95–102.

Frank, Daniel H. 1984. "The Power of Truth: Political Foresight in Thucydides' Account of the Sicilian Expedition." *Prudentia* 16: 99–107.

Freeman, Kathleen. 1959. *The Pre-Socratic Philosophers.* Cambridge, Mass.: Harvard University Press.

Fritz, Kurt von. 1967. *Die griechische Geschichtsschreibung.* Vol. 1. Berlin: Walter de Gruyter.

Gabrielsen, Vincent. 1986. "Φανερά and Ἀφανὴς Οὐσία in Classical Athens." *C&M* 37: 99–114.

———. 1994. *Financing the Athenian Fleet: Public Taxation and Social Relations.* Baltimore: Johns Hopkins University Press.

Gardner, Percy. 1913. "Coinage of the Athenian Empire." *JHS* 33: 147–88.

———. 1974. *A History of Ancient Coinage, 700–300 B.C.* Chicago: Ares.

Gauthier, P. 1971. "Les ξένοι dans les textes athéniens de la seconde moitié du ve s. av. J. C." *REG* 84: 44–79.

———. 1976. *Un commentaire historique des* Poroi *de Xénophon.* Geneva and Paris: Librairie Droz.

———. 1989. *Nouvelles inscriptions de Sardes II.* Centre de recherches d'histoire et de philologie de la IVe section de l'École pratique des hautes études III. Hautes études du monde gréco-romaine, vol. 15. Geneva: Droz.

Genette, Gérard. 1980. *Narrative Discourse: An Essay in Method.* Translated by Jane E. Lewin. Ithaca, N.Y.: Cornell University Press.

———. 1983. *Nouveau discours du récit.* Paris: Seuil.

———. 1988. *Narrative Discourse Revisited.* Translated by Jane E. Lewin. Ithaca, N.Y.: Cornell University Press.

———. 1990. "Fictional Narrative, Factual Narrative." *Poetics Today* 11: 755–74.

Georges, Pericles B. 2000. "Persian Ionia under Darius: The Revolt Reconsidered." *Historia* 49: 1–39.

Gernet, Louis. 1981. *The Anthropology of Ancient Greece.* Translated by J. Hamilton and B. Nagy. Baltimore and London: Johns Hopkins University Press.

Gillespie, C. M. 1912. "The Use of Εἶδος and Ἰδέα in Hippocrates." *CQ* 6: 179–203.

Goldhill, Simon. 1986. *Reading Greek Tragedy.* Cambridge: Cambridge University Press.

———. 1996. "Refracting Classical Vision: Changing Cultures of Viewing." In Brennan and Jay 1996, 15–28.

Goldstein, M. S. 1974. "Athenian-Persian Peace Treaties: Thuc. 8.56.4 and 8.58.2." *CSCA* 7: 155–64.

Gomme, A. W. 1920. "Notes on Thucydides, Book VI." *CR* 34: 81–85.

———. 1951. "Four Passages in Thucydides." *JHS* 71: 70–80.

———. 1956. *A Historical Commentary on Thucydides.* Vol. 2. Oxford: Clarendon Press.

Gommel, Jürgen. 1966. *Rhetorisches Argumentieren bei Thukydides.* Hildesheim: Georg Olms.

Green, Peter. 1970. *Armada from Athens.* London: Hodder and Stoughton.

Gregory, Justina. 1985. "Some Aspects of Seeing in Euripides' *Bacchae.*" *G&R* 32: 23–31.

———. 1999. *Euripides:* Hecuba: *Introduction, Text, and Commentary.* Atlanta: Scholars Press.

Grene, David. 1950. *Man in His Pride: A Study in the Political Philosophy of Thucydides and Plato.* Chicago: University of Chicago Press.

Gribble, David. 1998. "Narrator Interventions in Thucydides." *JHS* 118: 41–67.

———. 1999. *Alcibiades and Athens: A Study in Literary Presentation.* Oxford: Clarendon Press.

Griffin, Jasper, ed. 1995. *Homer:* Iliad *Book Nine.* Oxford: Clarendon Press.

Hainsworth, Bryan, ed. 1985. *The* Iliad: *A Commentary.* Vol. 3: Books 9–12. Cambridge: Cambridge University Press.

Halperin, David M. 1990. "The Democratic Body: Prostitution and Citizenship in Classical Athens." *Differences* 2: 1–28.

Hamel, Debra. 1998. *Athenian Generals: Military Authority in the Classical Period.* Leiden, Boston, and Köln: Brill.

Hardwick, Nicholas. 1996. "The Solution to Thucydides VIII 101.1: The 'Chian Fortieths.'" *Quaderni ticinesi di numismatica e antichità classiche* 25: 59–69.

Harris, Diane. 1991. "Gold and Silver on the Athenian Acropolis: Thucydides 2.13.4 and the Inventory Lists." *Horos* 8: 75–82.

———. 1995. *The Treasures of the Parthenon and Erechtheion.* Oxford: Clarendon Press.

Hartog, François. 1988. *The Mirror of Herodotus: The Representation of the Other in the Writing of History.* Berkeley and Los Angeles: University of California Press.

Hasebroek, Johannes. 1933. *Trade and Politics in Ancient Greece.* Translated by L. M. Fraser amd D. C. MacGregor. London: G. Bell.

Hatzfeld, J. 1951 [1940]. *Alcibiade: Étude sur l'histoire d'Athènes à la fin du Ve siècle.* Paris: Presses universitaires de France.

Hedrick, Charles W., Jr. 1993. "The Meaning of Material Culture: Herodotus, Thucydides, and Their Sources." In Nomodeiktes: *Greek Studies in Honor of Martin Ostwald,* edited by Ralph M. Rosen and Joseph Farrell, 17–37. Ann Arbor: University of Michigan Press.

———. 1995. "Thucydides and the Beginnings of Archaeology." In *Methods in the Mediterranean: Historical and Archaeological Views on Texts and Archaeology,* edited by David B. Small, 45–88. Leiden, New York, and Cologne: E. J. Brill.

Henderson, Jeffrey, ed. 1987. *Aristophanes'* Lysistrata. Oxford: Clarendon Press.

Herter, Hans, ed. 1968. *Thukydides.* Darmstadt: Wissenschaftliche Buchgesellschaft.

Hiller von Gaertringen, F., and G. Klaffenbach. 1924–1925. "Das Münzgesetz des ersten athenischen Seebundes." *ZfN* 35: 217–21.

Hinds, Stephen. 1998. *Allusion and Intertext: Dynamics of Appropriation in Roman Poetry.* Cambridge: Cambridge University Press.

Hirschman, Albert O. 1977. *The Passions and the Interests.* Princeton: Princeton University Press.

Hitzl, Konrad. 1996. *Die Gewichte griechischer Zeit aus Olympia.* Berlin and New York: Walter de Gruyter.

Holzapfel, L. 1893. "Doppelte Relationen im viii. Buche des Thukydides." *Hermes* 28: 435–64.

Hornblower, Simon. 1991a. *A Commentary on Thucydides.* Vol. 1. Oxford: Oxford University Press.

———. 1991b. *The Greek World, 479–323 B.C.* London and New York: Routledge.

———, ed. 1994a. *Greek Historiography.* Oxford: Clarendon Press.

———. 1994b [1987]. *Thucydides.* Baltimore and London: Johns Hopkins University Press.

———. 1996. *A Commentary on Thucydides.* Vol. 2. Oxford: Oxford University Press.

Howgego, Christopher. 1995. *Ancient History from Coins.* London and New York: Routledge.

Howie, J. G. 1998. "Thucydides and Pindar: The *Archaeology* and *Nemean* 7." In *Papers of the Leeds International Latin Seminar,* edited by Francis Cairns and Malcolm Heath, 10: 75–130. Leeds: Francis Cairns.

Huart, Pierre. 1968. *Le vocabulaire de l'analyse psychologique dans l'oeuvre de Thucydides.* Études et commentaires, vol. 69. Paris: Librairie C. Klincksieck.

———. 1973. ΓΝΩΜΗ *chez Thucydide et ses contemporains.* Études et commentaires, vol. 81. Paris: Éditions Klincksieck.

Hunter, Virginia. 1973. *Thucydides the Artful Reporter.* Toronto: Hakkert.

———. 1973/1974. "Athens *Tyrannis:* A New Approach to Thucydides." *CJ* 69: 120–26.

———. 1980. "Thucydides and the Uses of the Past." *Klio* 62: 191–218.

———. 1982. *Past and Process in Herodotus and Thucydides.* Princeton: Princeton University Press.

———. 1986. "Thucydides, Gorgias, and Mass Psychology." *Hermes* 114: 412–29.

Hussey, Edward. 1985. "Thucydidean History and Democritean Theory." In *CRUX: Essays in Greek History Presented to G. E. M. de Ste. Croix on His 75th Birthday,* edited by P. Cartledge and F. D. Harvey. London: Duckworth.

Immerwahr, Henry R. 1966. *Form and Thought in Herodotus.* Cleveland: Western Reserve University Press.

Isager, Signe, and Mogens Herman Hansen. 1975. *Aspects of Athenian Society in the Fourth Century B.C.: A Historical Introduction and Commentary to the* Paragraphe-*Speeches and the Speech* Against Dionysodorus *in the* Corpus Demosthenicum *(XXXII–XXXVIII and LVI).* Translated by Judith Hsiang Rosenmeier. Odense: Odense University Press.

Jay, Martin. 1993. *Downcast Eyes: The Denigration of Vision in Twentieth-Century Thought.* Berkeley and Los Angeles: University of California Press.

Jebb, Richard. 1907. *Essays and Addresses.* Cambridge: Cambridge University Press.

Johnston, J. 1932. "An International Managed Currency in the Fifth Century." *Hermathena* 47: 132–57.

Jonas, Hans. 1982. *The Phenomenon of Life: Toward a Philosophical Biology.* Chicago: University of Chicago Press.

Jong, Irene I. F. de. 1989. *Narrators and Focalizers: The Presentation of the Story in the* Iliad. 2d ed. Amsterdam: B. R. Gruner.

Jordan, Borimir. 1975. *The Athenian Navy in the Classical Period: A Study of Athenian Naval Administration and Military Organization in the Fifth and Fourth Centuries* B.C. Berkeley, Los Angeles, and London: University of California Press.

———. 2000. "The Sicilian Expedition Was a Potemkin Fleet." *CQ* 50: 63–79.

Jouanna, Jacques. 1980. "Politique et médecine: La problématique du changement dans *le Régime des maladies aiguës* et chez Thucydide (livre VI)." In *Hippocratica: Actes du colloque hippocratique de Paris, 4–9 septembre 1978,* edited by M. D. Grmek, 299–318. Paris: Éditions du Centre national de la recherche scientifique.

———. 1999. *Hippocrates.* Translated by M. B. DeBevoise. Baltimore and London: Johns Hopkins University Press.

Kagan, Donald. 1981. *The Peace of Nicias and the Sicilian Expedition.* Ithaca, N.Y.: Cornell University Press.

———. 1987. *The Fall of the Athenian Empire.* Ithaca, N.Y.: Cornell University Press.

Kallet, Lisa. 1999. "The Diseased Body Politic, Athenian Public Finance, and the Massacre at Mykalessos (Thucydides 7.27–29)." *AJP* 120: 223–44.

———. 2003. "*Demos Tyrannos.* Wealth, Power and Economic Patronage." In *Popular Tryranny,* edited by Kathryn Morgan. Austin: University of Texas Press.

Kallet-Marx, Lisa. 1993. *Money, Expense, and Naval Power in Thucydides'* History, *1–5.24.* Berkeley and Los Angeles: University of California Press.

———. 1994. "Money Talks: Rhetor, Demos, and the Resources of the Athenian Empire." In Osborne and Hornblower 1994, 227–51.

Kern, Paul B. 1989. "The Turning Point in the Sicilian Expedition." *CB* 65: 77–82.

Kierdorf, W. 1962. "Zum Melier-Dialog des Thukydides." *RhM* 105: 253–56.

Kitto, H. D. F. 1966. Poiesis: *Structure and Thought.* Berkeley and Los Angeles: University of California Press.

Kleinlogel, A. 1990. "Mythos, Rede und Fiktion im Geschichtswerk des Thukydides." In *Mythos: Erzählende Weltdeutung im Spannungsfeld von Ritual, Geschichte und Rationalität,* edited by Gerhard Binder and Bernd Effe. Bochumer Altertumswissenschaftliches Colloquium, Band 2. Trier: WVT Wissenschaftlicher Verlag.

Koch, Christian. 1991. *Volksbeschlüsse in Seebundangelegenheiten: Das Verfahrensrecht Athens im ersten attischen Seebund.* Europäische Hochschulschriften 3, 446. Frankfurt/Main: Lang.

Kohl, W. 1977. *Die Redetrias vor der sizilischen Expedition (Thukydides 6, 9–23).* Meisenheim: Hain.

Konishi, Haruo. 1987. "Thucydides' *History* as a Finished Piece." *LCM* 12: 5–7.

Konstan, D. 1987. "Persians, Greeks, and Empire." *Arethusa* 20: 57–93.

Kopff, E. Christian. 1976a. "Philistus Still." *GRBS* 17: 220–21.

———. 1976b. "Thucydides 7.42.3: An Unrecognized Fragment of Philistus." *GRBS* 17: 23–30.

Kraay, Colin M. 1976. *Archaic and Classical Greek Coins.* Berkeley and Los Angeles: University of California Press.

Kraay, C. M., and P. R. S. Moorey. 1981. "A Black Sea Hoard of the Late Fifth Century B.C." NC 141: 1–19.

Kraus, Christina Shuttleworth, ed. 1999. *The Limits of Historiography: Genre and Narrative in Ancient Historical Texts.* Leiden and Boston: Brill.

Krentz, Peter. 1989. *Xenophon:* Hellenika *I–II.3.10.* Warminster: Aris & Phillips.

Kroll, John H. 1998. Review of Hitzl 1996. *AJA* 102: 632–33.

Kurke, Leslie. 1991. *The Traffic in Praise: Pindar and the Poetics of Social Economy.* Ithaca, N. Y., and London: Cornell University Press.

———. 1999. *Coins, Bodies, Games, and Gold: The Politics of Meaning in Archaic Greece.* Princeton: Princeton University Press.

Lacroix, L. 1969. "La monnaie grecque et les problèmes de la circulation monétaire." *BAB* 55: 169–80.

Lang, Mabel. 1995. "Participial Motivation in Thucydides." *Mnem.* 48: 48–65.

Lateiner, Donald. 1976. "Tissaphernes and the Phoenician Fleet (Thucydides 8.87)." *TAPA* 106: 267–90.

———. 1977. "Pathos in Thucydides." *Antichthon* 11: 42–51.

———. 1982. "A Note on the Perils of Prosperity in Herodotus." *RhM* 125: 97–101.

———. 1990. "Deceptions and Delusions in Herodotus." *CA* 9: 230–46.

Lattimore, Richmond. 1939. "The Wise Adviser in Herodotus." *CP* 34: 24–35.

Lavelle, Brian. 1989. "Thucydides and *IG* I³ 948: ἀμυδροῖς γράμμασι." In *Daidalikon: Studies in Memory of Raymond V. Shoder, S.J.,* edited by Robert F. Sutton. Wauconda, Ill.: Bolchazy-Carducci.

Lawall, Mark L. 2000. "Graffiti, Wine Selling, and the Reuse of Amphoras in the Athenian Agora, ca. 430 to 400 B.C. *Hesperia* 69: 3–90.

Lederer, P. 1910. *Die Tetradrachmenprägung von Segesta.* Munich: A. Buchholz.

Leighton, R. 1999. *Sicily before History: An Archaeological Survey from the Palaeolithic to the Iron Age.* Ithaca, N.Y.: Cornell University Press.

Leimbach, Rüdiger. 1985. *Militärische Musterrhetorik: Eine Untersuchung zu den Feldherrnreden des Thukydides.* Stuttgart: Franz Steiner.

Leppin, H. 1992. "Die ἄρχοντες ἐν ταῖς πόλεσι des delisch-attischen Seebundes." *Historia* 41: 257–71.

Lévy, E. 1983. "Les trois traités entre Sparte et le Roi." *BCH* 107: 221–41.

Lewis, David M. 1958. "The Phoenician Fleet in 411." *Historia* 7: 392–97.

———. 1966. "After the Profanation of the Mysteries." In *Ancient Society and Institutions: Studies Presented to Victor Ehrenberg on His 75th Birthday,* edited by Ernst Badian. Oxford: Blackwell [= Lewis 1997, 158–72].

———. 1974. "Entrenchment Clauses in Attic Decrees." In ΦΟΡΟΣ: *Tribute to Benjamin Dean Meritt,* edited by Donald William Bradeen and Malcolm Francis McGregor, 81–89. Locust Valley, N.Y.: J. J. Augustin [= Lewis 1997, 136–49].

———. 1977. *Sparta and Persia.* Leiden: E. J. Brill.

———. 1987. "The Athenian Coinage Decree." In *Coinage and Administration in the Athenian and Persian Empires,* edited by Ian Carradice, 53–64. The Ninth Oxford Symposium on Coinage and Monetary History. Oxford: BAR [= Lewis 1997, 116–30].

———. 1997. *Selected Papers in Greek and Near Eastern History,* edited by P. J. Rhodes. Cambridge: Cambridge University Press.

Liebeschuetz, W. 1968a. "The Structure and Function of the Melian Dialogue." *JHS* 88: 73–77.

———. 1968b. "Thucydides and the Sicilian Expedition." *Historia* 17: 289–306.

Lloyd, G. E. R. 1979. *Magic, Reason, and Experience: Studies in the Origins and Development of Greek Science.* Cambridge: Cambridge University Press.

———. 1987. *The Revolutions of Wisdom: Studies in the Claims and Practice of Ancient Greek Science.* Berkeley, Los Angeles, and London: University of California Press.

Loomis, William T. 1998. *Wages, Welfare Costs and Inflation in Classical Athens.* Ann Arbor: University of Michigan Press.

Loraux, Nicole. 1985. "Enquête sur la construction d'un meurtre en histoire." *L'écrit du temps* 10: 3–21.

Luginbill, R. 1997. "Thucydides' Evaluation of the Sicilian Expedition: 2.65.11." *AncW* 28: 127–32.

———. 1999. *Thucydides on War and National Character.* Boulder: Westview Press.

Luschnat, Otto. 1942. *Die Feldherrnreden im Geschichtswerk des Thukydides.* Philologus Supplementband 34.2. Leipzig: Dieterich.

Lyne, R. O. A. M. 1994. "Vergil's *Aeneid:* Subversion by Intertextuality: Catullus 66.39–40 and Other Examples. *G&R* 41: 187–204.

Macan, Reginald Walter, ed. 1973. *Herodotus: The Fourth, Fifth, and Sixth Books.* New York: Arno Press.

MacDonald, Brian R. 1981. "The Phanosthenes Decree: Taxes and Timber." *Hesperia* 50: 141–46.

Mackie, C. J. 1996. "Homer and Thucydides: Corcyra and Sicily." *CQ* 46: 103–13.

Macleod, C. M. 1983. *Collected Essays.* Oxford: Clarendon Press.

Macve, R. H. 1985. "Some Glosses on Greek and Roman Accounting." In *Crux : Essays in Greek History Presented to G. E. M. de Ste. Croix on His 75th Birthday,* edited by P. A. Cartledge and F. D. Harvey, 233–64. London: Duckworth.233–264.

Mader, Gottfried. 1993a. "Rogue's Comedy at Segesta (Thucydides 6.46): Alcibiades Exposed?" *Hermes* 121: 181–95.

———. 1993b. "Strong Points, Weak Argument: Athenagoras on the Sicilian Expedition (Thuc. 6.36–38)." *Hermes* 121: 433–40.

Maele, S. van de. 1971. "Le récit de l'expédition athénienne de 415 en Sicile et l'opinion de Thucydide sur le rappel d'Alcibiade." *AntCl* 40: 21–37.

Malkin, Irad. 1998. *The Returns of Odysseus: Colonization and Ethnicity.* Berkeley, Los Angeles, and London: University of California Press.

Maloney, G., and W. Frohn. 1984. *Concordance des oeuvres hippocratiques.* St-Jean-Chrysostom, Quebec: Éditions du Sphinx.

Marinatos, Nanno. 1980. "Nicias as a Wise Advisor and Tragic Warner in Thucydides." *Philologus* 124: 306–10.

Marinatos Kopff, N., and Hunter R. Rawlings III. 1978. "Panolethria and Divine Punishment: Thuc. 7.87.6 and Hdt. 2.120.5." *PP* 182: 331–37.

Marincola, John. 1997. *Authority and Tradition in Ancient Historiography.* Cambridge: Cambridge University Press.

Martin, Thomas R. 1985. *Sovereignty and Coinage in Classical Greece.* Princeton: Princeton University Press.

Matthaiou, A. P. and G. A. Pikoulas. 1989. "ʼἜδον τοῖς Λακεδαιμονιος ποττὸν πόλεμον." *Horos* 7: 12–23.

Mattingly, Harold. 1967. "Two Notes on Athenian Financial Documents." *BSA* 62: 13–17 [= Mattingly 1996, 205–13].

———. 1968. "Athenian Finance in the Peloponnesian War." *BCH* 92: 450–85 [= Mattingly 1996, 215–58].

———. 1974. "The Protected Fund in the Athenian Coinage Decree (*ATL* D 14, par. 7f.)." *AJP* 95: 280–85 [= Mattingly 1996, 347–51].

———. 1977. "The Second Coinage Decree." *Klio* 59: 83–100 [= Mattingly 1996, 403–26].

———. 1979. "Periclean Imperialism." In *Perikles und seine Zeit,* edited by G. Wirth, 312–49. Darmstadt: Wissenschaftliche Buchgesellschaft [= Mattingly 1996, 147–80].

———. 1981. "Coins and Amphoras—Chios, Samos, and Thasos in the Fifth Century B.C." *JHS* 101: 78–86 [= Mattingly 1996, 435–52].

———. 1996. *The Athenian Empire Restored: Epigraphic and Historical Studies.* Ann Arbor: University of Michigan Press.

Maurer, Karl. 1995. *Interpolation in Thucydides.* Leiden, New York, and Cologne: E. J. Brill.

Maxwell-Stuart, P. G. 1973. "The Dramatic Poets and the Expedition to Sicily." *Historia* 22: 397–404.

McGee, Michael Calvin. 1980. "'The Ideograph': A Link Between Rhetoric and Ideology." *Quarterly Journal of Speech* 66: 1–16.

McGregor, Malcolm F. 1987. *The Athenians and Their Empire.* Vancouver: University of British Columbia Press.

McLennan, George R. 1977. *Callimachos:* Hymn to Zeus: *Introduction and Commentary.* Rome: Edizioni dell'Ateneo & Bizzarri.

Méautis, Georges. 1935. "Le Dialogue des Athéniens et des Méliens (Thucydide, V, 85–113). *REG* 48: 250–79.

Meiggs, Russell. 1972. *The Athenian Empire.* Oxford: Oxford University Press.

Meikle, Scott. 1995. *Aristotle's Economic Thought.* Oxford: Clarendon Press.

Meister, C. 1955. *Die Gnomik im Geschichtswerk des Thukydides.* Winterthur: Keller.

Mele, A. 1993/1994. "Le origini degli Elymi nelle tradizioni di v secolo." *Kokalos* 39–40: 71–109.

Meritt, Benjamin D. 1936. "Greek Inscriptions." *Hesperia* 5: 355–430.

———. 1945. "Attic Inscriptions of the Fifth Century." *Hesperia* 14: 61–133.

———. 1953. "An Athenian Decree." In *Studies Presented to David Moore Robinson on His Seventieth Birthday,* edited by George E. Mylonas and Doris Raymond, 298–303. St. Louis: Washington University.

Meyering, Theo. 1989. *Historical Roots of Cognitive Science: The Rise of a Cognitive Theory of Perception from Antiquity to the Nineteenth Century.* Dordrecht and Boston: Kluwer Academic.

Millett, Paul. 1998. "The Rhetoric of Reciprocity in Classical Athens." In *Reciprocity in Ancient Greece,* edited by Christopher Gill, Norman Postlethwaite, and Richard Seaford, 227–53. Oxford: Oxford University Press.

Mink, Louis O. 1987. *Historical Understanding.* Edited by Brian Fay, Eugene O. Golob, and Richard T. Vann. Ithaca, N.Y.: Cornell University Press.

Mittelstadt, Michael C. 1977. "Thucydidean Psychology and Moral Judgment in the *History:* Some Observations." *RSC* 25: 30–55.

Momigliano, Arnaldo. 1930. "La composizione della storia di Tucidide." *Mem.Accad.Torino* 67: 1–48.

Munn, Mark. 2000. *The School of History: Athens in the Age of Socrates.* Berkeley, Los Angeles, and London: University of California Press.

Murray, Gilbert. 1944. "Reactions to the Peloponnesian War in Greek Thought and Practice." *JHS* 64: 1–9.

Murray, Oswyn. 1966. "Ο ΑΡΧΑΙΟΣ ΔΑΣΜΟΣ." *Historia* 15: 142–56.

———. 1988. "The Ionian Revolt." In *The Cambridge Ancient History,* 2d ed., vol. 4, edited by J. Boardman, N. G. L. Hammond, D. M. Lewis, and M. Ostwald, 461–90. Cambridge: Cambridge University Press.

Musti, D. 1985a. "L'iscrizione del tempio G di Selinunte." *RFIC* 113: 134–57.

———. 1985b. "Pubblico e privato nella democrazia periclea." *QUCC* 49: 7–17.

Nelles, William. 1990. "Getting Focalization into Focus." *Poetics Today* 11: 365–82.

Nenci, G. 1987. "Troiani e Focidesi nella Sicilia occidentale (Thuc. vi.2.3; Paus. v 25.6)." *ASNP* ser. 3, 17: 921–33.

Nixon, Lucia, and Simon Price. 1990. "The Size and Resources of Greek Cities." In *The Greek City: From Homer to Alexander,* edited by Oswyn Murray and Simon Price, 137–70. Oxford: Clarendon Press.

Ober, Josiah. 1998. *Political Dissent in Democratic Athens : Intellectual Critics of Popular Rule.* Princeton: Princeton University Press.

O'Brien, D. 1970. "The Effect of a Simile: Empedocles' Theories of Seeing and Breathing." *JHS* 90: 140–79.

Oppermann, Detlef. 1985. *Aussenpolitik und antike Demokratie: Anmerkungen zu ihrem Verhältnis in perikläischer Zeit.* Frankfurt: dipa.

Orwin, Clifford. 1994. *The Humanity of Thucydides.* Princeton: Princeton University Press.

Osborne, Robin, and Simon Hornblower, eds. *Ritual, Finance, Politics: Democratic Accounts Presented to David Lewis.* Oxford: Clarendon Press.

Ostwald, Martin. 1988. ΑΝΑΓΚΗ *in Thucydides.* Atlanta: Scholars Press.

Packman, Zola M. 1991. "The Incredible and the Incredulous: The Vocabulary of Disbelief in Herodotus, Thucydides, and Xenophon." *Hermes* 119: 399–414.

Page, D. L. 1953. "Thucydides and the Great Plague at Athens." *CQ* 3: 97–119.

Panagopoulos, Andreas. 1989. *Captives and Hostages in the Peloponnesian War.* Amsterdam: Adolf M. Hakkert.

Parker, Patricia. 1990. "Metaphor and Catachresis." In Bender and Wellerby, 60–76.

Parker, Robert. 1987. "Myths of Early Athens." In *Interpretations of Greek Mythology,* edited by J. Bremmer, 187–214. London: Croom Helm.

———. 1994. "Athenian Religion Abroad." In Osborne and Hornblower, 339–46.

———. 1996. *Athenian Religion: A History.* Oxford: Clarendon Press.

———. 1997. "Gods Cruel and Kind: Tragic and Civic Ideology." In *Greek Tragedy and the Historian,* edited by Christopher Pelling, 143–60. Oxford: Clarendon Press.

Parry, Adam. 1969. "Thucydides' Description of the Plague." *BICS* 16: 106–18 [= Parry 1989, 156–76].

———. 1981. Logos *and* Ergon *in Thucydides.* New York: Arno Press.

———. 1989. *The Language of Achilles and Other Papers.* Oxford: Oxford University Press.

Patwell, Joseph Michael. 1978. "Grammar, Discourse, and Style in Thucydides' Book 8." Ph.D. diss., University of Pennsylvania.

Pearson, Lionel. 1985. "Tissaphernes' Extra Money." *Bulletin of the American Society of Papyrologists* 22: 261–63.

Pébarthe, Christophe. 1991. "Thasos, L'empire d'Athènes et les *emporia* de Thrace." *ZPE* 126: 131–54.

Pelling, C. B. R. 1991. "Thucydides' Archidamus and Herodotus' Artabanus." In *Georgica: Greek Studies in Honour of George Cawkwell,* edited by M. A. Flower and M. Toher, 120–42. BICS Suppl. 58. London: University of London, Institute of Classical Studies.

———. 1997. *Plutarco,* Filopemene e Tito Flaminino: *Introduzione e note.* Milan: Traduzione di Eleonore Melandri.

———. 1999. "Epilogue." In Kraus 1999, 325–60.

———. 2000. *Literary Texts and the Greek Historians.* London and New York: Routledge.

Perneé, L. 1980. "Des subsides à taux fixe ou/et à la proportionelle (Thucydide viii, 29)." *Revue de Philologie* 54: 114–21.

Plamböck, G. 1964. *Dynamis im Corpus Hippocraticum.* Wiesbaden: F. Steiner.

Pouilloux, Jean. 1953. "De rapports actuels de l'épigraphie et de l'histoire grecques." *AC* 22: 32–49.

———. 1954. *Recherches sur l'histoire et les cultes de Thasos.* Études Thasiennes 3. Paris: E. de Boccard.

Pouilloux, J., and F. Salviat. 1983. "Lichas, Lacédémonien, archonte à Thasos et le livre viii de Thucydide." *CRAI:* 376–403.

Pouncey, Peter. 1980. *The Necessities of War: A Study of Thucydides' Pessimism.* New York: Columbia University Press.

Pritchett, W. Kendrick. 1965. "The Thucydidean Summer of 411 B.C." *CP* 60: 259–61.

———. 1971. *The Greek State at War.* Pt. 1. Berkeley and Los Angeles: University of California Press.

———. 1974. *The Greek State at War.* Pt. 2. Berkeley and Los Angeles: University of California Press.

———. 1991. *The Greek State at War.* Pt. 5. Berkeley and Los Angeles: University of California Press.

Quinn, Trevor J. 1995. "Thucydides and the Massacre at Mycalessus." *Mnem.* 48: 571–74.

Raubitschek, A. E. 1963. "War Melos tributpflichtig?" *Historia* 12: 78–83.

Rawlings, Hunter R. 1981. *The Structure of Thucydides'* History. Princeton: Princeton University Press.

Rechenauer, Georg. 1991. *Thukydides und die hippokratische Medizin: Naturwissenschaftliche Methodik als Modell für Geschichtsdeutung.* Zurich and New York: Georg Olms.

Reden, Sitta von. 1995. *Exchange in Ancient Greece.* London: Duckworth.

Regenbogen, Otto. 1968. "Drei Thukydidesinterpretation." In Herter 1968, 10–22.

Reger, Gary. 1994. *Regionalism and Change in the Economy of Independent Delos, 314–167 B.C.* Berkeley and Los Angeles: University of California Press.

Reinhardt, Karl. 1966. *Vermächtnis der Antike: Gesammelter Essays zur Philosophie und Geschichtsschreibung.* 2d ed. Edited by C. Becker. Göttingen: Vandenhoeck und Ruprecht.

Renehan, Robert. 1982. *Greek Lexicographical Notes. Second Series. A Critical Supplement to the Greek-English Lexicon of Liddell-Scott-Jones.* Hypomnemata 74. Göttingen: Vandenhoeck und Ruprecht.

Rhodes, P. J. 1981. *A Commentary on the Aristotelian* Athenaion Politeia. Oxford: Clarendon Press.

———. 1988. *Thucydides: History II.* Warminster: Aris &Phillips.

Robbins, Emmet. 1990. "Achilles to Thetis: *Iliad* 1.365–412." *ECM* 9: 1–15.

Romilly, Jacqueline de. 1956. "La crainte dans l'oeuvre de Thucydides." *C&M* 17: 109–27.

———. 1963. *Thucydides and Athenian Imperialism.* Translated by P. Thody. Oxford: Oxford University Press.

Rood, Tim. 1998. *Thucydides: Narrative and Explanation.* Oxford: Oxford University Press.

———. 1999. "Thucydides' Persian Wars." In Kraus 1999, 141–68.

Rusten, J. S., ed. 1989. *Thucydides: The Peloponnesian War, Book II.* Cambridge: Cambridge University Press.

Rutherford, Richard. 1994. "Learning from History: Categories and Case-Histories." In Osborne and Hornblower 1994, 53–68.

Saar, H. G. 1953. "Die Reden des Kleon und Diodotus und ihre Stellung im Gesamtwerk des Thukydides." Ph.D. diss., University of Hamburg.

Ste. Croix, G. E. M. de. 1954/1955. "The Character of the Athenian Empire." *Historia* 3: 1–40.

———. 1956. "Greek and Roman Accounting." In *Studies in the History of Accounting,* edited by A. C. Littleton and B. S. Yamey. Homewood, Ill.: Richard D. Irwin.

———. 1972. *The Origins of the Peloponnesian War.* London: Gerald Duckworth.

Sanctis, G. de. 1930. "Postille Tucidide I: Il Dialogo tra I Melii e gli Ateniesi." *Rend. Acc.Lincei* 6: 299–308.

Sanders, Guy. 1984. "Reassessing Ancient Populations." *BSA* 79: 251–62.

Scanlon, Thomas. 1987. "Thucydides and Tyranny." *CA* 6: 286–301.

Schadewaldt, Wolfgang. 1929. *Die Geschichtschreibung des Thukydides.* Berlin: Weidmann.

Schneider, Christoph. 1974. *Information und Absicht bei Thukydides: Untersuchung zur Motivation des Handelns.* Gottingen: Vandenhoeck & Ruprecht.

Schoenhammer, Maria. 1995. "Coinage and Empire: The Athenian Standards Decree of the 5th Century B.C." Ph.D. diss., City University of New York.

Schuhl, P. 1953. "Adela." *Annales publiées par la faculté des lettres de Toulouse, Homo: Etudes philosophiques* 1: 86–93.

Schuller, Wolfgang. 1974. *Die Herrschaft der Athener.* Berlin and New York: Walter de Gruyter.

Schwartz, Eduard. 1919. *Das Geschichtswerk des Thukydides.* Bonn: F. Cohen.

Seager, Robin. 1967. "Alcibiades and the Charge of Aiming at Tyranny." *Historia* 16: 6–18.

Sealey, Raphael. 1973. "The Origins of *Demokratia.*" *CSCA* 6: 253–95.

Seaman, Michael. 1997. "The Athenian Expedition to Melos in 416 B.C." *Historia* 46: 385–418.

Segal, Charles P. 1962. "Gorgias and the Psychology of the Logos." *HSCP* 66: 99–155.

———. 1995. "Spectator and Listener." In *The Greeks,* edited by Jean-Pierre Vernant, 184–217. Translated by Charles Lambert and Teresa Lavender Fagan. Chicago: University of Chicago Press.

Segre, Mario. 1938. "La legge Ateniese sull' unificazione della moneta." *ClRh* 9: 149–78.

Shapiro, Michael J. 1986. "Literary Production as a Politicizing Practice." In *Form, Genre, and the Study of Political Discourse,* edited by Herbert W. Simons and Aram A. Aghazarian. Columbia, S.C.: University of South Carolina Press.

Simon, Gérard. 1979. *Le regard, l'être et l'apparence dans l'optique de l'antiquité.* Paris: Éditions du Seuil.

Sjöqvist, Erik. 1973. *Sicily and the Greeks: Studies in the Interrelationship between the Indigenous Population and the Greek Colonists.* Ann Arbor: University of Michigan Press.

Smarczyk, Bernhard. 1990. *Untersuchungen zur Religionspolitik und politischen Propaganda Athens im delisch-attischen Seebund.* Munich: Tuduv.

Smith, Charles Forster. 1900. "Traces of Epic Usage in Thucydides." *TAPA* 31: 69–81.

Snell, Bruno. 1953. *The Discovery of the Mind: The Greek Origins of European Thought.* Oxford: Blackwell.

Solmsen, Friedrich. 1975. *Intellectual Experiments of the Greek Enlightenment.* Princeton: Princeton University Press.

Sommerstein, Alan H., ed. 1987. *Aristophanes:* Birds. Warminster: Aris & Phillips.

Sosin, J. D., and J. F. Oates. 1997. "P.Duk.inv. 314: Agathis, Strategos and Hipparches of the Arsinoite Nome." *ZPE* 118: 251–58.

Spatafora, Francesca. 1996. "Gli elimi e l'eta del ferro nella Sicilian occidentale." In *Early Societies in Sicily: New Developments in Archaeological Research,* edited by R. Leighton. Accordia Specialist Studies in Italy, vol. 5. London: Accordia Research Center, University of London.

Stahl, Hans-Peter. 1966. *Thukydides.* Munich: C. H. Beck.

———. 1973. "Speeches and Course of Events in Books Six and Seven of Thucydides." In *The Speeches in Thucydides,* edited by Philip A. Stadter. Chapel Hill: University of North Carolina Press.

Starr, Chester A. 1970. *Athenian Coinage, 480–449 B.C.* Oxford: Clarendon Press.

———. 1984. In *The Minoan Thalassocracy: Myth and Reality,* edited by R. Hägg and N. Marinatos. Proceedings of the Third International Symposium at the Swedish Institute in Athens, 31 May–5 June, 1982. Stockholm: Goteborg, Sweden.

Stein, Jürgen. 1987. "Standortbewußtsein und Entscheidungskompetenz bei Thukydides und Aristoteles: Eine Untersuchung zur politischen Bedeutung des Begriffes 'gnome.'" Ph.D. diss., University of Cologne.

Stewart, Andrew. 1997. *Art, Desire, and the Body in Ancient Greece.* Cambridge and New York: Cambridge University Press.

Strasburger, Hermann. 1966. *Die Wesenbestimmung der Geschichte durch die antiken Geschichtsschreibung.* 2d ed. Wiesbaden: Franz Steiner.

———. 1968. "Thukydides und die politische Selbstdarstelling der Athener." In Herter 1968, 498–530.

Stroud, Ronald. 1994. "Thucydides and Corinth." *Chiron* 24: 267–304.

———. 1998. *The Athenian Grain-Tax Law of 374/3 B.C.* Hesperia Suppl. 29. Princeton: American School of Classical Studies at Athens.

Sutherland, C. H. V. 1943. "Corn and Coin: A Note on Greek Commercial Monopolies." *AJP* 64: 129–47.

Swain, Simon. 1994. "Man and Medicine in Thucydides." *Arethusa* 27: 303–27.

Syme, Ronald. 1958. *Tacitus.* 2 vols. Oxford: Clarendon Press.

Taylor A. E. 1911. *Varia Socratica.* 1st ser. Oxford: James Parker.

Tenger, Bernhard. 1995. "Phoroshöhe und Bevölkerungszahl. Die Athener Tributlisten als Indikator für GröBe der Einwohnerschaft einer Polis?" *Asia Minor Studien* 16: 139–60.

Thomas, Richard. 1986. "Virgil's *Georgics* and the Art of Reference." *HSCP* 90: 171–98.

Thompson, Wesley E. 1965. "Tissaphernes and the Mercenaries at Miletos." *Philologus* 109: 294–97.

———. 1968. "Some Thucydidean Parallels." *Philologus* 112: 119–21.

———. 1971a. "The Chian Coinage in Thucydides and Xenophon." *NC* 11: 323–24.

———. 1971b. "Thucydides 2.65.11." *Historia* 20: 141–51.

Thomsen, Rudi. 1965. Eisphora: *A Study in Direct Taxation.* Copenhagen: Gyldendal.

Tompkins, Daniel. 1972. "Stylistic Characterization in Thucydides." *YCS* 22: 181–214.

Tozzi, P. 1978. *La rivolta ionica.* Pisa: Giardini.

Tracy, Steven V. 1984. "Hands in Fifth-Century B.C. Attic Inscriptions." In *Studies Presented to Sterling Dow on His Eightieth Birthday,* edited by Alan Boegehold et al., 277–82. Greek, Roman and Byzantine Monographs, vol. 10. Durham, N.C.: Duke University.

Treu, M. 1954. "Athens und Melos und der Melierdialog des Thukydides." *Historia* 3: 253–73.

Trevett, Jeremy C. 1995. "Nikias and Syracuse." *ZPE* 106: 246–48.

Underhill, G. E. 1984 [1906]. *Xenophon:* Hellenica. Salem, N.H.: Ayer.

Vélissaropoulos, Julie. 1980. *Les nauclères grecs.* Geneva: Librairie Droz; Paris: Librairie Minard.

Vickers, Michael. 1996. "Fifth-Century Chronology and the Coinage Decree." *JHS* 116: 171–74.

Vickers, M., and D. Gill. 1994. *Artful Crafts.* Oxford: Oxford University Press.

Wade-Gery, H. T. 1931. "The Financial Decrees of Kallias." *JHS* 51: 57–85.

Walbank, Michael B. 1978. *Athenian Proxenies of the Fifth Century B.C.* Toronto and Sarasota: Samuel Stevens.

Walker, Andrew D. 1993. "*Enargeia* and the Spectator in Greek Historiography." *TAPA* 123: 353–75.

Wallace, Robert W. 1989. "On the Production and Exchange of Early Anatolian Electrum Coinages." *REA* 91: 87–95.

Wartofsky, Marx W. 1979. *Models: Representation and the Scientific Understanding.* Boston: D. Reidel.

———. 1981. "Sight, Symbol, and Society: Toward a History of Visual Perception." *Philosophical Exchange* 3: 23–38.

Wassermann, Felix Martin. 1947. "The Melian Dialogue." *TAPA* 78: 18–36.

Weil, R. 1906. "Das Münzmonopol Athens im ersten attischen Seebund." *ZfN* 25: 52–62.

———. 1910. "Das Münzrecht der ΣΥΜΜΑΧΟΙ im ersten attischen Seebund." *ZfN* 28: 351–64.

Westlake, H. D. 1958. "Thucydides 2.65.11." *CQ* n.s. 8: 102–10.

———. 1968. *Individuals in Thucydides.* London: Cambridge University Press.

———. 1969. *Essays on the Greek Historians and Greek History.* Manchester: Manchester University Press.

———. 1979. "Ionians in the Ionian War." *CQ:* 9–44 [= Westlake 1989, 113–53].

———. 1985a. "The Influence of Alcibiades on Thucydides, Book 8." *Mnem.:* 93–108 [= Westlake 1989, 154–65].

———. 1985b. "Tissaphernes in Thucydides." *CQ:* 43–54 [= Westlake 1989, 166–80].

———. 1989. *Studies in Thucydides and Greek History.* Bristol: Bristol Classical Press.

Wettergreen, J. A. 1980. "On the End of Thucydides' Narrative." *Interpretation* 9: 93–110.

White, Hayden. 1981. "The Value of Narrativity in the Representation of Reality." In *On Narrative,* edited by W. J. T. Mitchell, 1–24. Chicago and London: University of Chicago Press.

Whitehead, David. 1976. "IG I^2 39: 'Aliens' in Chalcis and Athenian Imperialism." *ZPE* 21: 251–59.

———. 1998. "Ο ΝΕΟΣ ΔΑΣΜΟΣ: 'Tribute' in Classical Athens." *Hermes* 126: 173–88.

Wilamowitz-Moellendorf, U. von. 1880. *Aus Kydathen.* Philologischen Untersuchungen 1. Berlin: Weidmann.

———. 1908. "Thukydides viii." *Hermes* 43: 578–618.

Will, Édouard. 1972. *Le monde grec et l'orient.* Vol. 1. Paris: Presses universitaires de France.

———. 1975. "Notes sur ΜΙΣΘΟΣ." In *Le monde grec: Pensée, littérature, histoire, documents: Hommages à Claire Préaux,* edited by Jean Bingen, Guy Cambier, and Georges Nachtergael, 426–38. Brussels: Editions de l'Université Bruxelles.

Wilson, Donna. 1999. "Symbolic Violence in *Iliad* Book 9." *CW* 93: 131–48.

Wilson, John R. 1990. "Sophrosyne in Thucydides." *AHB* 4: 51–57.

Winkler, John J. 1990a. *The Constraints of Desire: The Anthropology of Sex and Gender in Ancient Greece.* New York and London: Routledge.

———. 1990b. "*Phallos Politikos:* Representing the Body Politic in Athens." *Differences* 2: 29–45.

Wohl, Victoria. 1999. "The Eros of Alcibiades" *CA* 18: 349–85.

Worman, Nancy. 1997. "The Body as Argument: Helen in Four Greek Texts." *CA* 16: 151–203.

Yunis, Harvey. 1996. *Taming Democracy: Models of Political Rhetoric in Classical Athens.* Ithaca, N.Y.: Cornell University Press.

Zadorojnyi, A. V. 1998. "Thucydides' Nicias and Homer's Agamemnon." *CQ* 48: 298–303.

Zeitlin, Froma I. 1994. "The Artful Eye: Vision, Ecphrasis, and Spectacle in Euripidean Theatre." In *Art and Text in Ancient Greek Culture,* edited by Simon Goldhill and Robin Osborne. Cambridge: Cambridge University Press.

———. 1995. "Art, Memory, and *Kleos* in Euripides' *Iphigenia in Aulis.*" In *History, Tragedy, Theory: Dialogues on Athenian Drama,* edited by Barbara Goff, 174–201. Austin, Tex.: University of Texas Press.

GENERAL INDEX

INDEX LOCORUM

Compositor: G&S Typesetters, Inc.
Text: 10/12 Baskerville
Display: Baskerville
Printer and binder: Thomson-Shore, Inc.